HENRY WILLIAMSON

TARKA AND THE LAST

ROMANTIC

*The difference between the true poet in his poetry and in his
letters or personal intercourse, is just the difference between
the two states of the one man; between the metal live from
the forge, and the metal chill. But, chill or glowing, the
metal is equally itself. If difference there be, it is the metal in
glow that is the truer to itself. For cold, it may be overlaid
with dirt, obscured with dust; but afire, all these are
scorched away.*
Francis Thompson, 'Essay on Shelley'

(Printed on the title page of the 1947 Faber edition of
The Gold Falcon by Henry Williamson)

Henry Williamson by Charles F. Tunnicliffe, January 1934.

HENRY WILLIAMSON

TARKA AND THE LAST ROMANTIC

Anne Williamson

SUTTON PUBLISHING

First published in the United Kingdom in 1995 by
Alan Sutton Publishing Limited, an imprint of Sutton Publishing Limited
Phoenix Mill · Far Thrupp · Stroud · Gloucestershire

Reprinted, with corrections, 1995

First paperback edition, with corrections and additions, published in 1997 by
Sutton Publishing Limited

British Library Cataloguing-in-Publication Data

A catalogue record for this book is available from the British Library.

ISBN 0-7509-1492-0

Half-title page illustration: silhouette of Henry Williamson, cut at Southend-on-
Sea motor-cycle races, September 1919.

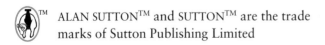 ALAN SUTTON™ and SUTTON™ are the trade
marks of Sutton Publishing Limited

Typeset in 10/13 Sabon.
Typesetting and origination by
Alan Sutton Publishing Limited.
Printed in Great Britain by
Butler & Tanner, Frome, Somerset.

CONTENTS

*To all members of the Williamson family
past, present and future,
but particularly to my beloved husband, Richard,
and our son and daughter, Brent and Bryony,
who have brought me such great happiness.*

ILLUSTRATIONS

PREFACE

In 1932 Professor Herbert Faulkner West wrote an essay on Henry Williamson entitled *The Dreamer of Devon*[1] in which he included the words:

> His mind turned too long upon itself, enjoying in its own solitude the inner landscape of the soul, the prey to imagined fears, dreaming of some Utopia which would give it adequate and complete compensation, soaring to a belief in an impossible and unearthly love, had woven for itself a set of ideals which clashed inevitably with the compromises the world of experience forces upon all men. So he was unhappy and indulged in a great deal of self-pity.

Professor West was actually describing Willie Maddison, hero of Henry Williamson's early tetralogy, *The Flax of Dream*, but he goes on to state that Maddison was Williamson. Although written many years ago, and allowing for the fact that Maddison is not totally Williamson, nor vice versa, the description holds: for it is a perfect description of this complicated, eccentric, and controversial man – soldier, naturalist, broadcaster, journalist, farmer, visionary and, above all, writer.

Until now this essay has had little prominence, due to the fact that it was privately printed as a small limited edition, but it shows great insight into Henry Williamson's character and writing.

A few years later Henry's portrait was painted by Edward Seago and this was reproduced in *Peace In War*[2] with its attendant essay, in which Seago states that he has painted a portrait of the man in paint and

> I hope that one day someone will do so in the written word. Whoever it is they will have a difficult task, for Henry Williamson will not be captured easily on paper. I think that his biographer will find that he is writing the life of more than one man, and it will not be easy to keep them from getting muddled. But if he fails to do so the portrait will lose by it. . . .
>
> I am certain that the various Williamsons are all of them very real, for I have never met a man more completely sincere, nor so steadfast in his search for truth. . . .
>
> There have been a few writers and painters in every age who have refused to shut their eyes to the truth underlying the modes or conventional thought-patterns of their time; who have said, 'These things are real; that is how we

shall put them down. Beauty in hand with Ugliness, and sometimes apart, but never will we mask them with the cloak of conventional thought to make them more palatable.' . . .

I admire those men who follow unflinchingly their own vision of truth, whether it be with, or though generally against, popular taste. But theirs is a hard road, and scarcely a happy one. Henry Williamson is one of them, and he, I believe, is not a happy man. I wish that he could find peace of mind, but I'm afraid that if he did the spark which burns fiercely inside him might die.

It was daunting to have the clearsightedness of these two men, and of many others who have written about Henry's work and life, before me over the months of writing this book about him, and I only hope that I have met their exacting standards and have managed to do justice to this many-faceted man. I have tried to be fair and objective and, above all, as truthful and as accurate as possible and hope that at least I have provided a framework – a skeleton, the bones on which flesh can be put in the future. Many books remain to be written about Henry Williamson, for the layers of meaning hidden within his life are very complex indeed. Trying to decipher his life is like opening an old and very voluminous knitting bag containing a garment made up into a complicated Fair Isle pattern, with the neat surface design on top very clear, and an equally neat but totally different pattern on the reverse: it is as if the many skeins of wool which went into the garment have been played with by several generations of very naughty kittens and twisted and tangled into a hopeless muddle, which only after hour upon hour of very patient unravelling will result in solid balls of single-coloured threads.

That was indeed my first task – untangling, not balls of thread, but very large piles of paper. When, towards the end of his life, Henry became incapable of looking after himself and was in the safe haven of a nursing home run by monks, my husband Richard (one of Henry's sons and named as his literary executor; other offspring were executors of his trust and his will in due course) and I went down to Devon and collected up all his papers: manuscripts, typescripts, letters, documents, everything. We brought it all back to our own house, where they resembled nothing so much as those tangled skeins of wool. For in his last years Henry, in searching for material for his last project (a massive script for the film of *Tarka* in which he used almost everything he had ever written and which would have made the longest film ever envisaged), had turned all his papers into a meaningless muddle. At this stage two large rooms were filled with this literary archive, one of which was our bedroom. To get into bed we literally had to clamber over boxes filled to overflowing.

My career had been as a librarian, and as I was used to dealing with books and papers the family appointed me manager of Henry's literary estate, working directly under Richard as the literary executor but, of course, responsible to them all. It took me two years' solid work to put even his manuscripts and typescripts into some semblance of order, first for the probate valuation and then for the list of material that was to be presented under the National Heritage Scheme in lieu of capital gains tax; for his estate had no money with which to pay this, and his beneficiaries (his family) did not want to sell off his manuscripts abroad piecemeal, which they could so easily have done (and made themselves a considerable amount of money, once the tax had been paid). They wanted everything to be kept as a repository for research purposes, as a monument to his life and work. In due course, their aim was fulfilled, and those manuscripts and typescripts have joined those which Henry Williamson himself presented to Exeter University in 1965,[3] where they may be consulted by bona fide researchers. It is at Exeter University also that is kept the growing archive of the Henry Williamson Society, formed in 1980 by a nucleus of his loyal readers (see p. 358).

But a huge pile of more personal papers remained which still fills one room of our house. Copies of all the most valuable have had to be made so that the originals can stay in the bank for safe keeping. It is now almost twenty years since I first started sorting out those papers; I still have not finished; I doubt if I ever will. I have had to rearrange much of the material in the process of writing this book, and the final cataloguing will no doubt see it rearranged yet again. This biography is based entirely on the documents to be found within this extensive literary archive; on the primary source material of Henry Williamson's own diaries and notebooks; on letters, both to him by his friends and literary peers (often themselves famous writers) and from him, for he frequently wrote several versions of his letters and often never actually posted them to the named recipient; on documents of all kinds; and, above all, on photographs, many of which have been reproduced in these pages.

I first met Henry Williamson on my wedding day. I had of course heard a lot about him beforehand, and it wasn't helping my nerves to know that he was to be present. He attended our very simple little ceremony, made himself charming to my aunt (who had brought me up, my mother having died when I was an infant) and sent Richard and I on our way afterwards by driving along behind us, head out of his car window, blowing great blasts on his hunting horn.

Two months later Henry proposed a visit to our tiny flat. I was so nervous that I went down with virulent tonsillitis (a habit of mine when under stress). Henry blandly ignored this, as he later ignored the debilitating mastitis I suffered after the birth of my first child when he had decided on a long visit because he wanted me to do some urgent revision work with him.

He visited us quite frequently (as indeed he did all of his family; but I think Richard and I particularly provided a literary empathy for which he was always desperate), sometimes for short visits in passing, sometimes for longer periods: sometimes alone, frequently in the company of whichever girlfriend was current at the time. We always made him welcome and tried to carry on our own affairs around him – not easy to accomplish. Once, Richard was engaged on a quite complicated project, to do with his work as a naturalist, with which I was helping him. Our two children were in the newly born and toddler stages, so life was quite hectic anyway. The deadline for the project was fast approaching and we ended up working in the kitchen of our small cottage most nights until the early hours, while Henry played his Wagner records (which he had brought with him!) at full volume in the next-door sitting room, every few minutes putting his head round the door to exclaim about how wonderful the music was. Our neighbour, a trainee farm manager who had to get up at dawn every day, was not very amused; but luckily took the larger view of the situation. We were all, however, very relieved when the visit was over!

Henry Williamson's writing stands on its own, but to gain any understanding of the writer the man has to be known, and there are some facets of his life and temperament that are perhaps difficult to reconcile with his writing. Henry himself made use of every single event and emotion in his life and transmuted it into his writings. He also left many precise notes of explanation among his papers – and, more importantly, he made sure it was all very carefully kept. He intended that it should all be made public and used for his biography in due course, even (particularly) those things that were to his detriment. It is perhaps beyond the scope of this biography and this biographer to analyse definitively what the root causes of his behaviour were and what formed his temperament, but I have attempted to explore this a little. The overriding theme must be that he was driven to a quest for perfection: this is apparent in the ceaseless searching after 'Barleybrights' – perfect female companions who belong to the realms of the gods rather than to real life; in the way he approached every task, always making it difficult, however simple it might have been in actual fact; and above all, in the constant rewriting and re-presentation of his work. It is perhaps encapsulated in his interest in, his passion for, the music of Richard Wagner, which draws on German myth and legend, particularly the great *Ring* cycle, *Parsifal*, and the story of *Tristan und Isolde*, which is also the story of King Arthur, Guinevere, Lancelot, and King Mark, and the overarching goal of the Knights of the Round Table – the search for the Holy Grail, which in itself is an allegory for Truth. If Henry had not been driven to this search for perfection, he would not have been the extraordinary writer he was. There can be no doubt that he *was* an extraordinary man and writer, whatever sense of the word one uses.

Henry Williamson was greatly influenced by a member of his family, his Aunt Mary Leopoldina, his father's sister, who wrote a book under the pseudonym J. Quiddington West, entitled *The Incalculable Hour*.[4] In her book she uses phrases and images that are immediately pertinent to the thesis of 'Dreamer of Devon', and which make the use of this phrase as a description and statement particularly apt, apart from Herbert West's use in his essay. For in her strange allegorical little work, Mary Leopoldina uses the term 'Master of Dream':

Thus it is that the Master of Dream comes to us in the Incalculable Hour; a swift weaving of shadows about our feet, a whisper against the ear, a strange leaping of thought to wed with thought; and the Portals of Dream are flung wide. . . .

The land of Dream would seem to belong to the past rather than the present. . . . And the land their dreams inhabit is a land of illusion, rainbow-lit with vain longings, where the splendour of a tradition that had outlived the passionate fire of the hearts that kindled it, fades slowly upon a grey horizon. Upon it is the shadow of a despairing love.

The Incalculable Hour, passim

As you read this biography, it will become clear that Henry Williamson's Aunt Mary Leopoldina could have written that passage about her nephew. If she was writing about herself, then they must have been very much alike indeed.

But it was George Painter, biographer of Marcel Proust, André Gide, William Caxton and Chateaubriand, who thought very highly of Henry Williamson's writing, who made the true analysis:

All great writers have . . . a sense of power and vision, a moment of grace and revelation made permanent – which is communicated from them to the reader. . . . It will be among the accepted facts of English literary history that our only two great novelists writing in the second quarter of the twentieth century, after the deaths of Lawrence and Joyce, were John Cowper Powys and Henry Williamson. . . . The peculiar quality of Henry Williamson is the piercing directness of his vision, the absolute identity of his own feeling and its communication to the reader, the clothing of a naked and terrible pain or joy in a noble and innocent prose, as keen as sunlight and as innocent as spring-water. He stands at the end of the line of Blake, Shelley and Jefferies: he is the last classic and the last romantic.[5]

The thing that everyone who met him remembers about Henry Williamson above all else is his tremendous energy. His personality was like a charged magnet. To be in his presence was to enter an enormously strong electrical field with its power to attract and lock on or repel and scatter to the four winds. Luckily for himself, and for us, he was able to earth that electricity in the pole of his writing.

Although mainly known as the author of *Tarka the Otter*, he did in fact write over fifty books, of which the fifteen-volume *A Chronicle of Ancient Sunlight*, based to a large extent on his own life, is a novelized social history of the first half of the twentieth century.

Henry Williamson lived and worked in North Devon for the greater part of his long writing life. He spent a brief holiday in the village of Georgeham immediately before the First World War and, enthralled by the wild Devon scenery so in keeping with his own sensitive and passionate nature, he vowed to return. Born in Brockley, his young life was spent in south-east London. His love of nature was instilled from an early age, and from the then semi-rural London suburb where he lived he had easy access on his bicycle to the nearby Kent countryside, where he roamed freely in the lanes and woods at weekends and during the school holidays. He recaptured the atmosphere of life in these early years of the twentieth century in the opening volumes of *A Chronicle of Ancient Sunlight*.

He was a soldier in the First World War, and there are several books detailing those traumatic years. His descriptions of life in the trenches based on his first-hand experiences are considered by many to be the finest of their kind.

After the war he spent a brief period as a journalist in Fleet Street, but with life in the family home proving difficult and with his first novel accepted, he decided to go and live permanently in that village of Georgeham in North Devon, the memory of which had sustained him during the war. Many of his early books and volumes of natural history sketches paint a portrait of the now long-vanished life of Georgeham and the surrounding countryside of North Devon. His detailed descriptions of natural history and his atmospheric evocation of the moods of nature, epitomized by *Tarka the Otter* and *Salar the Salmon* but evident in many other of his books and stories, are part of the great heritage of English natural history writings. Once established he bought a field on the hill above Georgeham, where he built himself a 'Writing Hut' which was to be his refuge for the rest of his life.

He spent the Second World War as a farmer in Norfolk, convinced that sound agriculture was the answer to England's problems. Again, his experiences, hopes and dreams are recorded in several books. After this war was over, he returned to live permanently in his Field, although he later bought a cottage in Ilfracombe as well. He then began the great work of his mature years, *A Chronicle of Ancient Sunlight*, an objective look at the history of this country in all its varied detail enveloped in the history of the Maddison family and in particular of Phillip Maddison, based on Henry Williamson's own life and family. For the next nineteen years he produced a volume nearly every year, each book averaging two hundred thousand words.

Henry Williamson was a man who drove himself unremittingly both in his writing and in his life. He believed himself to be a chosen one, destined to pass on the 'ancient sunlight', and he never ceased in his task. West and Painter captured the essence of the man each in their different ways: the Dreamer of Devon – the last Romantic.

Anne Williamson
1995

ACKNOWLEDGEMENTS

I am indebted to Herbert West, Jnr for permission to use extracts from his father's work, and to the Librarian at Dartmouth College, Hanover, New Hampshire for supplying copies of background information from the college archives; to the estate of Charles Tunnicliffe for permission to use extracts from his letters and illustrations; to the estate of Edward Seago for the use of material; to Colfe's Grammar School for extracts from the *Colfeian* etc.; to the estates of Walter de la Mare and Richard de le Mare for permission to use extracts from unpublished letters; to Fortescue Estates for use of letters from Sir John Fortescue; to the BBC for the use of the photograph in Chapter Six; and to the estate of R.L. Knights, photographer, Barnstaple, for permission to reproduce the photographs of Henry Williamson's wedding and William Rogers, Master of the Cheriton Hunt, and to John Fursdon for the use of photographs on pages 212 and 221. More precise acknowledgements will be found in the Notes.

I apologize to those people who appear in these pages as part of Henry Williamson's life whom it has not been possible to contact despite much effort; all have been treated sympathetically, and all are an essential part of the total picture. Conversely, it has not been possible to include every detail and every person so I further apologize if you should, but do not, appear in these pages.

I would like to thank John Gregory for reading the typescript and for his valuable suggestions. I would especially like to thank my husband, Richard Williamson, for his steady support and his forebearance with my necessary total absorption in this project.

Henry Williamson's Family Tree

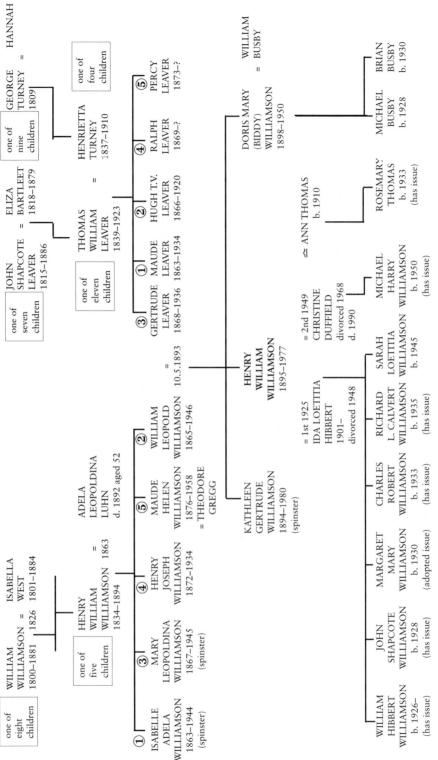

(A more detailed family tree with extensive background can be found in The Henry Williamson Society Centenary *Journal*, No. 31, (September,1995))

CHAPTER 1

EARLY DAYS

Over the Hill at night shone the stars of heaven; but they were seldom observed by those walking there, for northward lay the city of London. . . .

The gentle winds of evening in May, eddying from the chalk downs of north-west Kent and pushing back the smoke of London across the marshes of the river, brought the cry of owls, and sometimes, when the scents of lilac and hawthorn blossom were in the still air, the voices of nightingales answering one another across the moonlit spaces of the night. Occasionally when the wind was blown from the south-east, the chatter of warblers could be heard among the reeds of Randisbourne brook beyond the railway station half a mile away. . . .

One evening in late June of the year 1893 a solitary young man who regarded the Hill as a friend was walking up the Western slope to the elm trees upon the crest, to visit some strips of cloth, impregnated with a boiled mixture of foots sugar and beer, which he had pinned upon the bark an hour previously, for the purpose of luring moths thither. . . .

He reached the top of the slope, coming to the row of elms, where he paused to look around him, while feeling for his lucifer matches in a waistcoat pocket. The sky was starry, the wind warm and gentle, a good scenting night for moths. Squatting on his heels, he opened the front of his lantern, turned up the wick, and struck a match. With the lantern in his left hand and small net in his other, he moved to the first of the strips pinned to the bark of the nearest tree. Three woodlice and an earwig on that one.

At the fourth tree he gazed with unbelieving amazement at what he beheld in the circular and wavering beam of his lantern. There upon the strip of damp cloth was clinging a butterfly, whose colours and shapes at first perplexed him – the insect had definite deep brown wings shot with purple. It was exactly like the coloured woodcut in the old book given him by his grandfather – it was a Camberwell Beauty! Last seen in England nearly a hundred and fifty years ago, three of them being recorded as taken at Camberwell in 1748! A Camberwell Beauty! He gazed without power of movement.

The Dark Lantern, Chapter 1, 'Camberwell Beauty'

Those words are from the opening chapter of *The Dark Lantern*, written by Henry Williamson in the early 1950s. The scene he is describing was real and took place on Hilly Fields, Brockley, Lewisham in south-east London in 1893 and the man out in the starlight catching moths is based on his father.

Henry in early childhood, aged about five years.

Hilly Fields, Brockley, Lewisham, at the turn of the century. The view is taken opposite the house where Henry spent his childhood, and which features in some of his books.

The Dark Lantern is the first in a fifteen-volume series of novels with the overall title of *A Chronicle of Ancient Sunlight*, which charts the life of Phillip Maddison and his family and the way of life in England from 1893 until about 1953. It is well known that the *Chronicle* is fairly firmly based on Henry Williamson's own life and that of his family and friends, and describes throughout, albeit in story form and with some poetic licence, real events and real places. It is, in fact, a fictionalized social history of England in the first half of this century.

Henry's father, William Leopold Williamson, was born on 7 May 1865 in Ryde on the Isle of Wight, although his parents actually lived in London and were shortly to be established in Sutton, South London, where they remained until they died, towards the end of the century. (His mother seems to have gone to the Isle of Wight for the sole purpose of the confinement.) William Leopold first attended Grove Park School in Sutton but later was educated at the Thanet Collegiate School in Margate, Kent, for there is a school bill relating to him for summer 1877, although his name does not appear on the few school records now kept at the Margate Reference Library. He became a clerk, employed at a branch of the National Bank in Broad Street in the City of London, walking across London Bridge on his way to and from work every day, as we find Richard Maddison does in the *Chronicle* novels: 'he estimated he had crossed the flagstones of London Bridge, in the roar of iron wheel-bands and horses' hooves on granite, approximately fourteen thousand and five hundred occasions.'

Henry's parents, William Leopold and Gertrude Williamson.

William Leopold married Gertrude Leaver on 10 May 1893 at Greenwich Registry Office under rather odd circumstances, for it was without the knowledge of Gertrude's father, Thomas William Leaver. Gertrude's mother, Henrietta Leaver (née Turney) signed the marriage certificate, along with W.C. Cornish.

Thomas Leaver was against the liaison. He had some knowledge of the Williamson family and apparently did not approve of them. In the novels the reason given is that it was against bank rules for employees to marry until they had reached a certain status and salary, which seems a most draconian regulation. But the young couple determined to marry and, with the encouragement of Gertrude's mother, took advantage of Thomas Leaver's absence on holiday to do so. A very small family group attended the ceremony and then the pair had a brief weekend's honeymoon in the nearby countryside. William was twenty-seven, Gertrude twenty-five. Gertrude then returned to her parental home in Sutton in south-west London and the couple lived separately for several months, until after another weekend away in the early autumn Gertrude became pregnant and her father had finally to be told of the situation in a difficult scene.

This is all related in great detail in *The Dark Lantern*, where the young couple are Richard and Hetty. It does seem a very daring enterprise to have undertaken within the strictures of the respectability of the Victorian regime. The family were obviously more progressive than one would expect from their background.

William Leopold was from a fairly large family of brothers and sisters: Isabelle, born 1863; Mary Leopoldina, born 1867; Henry Joseph born 1872; and Maude Helen, born 1876. The most interesting was Mary Leopoldina, who features as Theodora (Dora) in the *Chronicle* novels. She was a very intelligent lady but although in the novels Dora goes to Girton College, Cambridge, the name Mary

Leopoldina Williamson does not appear anywhere on the college records, nor on those for Newnham College, a possible alternative.[1] Under the pen name J. Quiddington-West Mary Leopoldina wrote a book called *The Incalculable Hour*, inspired by a sojourn in Greece, which was published in 1910. Privately printed, and only forty pages long, it is a strange allegorical tale with deep mystical undertones, very visionary and very Romantic in derivation, rather like a female version of some of William Blake's work. This aunt was a great influence on Henry. The phrase 'The Flax of Dream' which he used as the title of his early tetralogy is actually taken from her book:

> Our land of heart's desire is woven of our thoughts and longings and emotions, and no two weave alike. And it is well if, returning thence, we bring with us gifts worthy of acceptance. For many to whom the Weaver gives the Flax of Dream, weave hurriedly, and the web is spoilt. It needs time to gather the joy and sorrow, the love and suffering, the wisdom that go to make a perfect design; and through all the weft of it must run the thread of self-sacrifice like a scarlet flame, touching it to inconceivable beauty.
>
> *The Incalculable Hour*

William Leopold's parents were Henry William Williamson, a house and quantity surveyor, and Adela Leopoldina Lühn. German by birth, thought to be Bavarian the only photograph of her shows Adela to be a lady of very striking appearance. It is believed that she fled to England about 1860 as a result of her family's early involvement in the unrest that was the prelude to the Bismarck wars

Adela Leopoldina Lühn, Henry's Bavarian grandmother.

in Germany, when it is thought that her father and brothers were killed and their *Schloß* (castle) burnt to the ground. It has not been possible to verify this story, which was included by Henry Williamson in a few pages of biographical notes found in his literary archive, in which he states it was told to him by his Aunt Maude, who was her daughter and would presumably have known this directly from her mother. The Bismarck wars did not really start until about 1866, but there was a lot of unrest and inter-state fighting in Germany before that time.

How Henry William and Adela met is not known but they were married in April 1863 by special licence in Lewisham parish church. This location, so relevant to Henry Williamson's own story, seems to be just one of those strange coincidences. Their first child, a daughter, was born seven months later. Whether Adela was already pregnant when they married is not known, although the special licence possibly points to such a supposition. It is equally possible that the baby was premature and that it was a difficult birth, which is why Adela went to the Isle of Wight, a known health resort, for the birth of her second child. They had a German nanny called Minnë, who probably brought up their children as Adela may not have been very strong. She died at the comparatively young age of fifty-two from diabetes. Her husband Henry William seems to have had the reputation of being a philanderer and an alcoholic. He died in March 1894, aged sixty, from injuries sustained from an accidental fall through a trap door, while inspecting new buildings of the Prudential Assurance Company in Newcastle-upon-Tyne.

William Leopold, as the eldest son, attended the inquest on behalf of the family. The verdict was straightforward 'Accidental death', but William Leopold was to complain to Henry in later years that his father had been said to be drunk at the time, and thus they were unable to claim compensation. Henry William died intestate, but letters of administration were granted to William Leopold, and the estate was valued at £116. Divided among his five offspring, each would have received a small portion – only £23. However, there does seem to have been some property as, two or three years later, a letter from a legal firm to William Leopold refers to the sale of property.

But there had certainly been money in the family in a previous generation. Henry William's father, William Williamson, had been a comparatively rich man, owning a great deal of property throughout south London, with stocks and shares also. Apart from these, his will details items such as liquors and wines, household effects, books, paintings, and musical instruments, all of which point to his being a man of substance. Apart from the main bequests, William left a small trust, the income devolved from the rents of a particular property, to be used for the education of his grandson William Leopold, hence the attendance at the Thanet Collegiate School. It is probably this property that was the object of the sale referred to above.

At the time of his death, Henry William Williamson's home address was Hildersheim, Cavendish Road, Sutton. The Leaver's family address was Wespelaer, Cavendish Road, Sutton. Young William Leopold was living in lodgings in Brockley at the time of his marriage, presumably to be nearer his place of work, and, after his mother's death there was little to keep him at home anyway, but in effect he married the girl next door – a fact well disguised by Henry Williamson in his novels, where he has Richard visiting 'some friends of Dora's who lived in a village in the midst of the herb fields to the west of Croydon'. Henry Williamson gives an idyllic description of the sight and smells of these herb fields, which would have provided a lucrative local industry, in *The Dark Lantern*:

> *From hedge to hedge in the morning sunlight lay acres of herbs of all colours and hues of the rainbow, from deep purple of lavender to bright yellow of fennel and dark red of valerian. But these colours were more vivid, more familiar and earth-bright than any band of spectrum, whether seen in the sky or on the cloth of magic-lantern. The marine blue blossoms of hyssop lay adjacent to the blazon of marigold, the Herb of the Sun; then came a field of Vatican sage with its heliotrope flower-heads, the Oculis Christi of Gerard; more hyssop, deep blue as the Mediterranean, and then paler blue licorice. And oh, the azure of the chicory, the heavenly azure of the rayed flowers, the very blue of remote sky, far beyond the highest lark. Then a field of opium poppies – she did not like them, they were different from other flowers, livid and fleshy in the midst of wavering cerulean blues and reds and shades of brown to palest pink of centaury. Sweet marjoram with its rose-purple flowers: how beautiful was its other name, mountain joy. And the rosemary! Grey bushes of rosemary as far as the distant hedge, acres and acres of grey-blue blossoms, 'dew of the sea', as the Romans called the flower. Colour after colour in succession, scent after scent dashing upon the fact out of the morning! Coriander, with flowers of pale mauve; tall angelica clothed in bright green leaves and white flowers; sweet cicely, smelling like myrrh, also clothed in white; tarragon, 'little dragon' said to be a cure for snake-bite or wound of wolf in olden time; a field of peppermint, both black and white varieties side by side. And the butterflies among them, thousands of butterflies, attracted alike to tall spikes of mullein with their clusters of primrose blossoms and lowly pale florets of thyme. And above all the big lavender fields, with the loveliest scent of all, her favourite lavender!*
>
> *The Dark Lantern*, Chapter 3, 'Behind the Cob's Ears'

Gertrude herself was born in 1868, and was also one of five children. She had an older sister Maude, two younger brothers Ralph and Percy, who would seem to have gone to South Africa to earn their living, and another brother, Hugh, two years older than herself, who is shown in the novels as the black sheep of the family, where he is supposed to have been sent down from Cambridge for a fairly minor misdemeanour. However, like Mary Leopoldina, Hugh Leaver's name does not appear on college records for either Cambridge or indeed for Oxford; although apparently he did, as in the novel, contract syphilis from which he died, slowly and painfully, in 1920.

Gertrude's father, Thomas William Leaver, was a Worcestershire man, born in Bromsgrove in November 1839, and educated at the famous Stratford-upon-Avon

Left: The Leaver family. From left to right: Charles Turney, Elizabeth Turney (née Boone), Gertrude Leaver (Henry Williamson's mother), and Thomas William Leaver (Gertrude's father). Right: Hugh Leaver, brother of Henry's mother.

Left: Captain William Leaver RN, Henry's great-great-grandfather. Right: Sarah Leaver, née Shapcote, Henry's great-great-grandmother.

Free Grammar School, which had housed William Shakespeare in earlier times. He became a manufacturing stationer, with a partnership in the large and respectable firm, Drake, Driver and Leaver Ltd (translated in the *Chronicle* as Mallard, Carter, and Turney), whose substantial headquarters were in Rosebery Avenue, London. This gentleman had a remarkable likeness to Edward VII, which Henry remarks upon in his novel. His father, John Shapcote Leaver, was a most interesting man and was involved in many of the institutions of Stratford-upon-Avon, including holding the very prestigious post of Secretary of the Shakespeare Trust. The *Stratford-upon-Avon Herald* printed a generous obituary praising his qualities when he died in 1886.[2]

John Shapcote had married Eliza Bartleet on 7 January 1839 at Tardebigge. The Shakespeare Birthday Trust archive contains the family bible, which has details of their marriage and births of their children. Eliza was born on 18 August 1818 and she was the daughter of William Bartleet, a needle manufacturer from a well-known and prolific family from Redditch. Research into this connection has revealed a most astonishing fact, for the maiden name of the mother of the novelist John Galsworthy was Blanche Bailey Bartleet, whose father was Charles Bartleet, also a needle maker from Redditch. In fact, Charles and Eliza's father were cousins – their fathers were brothers, whilst *their* father, the ancestor common to both branches, was William Bartleet (1723–95), married to Mary Milward. All this family were involved, to varying degrees of success, in the needle manufacturing business of Redditch. Galsworthy wrote some notes on his family which were included in *The Life and Letters of John Galsworthy*, H.V. Marrott (Heinemann, 1935), in which he shows that William Bartleet started this industry 'from which the growth and prosperity of that town dates', and that the family were held in high esteem in the area and were the local squires. This relationship makes John Galsworthy and Henry's grandfather, Thomas William Leaver, third cousins and thus Henry Williamson and John Galsworthy third cousins twice removed, not particularly close but definitely related. The two men, who were to be on such friendly terms in due course, seem to have been totally oblivious of their relationship.

John Shapcote Leaver's mother was Sarah Shapcote, who married William Henry Leaver, a lieutenant in the navy who is believed to have taken part in the battle of Trafalgar, and was in turn descended from a landed gentry family who originated at Knowestone, near South Molton, Devon. Sarah's father, John Shapcote, was a lieutenant in the Royal Navy who died at sea in 1790 whilst acting as agent on the *Neptune*, one of the ships conveying convicts to Australia. His somewhat infamous story is well tabulated in documents of the period. These facts were unknown to Henry Williamson but the name Shapcote meant a great deal to him. In later life he claimed his Shapcote ancestors as his true spiritual antecedents and his soul's birthplace as being on the Chains of Exmoor. The full family tree[3] certainly shows that some of Henry Williamson's roots are planted firmly in the rich red soil of Devon, and his claim that Exmoor was his spiritual home is truly justified.

Gertrude's mother was Henrietta Turney, whose forebears had once been farmers in Bedfordshire but more recently had been millers and bakers. We know that the infant Henry was taken to stay with these relations at their home at

Aspley Guise near Woburn Abbey when only a few weeks old due to his mother's ill health, and that his mother often took him to stay there during his childhood. These visits were to make a great impression on him and he drew heavily on these scenes of happy childhood memories in his early writing. In the novels the area is disguised as Gaultshire, deriving from the Gault clay that makes up the local soil. Henry was particularly friendly with his cousins Charles and Marjorie Boone, whose great-grandfather Abraham was the brother of his own great-grandfather, George Turney. George and Abraham came from a family of nine children all of whom lived in the Aspley Guise, Husborne Crawley, and Ridgmont area, and who had been millers and bakers and grocers, which seems a happy combination of family cooperation in making maximum use of the available source of income, but Henry Williamson keeps to farming as the family occupation in his writings.

All these family names and events were used, mixed up and cross-hatched, in the novels of A Chronicle of Ancient Sunlight, and it is of great interest to trace the real names and match them with often thinly disguised characters in the novels.

Gertrude's father, as partner in a large firm, was prosperous and was a well-travelled man, taking holidays in Europe, Russia and Canada, evidenced by several photographs and postcards in the literary archive. Gertrude accompanied her father on one journey at least, as we know from a short fragment from a 'Journal' that she wrote in a small plain autograph-size 'Log Book'. This began on 30 April 1891, when with her father and 'the boys' (her brothers, but she only refers to Percy by name) she left Sutton by train for Victoria to catch the express for Liverpool, thence to embark on 1 May on the passenger ship Parisian for Quebec, which they reached on Sunday 10 May, travelling on up the St Lawrence River by steamer. She was very sick on the boat to begin with, but later enjoyed the voyage. At one point she went to 'see the Steerage, very awfull and dirty, like cattle trucks. The 2nd. class not much better, a vast difference between 1st. and 2nd. classes.' On reaching Winnipeg she notes: 'not used to the cooking, seems very comical to have a lot of little side dishes placed around one's plate'. But there the fragment ends. In the Chronicle we read that Hetty's father took her to Canada to visit her brother Charlie who was learning to farm. Perhaps this visit to Canada was a way of removing Gertrude from the scene of a budding liaison with the young man who lived next door, an outward expression of Thomas Leaver's objections to their subsequent marriage. The move may have come too late, however, as there may well have been a secret understanding between the two young people even before Gertrude left for Canada.

Once the marriage between William Leopold and Gertrude became public, they managed to rent a small house near Hilly Fields, the setting which opened this chapter, at 66 Braxfield Road, Brockley. Their first child, a daughter, Kathleen Gertrude, was born on 13 June 1894. Henry William, the subject of this biography, named after his paternal grandfather, was born on 1 December 1895, and a third child, another daughter, Doris Mary, always known as Biddy, was born on 5 August 1898.

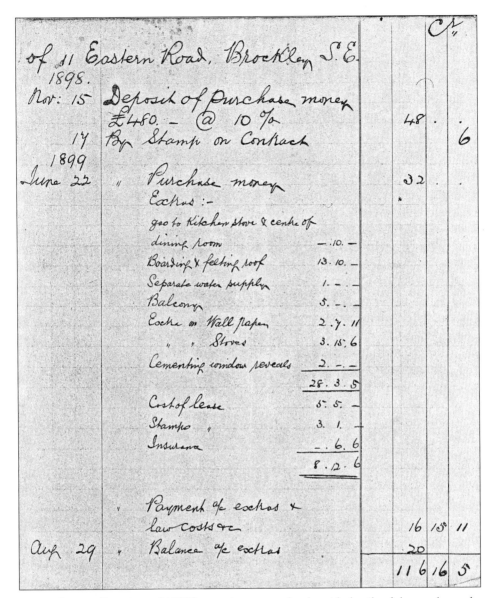

A page from William Leopold Williamson's accounts book, with details of the purchase of No. 11 Eastern Road.

At this time the family had left the original house and were living in Ladywell Road nearby, but on 15 November 1898 William Leopold put down a deposit of 10 per cent of the purchase money of £480 for a property being built next to Hilly Fields. It was part of a new development of typically solid Victorian semi-detached houses. This was 11 Eastern Road, Brockley (Lewisham) and in due course the family moved in – probably at the end of the following year. It was in this house that the main part of Henry's childhood and adolescence was spent. In fact Leopold and Gertrude were still living there at Gertrude's death in 1936, and Leopold stayed on for some time afterwards. The house was also called Hildersheim, after his parental home in Sutton, but this German name was removed at the outbreak of the First World War. The numbering was also changed at some point (possibly soon after the war) and the house became No. 21. It still exists and a commemorative plaque was affixed under the aegis of the Henry Williamson Society and Lewisham Council in 1984. Gertrude's parents, the Leavers, also moved here, buying No. 12, the adjoining house of the pair, which was not at all to William Leopold's liking. The two 'patriarchs' never got on, understandably after such a bad beginning. William Leopold supposedly never entered his father-in-law's house, and he was very jealous of his wife's frequent and lengthy visits next door. The top house was a little grander, with a turret, and was occupied by Stanley Nicholson. In his novels Henry calls this family the Rolls and the daughter of the house is Helena, for whom his character, Phillip, harbours a strong calf love.

The peculiarities attendant to their marriage must have been very bewildering to William Leopold. Having to keep his marriage secret for about six months after the event, and if he really did believe that he would also lose his job if the facts became known, must have been a tremendous strain. And when he did finally get his wife to himself she was, of course, already well into her first pregnancy. In the *Chronicle* Hetty undergoes the traumatic experience of having her revered father knock her down on hearing the news of the secret marriage and pregnancy of his beloved and, as he thinks, pure daughter, rendering her unconscious for some time. As Henry Williamson drew so closely on actual events this probably happened and Gertrude's delicate psyche must surely have been marked for ever. It was not the basis for a good marriage.

The picture we get of Henry's father from the novels is of a very stern and cold man. Henry Williamson's first wife, who knew Henry's parents well, bears witness to this as a true portrait, but interestingly, Henry's eldest son, William (Bill), has a very fond memory of his grandfather as a tremendous person for having fun and playing jokes. Bill remembers how William Leopold had a small brass 12 bore cannon, probably of the type used for starting a boat race. Once when his young grandson was visiting in about 1930, he fired it off secretly in the next room to make everyone jump, coming back into the room where they were gathered and smiling broadly at their looks of shocked surprise; Bill considered this the greatest prank a fond grandfather could ever hope to play. So William Leopold certainly wasn't entirely humourless as we are led to believe. Further evidence of his

Hilly Fields, Lewisham, at the turn of the century (taken from a Christmas Card by William and Gertrude Williamson).

Nos. 11 and 12 Eastern Road, where the Williamson family lived, with their Leaver in-laws next door at No. 12. Henry and other members of the family can be seen on the balcony.

character is contained in a letter to Henry from his Aunt Maude, William Leopold's sister, written at a much later date, in which she states that William Leopold was very happy as a young man, that the family were all very cheerful and they all got on together very well. According to Aunt Maude, William Leopold's character changed completely on his marriage, due to the 'lies' that that family involved him in.[4]

With his two sisters, Henry had a respectable lower middle-class, typically Victorian upbringing. His father was apparently strict, humourless, and out of touch with his son. William Leopold liked solitary pursuits, hence the long cycle rides, the collecting of moths at night and the flying of kites on the Hill; he played classical music on his old wind-up gramophone and is thought to have played the violoncello. Gertrude, on the other hand, seems to have been a very patient but over-anxious personality, for ever trying to appease her rather irascible husband.

The young Henry did not get on with his sisters, particularly Kathie. They quarrelled throughout their lives, and most of the many letters between them in his literary archive are unhappy. For example, Henry accused Kathie of manipulating first their mother, persuading her to spend much of her money for Kathie's own purposes, and then their father, by persuading him to change his will

Henry with his two sisters, Kathleen and Biddy, *c.* 1900.

and by selling books and destroying family papers. In her turn, to defend herself, Kathie would snipe back. Henry frequently told a story of how Kathie had pushed him on the fire when he was a small boy, but in her old age Kathie (with whom no one in Henry's own family really had any contact until after his death, due to his strictures) said that it was the other way round, claiming that he had pushed her on the fire in a rage and received a severe beating for it. Possibly they pushed each other! They were probably too alike in temperament, both convinced they were right, neither able to understand or make allowances for the other. Kathie appears to have had problems with her health, which it was hinted was due to the strain her mother underwent during the pregnancy, thus Gertrude tended to indulge her daughter. Henry was very jealous of this. Kathie lived to a ripe old age, outliving Henry by a few years. Right to the very end she was strong willed and somewhat eccentric, with the same dynamic eyes as Henry. And, although she spoke very kindly and understandingly of him, one could well imagine the clash of personalities as soon as they came together! Henry's younger sister, Biddy, would appear to have been of equally strong character. As a very young girl she apparently took her mother's part against her father, threatening to kill him if he went on bullying her mother.

Gertrude's little 'Log Book' from her visit to Canada was now taken over for other purposes. In it she wrote down a few of the children's sayings, and they made little drawings and notes from time to time. There are only a few jottings but they include three or four of the children's amusing phrases in Gertie's handwriting.

Kathie. 'Do tell Sonnie to be quiet, he keeps interubbering me so.'
Sonnie January 1900. [Sonnie being Henry, at age four]
   'Don't touch that dog, Kathie, it may get *incited*.'
   'I must be quick & put this bottle's head (cork) on, or it may catch cold.'
   'How does God put our skins on? does he sew them on with needle & cotton?'
   'Does God keep our skins in a box? He does our toe-nails, because I have seen them.'

Henry Williamson used some of this in *Donkey Boy*, the *Chronicle* novel which covers the period of his childhood. The 'Log Book' also contains Henry Williamson's first known story, in his own handwriting, which appears immediately after the following:

My dear Gertie you try and guess Who my Sweetheart is put it down here.

[and his mother wrote underneath]

May Monk but you must not spoil this book or take my brooches.
                                       G.E. Williamson.

[and the story follows]

Once upon a time there was a girl named May Monk and she went fishing with her brother her brother took her by the hand but when he sew a squirrel up in a tree he left hold of her hand and in going so he slipped & fell forward and to save himself caught hold of his sister & pulled her down and to all appearances killed her he was so frightened that he ran away meaning never to come back he ran strate into the forest where an old whitch lived he lay there all night thinking of his little sister and soon the old whitch found him next day took him and made him into a drunken pie and (drank) ate him and so he never went home again but he was so bitter that it killed the old monkey and that was the end.

There are several drawings and little wash sketches done by Kathie in this book and there is also a little water colour of some daffodils from 'Harry' to his mother, and a scrap of 'diary' from Kathie which she perhaps wrote to pass the time when unwell, and which again became source material for the novels in due course. A little verse, autograph book style, written by Gertie in 1909, can perhaps be seen as prophetic. One feels it was certainly heartfelt:

The story that the young Henry wrote in his mother's 'Log Book'.

Boys flying kites haul in their white winged birds
But you can't do that when you are flying words
Thoughts unexpressed, sometimes fall back dead
But God himself can't kill them when they're said.

The activities of his father and the atmosphere of the household were keenly observed by the little boy, who fifty years later and blessed with the gift of total recall, objectively narrated it all in *A Chronicle of Ancient Sunlight* whose early volumes – *Donkey Boy, Young Phillip Maddison*, and *How Dear is Life* – give a remarkably honest account of the whole family and of life as it was at the turn of the century.

Henry was a lively yet very diffident boy, with a difficult and complicated character. Frightened of his stern Victorian father, young Henry would prevaricate and lie his way out of trouble, which earned him many beatings, causing his mother anguish and tears, which only further irritated his father. This was a fairly common occurrence in Victorian times, of course, but it did affect the very sensitive young Henry to a marked degree and exacerbated his tendency to unhappiness. For both his Aunt Maude and Aunt Mary Leopoldina said separately in letters that he was born unhappy and had 'unhappy eyes' even as a baby. 'You were the unhappiest small boy I had ever seen.'[5] In Henry's literary archive there are a few pages of biographical notes that Henry himself wrote much later in life, probably in the mid-1960s, where he states:

I suppose I was unhappy ever since I could remember. I was afraid. To escape this fear I did 'unaccountable' things, for which I was punished by canings. I used to scream during this punishment. The word 'unaccountable' was my father's. He must have been puzzled – and maddened. The long dry grass in the field behind our garden fence often went up in flames and smoke during the August holidays. Once the local fire brigade was called out – rapidly clanging brass bell, rapid pounding of the grey's hoofs on flinty road, grinding wheels – flash of brass helmets, running out of flat hose with polished brass nozzle on the end – and then a conference. There stood Mr Gerrard, in a hat half top half bowler, red face, large drooping moustaches, conferring with an inspector of police and captain of Fire Brigade, while the men spread out, small branches of elm in their hands, to beat out the flames under the thick yellow smoke rising above the field – nearly 400 yards of fire in line, flames 2–3 ft. high, and roaring, advancing to the wooden fences of back gardens of the row of houses built in 1902.

I saw this from the window of the back bedroom overlooking garden and field. I was not visible. I was kneeling, crouching, peering not through glass but a 'crack' of ½" between window sash and lower framing: a terrified small boy, with the 'fascinated' feeling between the legs, slightly pleasurable in a remote way of stricture in fear-terror-despair of what I had done. Prison – reformatory – cat o'nine tails – Mother's heartbreak because 'Sonnie' was ruined for life – all these feelings culminating in the silent screaming away of my life as I knew it. 'Shall I kill myself?' Then to hide under the bed in the next room, my own small bedroom. Any moment the knock on the door, the gruff voice, the tramp of heavy feet. I lay on the oil-cloth, shuddering, too frightened for tears.

'Why did you do it, my son? You promised last year, you know, never to do it again? Why do you do these things, which get you into trouble, again and again? Do you want to be punished again and again? Then why, why, why, do you do these things?'[6]

Yet despite all this Henry seems to have had a very real sense of self-importance and of occasion from an early age. His large and expressive eyes are always arresting in every photograph, and his bearing upright. He stands out in group photographs; in the studio portrait taken with his casually dressed cousin (home on holiday from South Africa) Henry is in a high collar and gloves, very upright, very conscious of the importance of the occasion. It was this apparent conflict – deep sensitivity yet the need for self-importance – that later was to give him the qualities that made him a writer. All his life he was to swing from the heights to the depths.

Henry, aged about twelve years, showing his large and expressive eyes.

Henry and his cousin from South Africa, Tommy Leaver.

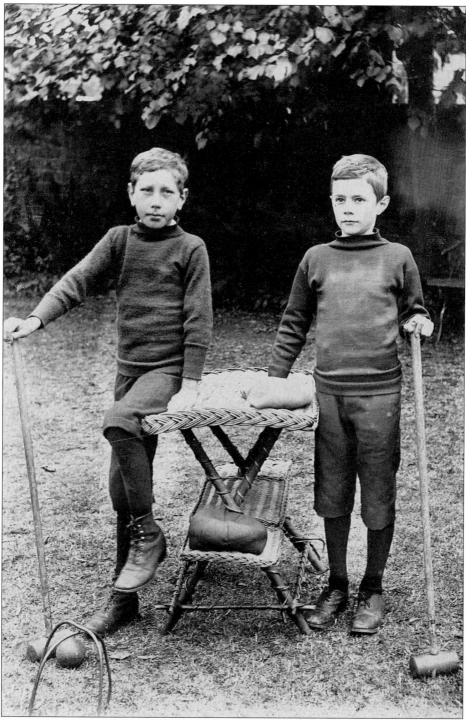

Henry and his cousin, Charlie Boone, at Aspley Guise, Bedfordshire.

But there were happy childhood times; particularly the visits to Gertrude's family in Bedfordshire with the social mix of relatives, and the greater freedom he enjoyed away from the pressure of his father's presence, and especially his friendship with his cousins Charlie and Marjorie Boone, who feature as Percy and Polly Pickering in the *Chronicle* novels. This Bedfordshire connection was to prove a lasting and vital influence on Henry Williamson. But Charlie was to die in the First World War. His death broke the heart of Henry's younger sister, Biddy, who was deeply in love with him. In the novels Phillip tends to be somewhat in love with Polly throughout their youth, and some sexual exploration takes place, as it obviously did in real life. The two cousins remained friends and exchanged amicable letters right up to Henry's death, and in some of Marjorie's there is an element of 'what might have been'.

From postcards and letters it is clear that the Williamson family spent their summer holidays over several years of Henry's childhood at Hayling Island on the south coast. Often William Leopold went off on his own cycling trips at these times, usually to the West Country. Such childhood holiday incidents are evocatively recreated in the following passage taken from *Donkey Boy*, the second volume of the *Chronicle*, where in Chapter 26, Hetty takes the children by train on holiday to Hayling Island. After a day or so Richard arrived on his bicycle, staying briefly before continuing on his way to the West Country.

> *From the station, where they said goodbye to the lady, they rode in a cab through the village and came among trees to a lane behind the common. The sea, the sea! There beyond gorse and brambles among patches of brown shingle could be seen a blue-grey placid level. Phillip was wildly excited. He kept jumping up and down; and out, as soon as the cab stopped at Sea View Terrace. The terrace was built opposite the Lifeboat House, about a minute's walk from the shingle slope to the sea. Off the children ran, to see the sea, having promised to be back in time for tea at half-past four. . . .*
>
> *Phillip ran in, just in time, breathlessly telling his mother that it was a wonderful place, with fishing boats, anchors, bathing tents, a life-saving apparatus, a real lifeboat in the house, and most wonderful of all, porpoises coming up black out of the waves quite near the shore.*
>
> Donkey Boy, Chapter 26, 'Hayling Island'

Henry's education began at Brockley School. Then in 1907 at the age of eleven, amid much anguish of spirit, he sat for and obtained a scholarship to Colfe's, the prestigious grammar school in Lewisham. He was put into Buff House. The Headmaster was Frank W. Lucas who had been appointed in 1895 and was to continue until 1923.[7]

The young Henry was not temperamentally suited to the confinement of school life, preferring to roam the countryside rather than to study, but he took a full part in the various sports, particularly cross-country running, where he ended up as captain of harriers. He also took part in rifle shooting and.

Colfe's Grammar School Harriers. Henry is sitting second left on the middle row.

Colfe's Grammar School Cricket Team. Henry is standing on the extreme left of the back row.

Colfe's Grammar School Rifle Team at Bisley.
Henry is on the left.

represented his school at Bisley. His name is mentioned in several issues of the school magazines *Colfensia* and the *Colfeian* and we learn that in June 1911 he came fifty-sixth in the Annual Cross Country Run (which was actually first man in for the Buffs), while in the 1912 Harriers Cross Country he was first for his house and third overall. In November 1912 he is reported as being in the Second XI football team and also in the cricket team, while in June 1913 we find him placed third in the hurdle race. After he had left school it was recorded that 'Buff House regrets the loss of H. Williamson as Captain of Harriers'. Although not a distinguished scholar, he was not a disgrace and is mentioned in the summer 1913 issue as having obtained 3rd class honours in the Senior Cambridge Examination held in December 1912. The writing of essays was his strong point even at this early age.

Apart from school activities, Henry was a boy scout, and the doings of the local troop feature in *Young Phillip Maddison*, even the supposed furtive sexual advances of the scout master towards the young boys. Among Henry's archive papers there is a copy of *The Flag*, 'The Quarterly Journal of the South Eastern Troop of Baden Powell's Boy Scouts' for June 1909 mainly written by 'A.R.P.', and in the margin Henry Williamson has written 'Arthur Reginald Price is Purley-Prout [the scout master] in *Young Phillip Maddison*', while on another page is a report of 'The Whitsuntide Camp' by 'A.R.P.' which states: 'The night proved very wet, and sleep was rather difficult on account of this and the talkative mood of a certain patrol-leader, who disturbed everybody, in spite of threats and warnings.' Henry has underlined this and written a note in the margin – 'HW'.

Henry left Colfe's on 30 May 1913, ending with the annual Visitation Day (when the governors 'visited' the school – more usually called Speech Day); he

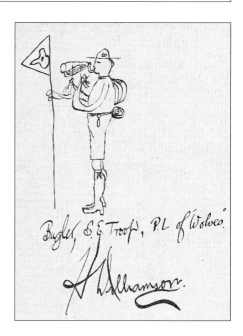

A cartoon sketch by the young scout.

wrote in his small Lett's schoolboy's diary 'Prize's decent' and noted that he had gained a Bramley Prize,[8] value 15 shillings and had chosen 'The Bible in Art' and two Dent's library books, while a further note – 'will try to get Jeffry's works' – shows that Richard Jefferies was already an influence at this stage, even if he could not spell the name correctly! He also obtained a sport's prize, value 1 shilling, which bought a pair of scissors which, the diary states, 'won't cut butter'.

On leaving, all boys were presented with a copy of *A History of Colfe's Grammar School* written in 1910 by Leland L. Duncan. A solid tome, the book plate pasted inside the cover shows the school crest and motto, 'Presented by the Governors, The Worshipful Company of Leathersellers to H.W. Williamson, 28.5.1913.' They are called 'The Company of Tanners' in the *Chronicle* novels and Leland Duncan is 'Sir Heland Donkin, the Big Bug in Whitehall'.

Meanwhile, Henry's older sister Kathleen was being educated at the Ursuline convent at Thildonck in Belgium. In *Young Phillip Maddison* we find the youthful Phillip being taken over to Belgium to visit his sister, Mavis, at her school. This visit is described in great detail including the meeting with the Mother Superior, Mère Ambroisine, which was the name of the real Mother Superior, as there is a school bill for Kathie signed by her. The young Phillip was very impressed by Mère Ambroisine, 'feeling that she was a wonderful person . . . when he looked up at her he felt good, feeling that when he had not been good, it was not really himself' (*Young Phillip Maddison*, Chapter 28, 'Jaunt to Belgium'). We learn here that Mère Ambroisine knew Phillip's mother when she was a little girl: so it would seem that Henry's own mother may have been educated at the very same convent. This is further borne out by a note in Gertrude's short diary of her trip to Canada, where they landed opposite Quebec in a village which 'reminded me strongly of Belgium especially as they mostly talked French'. There are further references in the novels to Hetty's education in Belgium; also the parental home in Sutton had been named Wespelaer, and Wespalaer (sic different sp.) is the name of the village where the convent is situated, which would all seem to support this supposition.[9] Kathie's early education in a Catholic establishment obviously made a deep impression on her, for she was certainly of the Catholic faith in her old age, although it is not known when she was actually converted. Biddy, the younger sister, was educated much more prosaically at a local ladies college in south London. Perhaps it was considered sensible to separate the two girls. Their fees were paid by Thomas Leaver, the maternal grandfather.

Although there is no record of it at this time, it is known that in 1912 the family took a holiday on the north Norfolk coast at East Runton near Cromer, for Henry Williamson wrote about it in *The Story of a Norfolk Farm*. Henry himself apparently cycled there, and on his way saw his first otter hunt at a mill somewhere beyond Colchester; he also made himself feel quite queasy eating cold pork and drinking strong cider at the inn where he stayed overnight. A letter from his mother written just before she died refers to this holiday, reminding him of how wet it had been and how their tent had been washed out by the torrent of rainfall.

It is obvious that Henry's love of nature was inherent. But it was nurtured by his roaming the Kent countryside, often by bicycle. Keston Ponds was one of his favourite haunts. He had always been out and about in the countryside and interested in natural history, but in his last year at school he obtained permits to have access to private woods, Holwood and Squerryes Park, spending all his spare time looking for birds and their nests, and making notes on what he saw. Aged seventeen Henry kept a diary for 1913 which gives us the flavour of his life at this time. It opens:

> Went several times in the Xmas holidays to H.P. with Terence, most times by myself. The roads were fearful, sometimes it took us 1½ hours to get to H.P. on account of the mud. [H.P. is Holwood Park]
> Saw sparrow hawks several times near 'haystack bank'. They did not hover like kestrels, but make a quick dash after their prey.
> *Saturday 8 February*
>   The eggs I hope to get at Sq. N's woods as (which I shan't get elsewhere) Snipe, merlin, woodcock, nuthatch, kingfisher, kestrel and many others.

The Terence in the entry is Terence Tetley, who is Desmond Neville in the *Chronicle*. He first appears in *Young Phillip Maddison* when he asks if he can join Phillip's scout patrol. They remained friends for several years, through the ensuing war, until they finally quarrelled apparently (from what one can deduce from a scattering of letters and their added notes) because Terence would not repay money that Henry had lent him, but there are hints that there may have been deeper reasons.[10] Other friends, comrades, and rivals mentioned in this diary are

Hose, Watson and Victor Yeates and his cousins Charlie and Marjorie Boone. They all appear as characters in the *Chronicle*, while Victor Yeates reappears later on in Henry Williamson's life. Extracts from his diary at this time mention several of his friends.

Wednesday 12 March

I am very relieved & not a little pleased that Watson send me a note today breaking off our friendly relations. I am very glad for it saved me making an obvious hint to a undesired & shallow gentleman.

Thursday 13 March

Learnt that Watson went yesterday to a new place. He says it is decent but refuses to say a word about it. However I shall soon find out.

Thursday 20 March

Left in evening for Mount Pleasant House. Arrived at Euston at 7.30. got to Woburn Sands 10 p.m. Marjorie met us at the station.

Friday 21 March

Very rainy day. Charlie's game of football spoilt. Shot all day at intervals into the fir plantation at the back of the garden. Got several chaffinches & one greenfinch.

Saturday 22 March

Went over Duke's Moors . . . Saw snipe, peewits many wild ducks, etc. etc. Ripping.

Sunday 23 March

Shot about in the morning. Shot a teeny weeny little cole tit. In afternoon went to Duke's Park. Saw much ripping birds & thousands of deer. Saw pair of wild geese. Lovely day & lovely time.

Monday 24 March

Shot the other cole tit this morning. I now have the pair which I shall mount. Last day. Feel sorry that I must go back to rotten London.

Friday 11 April

Hippodrome in evening with Smith, Yeates & Terence.

Friday 18 April

Went to Hippo again in evening with Yeates & Terence.

Saturday 19th April

Went by myself to H.P. Searched every hollow tree. Found barn owl.

Sunday 20 April

Went with Charlie to F.G. Wds. Saw place where woodpecker was boring. Found newly built tree-creepers' nest in stump. . . . Am afraid [it] will be found by Hose.

Monday 21 April

Squire Norman's by myself. Went with decent Keepers. Got moorhen's eggs & saw young.

Wednesday 23 April

Went to Sq. P. [Squerryes Park] by myself. Found plovers nest: 4 fresh eggs.

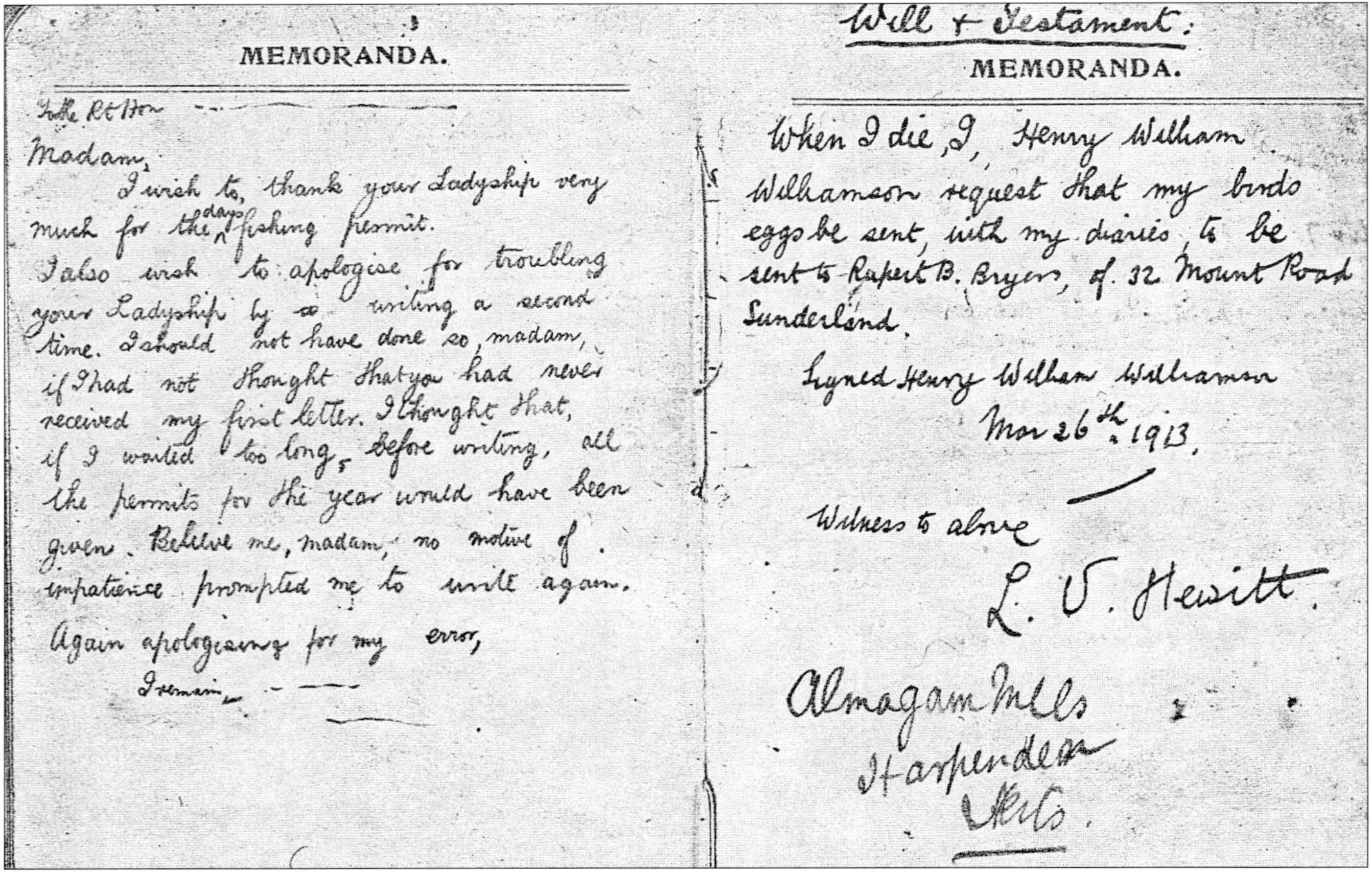

Will + Testament:

MEMORANDA.

3
MEMORANDA.

Madam,

I wish to thank your Ladyship very much for the [fishing] permit. I also wish to apologise for troubling your Ladyship by so writing a second time. I would not have done so, madam, if I had not thought that you had never received my first letter. I thought that, if I would be too long, before writing, all the permits for this year would have been given. Believe me, madam, no motive of impatience prompted me to write again.

Again apologising for my error,

I am—

MEMORANDA.

When I die, I, Henry William Williamson request that my books etc be sent, with my diaries to be sent to Rupert B. Bryon, of 32 Mount Road, Sunderland.

Signed Henry William Williamson
Mar 26th, 1913.

Witness to above
L. S. Nesitt
Amgam Mills
Harperdean
Herts

Henry's Will and Testament from his 1913 diary, and a draft letter about one of his permits.

One of Henry's great friends was Rupert Bryers, who appears under his real name in *Dandelion Days*. In the back of this 1913 diary Henry has written out his 'Will and Testament', dated 26 March, leaving his birds' eggs and diaries to Rupert Bryers, which ties in with the entry for 26 February: 'Have felt for a long time that I shall die soon. Motor bus, I think. Dreamt of it last night.' There is a letter, dated 16 April 1913, from Rupert Bryers who, older than Henry Williamson, had already left Colfe's and was at this time living in Sutherland. The letter mainly refers to birds and nests that he has seen, and is signed 'Your old companion, Rupert Bryers'. In a small address section at the back of the 1913 diary, next to Rupert Bryers's name, Henry has written 'Oh!! Oh!! Those glorious days to appear no more!!!! Oh, what heart sorrows.'

Henry's premonitions of an early death did not materialize. Instead, it was Rupert Bryers who was to die shortly after the First World War started and of whom Mr Fitzaucher, their housemaster at Colfe's, was to write to Henry when his book *The Dandelion Days* was published in 1922. Fitzaucher was glad to find from the novel that Bryers had held him in some affection.

From Saturday 22 February to Wednesday 14 May 1913, the young Henry also kept a more detailed nature diary in an exercise book. Certain phrases show promise of the writer to be: 'The buds on the beech trees, so late generally in bursting into leaves, are now hovering between budlife and flower-hood. I heard a nightingale singing low notes, like a flute bubbling in water.' These notes appear as a nature diary that Willie is keeping in *Dandelion Days* and were later used directly as 'A Boy's Nature Diary' in a revised edition of *The Lone Swallows* published in 1933.

In an article called 'The Last Summer' which Henry Williamson wrote in 1964 for the *Sunday Times Magazine*[11] to commemorate the fiftieth anniversary of the outbreak of the First World War, he writes that he was 'a dreaming youth', whose 'dream lay in the countryside of north-west Kent'. He explains how he used to visit the 'Seven Fields of Shrofften' (Shroffield, where in the novels Richard and Hetty have their brief honeymoon) which 'sloped to the grey Bromley road'. Although by 1914 these places were becoming increasingly developed and suburbanized, partridges were still to be seen there, with roach in 'the little cattle-drinking ponds, each inhabited by its pair of moorhens' and trout in 'the watercress beds by Perry's Mill', although the Ravensbourne was dying the nearer to the Thames it flowed. He speaks of his 'own woods or preserves' further into the country, as being 'safe'. He had written to the landowners and gained permission to visit Holwood Park at Keston, Squire Norman's woods at the Rookery and Shooting Common, High Elms near Downe, Dunstall Priory near Sevenoaks and Squerryes Park at Westerham: no mean achievement for a schoolboy. How little could those who issued the permits have realized to what it would lead, for Henry Williamson's feelings and the adventures of his schooldays at the close of the Edwardian era would be marvellously recaptured in *Dandelion Days* published originally in 1922 and the second volume of his early work, the tetralogy *The Flax of Dream*, whose hero is Willie Maddison, where Colfe's is

<u>Part I.</u>

<u>Official diary of observations made in 1913,</u>
<u>as supplementary to pocket diary (fuller</u>
<u>account here).</u> a Boy's Nature Diary

Sat. Feb 22nd. Went to H. P. by myself. Arrived
at 3 o'clock. Saw woodmen clearing paths.
The one that told me about the sparrow-hawk's
nest last August, told me that he had seen
two young tawny owls sitting on old
ash tree near stack two months ago.
This seems to me to be unusual. Tawny
Owls nesting in early January! Still, the
abundance of field mice and voles, and
the mildness of the weather doubtless
account for this. (I have examined scores
of cast-up "pellets" both of the barn and
tawny owls, and the contain the bones and
fur of house + field mice, shotailed
field voles, and young rats. Occasionally
I have found evidence of sparrows being
eaten). This proves to me that (at least in.

A page from Henry's 1913 'Nature Diary'.

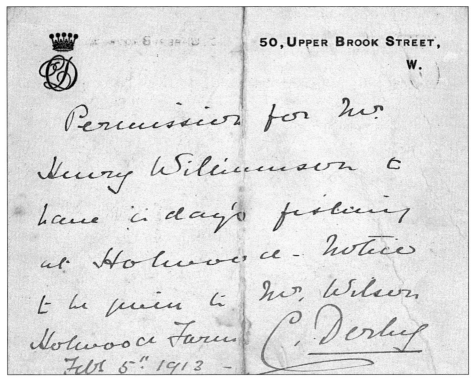

Henry's permits for Holwood and Squerryes Parks.

Colham Grammar School and the Headmaster, Mr Lucas, is Mr Rore. The same era is covered in *Young Phillip Maddison*. (Willie and Phillip are cousins in the books but in reality they are both, of course, extensions of Henry Williamson himself.)

When Henry first published *The Flax of Dream* books in the early 1920s his penetrating portraits of the staff and the daily life of the school were supposedly not very well received at Colfe's; hardly suprising, for no one likes their weaknesses and character to be so exposed, and the time-gap was still very short. Moreover Henry Williamson was also expounding an alternative and radical scheme of education via the chief character, Willie Maddison's 'A Policy of Reconstruction', which by inference, and more, suggested the old regime was the root of all evil. His ex-Headmaster, F.W. Lucas, did write him a mild reprimand, suggesting that the school's method of education had been really quite progressive, for example in allowing the Natural History Club, which permitted the boys a certain autonomy. But there is also in Henry Williamson's literary archive, a small number of most cordial letters from F.W. Lucas, and several very warm and friendly ones from his old housemaster, R.A. Fitzaucher, Mr Rapson in the novels, known to the boys as 'Rattlethrough', who wrote to Henry in 1922: 'You must not deprive me of the small piece of vanity, that I *am* the *original* of Mr Rattlethrough . . . it would be a blow to me if I felt there was a doubt on this point. I think the caricature immensely clever & killingly funny!' Today Henry Williamson is considered an honoured 'Old Colfeian' and the school is very proud to have been his Alma Mater.

His revisions of *Dandelion Days* in the late 1920s toned down his criticisms and deleted the somewhat caricature elements from the stories. By the time he came to write the *Chronicle* series in the 1950s the distance of time, his own maturity and firm grasp of structure and style enabled him to do a profounder justice to the whole era. He did say in many articles and prefaces to books that he had not enjoyed his schooldays, that they were an extremely unhappy time and particularly that the educational system prevailing at that time was iniquitous. (He certainly was not the only one to think that, but he did give extremely public utterance to his theories.) One of the chief remits of *The Flax of Dream* was to state this. Willie's 'Policy of Reconstruction' embodied Henry's thoughts on how to deal with the world after the end of the First World War, how to improve things for the future. But really the picture that emerges from his tales of his schooldays is that it was quite a reasonable time and that overall he had a lot of fun. It certainly gave him good material for some superb writing.

Having spent the last months at school in the commercial class to learn book-keeping, Henry left Colfe's at the end of May 1913 and commenced work two months later as a clerk in the Sun Fire Insurance Office – thinly disguised in the *Chronicle* as the Moon Fire Office. There are no real entries in his diary after that date, just the odd jotting of an appointment and suchlike sundries, from which we learn that his first wage of £5 was paid on 26 September. He then received another £5 on Tuesday 11 November (Martinmas), and also an extra £3 7s 6d for

THE SCHOOL STAFF, December, 1923.

Front line Worthy, "Rapson", Mr Snable, Mr Rose, or Rev Maycaster, Mr Tymon or Taffy, Mr Kennett or Bennett, Kellard chemistry master

Staff at Colfe's Grammar School. Henry has marked the names of those who were his masters.

Colfe's Grammar School.

May 30	Goldcrest	Small nests pendulated in branches of fir-tree. Several nesting here. Some reached young ones.
May 18–30	Wagtail (yellow-grey) 5	On hole in wall (built of slabs of some sort) in ledge of quarry (where birds have failed to nest 4 times this year). Each time robbed (by boy). Sat moderately lightly. Sits again on nest like in another; lives in another. Nests similar to preceding.
May 30.	Buzzard, Common (very rare).	On wood near mansion at Spaxcombe. Wood was looking or side of hill composed of good fir, oak and beech. Built a thing across where buzzard out, buzzards nests for many years. Difficult climb too, nest was situated thus, on horizontal branch. Three large eggs, near at hand. One like slightly crackled. Another was squarely marked at all. The old birds settled at some distance, and uttered

May 30.	Buzzard. plaintive cry: like a large kestrel. There are several pairs about here: they can often be seen soaring over the hills. The nest was, I believe, several nests of different years.

H.W. was a soldier 2½
Brought later, in
France 5½ months etc.
And front, front,
front, the last
always at front,
died and for
ever and
ever for ever

The final page from Henry's boyhood 'Nature Diary', written in 1914.

overtime. It seems logical that he would have commenced work on the previous quarter day, which would have been Lammas Day – 1 August; but that coincided with the Bank Holiday weekend, so possibly he did not actually start work until Tuesday 5 August.

At the end of August Gertrude took her two daughters, Kathie and Biddy, to the Channel Islands for a holiday. Postcards home to William Leopold are from Jersey, Guernsey and Sark and include one or two from the girls, but are mainly from Gertrude to her husband. Left to themselves, Henry and his father would appear not to have got on very well together, but Gertrude cannot have helped the situation by constant remarks about the lack of letters from her son – on postcards which he no doubt saw. This is the first proof of the friction between mother and son which was to be seen frequently from then on.

August 29 1913 – Homelands, Guernsey. [picture: Fermain Bay]
We have come here today, it is nicer. Why hasn't Harry written?
Much love GEW

August 30 1913 – Homelands, Guernsey [picture: Cobo Bay]
Hope you are alright. Tell Harry to write at once.
Shall be home next Saturday. Much love GEW

September 3rd. 1913 [picture: La Coupee, Sark]
We went here yesterday. It was quite calm & I was sick, the only one on board.
I am sorry about the boy, very. There are so many fathers with boy only here. It is a pity H. cannot be as companionable as they. Much love to both, shall see you on Sat.

Sept. 3rd. 1913 [picture: Icart Point, Guernsey]
We are going here this afternoon. The girls have gone for the day & we follow on. The air is more bracing here than Jersey & the scenery grand. Shall be glad to see you both. Have not heard from H. at all.

Having settled down to his job, Henry decided to enlist in the 5th Battalion, City of London Regiment, Territorial Forces, in January 1914. He was attracted, he said, by the £4 grant paid by his employers to every clerk who joined the territorials, and by the thought of the month's summer camp for regulation training, salary paid. He was expected to attend three drills a month.

At Easter he was with his cousins at Aspley Guise in Bedfordshire, his diary recording that he saw swallows, warblers, etc. there on Sunday 12 April. Then in May 1914 Henry went on holiday to North Devon to stay with his aunt Mary Leopoldina who rented a cottage in the isolated village of Georgeham in North Devon. His diary entries for this holiday start on 16 May: 'Sparrowhawk & 2 missle thrushes in field, Barn owl in cottage roof, 'Cob', Nightjars reeling. Cuckoo on gate. Stonechats; hopeless watch for nest.'

For the first time he climbed the hill leading north out of Georgeham, past the confluence of lanes at the top, and past the little copse, where he stopped and leaned over the field-gate to admire the view of the distant estuary of the Rivers Taw and Torridge. However beautiful he found it at that time, he certainly could not have known the great importance this place was to have in his future life. He wandered on down the other side of the hill to the woods at Spreycombe where he found: 'deserted tin mines (? silver) works and cottages (wagtail owl out). Caves. Cuckoo flying. . . . Barking cry of buzzard and crow's shrieks when he saw him.' On another day he ventured in the other direction: 'Mist over sea "Saunton Marshes" (= Braunton Burrows) – Ringed Plover Goldcrest. 3 nests. Seagulls down cliff. Cat & chicken at Croyde. Gorse fires.' And back to Spreycombe: 'Buzzard in Fire-tree. Aerie. Many years nests. 3 eggs – nearly hatched. Luck.' Until on 1 June, Whit Monday: 'Home. Baggy Point for farewell. Gulls on nest. Cormorants.'

This was a very happy and idyllic time for this impressionable and emotional young man. He immediately fell in love with the area's wild cliffs and moors and it made a great impression which was to have a lasting effect, forever heightened by the abrupt and imminent change to his world brought about by the declaration of war. Thoughts of this place sustained him through the ensuing hostilities. He returned for short visits whenever possible and it was to provide the haven to which he would flee after that war was over. At the end of his childhood 'Nature Diary' he added in later years:

> H.W. was a soldier 2¼ months later; in France 5¼ months later
> And Finish, Finish, Finish, the hope and illusion of youth,
> for ever, and for ever, and for ever.

CHAPTER 2

THE WET FLANDERS PLAIN

The First World War was a crucial period in Henry Williamson's life, forcing him to witness terrifying if thrilling battle scenes, providing male comradeship and the opportunity to enjoy wild and extravagant leaves, as well as an escape from his overbearing father. It may have scarred him psychologically; it certainly left its mark deep within him; but it gave him a *raison d'être*, a focus for his tremendous energy, and the inspiration for a series of books which are considered by many to contain the best descriptions of trench warfare ever written. For it is a *tour de force*, of the intellect and of the imagination, to have captured the whole experience of the war within five volumes of *A Chronicle of Ancient Sunlight*,[1] their continuous thread of story weaving in and out, from the front lines of battle to the suburbs of London, from the barracks of home-based battalions to the first hesitant fumblings of sex and idealistic love, creating a whole tapestry so true in detail, so convincing in content, that we know exactly what it was like to have lived in that time.

Those books were written in the 1950s in his mature years, when he had had time to come to terms with his war experiences, but he first wrote of them at the end of the 1920s in two other important books, *The Wet Flanders Plain* and *The Patriot's Progress*.[2]

It has been said by some critics of Henry Williamson that he never took any part in the First World War whatsoever; that everything he wrote was plagiarized from other people's work, particularly from the official war records. There are others who have taken every word he wrote literally, as gospel truth, believing that every detail of battle and incident in his novels must have happened, and did happen, to Henry Williamson himself. The reality lies somewhere between the two extremes. Henry Williamson did take part in the war; he enlisted in 1914 and he was present at some of the battles he describes in his novels, but some of his information has been gained from other sources. Where he was not himself actually present, his research into the minutest detail was meticulous and painstaking. Henry himself explained the situation in his 'Author's Note and Dedication' in the front of *A Fox Under My Cloak*, the fifth volume of *A Chronicle of Ancient Sunlight*:

Many of the scenes in this novel are authentic, including those which are based on incidents recorded in the Official History of the Great War, etc. Each of the characters in this novel had an existence in the 1914–18 war, though not all necessarily acted or played their parts in the times and places mentioned in the

Henry Williamson, 1917.

story. In particular, the author dedicates this volume to Captain Douglas Bell, MC, his old school-fellow and comrade-in-arms, wounded at Lone Tree during the battle of Loos, 1915.[3]

War was declared on 4 August 1914. The core of the regular army was the British Expeditionary Force (BEF) of six brigades of cavalry and six infantry divisions; plus the territorial force (314,000 non-professional soldiers); plus the home defence army consisting of fourteen mounted brigades and fourteen infantry divisions. Henry Williamson had already enlisted and his battalion, known as the London Rifle Brigade, was mobilized on 5 August 1914.

A very young and raw Henry, aged eighteen years and eight months, a private in P Company, No. 9689, in an emotional flux of excitement and trepidation, was swept along in the tide of men that flowed out of London for training, first at Bisley, where he had previously been in happier times with his school rifle team for competitions, and then at Crowborough Camp, Sussex.

His letters home, mainly to his mother, were all kept so there is a very personal record of much of his life in that dreadful war. From Bisley he wrote to her on 24 August 1914:

Dear Mother,
We are in this camp now. We sleep twelve in a tent like sardines, and have an awful time all day with marching in full kit, on Sat we marched thirteen miles with full kit, 70 lbs in the hot sun and dust, marching from 7.30 – 1.30. . . . Will you make me a blue woollen cap to sleep in covering the ears and head. . . .

love to all HWW.

And on 29 August 1914:

Dear Mother,
Thanks very much for the things you sent me. The cap is very nice at night . . . the LRB has volunteered for foreign service. You must not mind my going abroad . . . about one fifth will return alive. . . . It is very hard to leave home and friends and have only a memory of them left. I wonder if I shall ever see Holwood Park again, and play tennis on the Hill? I wonder but it is in higher hands than mine. I must close now, with great love to yourself and all the others, Your loving son, Harry.

Then a few days later, on 2 September:

Dear Mother,
Thanks very much for the socks, But really I have four pairs, and I daren't wear the pair you sent me for marching, because the seams in them would blister my feet terribly. But I shall sleep in the last pair. Can you send me my woollen sweater, I am very cold at night. . . . Give my love to Granpa and Uncle Hughie,

and to father and Bids and Kath and to yourself and all. Love from your
affectionate son, Harry.

And on 5 September:

Dear Mother,
Thanks for the jersey. . . . Will you come and see me here if I can't get leave, I
will write when. . . . Tell father to look after my bike for me. Don't touch my
eggs or my diaries – they are both sacred to me as remenisences [*sic*] of happy
days. We rise at six. One hours Swedish. 8 – Breakfast – 'Tea' (green water with
grease but drinkable to we 'sojers') Bread, fat, 'jam' (turnips). Drill, scurmishing
[*sic*] 8.30 to 1. 1 Dinner ('skilly', meat, potatoes, bread in a stew – good stuff).
2–4 Drill +c. 4 'Tea' Bread, jam. Muck about till 9.15. Same monotonous stuff
every day.

Letters in HWLEA

Henry had also written to his old school mentors for he received encouraging
letters from Leland Duncan and also F.W. Lucas on school headed notepaper:

My dear Williamson,
Many thanks for your most interesting letter. The hardships will not be without
their use & when you get fit, – why, glorious. I speak having suffered in many a
weary walk & climb & ride. Tasks of fatigue are wisely taken at intervals.
I regularly take them now. This mention to cheer you in your trial with thoughts
of the ultimate gain & the pleasant memories.
    Very many old Colfeians have taken the post of honour. We hope to make a
roll of all such for undying memory.
    Never was there a more righteous war – civilisation against despotism. None
of us can survive with honour unless there is victory.
    It is quite possible the war may be short. What sort of soldiers are made by
scurging & spitting in the face? There can be no ideals. The cry of 'Fatherland'
has no inspiration for men thus treated.
    You & all Colfeians will bravely face your Destiny, as we must all. And we
must hope & trust though all the strings of our lyre be broken.[4]
    Please remember me most kindly to all the fellows & to them & to you my
kindest wishes. And when you lie in the field amid all the panoply of war,
seeking memories of the past ere sleep falls upon you, think that my thoughts
will be with you nightly in my solitary walk between 10 & 11 p.m. with regrets
that I cannot be with you to share your fighting & hardships.

Kindest wishes. Very truly yours, F.W. Lucas
Letter in HWLEA, dated 7 September 1914

On 16 September the company were on the road again, marching en route from
the camp at Bisley to the one at Crowborough, Sussex, where Henry quickly

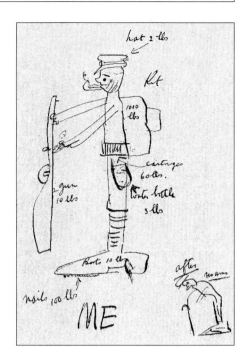

Henry drew this sketch on the back of a
letter home after marching out of London to
the training camp in August 1914.

found that his specially ordered thick-soled boots were useless for marching, as he
wrote in *How Dear Is Life* where Phillip sets out on the same journey:

*Phillip's faith in heavy-nailed campaign clumps was gone by the time the
battalion reached the granite-setts of London Bridge at half-past six on the
summer morning. The sun was already hot in the eastern sky above Tower
Bridge. There were few people about to cheer the skirl of pipes and tramp of
feet; but enough to make him proud of being a London Highlander, to forget
his disappointment over the boots. But by the time the battalion had marched
over similar jarring setts along the tram-lined Kennington, crossed Clapham
Common, and reached Wandsworth, the Brigade rendezvous by the windmill on
Wimbledon Common, the skin of his feet was broken and raw in a dozen
places. Fortunately they piled arms, and could lie on the grass.*

How Dear Is Life, Chapter 13, 'Elastic-sided Highlander'

Reveille had been at 5 a.m., with only coffee and biscuits. At 6 p.m. they were
dismissed and were able to wash, and patch up their heels with the black plaster
called 'New Skin'. Eventually after queueing for an hour they managed to get
some fish and chips. The following day's march, which started in 'great spirit in
the bright air of the morning' soon turned into a nightmare of heat and dust and
the burden of heavy awkward equipment, all of which increased proportionately

as the day progressed. The cartoon he drew on the back of one of his letters makes it amusing in retrospect. It cannot have been very amusing at the time.

The march over, conditions seem to have been pretty grim on their arrival at Crowborough – no tents and the food abominable – as he wrote to his father:

Dear Father,
Thanks very much for the decent letter and the 10/- . . . We arrived here in the bleak, cold windy spot. Wind continual, with a fine gritty dust. We arrived at 3pm and ate our 'emergency ration' ¼ lb bread and cheese. Rain. Wet through and thoroughly hungry, we slept all night on the damp ground under the stars. Breakfast – undrinkable 'tea' (no milk or sugar) and one slice bread. For dinner uncooked boiled mutton. Half the chaps couldn't eat it but I wolfed 2 lbs of it. For tea, no milk or sugar, and 3 Huntley & Palmers lunch biscuits. No drinkable tea today – and three loaves per twelve men for all day. Result today – several men high temperatures and delirious. It's pretty awful. Be sure that if I go abroad, I will fight like a devil and a Williamson against these barbarians who are doing the Fiend's own hellish work in wrecking the peace of Europe, and causing grief and anguish in millions of homes.

Letter in HWLEA, dated 19 September 1914

But conditions improved; 'We are enjoying ourselves now – are fit & 20 miles march is nothing. Good food.' Hard training was going on continuously and Henry was constantly expecting the LRB to be sent abroad and equally constantly hoping to have some leave. The family went to visit him at Crowborough. Many letters show petulance and tetchiness that his every request was not immediately seen to; due to nervousness no doubt, but his poor mother must have found some of the letters rather hard to take. For instance, he had asked for a lamp to be sent but his mother was obviously unsure about it and did not deal with the request, and so received a very curt and sarcastic note:

We have to burn candles, so a little oil lamp to burn steadily would be a blessing. Still, as you are uninclined to get one as I particularly asked you, perhaps I had better write to other people for it. So please don't trouble any more about it. I will arrange for it & any other little necessities of life that help to improve the existence here. If there are any little debts owing to you from me, please deduct them from the sum that you have. Also do you think it advisable to get rid of my suits and saleable things at home. In all probability I shall never have need of them again. There is some talk of us going away at dawn tomorrow. If that is so then it is goodbye for most of the chaps for ever. So if you hear of our departure you mustn't mind at all. . . . Hope that you are all well and comfortable, I remain Your affectionate son, Harry.

Letter undated

Then on 29 October 1914, the waiting was over:

Dear Mother,
Come on Friday with Father, in time for tea at the Camp here, the LRB is one of several regiments for the Front in France.

And a postcard written in another's hand from Crowborough on 5 November 1914:

'Just off. Quite well – HWW'. Williamson wished me to send the above message. He seemed well & happy. Signed W. [?] Blelarks

Letters in HWLEA

The troopship *Chyebassa* took them to France on 4 November 1914. They landed at Le Havre, then went by cattle truck on a two days' journey to St Omer where they were billetted in the convent. The arrival in France seems to have been chaotic. A small official book produced by the London Rifle Brigade in 1916, under censorship regulations, describes the dismal and dirty artillery barracks where the battalion were eventually billetted.[5]

Henry's first letters home were calm and cheerful, and plainly factual, one written on 19 November and date-stamped 24 November 1914 cleverly getting round the fact that he was not allowed to give his whereabouts, stated:

Dear Mother,
I received several letters from you lately. We have moved about a lot since last writing, and we are now in a little village in the country we visited two years ago with Uncle Percy & Grandfather. You remember? [i.e. Belgium, when they visited Kathie's school near Wespalaer.] All day & most of the night huge detonations shake the air around us, and the sounds are rather awe-inspiring at first.

The official book states, 'Training which consisted of trench digging and artillery formation, was carried out daily regardless of the weather', and on 19 November, 'the Battalion moved one stage nearer to the firing line in a snow-storm'. It records for 20 November, 'At dusk on this date the Battalion proceeded via Ploegsteert to the trenches.' Henry's postcard home of 6 December fills out the reality of this bald statement:

Quite well but rather seedy; just returned after 3 days in trenches – flooded out by rain – Rotten time this time; continually shelled and maxims and rifle fire. Thank Auntie B. & Mary & Effie for parcels & Granpa. Have got fur coat. Send choc, sweet *cake*. sardines, milk etc. Love Harry.

And again on 13 December:

As I write I am sitting by the stove of a little cottage in the Belgium village of ——. Last night we returned from the trenches (for the third time). It has been awful in the trenches. For two days and nights we have been in nearly 36 inches of mud and water. Can you picture us sleeping standing up, cold and wet half way up our thighs, and covered with mud. As we crept into the trenches at dead of night, the Germans sent up magnesium flares, and we had to crouch flat while scores of bullets spat amongst us.

On the 21st:

Dear Mother,
How are you all at home? I expect that by the time you get this you will have had Xmas. . . . We have progressed here perhaps 200 yds in 2 months. But the Germans can't stop us. I have received a parcel containing choc & sweets from the CSSA which I presume is from Father. Thanks very much. Love Harry

Letters in HWLEA

So Henry Williamson spent the Christmas of 1914 in the trenches in Belgium and was present at the famous 'Christmas Truce' as we learn from his pencilled letter home dated 26 December 1914, a small Union Jack pinned to the top of the page:

Dear Mother,
I am writing from the trenches. It is 11 o'clock in the morning. Beside me is a coke fire, opposite me a 'dug-out' (wet) with straw in it. The ground is sloppy in the actual trench, but frozen elsewhere. In my mouth is a pipe presented by Princess Mary. In the pipe is tobacco. Of course, you say. But wait. In the pipe is German tobacco. Ha Ha, you say, from a prisoner or from a captured trench. Oh, dear, no! From a German soldier. Yes a live German soldier from his own trench. Yesterday the British and Germans met & shook hands in the Ground between the trenches, & exchanged souvenirs, & shook hands. Yes, all day Xmas day, & as I write. Marvellous, isn't it? Yes. This is only for about a mile or two on either side of us (so far as we know). It happened thiswise. On Xmas eve both armies sang carols & cheered & there was very little firing. The Germans (in some places 80 yards away) called to our men to come and fetch a cigar & our men told them to come to us. This went on for some time, neither fully trusting the other, after much promising to 'play the game' a bold Tommy crept out & stood between the trenches, & immediately a Saxon came to meet him. They shook hands & laughed & then 16 Germans came out. Thus the ice was broken. Our men are speaking to them now. They are landsturmers or landwehr, I think, & Saxons & Bavarians (no Prussians). Many are gentle looking men in goatee beards & spectacles, and some are very big and arrogant-looking. I have some cigarettes which I shall keep, & a cigar I have smoked. We had a burial service in the afternoon, over the dead Germans who perished in the 'last attack that was repulsed' against us. The Germans put 'For Fatherland & Freedom' on the cross. They obviously think their cause is a just one. Many

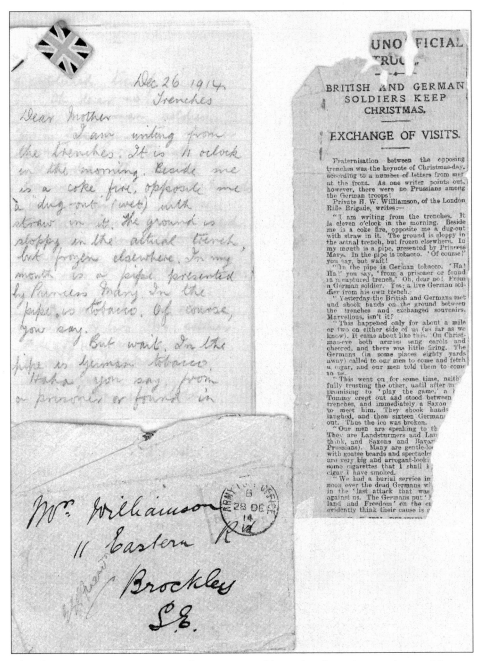

The Christmas Truce, 1914. Letter from Henry to his mother from the trenches on 26 December 1914, and its subsequent printing in the *Daily Express*.

of the Germans here are, or were, waiters. Thank Efford for his chocolate. Auntie Belle for the cigarettes. I have had an awful time with swollen feet and my toes are frostbitten now. But it is all in the days work, as is working all night at digging or etc etc & sleeping in wet and mud. Where we are billetted (8 of us in a cottage in a town which is shelled now and again) we have a good time. There is a family of Belgians here whose house had been destroyed, and the old mother, about 56 yrs old, is very jolly and resourceful, as well as comical. . . .

[The rest of the letter is missing]

Letter in HWLEA

Unknown to Henry, his father arranged to have this letter printed in the *Daily Express*. It is the first known published example of Henry Williamson's work. He was quick to see the potential that publication brought about, which no doubt made him a centre of interest, and was soon planning a further episode.

Letter of 9 January 1915:

Dear Mother,

I am just writing a little letter to you now quite personal. By the same post I am sending another of general interest. I see that my letter of Xmas Day has appeared in the Daily Express. Perhaps you would send it to the same paper but I think that the Daily Mail is better.

Letter of 10 January 1915:

Dear Father,

I will in another letter, sent simultaneously with this one, endeavour to tell you what this war looks like, and the battlefield to the observer.

A cutting from a newspaper with these letters would appear to be the printed version of the item referred to above. It is very worn now, and is undated and untitled. William Leopold obviously arranged for its printing but it is not possible to say which paper he did indeed choose. The first part is missing but it continues:

. . . . The men are quite proud of Plug-Street. [Here HW has written in the margin – 'L.R.B. & Prussian Guards Nov 27 – Dec 14']

So much for the lighter side of the story. There is, alas! a grimmer tale belonging to it. Here has been, on a small scale, some of the most desperate fighting of the war. For months there was a bitter and bloody struggle for this position, which is of very considerable military value, and as late as last December the Germans inflicted heavy losses on the gallant garrison. They have little chance now of calling Plug-street their own, but more than once it has been touch and go.

Even today the sniping goes on continually, and occasionally the wood is shelled.

The Watch

Plug-Street represents, in epitome, the soldier's life in the sort of siege warfare that has reigned on the British lines for weeks and months past. Perhaps it is a little better than the weary vigil of the low-lying trenches. There is at least more air and freedom. Death, if it comes, may seem less terrible under the shadows of the trees than in the foul mire of an aritificial burrow. But is is terribly wearing. To peep over the parapets on the outskirts of the wood is simply to invite death. To be in the wood at all is to know that at any moment the predestined bullet may find its mark. There is more cheerfullness, certainly there is more real good friendship in Picadilly, Plug-street, than in Picadilly, London.

The fraternization on Christmas Eve 1914 made a deep and lasting impression upon Henry Williamson; he saw that war was created by greed, misplaced zeal and bigotry. He could never forget that the German soldiers thought as deeply and sincerely as the English that they were fighting for God and Country. (Also there is a note among the papers in his literary archive to the effect that after the war was over, his Aunt Maude pointed out to him that he had been fighting his own cousins.) All these factors affected him very deeply and determined his life's work: to show the world that truth and peace lay in beauty and the open air.

He was eventually to write up the Christmas Truce in the compelling and moving chapter in *A Fox Under My Cloak* entitled 'Heilige Nacht', where, although a little allowance for poetic licence must surely be made, we are projected into that scene:

It was most strangely quiet when, with posts, rolls of wire, hammers and staples, and R.E. wooden betels, they picked their way on the path of frost-cobbled mud leading to the open grey blankness beyond the wood. No flares were to be seen any-where in the silent night. Not a shot was to be heard over the frozen battlefield. Did the silence mean that they were to be trapped? Were the Germans waiting until they were all out in front of the wood, before mowing them down with machine-guns?

Their breath hung in the still air as they crept over the hard silver ground to their tasks, rifles slung, free of all equipment save a cloth bandolier across the front of their goat's-skin jerkins. Soon they were used to the open moonlight, in which all life and movement seemed unreal. Men were laying down posts, arranging themselves into parties to hold and knock; others preparing to unwind the rolls of wire.

Not a shot was fired; not a sound came from the Germans. The unbelievable soon became the ordinary so that they talked as they worked, without caution, while the night passed as in a dream. The moon moved down to the top of the wood behind them; always, it seemed, they had been moving bodilessly with their own shadows. . . .

Sometime in the night Phillip saw what looked like a light on top of a pole put up in the German lines. It was a strange sort of light. It burned almost white, and was absolutely steady. What sort of lantern was it? It was part of the strange unreality of the silence of the night, of the silence of the moon in the sky, of the silence of the frost mist.

Suddenly there was a short quick cheer from the German lines, Hoch! Hoch! Hoch!, and with the others he flinched and crouched, ready to throw himself flat; but no shot came from the enemy lines. Other cheers were coming across the space of No Man's Land. Then they saw dim figures on the German parapet, about more lights; and with amazement he saw that it was a Christmas tree being set there, and around it were Germans talking and laughing together. Hoch! Hoch! Hoch! They were cheering. Then from the German parapet a rich baritone voice had begun to sing a song Phillip remembered from his nurse Minny singing it to him. Stille Nacht! Heilige Nacht! – Tranquil Night! Holy Night!

The grave and tender voice rose out of the frosty mist; it was all so strange; it was like being in another world, to which he had come through a nightmare; a world finer than the one he had left behind, except for beautiful things like music, and springtime on his bicycle in the country.

The next day Phillip walked into No Man's Land and found himself face to face with living Germans, men in grey uniforms and leather knee-boots – a fact which was as yet almost unbelievable. Moreover, the Germans were actually, some of them, smiling as they talked in English. He moved on to where some Germans were digging a grave. An officer read from a prayer-book, and the Saxons stood to attention with round grey hats clutched in left hands, the English men stood to attention also. The Germans had made a cross from ration-box wood, marked in indelible pencil:

> *HIER RUHT IN GOTT EIN UNBEKANNTE DEUTSCHER HELD*
> *'Here rests in God an unknown German hero.'*
>   *A Fox Under My Cloak, Chapter 3, 'Heilige Nacht'*

In mid-January 1915 Henry Williamson became ill. He wrote to his mother:

I write hurriedly to let you know that I am now on my way to base, where I shall be in hospital. I am suffering from a rather bad form of enteritis accompanied by rotten pains in stomach and head and am very weak. I have been rotten for 3 weeks. I am very thin and pale but am not downcast. I am writing in the Red Cross train – the arrangements for 'malades' on it are ripping & the authorities are kindness itself. Will drop a card later. Yours affectionately, Harry.

> Letter in HWLEA, dated 17 January 1915

This was followed by a further postcard from the hospital itself on the coast, in which he asks for tobacco and cigarettes to be sent 'as soon as poss'. From there

On first returning from the trenches in January 1915 – with dysentery, trench feet, and torn overcoat.

he was shipped back to England. His official record gives his date of return as 26 January 1915. A note on a 1973 envelope into which he had placed a photograph, states that he was taken to Ancoats Military Hospital in the Midlands in February 1915, and returned to his home early in March 1915.

His older sister Kathie, speaking in her old age after his death, described Henry's appearance on his return thus: 'He was a terrible sight; when he appeared at the bottom of Eastern Road we couldn't recognise him. He was very pale and thin. He looked like a scarecrow; his uniform greatcoat was torn and covered in mud. He had dysentery and red puffy swollen feet from being constantly wet and frozen.'

In *A Fox Under My Cloak* Phillip's home-coming in the same circumstances is described as strained, and no doubt so was that of Henry. He had been through searing experiences in those two months in the battlefields, and ordinary homelife would have taken much adjusting to. His father had become a sergeant in the special constabulary set up for air raid warden and Home Guard type duties, and he was engaged in tiring tasks undertaken after a full day's work at his bank in the City, and which on several occasions a week went on until midnight. He took this work very seriously and recorded all the details in a little notebook. Henry had written him a long letter from the battlefield just before being invalided home, telling him to:

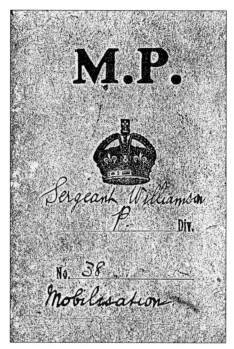

William Leopold Williamson in the uniform of Sergeant of Special Constabulary during the First World War, and his notebook.

Chuck the official constable work. Also the Defence Force you mention (composed of elderly men, I presume?) may be very nice as a sort of hobby but, believe me, in case of invasion they would be no use whatsoever.

He goes on to give a graphic description of just how useless they would be, and exactly what would happen to them and London, if the Germans invaded. He was, of course, writing with all the experience and evidence of bombardment, but not surprisingly William Leopold did not take very kindly to such criticism. He was further disturbed to find his son went out drinking with his friends, a natural enough desire on the part of someone back from the horrors of the front, but not approved of by his father.

Henry wrote to his old school about his experiences, and his letters appeared in an issue of *Colfensia*:

WAR NEWS

17th March 1915

. . . I was invalided home about two months ago, but am now cured, although, of course, I am not now very strong; my nerves are a bit 'joggy', too.

Trench work is rather monotonous. We relieve men holding them, and are relieved ourselves in turn, regularly.

The first time we went in the trenches we were mixed up with regulars, being, of course, rather nerve-shaken. But the feeling of nervousness soon left us, and we set to work to pump the trenches. I must tell you the actual trenches were two feet deep in mud and water, and the harder we pumped, the deeper grew the water (or so it seemed to us). In the trenches we do one hour 'on' sentry, and one 'off'. This is throughout the hours of darkness. During our one hour 'off' we pump, dig, fix up wire in front (we were about 90 yards from the Germans), fetch rations and numerous other jobs. You can imagine then, that after three or fours days of this the strain is rather acute. The fact of no sleep, and legs, and, in fact, all the body, wet through, does not help to improve the situation.

Now and then we get a shell or two over, and, when very lucky, an attack. We are literally overjoyed when they attack us, for it means a great shooting practice. They attack shoulder to shoulder, and *march* on our trenches. When (and if) they get within twenty yards they open fanwise, and some sections lie down to allow a clear path for the Maxim fire.

But, generally, they get to the barbed wire entanglements, and there they stop. It is a fine sound to hear thousands of rifles and machine-guns all cracking at once, and now and then a 'rafale' of several batteries of French 75mm. guns.[6]

Recovering strength, the young soldier soon applied for a commission, which was granted on 10 April, and this appeared in the Army List for May 1915 – 'Williamson, H.W., Temp. 2nd. Lieut., 10th Service Btn., The Bedfordshire Regiment.' (He wanted to be with his Bedfordshire cousin Charlie Boone, but they were fated not to meet up and Charlie was killed in action in 1916.) Henry then attended an officers' instruction course between April and September with the 4/1st Cambridgeshire Regiment at Newmarket.

Henry implies in his novels that he did not find the transition to officer very easy. He lacked the background and social graces to carry it off with nonchalance and his efforts to do so meant he committed several 'social gaffes' which were noted by his seniors, and which made him feel very uncomfortable and gauche. For example, he frequently told the tale of how at his first mess dinner he was offered a dish of asparagus; he helped himself liberally to the delicacy, almost emptying the dish, saying, 'Oh, good, I like asparagus.' To which the mess waiter replied very drily, 'Yes sir, and so do the others.'

On 9 October 1915 he was attached to the 25th (Reserve) Battalion, The Middlesex Regiment, newly formed at Crystal Palace and in November the regiment moved to Northampton. At the beginning of January 1916 (see Army List p. 1563) he was transferred to 208th Company, The Machine Gun Corps, 62nd Division, 187 Brigade, and for the greater part of 1916 he was training as a transport officer which included attending riding school and learning about the maintenance and firing of machine guns.

During this period Henry acquired a motorcycle: a Norton – LP 1656 – which he named 'Doris II'. In the *Chronicle* novels it appears as 'Helena', after the desirable but remote Helena Rolls, daughter of the well-to-do family who lived in his home street and who in real life were the Nicholson family; whom he yearns after but who is unobtainable.

His motorcycle gave him greater freedom of movement. It also gave him trouble and got him into trouble. Throughout his life Henry had problems with the engines of any vehicle he owned. He seemed to expect them to be perfect and was very impatient when they were not, while his understanding of mechanical things had many gaps, so he was forever spending vast amounts to have experts overhaul the latest acquisition.

In August he was given leave and went on holiday on his motorbike to Devon, to stay at the cottage in Georgeham with his friend from school days, Terence Tetley. A photograph shows them entirely relaxed, swimming naked at Putsborough Sands. Henry and Terence were somewhat wild at this point. For instance, there are notes attached to a photograph of Terence, who is standing next to Henry's motorcycle outside 11 Eastern Road in the early summer of 1916, captioned 'Terence Tetley, the original of Desmond Neville' and 'Terence & Me – Top hat on Sunday & broken boots. Flowers & Condy's Fluid. Horses on hill. Girls in flat.' This was an *aide-mémoire* for a scene he would write in the *Chronicle* about a 'drunken' episode in the summer of 1916 when the two of them went on the Hill next to Henry's parental home, about 3.30 a.m. one Sunday morning, where, as the note continued:

we (idiotically) broke into a lavatory & then scattered the Condy's Fluid about on the flowerbeds as a 'protest' against smug and self-righteous civilians. The

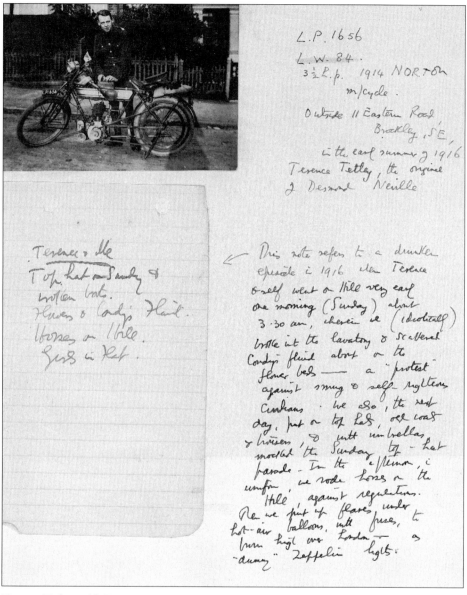

Terence Tetley, with Henry's accompanying notes.

Henry and Terence Tetley.

next day we put on top hats, old coats and trousers and with umbrellas mocked the Sunday top-hat parade. In the afternoon in uniform we rode horses on the Hill against regulations. Then we put up flares under hot-air balloons, with fuses, to burn high over London – as 'dummy' Zeppelin lights.

At some point Henry wrote to the *Motor Cycle* magazine extolling the virtues of his Norton and this letter was used by Norton in an advertisement which appeared in another magazine, *Motor Cycling*, on 17 October 1916. There is also a scattering of cuttings which show he was having trouble with what he called 'Konking on Hills' and was carrying on a correspondence in the press trying to discover the cause:

KONKING ON HILLS

Sir, – I should be greatly obliged if any of your readers could account for the following phenomenon which occurs with a well-known long-stroke single-cylinder motor cycle engine. It has puzzled me for a considerable period, and I confess I am beaten.

When I start from cold, the acceleration is terrific – the engine will roar away in fine style – with no suspicion of a konk or a knock. But if I have been running for a short time – say ten minutes – and I stop for a minute and then start again, while the engine is picking up a series of tremendous konks occurs, as though the cylinder were being hit by a hammer.

Now I have often been prevented from climbing a stiffish hill owing to this wretched konk. If I can manage to rush the hill I shall get up all right, but if I slow down whilst climbing I cannot manage to get up at all; but if I stop halfway up the hill, and allow the engine to get *absolutely cold* I shall roar up the hill without the slightest difficulty.

I have noticed that when these konks occur, a cloud of bluish smoke always comes out of the exhaust pipe, following the stroke of the piston; I have checked it several times. The ignition is timed correctly. Mixture right. I have tried bigger jets, smaller jets, extra air, etc. There are no airleaks. The cylinder never gets at all hot. I am certain the plug points do not get incandescent, and there is no doubt that it is not a carbon particle.

Can any of your readers tell me why this is? The engine, by the way, is 100 x 79.

H.W. Williamson (Lt. M.G.C.)

The Norton advertisement which used Henry's letter of praise.

There are two letters of reply which appeared in a later issue, but no indication of whether they were helpful in curing the problem. There is another cutting showing that he wrote to a paper a letter headed 'Motor Cycling Munition Workers' which refers to 'young male strikers at Woolwich . . . these weedy and narrow-chested youths fooling about with girls on their motor cycles. . . . When the boys come home I expect these wretched creatures will have a rather unpleasant time.' This brought a very tart reply from one of the said strikers:

> Does it strike H.W.W. that these 'narrow-chested weedy youths' are the men who make it possible for himself to move into action? These wretched creatures have worked night and day to provide munitions, and their brains and energy provided the country with the necessary war material. . . . I wish H.W.W. a safe return.
>
> Munition Worker

Also pasted into this exercise book is a further cutting headed 'YOUNG BLOODS IN THE ARMY WARNED' which relates how Lieut. Wm. Williamson, stationed at Newmarket, was summoned for driving a motorcycle at a speed dangerous to the public on 26 August 1915. He was fined £1. An entire 6 inches of column space were devoted to this item. This incident is related in A Fox Under My Cloak in the chapter entitled 'Life is Fun'. The impression one gains from this carefully pasted-up booklet is that Henry Williamson had discovered that getting into print was enjoyable.

On 1 November 1916 Henry was promoted to the rank of lieutenant with the Machine Gun Corps. The promotion appeared in the Army List, (p. 1565) in the following February, but it was notified in the London Gazette of 21 December, as stated in a letter from his bankers – he had written to ask them to amend the rank on his account and they used the notice as proof.

At the beginning of 1917 Henry Williamson was transport officer with the MGC 208 Company at Grantham where, apart from his duties with the horses and mules, he enjoyed visits to the pictures and the theatre, drinking sessions with his fellow officers, and taking out various young ladies. The unit was supposed to proceed to France on 1 February, but this was delayed. Finally they left Grantham on Saturday 24 February arriving at Southampton at 6 o'clock on the Sunday, 'No casualties [i.e. among the mules and horses]; left the dock at 7 and anchored in the Harbour', leaving at 3 p.m. on Monday 26th, and reaching 'Havre without incident at 2 in morning. Went to Rest Camp.' They arrived at the front on March 1.

The Henry Williamson Literary Estate Archive contains his diary, a detailed army correspondence book and a field message book, and his letters home to his mother, all covering this period. Between them they give a vivid picture of his life at this time.

Diary, Monday 12 March 1917: Artillery ominously quiet early morning. Davy wounded by bomb. Am taking Ammunition through Miramount tonight. Have

Henry in officer's uniform, 1917.

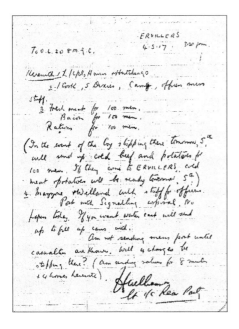

A page from Henry's 'Army Correspondence Book', 1917.

a presentiment. 3 letters from home. Took 16 pack mules through Miramount. Got lost. Lost 2 mules. Arrived back at 3 o'clock dead beat. Sent cheque to WLW £20. Bagdad [*sic*] falls.

Letter, 12 March 1917: Dear Mother, Am quite well and fit – I have had more during the last week than I got in 4 months in the Flemish sector. By God its awful – we are shelled day and night – the roads are barraged and 12 inch hows [howitzer shells] knock hell into us all day & night but *our* guns knock the Bosche to hell and back.

Diary, 15 March 1917: Bombardment of our heavies all day, of [?]. Very busy finding billets at Engelbelmer. Saw 34 and 213 MGC. Bombardment intense at night. Achiet le Petit the objective. Up all night driving.

Army Correspondence Book, 15 March 1917: To T. Sgt. Two empty limbers will leave here by 12 today for Coy. HQ. Each limber will have 6 mules and 3 drivers. Double feeds will be carried and each driver will take the unexpended portion of the days rations. Time of return will be probably late in the evening. The picket will have tea ready for these drivers when they return. The CQMS will have rations for 20 men in a bag labelled Lt. Horsley, B Section, which will proceed with the limbers. HWW. Lt. MG.

This continues with daily jottings of which the following are short extracts taken at random, showing the intensity of the situation: 'Bombardment intense at night'; 'Up all night driving'; 'Bosche poisoning wells'; 'Rode up too near Bosche lines'; 'looked around [Gommecourt] everything burnt & destroyed'; 'Brigade going over the top shortly'; 'Rode a buck jumping mule'; 'Saw Hindenburg Line & dead Bosches'; 'Arras bombardment intensive;' 'Beginning to feel the strain a bit – head aches like hell.'

Among Henry's papers there is a document entitled '62nd. Division Order No. 36', which contained the secret orders for the attack on the Hindenburg Line, dated 13 April 1917, of which this is copy number 19, allotted to 208th M.G. Coy. with an 'Order of the Day' dated 1 May 1917; it states:

> As the Division will shortly be going into action to take part in its first great battle, the Divisional Commander desires to assure all ranks of his complete confidence in their ability to defeat the German troops opposed to them. . . . That the 62nd (West Riding) Division will maintain its reputation for staunchness and grit – qualities for which Yorkshiremen have ever been famed – that they will gain all objectives and hold them against the most determined counter-attacks, is the firm conviction of the General Officer who is proud to be their Commander.
>
> Signed: Major General, Commanding 62nd (West Riding) Division

In the attack on the Hindenburg Line, the 62nd Division was given special responsibility for the capture of Bullecourt. Entries in Henry's diary continue: 'Last night attack on H. line. Cavalry up & RHA – working all night'; 'lots of Bosche planes over'; 'Bosche breaks through on our right, Coy. standing to. Raining again. Will this bloody weather never improve? Heavy shelling.' The entry for 3 May reads: 'Z day. Zero hour, 2.45. Intensive barrage right up North & down to Bullecourt. Rumours of failure – prisoners in cages – walking wounded. 3/4 Coy missing at evening. Mountford killed. Coy. badly mauled. Have been very lucky.' On 27 May he writes: 'B'de out of line. Taking rations to Bullecourt tonight. Shelled a bit and about 200 phosgene gas shells over.' For 8 June: 'Went sick this morning, Medicine & duty. Raining. Gassed at B.' For the 9th: 'Admitted to Field Ambulance Hospital'; 'Put on board train for Rouen.' Then, on the 17th: 'Am leaving today for hospital ship, to Sussex Lodge Hosp., London.' And finally, on the 21st: 'Home. Saw all. Very nice reception'; 'Saw board, 1 month leave'.

On the 29 June he travelled to Falmouth in Cornwall, to Trefusis, a house commandeered for use as a convalescent home for sick and wounded soldiers and which still exists today. At his next board he was granted three months' convalescence leave. A very terse diary entry for 3 July states, 'Began story'.

There are several photographs of Henry during this period at Trefusis in which he appears very relaxed, playing tennis, going boating, and becoming friendly with the nurses; gradually he recovered his health. It must have been a complete haven from the hell of bombardment in the trenches. The original Trefusis was built in 1447, in the solid manner of that time. Due to the quirks of fate of the family who owned it, it became eventually very dilapidated and was actually rebuilt in 1890, but keeping many of the features of the original.[7] Looking at the drawings, plans and general description of this house gave me a distinct impression of *déjà vu* – in particular the Tudor doorway and massive Tudor mantelpiece. For it would seem almost certain that it is this house which Henry Williamson used in *A Chronicle of Ancient Sunlight* as the basis for 'Fawley House', the home of Captain William Maddison, 'the family home since before the Wars of the Roses, in the fifteenth century'. It is described in Chapter 5 of *The Power of the Dead* as a fortified, square building with a wide oak staircase, more than ten bedrooms, rooms built in Stuart times around a raftered dining hall with minstrel gallery and great open stone fireplace. All of which fits the description of Trefusis. And, of course, we have the final clue of the pun, a favourite Williamson ploy, in the name of the house in the novels – Fawley House – which is the name of the River Fal, the estuary overlooked by the real house lengthened to a West Country drawl, Fa–w–ley.

Although Henry Williamson used the episode of convalescence at Trefusis in *A Test To Destruction*, where in Chapter 4, 'Algerian Wine Party' and Chapter 5, 'Relapsed Hero' Phillip convalesces at 'Tregaskis House' near Falmouth, he did not describe the house at all in detail. By the time he wrote these volumes he had decided to 'lift' this house and locate it, as the family home, in his imaginary village of Rookhurst, which in his first book, *The Beautiful Years*, is set rather vaguely in the 'West Country', but in the later writing of the *Chronicle* is rather more firmly placed in mid-Dorset – by his reference to local landmarks evidently somewhere just west of Salisbury. In the mature writing he is more sure of the effect he wants to achieve.

At the end of his convalescence leave Henry noted in his diary, on 15 October, that he joined the 3rd Bedfordshires at Felixstowe. But at the beginning of 1918 he stated that the medical board still kept him on home service only, and he 'Began Musk. [Musket] Course' on 28 January 1918. At this time he frequently noted that he had received letters from and had written to Terence Tetley, and he sent him several sums of money. Then eventually fresh orders were received and his diary entry for 27 March reads: 'Ret. Felixstowe. 5 a.m. Left for Victoria 9.30 a.m. Crossed to Boulogne 11.30 p.m. To IBD at Etaples. Up the line tomorrow, to 8th Battalion.'

This period of the war is described in *A Test To Destruction*, Part II, 'Action', where he covers the whole of that terrible spring German offensive when the British were pushed right back with very heavy casualties, and the war was almost lost, until the German attacks unaccountably lost their impetus.

Phillip was returning with the R.S.M. through the misty darkness of the moonless night, having visited the battalion working and wiring parties up the line, when gas shells began to swoop over along the whole front. They splashed yellow, oily liquid from the soft bursts. No high explosive fell. Out of damp darkness there swooped the softly spinning containers, each woo-er-woo-er followed by a slight plop on arrival. . . . Phillip could not sleep, but lay with the old helplessness of himself, in command of an untrained incoherence of men whose officers he hardly knew. . . . At last the working parties came in. Some of the young soldiers were crying, burned about the face and hands with mustard gas, which had raised blisters, some of them half-an-inch thick. Forty-two other ranks went to the First Aid Post.

* * * *

As the long, slow Red Cross train was crawling south-west towards the railway junction at Hazebrouck, through which all trains to and from the bases had to pass, the German guns bombarding Bailleul five miles away seemed to be shaking the coach. The wind being slight, when the train passed through an area of wood smoke, fumes entered the white dormitory reawakening fear and pain that it had been set on fire. Phillip sobbed within the flaming hell of his bandage mask, but no relieving tears fell, only gummy stabs of 60–pounder flame.

A Test To Destruction, Chapter 9, 'St. George I'

Henry Williamson was involved in the battle for a very short time, a mere three weeks. Unfortunately, the diary entries for those three weeks have been torn out so it is not possible to know what he actually did and thought during this period. The next entry is for 18 April; it states: 'Left Hall-Walkers hospital in Regent's Park. Board at Caxton Hall, in week's time.' So he had been returned 'with a

In relaxed mood towards the end of the war.

blighty one', but there are no details other than that he was given one month's convalescence leave at the next board.

On 15 May he was sent back to Felixstowe to rejoin the Bedfordshires, the diary entry for that day recording 'Posted to 'C' company. Know no-one', and on 20 May: 'Asked for medical board. Want to be in France. No life in England', but the entry for 18 June reports, 'Board gave 3 months Garrison Duty. I asked to be sent out, but they said I was still shaky.'

At this time apart from his army duties he was playing a great deal of tennis and going for early morning swims, often with his commanding officer, Lord Ampthill – 'he a bearded viking' – no doubt in an effort to get fit again. For some time there had been sporadic notes in his diary referring to stories he had written, and was sending to his current girlfriend, and on 14 August he noted: 'Began my book again after 5 months interval.' There are several quite detailed references to this during the early part of September, with, it would seem, a whole chapter being written each day – 'Writing at night. Door locked.' This was his first version of what was eventually to become the initial volumes of *The Flax of Dream* tetralogy.[8]

On 27 September he recorded that 'the M.O. sounded my lungs and said I have a dull patch', but the following day he was elated: 'Am going to India! My transfer to Indian Army came through! B1 category no bar!' On 2 October he wrote, 'Heard about embarkation' and on the following day, 'Lord Ampthill spoke to me awfully nicely about leave. He said I could go tomorrow.'

While on leave at home he typed out his manuscript using an upstairs room in his grandfather Leaver's house next door as a study. A telegram recalled him to Felixstowe where he heard he was to sail on 4 November. On Thursday 31 October he recorded that he 'gave a farewell dance at St. Peter's Hall. Bubbly etc. Went very well.' No doubt such an extravaganza was considered the thing to do. However, his celebration was a little premature for he wrote on 3 November, 'Orders cancelled. Won't sail – awaiting fresh orders', and a few days later, 'War ending.' Then, on Monday 11 November 1918: 'Armistice signed at 5.30 this morning. PEACE! Bands playing, guns, sirens, etc. etc.' and on the 19th: '20 German submarines to enter Harwich tomorrow at 12 a.m. No cheering. Saw scores, painted dragons on bows, saw-edge to cables over conning towers etc. Crews all to attention entering Orwell estuary.'

Henry captured these scenes of the end of the war in his novel *A Test To Destruction*:

The order to stand by to proceed to Taranto in Italy and thence to embark for Suez and the East was cancelled. This was followed by notification that no officers were required for the Indian Army. Every breakfast time there were maps in the newspapers, with half-familiar names – Valenciennes, Bruges, Mormal Forest – MONS. It was over.

But all was not yet done with. The officers paid an informal visit to the sergeants' mess, where each drank one glass of beer, standing, the gracious

William Leopold with his children, Henry, Kathie and Biddy, at No. 11 Eastern Road at the end of the First World War.

bearded face of Lord Satchville rising above all. At night toasts were drunk in the officers' mess, before all stood on their chairs, one foot on the table, and with linked arms sang Auld Lang Syne.

Up went the Very lights, scaling off the edge of the sea; off went slabs of gun-cotton, mock shells of practice battle, tracers flicked away over the waves until stopped by a calm-spoken 'Hen' Henley; down went the hot Irish whiskeys; up came the carpets. The party ended in a midnight bathe, fully clothed, Phillip leading half-a-dozen of the pack into the sea. . . .

Phillip watched with others on the sea-wall. The submarines came in flying the Imperial German flag, red white and black, conning towers open and crews in white standing to attention upon the lower decks. From each bow, rising at an angle of about thirty degrees, was extended a great jagged saw fixed to a cable which rose over the conning tower and sloped down to the stern – for cutting and passing through steel nets which were said to stretch from Dover to the French coast. But more immediately startling were the figure-heads on the bows – Chinese dragons painted red and yellow, blue and white serpents, black wolves with open jaws, sharks' heads, and even the profile of a red-faced laughing giant. They entered the harbour in line astern, two hundred yards between each craft. Some were rusty; they were of varying sizes; many of them had small quick-firing guns, but one, half as long again as the small fry, had what looked like a 6-inch gun. Not a movement among the crews, only the ribbons of their caps fluttering in the breeze; not a word from the on-lookers as the U-boats went by in procession to surrender.

Such weariness; such sadness.

A Test To Destruction, Chapter 18, 'Nightshade'

CHAPTER 3

METAMORPHOSIS

As the war ended Henry Williamson was almost twenty-three. The relief he felt (in company with every soldier) that the fighting was finally over must have been overwhelming, but possibly not to be shown openly; for to admit relief would be to admit the intensity of the inner tension of fear. But other emotions, too, were at the forefront: the loss of comradeship; the loss of adventure; the loss of a certain privilege and prestige. Henry shows us his feelings at that time through the medium of Phillip in the *Chronicle*:

> *It was over. It was ended. He sat in his bedroom of 9 Manor Terrace, at noon on 11th November, and mourned alone, possessed by vacancy that soon the faces of the living would join those of the dead, and be known no more.*
>
> A Test To Destruction, Chapter 18, 'Nightshade'

Temporary infantry officers were invited to stay with the forces for a period of one year, at increased rates of pay. Henry decided to do this, but as, according to bank book entries for October 1918, his pay was £17 15s. 0d. and his pay for March 1919 was for the same amount, the increased pay offer does not seem to have materialized! The beginning of 1919 sees him first at Shorncliffe and then at Folkestone, on fairly undemanding duties with the No. 1 Dispersal Unit, which organized troops returning from the front.

During this year his pre-war employer, the Sun Fire Insurance Office, wrote to him, first in March, asking when he was going to be demobilized and return to his old job, but he did not reply, and after three similar inquiries, they asked him to refund the salary that was paid to him throughout the war, though there is no evidence that he did so. Henry could not face returning to what he knew very well would be a very hum-drum existence after the traumatizing experience he had undergone.

On 7 June 1919 he ordered a new Brooklands Road Special Norton Motorcycle No. 8, a transaction completed on 16 June – total cost 73 guineas, with an additional 6 guineas for a Phillipson Pulley – quite an expensive machine. A paragraph appeared in the London *Evening News* sometime in June 1919 stating that Lieut. H. Williamson had won the 'flying mile motorcycle race near Folkestone':

FAST MOTOR-CYCLING

In the motor-cycle race 'flying mile' held this morning near Folkestone Lieut. H. Williamson, of the Bedfordshire Regiment, was first; Sergt. R. Fairley, K.R.R., second; and S. Mercier third.

Emerging from the chrysalis, 1921.

The winner's speed was at the rate of 72⅓ miles an hour.

Newspaper cutting in HWLEA

But apparently the story was made up as a joke, as he later wrote in 'Confessions of a Fake Merchant', an essay on his time in Fleet Street.[1] Whatever the truth, it is apparent that he found the fast machine exhilarating.

At some point during the spring or early summer, he was browsing in a bookshop in Folkestone when he found a copy of Richard Jefferies' *The Story of My Heart* and read in rapt attention to the end; the book was for him a revelation of total truth. For here he found writing that mirrored all his own visionary thoughts. Published in 1883, and subtitled 'My Autobiography', the book is not what is normally thought of as autobiography. There are no facts, no dates, no points of reference; instead, an outpouring of mystical and spiritual growth.[2]

For Henry Williamson this book was his Revelation on the Road to Damascus. His eyes were opened. He determined to tread the same authorial path as Jefferies; his aspirations were strengthened and deepened, and it was from this time that he seriously strove to be a writer. Another paragraph appeared in the London *Evening News*, marked in his journal 'early summer 1919', giving a quotation from Jefferies as his example of 'The Most Beautiful Sentence', presumably a column which was appearing regularly. This particular column includes quotations from II Samuel, a verse of Rupert Brooke's 'If I should die . . . ' and Henry's offering:

Henry astride his Brooklands Road Special Norton.

My Heart Opens Wide

'Softly breathes the sweet south wind, gently the yellow corn waves beneath; the ancient, ancient sun shines on the fresh grass and the flower; my heart opens wide as the broad, broad earth. I am in eternity now; I am in the midst of it. It is all about me in the sunshine; I am in it as the butterfly floats in the light-laden air.' (Richard Jefferies) – H.W. Williamson (Lieutenant, The Bedfordshire Regiment), Folkestone.

Evening News, June 1919

There, quietly tucked away in this cutting from early summer 1919, is the source of the phrase which he was constantly to use – 'the ancient sunlight' – his title for the great work of his life, *A Chronicle of Ancient Sunlight*. The original quotation comes from the third chapter of *The Story of My Heart* in which Richard Jefferies describes how he used to walk up to a tumulus on top of the hills and his affinity for the spirit of the man whose body was interred within. Henry's quotation uses two sentences that are actually separated and transposed in Jefferies' lyric prose. Henry's second sentence, 'I am in eternity now', comes first and then a few pages further on comes the first part of his 'Most Beautiful Sentence', except that he changed the tense: 'Softly breathed the sweet wind, gently the yellow corn waved beneath; the ancient, ancient sun shone on the fresh grass and the flowers, my heart opened wide as the broad, broad earth.' Thus we can see clearly the sentiments with which Henry most closely identified: the mystic union between the eternal sunlight and the long history of the earth.

Earlier in the book Jefferies writes:

I came to feel the long-drawn life of the earth back into the dimmest past, while the sun of the moment was warm on me. Sesostris on the most ancient sands of the south, in ancient, ancient days, was conscious of himself and of the sun. This sunlight linked me through the ages to that past consciousness. From all the ages my soul desired to take that soul-life which had flowed through them as the sunbeams had continually poured on earth.

Richard Jefferies, *The Story of My Heart*

This kind of writing was not to endear Jefferies to the establishment; in those days it was possibly even considered blasphemous. Henry Williamson related later how, even in 1925, he was told it was 'a dangerous book'. Jefferies' mode of writing was, perhaps, ahead of his time; if nothing else, he predated the 'stream of consciousness' novels of James Joyce and Virginia Woolf: yet he was not striving to be of a literary genre, rather to write the truth as he saw and felt it. Henry Williamson took on this ethos of portraying 'truth' as if it were a cloak that Jefferies had bequeathed him and which he wore for ever afterwards.

During his time at Folkestone Henry Williamson became very involved with the wife of a senior officer (away in Germany on army duties), referred to as Mabs B., who had a reputation for 'fast' behaviour. Henry based his fictional character Eveline (Evelyn) D'Arcy Fairfax, known as Eve, on Mabs B., and as such she appears as Willie Maddison's lover in *The Dream of Fair Women* (of *The Flax of Dream* novels) and Phillip also is involved in an unhappy and disastrous relationship with her in *A Test to Destruction* in the *Chronicle* series. In real life, family and friends exhorted Henry to have nothing to do with this lady, who appears to have been a devourer of men although it seems that some of her behaviour arose out of her own unhappiness. In the late summer of 1919 the couple spent a short time on holiday together in Georgeham in Devon.

The Georgeham cottage seems to have been always available to Henry. Although there is no actual evidence, it is possible that his Aunt Mary Leopoldina had a permanent lease on it, or even owned it, as a letter from Henry to his mother refers to the cottage and he is 'glad that it isn't let as I want it in late August'. He certainly made several journeys there before he actually went there to live in 1921. This occasion 'in late August' refers to his holiday in company with Mabs B. He made up a most complicated story to account for her presence for the benefit of the local people which can only have fooled the most naive – that Mabs was the sister of his dead wife, at the mention of whom crocodile tears would start from his eyes. The wife of the vicar of Georgeham was completely taken in; of course when the truth eventually came out, Henry's reputation suffered accordingly.[3]

Henry was then shunted off by the army to a camp in Staffordshire. There was little to do at Folkestone, and he was possibly making quite a nuisance of himself, drowning his deep unhappiness over Mabs B. in an excess of drink and difficult behaviour. Almost immediately he was asked to 'hand in his papers', because, as he wrote in the *Chronicle*, he refused to dine in the officers' mess, which was obligatory, and stayed in his room writing.

Henry Williamson was demobilized at Crystal Palace on 9 September 1919. In *A Test to Destruction* Henry describes how Phillip (and doubtless Henry himself) travelled down from Staffordshire on his motorcycle, calling in to see the relations at Aspley Guise on the way, arriving home so late that everyone has gone to bed. As he does not want to disturb them, he sleeps out on the Hilly Fields:

> *It was late to wake them up, so he [Phillip] lay under the bushes on the Hill and shivered all night on the edge of sleep, thinking that at last he was free, that nothing would ever be as bad as the battlefields, because he could go home in the morning.*
>
> *A Test to Destruction*, Chapter 20, 'Spectres of the Mind'

Henry received a lump sum and, because of his impaired health, a disability pension. A regular amount of just over £13 paid into his bank account at this time was possibly this pension. His bank and post-office books for many years were headed 'Captain H.W. Williamson', a small vanity he seems to have found necessary. In the same way he always maintained after the war was over that he had been under age when he enlisted. Perhaps this tale was originally told to impress a girlfriend, but once uttered proved impossible to deny. Thus he had to lie about his date of birth, which must have been quite difficult at times. Reference books still attribute to him the wrong year and place of birth, which he also tended to camouflage.

He found adjustment to civilian life difficult and was known to be drinking too much. His grandfather, Thomas Leaver, was asked to intervene and wrote him a stern letter. There was, of course, the awful example of Thomas Leaver's own son, Henry's Uncle Hugh, ever present before him. His wild ways had brought him in contact with syphilis from which he was then rapidly degenerating to a painful death. And, of course, Henry's own namesake, his paternal grandfather, had also taken to a life of over-indulgence. The family were very concerned that Henry would follow in their footsteps. However, it may well have been that he was not drinking to excess, but rather that, in his weakened condition, a very little alcohol had a disproportionate effect. There is no doubt that he was behaving a little wildly at this point, presumably in reaction to his war-time experiences and his present restricting circumstances.

My dear Boy,

I spoke to your mother last night about your incipient but regrettable propensity for *strong* drink – There's nothing stationary in this world – our lives, characters, thoughts are always rising or falling & perhaps the most insidious & awful in its results is drink but not that alone – indiscretions. Thoughtless folly of all sorts is paid for in months and years to come in the most painful suffering – now – my dear Harry, have the strength of mind to disregard the habits & utterances of any companions – you will learn with experience how rare commonsense, thought & conscience is but you can never visualize what remorse & physical suffering is accrued by acts lightly & thoughtlessly made in youth – act then *now* & firmly resolve not to drink any spirits except a medicinal dose under exceptionable circumstances such as a little rum after severe exposure & trench work – if you are beyond the influence of reason – think of your mother & her noble conduct & example & how she has sacrificed herself to start her children on the road to happiness & think of the result of your folly to her – she is not strong & the consequences of your folly may be far more awful than you think *now* – I have a little money for my children & their children & I have not exercised self-denial & much thought & work to have that money fooled away – you have the potentiality of a successful & with moderation in all things a happy life, be Master of your mind & don't throw your chance away.

[and added underneath in Henry's handwriting]

This letter was, apparently, not finished by T.W. Leaver in 1918, when he wrote it for me & left it with my mother. In the novel I have ante-dated the period. HW. 10 May 1956.

Letter in HWLEA, undated

So home life was resumed, uneasily for everyone. His sister Kathie had joined her father's bank while the younger sister, Biddy, was studying, either for a degree or for a certificate in teaching. The girls probably resented their brother's presence at home, bringing as it did irritations and squabbles and taking a lot of their mother's attention and energy. His father, older, tired by his own war efforts, and now more entrenched in his opinions than ever, did not intend to tolerate wild behaviour. The two were diametrically opposed and could rarely agree.

Towards the end of the year Henry attended, with his mother and sister Biddy, the wedding of his cousin Marjorie, the sister of Charlie Boone, to her cousin William F. Turney. As described in *A Test to Destruction* (Volume 8 of the *Chronicle*), it does not appear to have been a very happy occasion, even allowing

Henry in his 'suit of khaki barathea dyed navy blue' and 'yellow silk tie' at the wedding of his cousin, Marjorie Boone, to William F. Turney, November 1919. Henry is standing just right of centre beween his mother and his sister, Biddy.

for the fact that Henry might have been jealous. Perhaps the man Marjorie really loved died in the war, or she really was still in love with her very handsome young cousin Henry, who had seduced her at an impressionable age. In the photograph of the wedding we can see that Henry is wearing the suit he describes in Chapter 21 of the novel; 'Mother, Doris and I went down from Euston for Polly Pickering's wedding. I wore the suit of khaki barathea dyed navy blue, which I had made in Folkestone (and haven't paid for), with a yellow silk tie bought in the Burlington Arcade.'

Kathie and Biddy too seem to have had relationships that ended disastrously during the war. Kathie never married but there was a photograph of a group of First World War Guards' officers among her possessions when she died that by its condition had once been pinned up for a long time, and probably contains the image of the man she loved who probably died in the war. As regarding Biddy, Henry noted in his 1920 journal that 'When Charlie Boone died, I think the heart of my younger sister broke, for ever.' Biddy's subsequent marriage to William Busby was not to turn out happily, and she was eventually left to bring up her two sons on her own, after her husband abruptly walked out.

Henry's diary entry for 8 January 1920 states: 'Obtained job on Times.' This was as a canvasser in the Classified Advertisements Department of *The Times* whose chief was Major Pemberton (son of Max Pemberton). Henry's grandfather, Thomas Leaver, had obtained an introduction for him via Vansittart Bowater, a colleague known from his work in the stationery firm, to Lord Northcliffe, head of *The Times*. It is very difficult to envisage Henry Williamson doing such routine work, but it would have given him an entrée to the coterie of Fleet Street.

But his main introduction to the literary set came when he was invited to join the Tomorrow Club. Its founder was a most extraordinary woman, Mrs C.A. Dawson Scott, known as Mrs Sappho within her circle, who had, on account of her own struggles to become a writer, decided in 1917 to form a club to help and encourage aspiring young writers who showed promise; a place where they could meet, talk and listen to lectures by distinguished authors, among whom were J.D. Beresford, John Galsworthy, and Walter de la Mare. This club was to be the nucleus of PEN, the renowned society for 'Poets, Essayists and Novelists', whose first president was John Galsworthy.

Marjorie Watts, daughter of Mrs Dawson Scott, has written two books about her mother and PEN, and quotes a letter from Henry Williamson:

I, a mere vagrant of 1920, see only the (to me) intense days of its inception in Long Acre and later Caxton Hall; in both places I was a mere literary spiv, externally at least. And I remember, later, the beautiful sands of Constantine where I stayed with my bride, and we all – Dennis Arundell, Herman Ould, your mother and me – walked barefoot around Trevose Head and elsewhere along the breaking blue sea. And the dim-seen mullet, salmon and bass on the shelly sea-floor, pursued by seals . . . and the new potatoes clustered in a nest. . . . Looking back, one sees all things *en clair*. The sad thin figure of the Rhodes scholar,

Colby Borley – T.S. Eliot speaking – Swinnerton – G.B. Shaw – May Sinclair – the thrilling afternoon when Lauritz Melchior sang and revealed a great talent. And of course the excellent Alec Waugh, Violet Hunt . . . What a cluster of talent your mother drew about her, then and later.[4]

In his diary entries for the period, Henry alternated between enthusiasm and sarcasm for the activities of the Tomorrow Club; and he was somewhat scathing about Mrs Dawson Scott's lack of praise for his own first book.

Abandoning his conventional diary for this year, which tends to consist of jottings of addresses of the many people he met interspersed with little phrases and notes for his stories, with very occasional reminders of appointments, Henry kept instead a 'Journal' in a large folio filing book. Ostensibly a 'Nature Diary', this valuable document records his every thought from the beginning of February 1920 to mid-1922. From its cover and from many references within the entries, we find him in an almost mystical communion with Richard Jefferies:

Henry William Williamson
Naturalist and Disciple
of
THE MASTER
RICHARD JEFFERIES

While on the following page he wrote:

I am in Eternity NOW
Richard Jefferies
I am in Eternity now
Henry Williamson

The spirit of Jefferies communes with the subconscious spirit of Williamson in this Journal. 1920

Here too are the first drawings of the symbol of an owl, which meant so much to him and which, drawn out in a formal design, was to form his colophon; it would appear at the end of his first and every subsequent book, except one.

This journal was source material for much future writing. For instance, the entry for 9 February 1920 is transposed word for word in his novelized diary entry in *A Test to Destruction* (written and published in 1960) for Thursday 6 November 1919, immediately after the wedding scene just mentioned: 'Very sulky and rude to my patient, silver-haired Mother, I am conscious of being a perfect swine, but can't help it'.

But writing his journal was not his only interest. On 27 April he received a letter from Norton Motorcycles about a new engine for his Brooklands Road Special (after one year!) which ends:

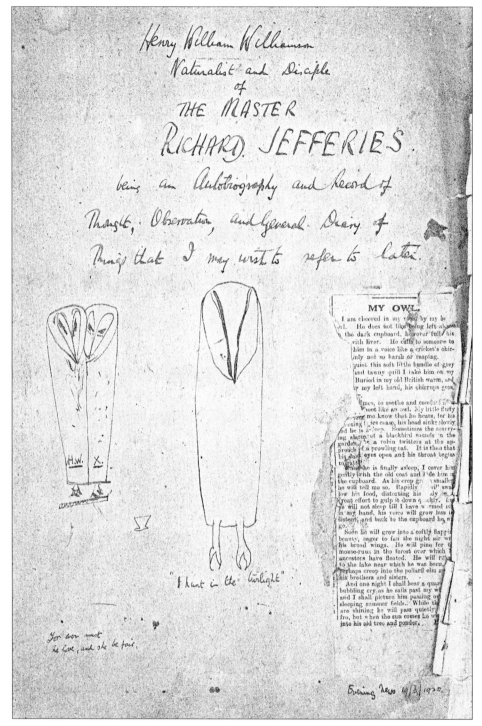

The cover of Henry's 1920 'Journal', with the 'Owl' article.

Gertrude Williamson in 1920: 'my patient,
silver-haired Mother'.

We note that you have been fined nine times, and suggest that you try going fast
through Kingston when no doubt the magistrates will have much pleasure in
raising your record to double figures.

Assuring you of our affectionate regard at all times . . .

His motorcycle was being driven fast and furiously.

Earlier in the month he had met a new kindred spirit, whose parents lived in
Folkestone, and who from a slight reference in one of Henry's notes, would appear
to have been a cousin of Mabs B. ('Eveline'). His journal reads: 'I am constantly
thinking of a girl I met, who is more like me than anyone I have yet met – I mean,
she loves the wild things. Her name is Doline Rendle. I believe I shall love her –
but God protect me from another "disappointment".' (Gwen)Doline was the
model for 'Spica' of *The Sun in the Sands*, after the star Spica Virginis. She was
also the original of Mary of *The Dream of Fair Women* (although for his later
volume *The Pathway* Henry was to base this character on his future wife). Doline
was a remarkable girl. Her many letters, frequent over this time until he met his
future wife in 1924, but sustained in friendship throughout his life – she was
godmother to one of their children – recreate her intelligence, her insight, and her
forthright character. Her letters show that she stood no nonsense from Henry,
roundly telling him he was self-pitying and self-righteous but encouraging his
writing and making constructive criticism which he obviously found helpful. She
made it clear that she was not in love with him; but he could not accept her solely
as a friend and made the situation fraught with an emotional see-saw. She was
very young when they first met, possibly only seventeen, and her mother, although

Doline Rendle: 'Spica Virginis'.

sympathetic to Henry as a person and a writer, did not welcome his attentions to her daughter which Henry remarked on rather bitterly several times.

But towards the end of April 1920 he received a letter from Curtis Brown Ltd, International Publishing Bureau, whom he had previously approached, and one of whose staff, Andrew Dakers, became his agent. Dakers wrote:

> I have read with great interest your book *Flax of Dream* and have also had a reader's opinion of it, which coincides with my own, that it is beautifully written and a good story. Much, however, will depend on the ending . . . [Only the first two parts had been sent]
> [At the end Henry added] 'that is encouraging, at all events.'
> Letter in HWLEA, dated 28 April 1920

This version was not actually published but remains a most interesting document showing Henry Williamson's rapid development as he sloughs off his caterpillar skins in increasingly maturer assurance of his writing skill.[5]

At the beginning of May on a visit to his beloved woods in the countryside near his home, he recorded in his journal how he found that the town dwellers and cockney children on a day out had desecrated the bluebells, trampling everything flat and leaving litter. At first sad and angry at the destruction, he then realized that 'all their faces were happy'. This incident was reworked and published as an essay, first in the *English Review* and then in his book *The Lone Swallows* in 1922.

His diary entry for 9 May describes how he took a baby tawny owl from its nest to keep as a pet – 'I climbed up the tree and put my hand in the hole. There were two grey fledgelings. I brought one home and as I write he is "shrilling" for his parents.' The next day's entry states, 'My owl is a pathetic little dear: very gentle and lost looking. When I whistle deeply he squeaks back at me.' On 11 May he wrote this up as a story which was published in the London *Evening News*. He pasted the cutting on to the front of his journal, next to his drawings of owls, and although it is a little shabby and blurred now (see p. 72), it is still just possible to make it out, with a little guess work over a few words.[6]

MY OWL

I am cheered in my room by my baby owl. He does not like being left alone in the dark cupboard, however full his belly with liver. He calls to someone to [cuddle] him in a voice like a cricket's chirrup, only not so harsh or rasping. To quiet this soft little bundle of grey [fluff] and tawny quill I take him on my [lap]. Buried in my old British warm, and [cupped] by my left hand, his chirrups grow [quieter].

Sometimes, to soothe and comfort him I [pretend] to hoot like an owl. My little fluffy owlet lets me know that he hears, for his wheezing cries cease, his head sinks slowly and he is asleep. Sometimes the scurrying alarm of a blackbird sounds in the garden, or a robin twitters at the approach of a cat. It is then that his dark eyes open and his throat begins to rattle.

When he is finally asleep, I cover him gently with the old coat and hide him in the cupboard. As his crop grows smaller, he will tell me so. Rapidly he will swallow his food, distorting his body in a great effort to gulp it down quickly. But he will not sleep till I have warmed him in my hand, his voice will grow less insistent, and back to the cupboard he will go.

Soon he will grow into a softly flapping beauty, eager to fan the night air with his broad wings. He will pine for the mouse-runs in the forest over which his ancestors have floated. He will return to the lake near where he was born, and perhaps creep into the pollard elm among his brothers and sisters.

And one night I shall hear a quavering bubbling cry as he sails past my window, and I shall picture him passing over the sleeping summer fields. While the stars are shining he will pass quietly to and fro, but when the sun comes he will creep into his tree and ponder. H.W.

Evening News, 19 August 1920

During the first fortnight of June Henry was again on holiday in Georgeham. His diary records: 'So much I have seen; so much achieved; so much thought; How then can I write the thoughts that arise from the stored colours and sounds in my head.' And after his return, on 27 June: 'Tonight I have been writing some more of the first chapter of the "Beautiful Years".'

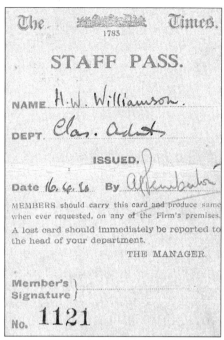

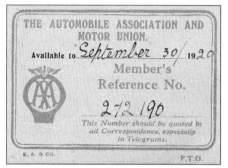

Press cards tucked into the flap of Henry's 1920 diary.

By August he was writing regularly for the *Weekly Dispatch* under the editor Bernard Falk, a column on light cars entitled 'On the Road',[7] some of which were a little thin as his knowledge of cars was rather superficial. He also contributed some nature notes for this paper, for the London *Evening News*, and occasionally for the *Observer*, and was gradually expanding his range. These articles were carefully pasted into his journal.

But by mid-September the *Weekly Dispatch* was in financial trouble and cutting back on staff; his diary records: 'out of work – a poor bloody freelance, What hopes? But who cares a damn.' But it's an ill wind that blows no good. He now had time to write and *The Beautiful Years* was finished by December; Dakers liked it, and wrote encouragingly 'a novel of the first rank'.

As 1921 opened Henry Williamson wrote in his diary:

For the past three months I have been existing on £2/2/- a week, by writing 400–500 words of motor notes every Sunday in the Weekly Dispatch. That is now ended, and I am quite a pauper. Dakers says I will do great things – but meanwhile I lie in bed till 9 & 10 in the morning, running to seed, forming vicious habits of loafing, then spasmodically walking 20 miles in a day, then being idle; writing 5000 words one night and 500 the next week. I am writing newspaper articles but cannot 'potboil'.

It was a difficult time for him, and for those with whom he came in contact, his family and friends. Moody and introspective, nervous to the point of paranoia, he lashed out at everyone and lamented his troubles in his journal. In effect he was in the chrysalis stage, seething and boiling within himself as all his being was rearranged. Then, on 21 February, he wrote:

Publication for *The Beautiful Years* is settled with Collins, the contract signed, the £25 in advance of Royalties paid over. I have been lucky in finding a publisher so soon; and Dakers, bless him, says my work is so 'striking' that any publisher's reader would sit up and take notice. Publication in September of this year. I want to rewrite part of the climax chapter called 'Fire' in order to make it more passionate (but not à la D.H. Lawrence)

At home matters came to a head and after yet another quarrel with his father, Henry, now just over twenty-five years old, left home and rode on his beloved Norton motorcycle to his beloved Devon – 'to my cottage'; drawn by the magnetism of that ancient area; drawn by the happiness he had felt before the war and on subsequent visits; drawn by his Shapcote forebears to his spiritual home. Oddly, he did not enter this momentous event in his journal – jumping straight from a long entry dated 12 March, which relates a rambling story concerning the Tomorrow Club, to a new paragraph:

I am now in Devon. I've left London; all my eggs (egos) are in my one basket of literature; I've got £12 in the bank. Meanwhile, I work. Today I heard about thirty linnets singing in a hedgerow, and their song was sweet. The owls are still in my cottage; beautiful mascots!

'My cottage' was, of course, the one next to the church in Georgeham, which he was already renting for £5 a year,[8] Although the exact history is a little obscure it is thought originally to have been called Church Cottage. Henry named it 'Skirr' after the calls of barn owls living in the space under the thatch. In *The Sun in the Sands*[9] he relates the story about his reason for going to Devon and describing the final altercation he and his father had about his behaviour and how it ended with his father telling him to leave the house, shouting: 'I can stand no more.'

But, of course, with the knowledge that his book had been accepted, Henry could see his way clear to continue, and he was ready to leave. He had hidden in the darkness of his chrysalis long enough; the time was ripe to burst out from its toughened skin, from the narrow life in the family home, from his father's disapproval of everything he did, and to spread his wings like a brimstone butterfly emerging into the March sunshine.

I was on my Norton, going down to my cottage in Devon, an author with a marvellous happy life before him, for I had ever renounced love for art. Spica had not believed in me; her mother had told me to go, to achieve success, not

Skirr Cottage, Georgeham, North Devon, 1921.

Outside Skirr Cottage, 1921.

everlastingly talk about it: to let others discover for themselves any talent I might possess. Neither Spica nor Spica's mother had realised how I had been doing hateful work all the week for the Sunday newspapers, and then, emptied out, had gone to the table in my room at night and written my book. I recalled with pain the occasion of the final scene of rejection. The dawn was glimmering on the Thames as I rode along the empty streets with the deep drum notes of the exhaust to gladden me, proud of my Norton's graceful design, its tank of silver-and-black lined-out with red, away to Maidstone and the Dover road. I must blind, faster, faster, to sit beside Spica at breakfast! For two things only had life a purpose; for my love, called Spica; for my writing, which was for Spica. In myself, I believed, was a power and vision and truth clearer than in any other writer in the world, except in Richard Jefferies, William Blake, and Francis Thompson.

The Sun in the Sands, Chapter 4

Once established in the cottage, it is obvious from various correspondence and photographs that his mother visited him at Georgeham on more than one occasion in those early days, and his sister Biddy and Bill Busby too.

At the end of May, a letter from Andrew Dakers (now with his own agency) referred to Henry's new growth of beard, and to his employment as a reviewer, which would bring him much needed funds.

Enjoyed the sight of your beardedness which looks comfortable at any rate. Walter de la Mare's note on your work is good. This year seems to be a

A bearded Henry.

Bill Busby, Biddy and Henry's mother outside Skirr Cottage, 1921.

fortunate one for you. It is to the credit of the Sat. Review to have selected you to do some of their reviewing.

Just before he left for Devon, Henry had been to an 'At Home' at the house of J.D. Beresford, one of the members of the Tomorrow Club. Beresford was himself a prolific author, but more importantly for Henry, he was a reader for Collins and responsible for recommending that they should publish Henry's first book. Henry describes the occasion in his journal:

A few celebrities present, including Walter de la Mare: He is a nice fellow, but doesn't know much about nature study; he didn't know the difference between a coltsfoot and a cowslip. However, his poetry is, I think, really beautiful. He is one of the *rare* ones. I got permission to dedicate 'The Passing of the Blossom', appearing in the May *English Review*, to him.

'The Passing of the Blossom' is of course the story of the desecration of the bluebells by the cockney children referred to previously. Walter de la Mare wrote to Henry Williamson on 26 April: 'I am looking forward very much to "The Passing of the Blossom" and proud to be its godfather', and in another letter:

. . . What a delight it has been to have, & read, your paper in the English Review. It is – if I may say so – a fresh and living piece of writing, & the first I

Henry on the cliff path to Baggy Point
overlooking Putsborough Beach.

hope, of many. The only quite insignificant criticisms that occur to me – if you
will forgive them – are 'the little poet'. Somehow it doesn't seem to be a
compliment to the long-tailed tit; and the 'dear children' – the word here hasn't
quite body enough. The whole thing is delightful in thought and feeling; I do
hope you will let me know when more of your work appears. It's a proud
godfather that writes this; & he treasures the owl. Yours very sincerely, Walter
de la Mare.

Letter in HWLEA, dated 21 May 1921[10]

Such kind encouragement from such an eminent writer must have been balm to
Henry's extreme nervous psychological state. The story also appeared under the
title 'London Children and Wild Flowers' in *The Lone Swallows*, where it is
dedicated to 'W. de la M.'. The following extract will perhaps distil a little of its
essence:

*In some woods near London the nightingale still returns, the jay lurks, and the
mysterious nightjar wheels when the chafer-beetles flit against the oak leaves at
twilight. And yet, less than half a mile away, is a busy tram terminus. The wild
things in freedom love their haunts and are not easily driven away, but in the
higher wood – beautiful in spring with apple blossom, uncurling brakefern,
silver birch and sheen of bluebell – no birds sang as alone I walked among its
violated sanctities. It was the hour of solitude, when the sun almost was*

quenched and the moon had not yet come above the dim hills. The paths were beaten into mire by the passing and repassing of a thousand feet, acres of bluebells had been uprooted and taken away, many trampled and crushed, or gathered and cast carelessly on the paths. The apple blossom was stripped from the trees. In his instinctive effort to possess beauty, man invariably destroys it – for is not all beauty ever elusive? It is the subconscious, or deeper than subconscious, realisation of this elusiveness of beauty that causes the sadness of its contemplation – the blossoms were gone, a whole spring-life of them, carried away by the people who had come from Walworth, Shoreditch, and Woolwich. Branches of those graceful trees, the silver birches, had been torn and wrenched off; not content with decimating the flowers, grasping hands had broken the smaller trees. A week ago, before the fatal beauty of the apple bloom had drawn the hordes from their strongholds, I found dozens of thrushes' and blackbirds' nests – some with eggs, others with fledgelings – all these disappeared on that Sunday. No beauty remains inviolate for long. . . .

I was filled with ecstasy and wanted to shout my joy aloud. Here was a manifestation of my hopes for the happiness of mankind. The tram drew nearer London with its ragged children; and I was filled with gladness, even though the buttercups had gone from the meadow, and the wandering bees sought in vain in the woods for the loveliness of bluebell and apple-blossom. For every year the flowers come, the wind rushes over, the silver-burning sun swings across the sky, but never enough of these do the little ones in the city see.

The Lone Swallows, 'London children and Wild Flowers'

At the end of June Collins advanced another £25 royalties, all of which Dakers generously passed on. 'I will defer taking my commission until some more money becomes due to you as I know you are wanting spot cash pretty badly.'

The Beautiful Years, the first volume of the tetralogy *The Flax of Dream* was published at the beginning of October. It tells the story of a lonely little boy, Willie Maddison, whose mother died giving birth to him, growing up in the quiet countryside village of Rookhurst, set in the West Country in the early years of the twentieth century, in the care of a father so wrapped up in his own grief that he is unable to communicate with the highly strung child. Willie finds refuge in the countryside around his home and comfort in the faithful care of Biddy, the family cook, but is wild and impish in his ways. He has a stolid friend of his own age, Jack Temperley, from a neighbouring farm, who shares his adventures. He gets to know Jim Holloman, ostensibly the crow-starver, but whose rapt English rustic character is actually a tribute portrait of Richard Jefferies. Jim has an idealist love affair with Dolly, the maid from the Temperley's farm, before he dies, carried away in a mud slide of marl into the lime quarry where he was camping overnight with Willie, and his body is never found. Willie himself, at the tender age of eight, feels the first stirrings of calf-love for Elsie Norman, daughter of a well-known local artist and we meet her friend, Mary Ogilvie, who is to play a major part in the final volumes of the tetralogy. Towards the end of the book Willie has to brave the terror of attending Colham, the local grammar school. Clearly, this first book is based very closely on Henry's own experience, but with the background and the location transposed.

Henry was disappointed to find little immediate reaction in the press, but during November Durrant's Press Cutting Agency began to forward reviews. They were on the whole favourable; the book was well received, the following remarks being fairly typical: 'a book of moving poetry'; 'a labour of love'; 'a true poet of nature'; 'memorable'; 'real literature'; and from S.P.B. Mais (himself a noted author, who was to be one of Henry's most loyal friends) 'a first novel of quite unusual distinction and beauty'.

Henry Williamson's first mention of an otter appears in a short series of articles which appeared in the *Sunday Express* in December 1921 and January 1922 where he describes his life in 'Scarecrow Cottage' (Skirr Cottage, of course). Throughout his life Henry would claim that he had rescued an otter cub and kept it as a pet. These articles mention the presence of an otter cub among several animals that lived with him in his cottage, which would tend to confirm that he kept such a creature in these very earliest days in Georgeham. However, Henry's first wife has no knowledge of it at all, and although there are various photographs of Henry with his dog, Bill-John, and with his cats, there is none of him with an otter. There is, however, one small item in his literary archive which provides a clue to this mystery: a two-page extract (sadly the remainder is missing) from one of his stories that was printed in an (unknown) American magazine in 1923. Entitled 'The Man Who Did Not Hunt', it tells the story of the rescue of an otter cub by a man crippled in the war, who enlists the help of another person, the writer of the story. Henry has revised these two pages quite heavily and added at the top a new title, 'Zoë'. 'Zoë' was published in *The Peregrine's Saga*. The man named in both versions is called Captain Horton-Wickham, which one would presume to have been fictional. But many years later, on 18 July 1942, Henry happened to walk back to his field above Georgeham from Braunton, as he recorded in his diary, 'by way of Heddon Mill & the steep hill – with its memories of going to see Horton-Wickham & the tame otter Zoe in 1921'. Thus Horton-Wickham would seem to be the name of a real person, and the source of the pet otter story; the basic details of which may well be true. Henry also narrated this story in one of his broadcasts in the 1930s.[11]

Henry always maintained that his first books did not sell, in fact that they never made enough money to cover even the small advances he was given. Nevertheless, it is fairly certain that, although he was not an instant 'best-seller' the books did in fact sell much better than he made out.

The people of Georgeham regarded their new resident with suspicion; he was considered an outsider; he was 'strange' – 'mazed'. Yet his portrayal of their village, their conversations, their customs, parish meetings, and country sports, was unerringly accurate, wickedly funny, yet sympathetic; and captured just in time, before the hustle and bustle of modern life had sullied the pure essence of that bygone era. But the publication of the books based on Georgeham was not

'Metamorphosis'. Emerging into the
sunshine and freedom on Putsborough
Beach.

immediate; he was still storing up his impressions, only later would they take
shape in the form of the *Village* books.

Certainly Henry Williamson must have presented an extraordinary sight to the
inhabitants of the quiet Devon village, a place which had changed little in the
previous hundred years. An ex-officer but dressed so casually that he often wore
no shoes, he slept out in summer, swam naked, threw apples at passers-by, and
wrote long into the night. His 'strangeness' was compounded by the friends that
appeared from London, especially the young ladies. The particular young lady to
console him for Doline's 'coldness' was Lois Martin. His 1922 diary opens with
'WILLIAM LOVES LOIS'. Lois was 'small, red, musical,' the original of Diana
Shelley of *The Flax of Dream* novels. But before long Henry was once again in 'a
stupor of misery' and yet another relationship was over.

During 1922, sustained by sporadic newspaper articles and stories in magazines
– 6 January, £4 4s from the Sunday Express, and on the 20th, ditto & again on
10 February; 21 February, £18 18s from Pearson's for 'Bill Brock'; £18 18s from
the 'Royal' for 'Li'l Jearge' (less commission); etc. – he continued to work
furiously on his books. That year, *Dandelion Days*, the second volume of *The Flax
of Dream* was published. Also published this year was *The Lone Swallows*, [12] a
collection of nature essays (some of which had already appeared in magazines)
dedicated, most appositely, to Richard Jefferies: 'The beautiful swallows, be tender
to them, for they symbol all that is best in nature and all that is best in our hearts.'
He had offered the dedication to Lois Martin but her casual acceptance, 'By all
means', infuriated him and her subsequently discovered 'two-timing' blighted their
relationship, bringing about its inevitable end.

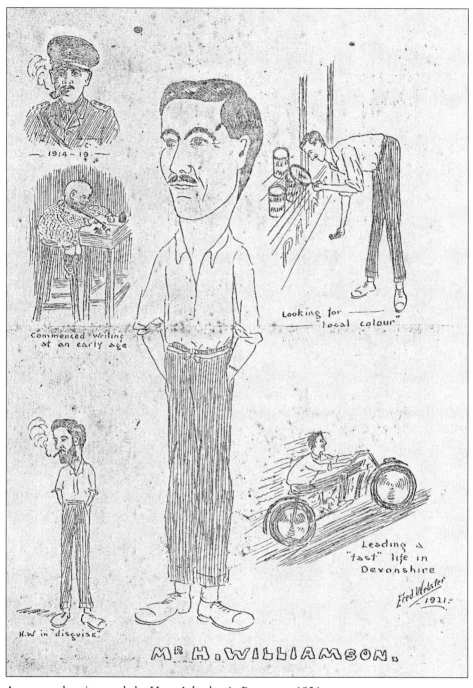

A cartoon drawing made by Henry's barber in Braunton, 1921.

Neither his journal nor his diary mention 'Julian Warbeck' who featured so strongly in his life in these early Georgeham days. 'Julian', a friend from the tail end of the war who lived with his parents near Henry's family home in London, shared the cottage in Georgeham for several months at this point, his parents apparently being glad to be rid of his presence as Henry's were of him! 'Julian' was a poet, a follower of Swinburne, drank beer ad infinitum, generally created mayhem, and totally irritated Henry as a living companion. Strangely, for Henry did leave clues about the identity of most of his characters, we only learn of all this from the books and from one archive photograph labelled 'Original of Julian Warbeck'. Until in a diary entry for 12 March 1933 where, writing of an incident that has just occurred, Henry notes: ' . . . reminded me of Frank Davis, the original of Julian Warbeck in *The Pathway* . . . '.[13]

In the summer of 1922 on the beach at Putsborough Henry met Esther Stokes, a widow with three children, one of whom, Mary Graham Stokes, became Annabelle of *The Sun in the Sands*. Henry recorded in his diary:

> . . . [She] is sixteen and a half years old, and immature. The first glance showed me one untouched by life. Brown eyes that looked straitly at you, without challenge or humility, wonderment or interest. She was still at school, of course, and on vacation.

On 20 September 1922, the summer vacation over, he saw her off to her school in London. Once again he is yearning for that which in his heart he knows he cannot have, or possibly does not really want: for to yearn was to suffer and to suffer was to write.

And indeed writing did continue apace. His income from short stories was small but steady and 1923 saw the publication of *The Peregrine's Saga – and Other Stories of the Country Green* (later subtitled *And Other Wild Tales*) containing 'Chakchek the One-eyed' and the totally charming moral 'A Weed's Tale', and he was working hard to complete the third novel of *The Flax of Dream*. Andrew Dakers was at all times supportive, tactful, gently chiding, guiding:

> A writer of your type has got to write certain things *out of himself*, they may not always be pleasant or popular, but write them you have got to, in order to release the more important and permanent stuff that's in you. Belief in oneself is a pendulum, & in order to swing it must be touching zero-point occasionally. If you need public encouragement to carry you through to your ultimate work, my advice is that you should write a *novel* of animals and birds, innocent of any moral or intention, but just a *jeu d'esprit*. Remember I always said your success would come slowly, even if it's hard to endure the waiting – it's ultimately worth it. Think of Conrad, Meredith, Hardy, and set your teeth, straighten your back-bone & bid the reviewers stew in ink. You'll come through, *certainly* if you simply remain tough in the face of adversity, & keep true to yourself.
>
> Letter in HWLEA, 31 October 1922

Frank Davis, the 'original of Julian Warbeck' (an important character in Henry's books).

Henry wrote on the back of this photograph: 'NB The punctured tyre of the old Norton which being inoperative, was discarded for a horse, Summer 1922, Devon'.

Henry and Mary Stokes at Braunton Tennis Club, 1922.

Andrew Dakers (Henry's first agent) and Henry on the beach at Putsborough, 1922.

During 1923 Dakers was negotiating publication of Henry's books in the United States (he was already being published in American magazines); this was finally settled with Dutton, who, under the aegis of John Macrae, were to prove very supportive and who published all the early books.

March 1923 brought the débâcle of the Braunton Tennis Club Fancy Dress Dance, a most correct affair within the realm of local society. Henry had not appreciated the niceties of etiquette with which such events were surrounded – or he had decided to ignore them – and managed to make a total fool of himself, as he relates in *The Sun in the Sands*:

How many times have I writhed in bed at night, remembering my sudden idiotic appearance at that dance in home made costume assembled from pyjamas, riding boots, leather jerkin, with my face white-washed and burnt-cork black circles round my eyes, a baby's woolen cap on my head stuck with two turkey feathers, and carrying in my mouth a moth-eaten lambskin tied with rope in the shape of a mouse! Village boys cheered as I arrived on my Norton. Quickly up the wooden steps I ran: it was an interval between dances; uttering a great screech, I announced myself as a Barn Owl.

The Sun in the Sands

As so frequently happened, it was one of Henry's jokes that spectacularly failed to impress. He was denounced as a drunken outsider and was subsequently ostracized by the local worthies. Dakers wrote to comfort his bruised ego: 'The mob spirit – and these people are a part of it – always goes to torture & crush the solitary spirits who have risen above it.'(Letter in HWLEA, dated 5 April 1923)

But one person did not shun him: the Braunton doctor, Frederick Elliston Wright, himself quite a character, and an accomplished naturalist, and author of a learned monograph on the plants of the famous local sand-dunes, Braunton Burrows. Together they went on many expeditions, and Henry Williamson no doubt acquired his knowledge of local natural history from him. For Henry was not a trained naturalist, and his knowledge was at times a bit ragged and narrow, indeed, it is possible to find many errors of fact within his work. But these pale into insignificance within the context of the whole. For it is his enthusiasm, his depth of feeling, and his ability to crystalize all this in felicitous literary expression that lifts his descriptions of nature into something much deeper and more powerful, into what can be recognized as a universal truth.

His story, 'A Weed's Tale' in *The Peregrine's Saga* encapsulates the essence of his powers, giving us a parable equal in depth of meaning and intensity of spiritual uplift to any one might find in the Bible. The following extract by necessity is much compressed from the original story.

A rook flying over a thatched cottage to its elm-top colony had in its beak a stick, found nearby. Something became dislodged from the stick, and fell. It was a small brown seed. A swallow caught it as it passed, but finding it uneatable, he dropped it, and it continued to fall until it came to rest on the cap of a grey-beard man who was smoking outside his cottage. For several moments it remained there, while the old cottager puffed his clay pipe.

Removing his cap to scratch his head, the brown seed completed its journey to the earth. It fell behind the rusty iron scraper fixed beside the threshold. Nothing interfered with it during the months of summer and autumn, and when the New Year came it had been washed by rain into a crevice between the cobblestones, and the mud from the boots of the old man had buried it three and a quarter inches from the light. It was a seed of Rumex sanquineus, *a Bloody-veined Dock, belonging to the sorrel family, common weeds of the countryside. . . .*

The sweet sunshine of a spring day gave warmth to the old man's back as he laboriously dug up the weeds and grass growing between the cobblestones of the path by his back door. Coming to the bootscraper, he attacked the thick stem of a dock. Its roots went down deep under the cobbles, and in his anxiety to dig up all the root he jabbed the thumb of his left hand, spurting red blood.

But he had not killed the weed. Between the cold stones, in damp darkness, lay the mangled root. Seven springs and summers had it started to build its tower towards the sky. Always its striving had been in vain. Seven years ago it had arrived beside the scraper, and no seed had it been able to make. Seven immense strivings had ended in failure. During the first spring it had put down a tap root, a feeler into the earth, for within the brown seed was a will, an unswervable determination. It worked patiently, thrusting a slow and minute tunnel with its root, feeling a way between the stones. The following spring it sent upwards out of its root, a green tower. The tower was broken. A third spring came; the root was now thicker and ventured forth a greenshoot which by June supported seventeen leaves, veined with crimson, and several hundred green seeds. They perished, burnt on the weed fire of the old man. Once more the sappy vitality of the dumb and gestureless root ebbed almost to nothingness. Again and again, every year this happened. Two grubs found the root and started to eat it; half its heart was consumed and rot set in to the remainder. The old root was abandoned, and three fresh shoots sent out, to wind themselves among the cobblestones. Despite all vicissitudes, the weed thrived. Until a new enemy arrived during the eighth spring, just as the green expedition was beginning. A meagre stream of a blue and red crystal liquid decimated all the new growth, shrivelling worms and tender frame and web, pressing round the root itself. All fruitfulness of the soil was poisoned by the paraffin.

That summer no rain fell. May became June, a month of intense heat and light pulsing from the blue sky. The weeds benefited by the sunny generosity, in spite of hoe and rake. The old man's energy flagged. He rarely left his cottage. July and August passed. No rain came. Until a night of violent storm, which gave the old man much hard work in clearing up. A week later the old man was found fully dressed but for his boots, dead in his bed. On his grave the following year were found growing, as though in faithful and compassionate memory, a score of young Rumex sanquineus.

The Peregrine's Saga, 'A Weed's Tale'

CHAPTER 4

THE OTTER'S SAGA

By the mid-1920s Henry Williamson's writing was prolific and penetrating; not yet in its prime, but powerful enough for him to be taken notice of. But he was on a constant see-saw of emotions, at times in fearful deep gloom about his ability ever to succeed, at others arrogantly asserting that he was the greatest writer ever born and the world was a fool not to see it. Impatient for success, he was fearful of its outcome, furious at its non-appearance, dejected by its apparent will o' the wisp nature.

In May 1924 Henry went on a walking holiday in the Pyrenees in the company of two friends, D.B. Wyndham Lewis (Dominic Bevan) and J.B. Morton (Johnny) who, one after the other, wrote for several years for the *Daily Express* as 'Beachcomber'. These two had planned to follow a great walk once undertaken by their hero Hilaire Belloc. Henry, feeling low and grieving over yet another unrequited love, asked if he could join them. A small newspaper cutting (undated), noted in Henry's handwriting to be from the *Daily Graphic* by S.P.B. Mais, chronicles their journey.

Words from the Wilds

I have just received a postcard from the three literary wanderers in the Pyrenees, Henry Williamson, J.B. Morton and D.B. Wyndham Lewis. They say:

'We haven't slept a wink for a week. Last night we walked in snow over 40 miles (Frankly I don't believe that.) Civic guards raid us in the forest, thinking we were bandits they were after. We have heard wolves howling at night, and seen the eagles soaring at immense heights.

We are a ragged band, blistered feet, collarless, unshaven, bottles sticking out of pockets and weighed down with packs. If nothing more is heard of us, we rely upon the DAILY GRAPHIC to fit out a relief expedition.' . . .

MR LONDON

S.P.B. Mais (Petre Mais), a great friend of Henry's, was himself a prolific writer. 'MR LONDON' was a rival to 'Beachcomber'.

The Pyreneean holiday over, life resumed its normal tenor. June 1924 saw the publication of the third volume of *The Flax of Dream*, *The Dream of Fair Women*, written the previous year and subtitled 'A Tale of Youth after the Great War' (although this was dropped when the book was revised). This was Henry's

Henry at the time of writing *Tarka the Otter*.

first book to be published by Dutton in America, although they brought out the revised versions of the earlier volumes of *Flax* in due course. It is the story of Willie Maddison's life in a remote Devon cottage, known as 'Rat's Castle' by the locals and is an idealized version of Henry's own early days in Devon. The names of the various sections in *The Dream of Fair Women*: 'The Weaver and the Flax', 'The Scarlet Thread', 'The Broken Web', and the overall title, *The Flax of Dream*, all derive from his Aunt Mary Leopoldina's *The Incalculable Hour*.[1] Apart from using her work as a source for his title, although very different in content, these four books are infused with a similar, Romantic Blakeian vision, particularly when the pendant volume, *The Star Born*, is considered together with the tetralogy. Although published much later, and underrated by the critics, it is meant to be taken together with the *Flax*, as it purports to be written by Willie Maddison, and is a surrealistic vision of the world.

But by the time *The Dream of Fair Women* was actually published, Henry was pursuing other lines, both literary and amatory. First, however, there was a small diversion. During the summer of 1924 Henry acted as tutor to a young boy, Patrick Foulds, whose parents had to travel abroad (the father was a composer), and had left their offspring in the care of a locally well-known Miss Johnson of Georgeham. 'Tutor' was a rather loose term for Henry's interpretation of his duties. Rather, he gave the boy books to read, *Bevis* by Richard Jefferies in particular, and took him out and about on nature rambles, and indulged in his usual slightly wild ways, which included shooting at chimney pots with his small

Henry with his friend Petre Mais outside Petre's house near Brighton.

gun, a trick which apparently greatly amused the young Patrick. Eventually his parents heard of this rather unorthodox interpretation of scholastic duties and ended the arrangement. Years later Patrick was to become the model for the boy in Henry Williamson's last book *The Scandaroon*. Interestingly, a letter to Henry from 'Your affect. cousin Dolly', and dated 24 October 1923 states, 'I am glad you have two pupils, at any rate it prevents that "unemployed feeling".'[2] The 'two pupils' must have been Patrick and his sister as there is no evidence of Henry having had any others, although October 1923 is a little early to fit the known facts. This extra occupation would have made a welcome addition to Henry's income.

During 1923 Henry had formulated ideas for a tale about the life of an otter (which no doubt arose out of the story of and connection with 'Zoë') and by the summer of 1924 this story was well under way. After his Pyreneean adventure he set to work seriously. In order to obtain accurate information he took to following the local hunt, the Cheriton Otter Hounds, who hunted otters along the waterways of the West Country, and particularly the Rivers Taw and Torridge, whose waters meet in the estuary beyond Barnstaple.

The huntsmen made a colourful scene, dressed in white breeches, dark blue cloth coats and waistcoats, white stock, dark blue worsted stockings with 'white' (actually pale grey) bowler hats, known as 'pot hats' and, of course, heavy boots. They carried long polished poles about five or six feet long incised with cuts to note particular kills. At this point their master was William Henry Rogers, 'Squire' Rogers, of Orleigh Court, Bideford, a well-known and well-liked figure, and the

Cheriton Otter Hunt. William Rogers, Master of the Hunt, is on the left. *Tarka the Otter* was dedicated to him.

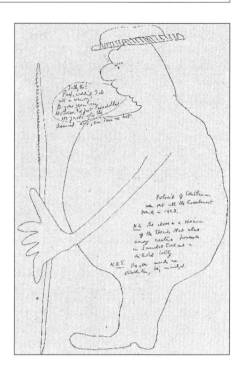

A cartoon drawing by Henry of a Hunt
follower.

Huntsman, the man who actually controlled the hounds, was Tom Allison. A
printed list of the pack show that the oldest hound was Dreamy, born in 1915.
Henry obviously did not feel 'Dreamy' sounded sinister enough for his purposes,
hence his own name for the chief hound in *Tarka the Otter* – Deadlock.

Henry Williamson wrote in a special preface to the limited edition of his book
The Pathway[3] how in June 1924, on one of these otter-hunting expeditions, he
found himself walking behind an old man who reminded him of Richard Jefferies.
When he remarked upon this to the old gentleman, to his surprise the latter
responded that he possessed all of Jefferies' books. Then, as they continued to
push through the heady, sweet-smelling foliage of wild Himalayan balsam, yellow
buttons of tansy and tangles of bramble along the bank of the River Torridge,
Henry noticed a girl nearby. He remarked, 'These brambles remind me of Bevis
and Mark walking by the New Sea.' To which the girl replied, 'Are you sure it
wasn't the Mississippi?' *Bevis*, by Henry's beloved Richard Jefferies, was her
favourite book. Henry Williamson was amazed to find people who knew and
loved Jefferies' writings.

The girl, Ida Loetitia Hibbert, was the daughter of the old gentleman Charles
Hibbert, who was one of the hunt officials.[4] Born in 1852 Charles Hibbert was
already over seventy when Henry Williamson met his daughter. Apart from his
portrayal in the *Chronicle*, he was also the model for Sufford Chychester in *The
Pathway*. (One branch of the Hibbert family had married a member of the

Chichester family, of whom Francis Chichester, the lone yachtsman, was part, hence the transposed name.) The Gainsborough portraits of Chychester's forebears in that book really were of Hibbert forebears, although this branch of the family only owned copies, Charles Hibbert being descended through younger sons. The diary entries supposedly written by Sufford Chychester are exactly in the style of his model's real diaries, for Charles Hibbert was a man of few words.

Charles Hibbert of course also appears with his daughter in *Tarka the Otter*. It is they who sit on the bank among the balsam flowers when the dragon-fly lands on Tarka's nose making him sneeze which gives away his position and the old gentleman lifts his hat and gives the old cry 'Tally Ho'. He was much liked and respected in the otter hunting fraternity. 'Squire' Rogers was known for composing little verses about the hunt, which were sung to a well-known tune; one of these referred to Hibbert and Henry and Ida Loetitia.

> Here's to Mr Hibbert
> If he'll pardon me the libert-
> y of introducing him into my song, boys.
> Here's to Henry and to Ida
> Who's a very dashing rider
> On the Norton motorcycle going strong, boys.[5]

Charles Hibbert's wife, Margaret Dora, twenty years his junior, had died of tuberculosis in 1918, when Ida Loetitia was seventeen and the girl had had to leave her boarding school at Wantage to take on the duties of chatelaine of the household, a role she did not relish. For Ida Loetitia, brought up with three brothers and in her early days with servants to do all the household chores, was more interested in the gentle things of nature, preferring to roam the lanes and hedgerows rather than prepare meals and see to household tasks. Life was very sheltered in the tiny Devonshire hamlet of Landcross where they lived, and Loetitia's social life restricted in the extreme; her choice of escort very limited. Otter hunting provided a rare opportunity to get out and meet people and to join in the various associated social events, which included the Hunt Ball.

Henry decided that this shy, dark-haired, strikingly beautiful girl was his perfect soulmate. By the end of July they were exchanging letters and meeting on a regular basis. 'Gipsy', as she was called on account of her dark looks, was a simple, unsophisticated person, with no nonsense about her. She loved her 'Willum' from the start, and having given him her heart, remained loyal to him throughout their tempestuous marriage and, at times, a very difficult life, continuing friends even after their divorce and his remarriage, until the very end. She is immortalized as Lucy Copleston in *A Chronicle of Ancient Sunlight*.

Meanwhile Henry was working hard on his book. Apart from the 'Zoë' incident, his first ideas for writing about an otter came from his reading of *The Life of an Otter* by J.C. Tregarthen.[6] As he wrote later to T.E. Lawrence, 'I thought I could improve on the original crib taken from "The Life of an Otter"'

Ida Loetitia Hibbert, Henry's fist wife.

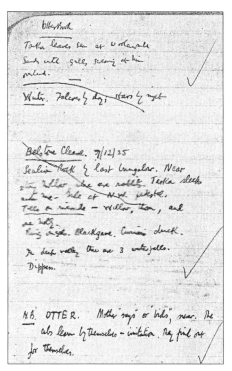

A page from Henry's notebook, 1925.

(letter in HWLEA, 8 March 1928). One of his notebooks also has details of watching otters in London Zoo. He also worked in several real-life events which he read about in the annals of the Cheriton Hunt written by the Master of the Hunt, William Henry Rogers.[7] There is one story of a very long hunt which started at 7.30 a.m. and continued until 6.50 p.m. which, although Henry changes some of the details, is the basis for the long hunt endured by Tarka at the end of the book. William Rogers was very helpful in providing Henry with information and correcting mistakes of etiquette and ambiance of the hunting fraternity, and in due course *Tarka* was to be dedicated to him in recognition. But none of this detracts from Henry Williamson's masterly achievement in rendering the convincing drama of his 'little water wanderer', where reality and imagination bond together recreating the inevitable and poignant climax of a totally authentic tale – the saga of an otter.

Before very long in the real lives of Henry and Ida Loetitia marriage was discussed. Henry probably proposed during the Cheriton Otter Hounds Ball held on 20 August 1924 as he has made a little note and sketch in his dance engagement card: 'This is *the* evening. . . . Let us keep this dear card.' Soon Loetitia, as she preferred to be known, was sorting herself out a simple trousseau, having fortunately just received a legacy of £200 from a great aunt, and seeing to

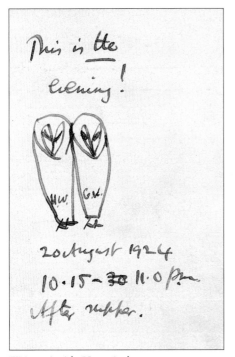

Written inside Henry's dance engagement card from the Otter Hunt Ball, 1924.

Henry and Loetitia at the time of their engagement.

the arrangements necessary for a wedding dress, while staying with her cousins in Sidmouth. A notice of the forthcoming marriage appeared in the national press, possibly round about Easter 1925.

MR H. WILLIAMSON AND MISS IDA HIBBERT

The marriage of Mr Henry Williamson and Miss Ida Hibbert will take place at Landcross Church on the 6th. May, at a quarter past one o'clock.

Henry wrote to his mother on 23 February 1925:

'We have fixed up the wedding on May 7 [*sic*], it will be the smallest and most informal affair, not even printed invitations being sent out.'

Gipsy thinks that it will be rot for Father to bother to come in a topper and frocker, as her Pa is going in a bowler and grey lounge suit, so I think that will be about the order of the day for men. I of course being the groom will wear a shiny headgear.

Meanwhile Henry had come to know the Hibbert family well as he now spent much of his time at Landcross, his only real way to see his bride-to-be. To his total amazement and horror, he discovered that their business affairs were in complete chaos, and he set himself the task of reforming them and their finances. What he did not realize was that they were perfectly happy with their situation and therefore resented Henry's interference in their affairs and ignored his advice, sending him into paroxysms of frustrated anger over what he considered such a decadent attitude. There was no understanding possible between such opposing and extreme examples of human nature. Henry portrays the Hibberts, rather unfairly, in a most unfavourable light in his writings. Jealousy and envy were probably at the root of this: envy of their family background being, as he saw it, wasted; jealousy of the very close relationship between Loetitia and her brothers, from which he felt shut out. All three brothers eventually emigrated to Australia and were very successful in their new lives, although Robin would return for a while.

Henry and Loetitia were married at the tiny church at Landcross on 6 May 1925. Henry's best man was Richard de la Mare, son of Walter, who was making a career for himself in publishing, working at that time for Selwyn and Blount Ltd., whilst Loetitia's bridesmaids were her cousins Mary Frances Hibbert and her

Wedding photograph. From left to right, Henry's mother, Mary Hibbert, Richard de la Mare, Henry, Loetitia, Charles Hibbert, 'Titia Hibbert. (Courtesy of Knights of Barnstaple)

younger sister 'Titia, daughters of Lt. Col. George Frederick Hibbert, younger brother of Loetitia's mother. It was a simple affair, and Loetitia's Girl Guide troop formed a guard of honour. The absence on the photographs of Henry's father would seem to imply that, in the end, he did not come.

To begin their honeymoon the bride and bridegroom drove across Exmoor with a new side-car fitted to the motorbike, to Higher House Farm at Wheddon Cross, near Dunkery Beacon. Henry wrote some notes under one general heading '6 May 1925' which show that he was more interested in natural history detail than his new bride:

> . . . The moor above us is untamed, and black with wind-blasted heather stems. The lower slopes of Dunkery, which is separated from the ancient moor by a hedge of beech, is brown with old bracken as though with the rust of all man's iron machinery which has failed to tame it. The moor seen from the Exford-Minehead road is a black strip, black as a rock spider and as savage. It remains through all the frosts and snows and rains, blasted by the wind and the sun. . . .

But the real object of the honeymoon was to return to the battlefields of the First World War, which seems rather a morbid occupation for what is supposed to be a happy time, especially for someone so sensitive. He was, perhaps, hoping that the company of his new and gentle wife would exorcise the ghosts and the trauma of that terrible time. His notes (undated) continued:

> Walked from Albert to Beaumont Hamel. Explored Y ravine and was drenched by rain. . . .
> Tall black dead trees, branchless, standing in marsh. At evening a chorus of bullfrogs began – but No gunflashes lit the whitewashed walls of our room, the

On honeymoon at a farm near Dunkery Beacon, Exmoor.

Dunkery Beacon, Exmoor, 1925.

trains from Arras rattled noisily past the windows, and a star moved beyond. The dugouts of Y ravine have subsided, the timbers break with a touch. . . .

Rifle barrels and holed helmets rust in the grasses. Rust and mildew and long green grass and frogs. The Ancre flows swift and hostile as before, gathering its green duckweed into a heaving coat, drowning its white water crowsfoot. . . .

What is to be found in the valley now? The answer is nothing. . . . Hindenburg Line. Walked from Achiet. Remembered. Trenches filled in but dugout shafts remain. . . .

Written at Neuville St. Vaast. 2pm. 30th May 1925. Have just seen the German cemetery at La Maison Blanche, at the Bethune–Arras road. 36000 BLACK CROSSES with white names and numbers thereon. Packed close together, two by two, back and front, the wooden crosses are planted in chalk. No flowers grow here, except the strays of the old battlefield, charlock, poppy and bindweed. They look in disgrace and unfriended. . . .

Black, black, black, thirty-six thousand of them, stuck in the white chalk. But there were larks above.

The honeymoon over, the couple returned to Skirr Cottage in Georgeham. Soon Loetitia realized she was pregnant; the cottage seemed too primitive for the coming winter so they took over the lease of Vale House a few yards up the road,

Henry among the thousands of crosses marking the war dead.

which became conveniently empty at this time. This house was owned by a Mrs Lamplugh, wife of the Revd Lamplugh who was vicar of a parish in Barnstaple and whose son Aubrey Lamplugh and his wife Ruth had lived for two or three years previously in Chertsey Cottage opposite the church in Georgeham. Henry had become very friendly with the Lamplughs long before his marriage,[8] spending considerable time at their house reading his latest work out loud (a life-long habit of his).

The house needed a little refurbishment but after some plastering and whitewashing, Henry settled into an upstairs room jutting out over the garage to continue writing his otter book in earnest. In his little pocket notebook the general heading 'Otter Book' soon changed to 'The Otter's Saga' and then became 'Tarka'.

In early 1925 Henry had written to Walter de la Mare, with whom he had exchanged several letters since their first meeting in 1921 and with whose son he was very friendly, to ask if he would approach Sir John Fortescue and inquire if he would write an introduction to Henry's 'Otter' book. The Earl of Fortescue's family seat was nearby at Castle Hill, Filleigh, South Molton, Devon, and his brother the Hon. Sir John Fortescue was engaged in writing a multivolume *History of the British Army*. More important to Henry was his earlier book, *The Story of a Red Deer*[9] written at the end of the nineteenth century, which Henry greatly admired and he therefore thought that Sir John would be an appropriate person to grace his own work.

Walter de la Mare wrote to Henry on 2 April 1925 saying that although he only knew Fortescue slightly, he had written to him and would relay the reply as soon as it arrived; a further letter dated 8 April shows that the reply was favourable. Henry sent his typescript forthwith. At this time Sir John Fortescue was librarian at Windsor Castle and his first letter to Henry dated 4 May 1925 is on Windsor Castle headed notepaper.

> Dear Sir,
> I return your story with many thanks, & with apologies for the delay of a very busy man. I read it once & liked it well; twice & liked it better. I am willing to write a little introduction for you, if you wish it, but I think the book striking enough to stand without need of any such prop. You have taught me more about otters than I have ever dreamed of, & of many other creatures besides otters, and I am very grateful to you. I must add also my congratulations. . . .
> [he then offers one or two suggestions for corrections and notes about style]
> Very truly yours. J.W. Fortescue
Letter in HWLEA, dated 4 May 1925[10]

This letter must have arrived on Henry's wedding day, and he would have felt very elated after the lack of response he felt there had been from all quarters. But the matter actually stayed in abeyance for some time and it was another eighteen months before the introduction was actually written.

By the end of 1925 business letters from Andrew Dakers, Richard de la Mare at Selwyn and Blount, Constant Huntingdon at Putnam, and American publishers show that *Tarka the Otter* was finished and Henry was looking for the best deal. He had earned little money that year with no new book published, his income being derived from stories in magazines, especially in the American market, and from American editions of his books and, in England, from cheap editions of books already in print. Henry had thought to place the book with Selwyn and Blount – indeed the file of business letters shows this to be well under way in September 1925, but then a letter from Richard de la Mare warned him that the firm was in financial difficulties and advised him to withdraw and look elsewhere.

At the beginning of December 1925 a letter in the files from the Royal Literary Fund indicates that Henry had applied for a grant to cover the cost of his wife's forthcoming confinement – an indication of their straitened circumstances; success had still not arrived.

Henry and Loetitia spent that Christmas at Landcross with the Hibbert family, but this was a mistake and did not improve family harmony. Throughout his life, Henry always found Christmas a very difficult time, for his memories of the Christmas spent in the trenches during the First World War were always uppermost. He felt much anguish as these memories overwhelmed him, and the fact that for other people this was a jolly occasion jarred on his spirits. Apart from this there was also the fact that he was not in sympathy with the attitude of 'Pa' and the 'Boys'. It was not a happy Christmas.

A few weeks later Henry rushed round to his friends Aubrey and Ruth Lamplugh to say that Loetitia's labour had started. Dr Wright, his Braunton botanist friend who was also the family doctor, did not consider the matter urgent enough to interrupt the skittles match in which he was engaged at the time. One can imagine the frenzy that the delay put Henry in! It had been arranged that Aubrey Lamplugh would transport Loetitia to the small nursing home in Braunton in his Trojan car, the motorbike and sidecar being considered even by Henry as too primitive a form of transport for a woman about to give birth. The child, a son, was born on 18 February 1926 and was named William Hibbert, but known to all throughout his childhood as 'Windles'. A bulletin for Georgeham Parish Church records the holy baptism of William Hibbert Williamson on 14 March. One of the godfathers was Henry's uncle, Henry Joseph Williamson, who on arriving at Georgeham for the ceremony upset Henry by complaining about his beard and saying his appearance was too scruffy for the occasion. Henry Joseph also arrived with a case of stout for Loetitia which he recommended to build up her strength. Knowing she loathed the stuff, Henry surreptitiously drank it on her behalf but his uncle was suspicious, and thus Henry had another black mark against him! 'To my Uncle I was perverse and not quite straight – witness the shifty way I had drunk Loetitia's medicinal stout in the dark larder, and when questions were asked, had kept silent.' (*The Children of Shallowford*, 1939).

Loetitia was not at all well after the birth of her child, succumbing to an infection, and was unable to feed the baby. Consequently it did not at first thrive,

Henry's mother visits the new baby.

but she says that stories of how Henry sat up at night nursing him while writing *Tarka* by the light of his candle are very exaggerated. She can remember one such occasion only! When Loetitia was better she was, naturally, busy caring for the baby. Henry had not foreseen the difference a child would make in their relationship and essentially was jealous – although he may not have recognized his emotion for what it was at the time – as his father had been jealous of his children years earlier. He had become used to doing exactly what he wanted when he wanted. He also wanted, needed and expected, total attention from those around him and could not see why this could no longer be so. He had grown used to his wife being able to go for a ramble whenever he wanted a break, and to instantly dropping whatever household occupation she was engaged upon to listen to him read his latest pages, which was how he 'fixed' his writing in his mind, or to hear what he considered to be a not-to-be-missed item of music on the wireless or gramophone. He became very irritable and depressed when he found she now had other priorities. But he was honest and objective enough to describe some of his share of the problems when he came to write the *Chronicle*.

He was continually working on *Tarka*, honing and refining: he always maintained that it was rewritten seventeen times, but only seven versions exist, although there is no doubt he was constantly correcting and reworking it over

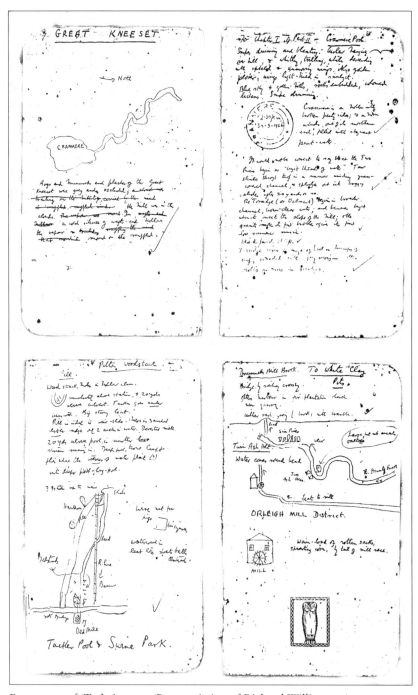

Four pages of 'Tarka' notes. (By permission of Richard Williamson)

some three or four years so he may well have gone over it for corrections seventeen times. His attention to detail was certainly exacting. Henry Williamson did indeed tramp every inch of Tarka's route, wanting his tale to be authentic and perfect. For example, a month after Windle's birth, Henry accompanied by 'Bin' (Loetitia's younger brother, Robin), anxious to get the Dartmoor scenes exact, walked up to Cranmere Pool (a remote, wild, boggy area high on Dartmoor only reached with some difficulty) on 30 March 1926 and wrote in the visitor's book which was kept there.[11] From there he sent a postcard to his wife addressed to her at 'Owlery, Georgeham'; 'Nice walk – you come in summer with me. Spurred otter. HW'

At the beginning of 1926 there was a quarrel with Collins over a new edition of *The Peregrine's Saga*. Henry wanted to incorporate corrections; the publishers declined – such refinements were too expensive for the cheap edition being contemplated. In the end Collins did accede, but Henry had already decided he had outgrown them, for he was negotiating with Putnam over the forthcoming *Tarka*, and it was Putnam – not without a considerable turbulence as can be deduced from the business letters file – that published *The Old Stag* in October 1926. Dedicated to 'Windles' Mother', it is a collection of stories that had already appeared in magazines mainly in America, and contains many of his finest pieces.

Henry's entry in the Cranmere Pool Visitors' book, 1926. (Reproduced with the kind permission of Devon Library Services)

Work on *Tarka* had continued. In the spring of 1926 Henry had sent a revised typescript to Sir John Fortescue for the latter writes, 'I return the typescript of Tarka with many thanks. I have read it aloud to my wife & we have enjoyed it greatly.' And there follows a few suggestions for amendments. In August 1926 he writes again: 'I send you my introduction to your Tarka. I do not know when I have found anything so difficult to write, & I am far from satisfied with it.'[12] It was actually exactly what was needed, and Putnam was certainly very pleased with it, for Constant Huntingdon wrote 'Thank you for sending Sir John Fortescue's Introduction to Tarka. Of course it is extraordinarily good. I do not see how it could be better. . . . He is right in singling out your powers of observation for special attention. I suppose you just take it for granted but I assure you nobody else could do the same.'

Two other important things happened to Henry Williamson at the end of 1926 which are of particular significance. The first concerned his comrades from the First World War. On the 4 November he attended a dinner at the Connaught Rooms in Great Queen Street, London for a reunion of those survivors who had travelled out to France on 4 November 1914 on the troopship *Chyebassa*. On the back of his menu from the occasion are the signatures of the survivors of 'P' Company, Henry Williamson's comrades in arms.

Henry wrote about this occasion in a little pocket notebook, following immediately on from the notes he had previously made on his honeymoon trip to the battlefields in 1925. This must have been deliberate and indicates a significance of association and purpose. He was preparing to write about that war. Headed 4 November 1926, he recorded: 'Attended the re-union of the original L.R.B. survivors – "Chyebassa dinner", named after ship that took us from Southampton to Havre on 4/11/14.' There follows a carefully drawn map, copied from 'Lt (now Capt.) Fursdon's map he sketched for me . . . of Plugstreet wood & trenches'. Then there are short descriptive comments on the men he either knew personally or singled out as worthy of note: 'D.H. Bell – 'keen, dark, double-life . . . twelve years after, he showed curious double strain . . . ; Hollis – slow of speech, red face, just as in 1914. . . ; Blunden – lance-corporal Blunden. Slight impediment in speech. Small narrow face, dark, close-set eyes; deliberate. Root of an oaktree. Arm off now. . . .'

One immediate outcome of the reunion was the renewal of contact with Douglas Bell, an old Colfeian, who asked Henry for his help with a book he was planning to publish. Henry was always very generous to other writers and helped several to get their work in print. He was grateful for help he himself had received and was conscious of his responsibility to help others. He read Bell's manuscript, which was in fact his war diary, made several suggestions, and sent it off to Richard de la Mare now at Faber and Gwyer, writing an introduction for it in due course. *A Soldier's Diary of the Great War* was published anonymously in 1929. Involvement with that book may well have crystallized Henry's own thoughts on the war.

The other occurrence in that autumn of 1926 was not in itself significant but it led to an important incident in Henry's life. On 29 November Henry visited John

Galsworthy, which is known because the latter wrote two letters later that day. One was to Henry himself. From this it can be discerned that the two men had discussed literary matters and it would seem that Henry was depressed about the reaction he was receiving to his otter book, for Galsworthy offered Henry gentle encouragement and stated that he had written to Edward Garnett about him. The letter to Garnett recommended Henry's writing and mentioned the new book in process about an otter:

> Do you know the work of Henry Williamson? It's uneven but at its best extraordinarily good I think. A strange and sensitive nature lover and worshipper of Jefferies and Hudson. . . . The Old Stag is his best book, but he's got one in Press on the life of an otter that he thinks best. . . . If you like it (The Otter Book) give him a word of encouragement. He can see and he can write. . . .[13]

Edward Garnett was an author and well-known critic who had been instrumental in encouraging and establishing several writers, including Joseph Conrad, W.H. Hudson, D.H. Lawrence and E.M. Forster and was at this time consultant editorial advisor to Jonathan Cape. Galsworthy's introduction started a friendship between Henry and Edward Garnett which was to prove of great significance to Henry; for Edward Garnett was also a great friend of T.E. Lawrence – Lawrence of Arabia – whom he had advised on *The Seven Pillars of Wisdom* and Garnett was to be the catalyst for the friendship between Lawrence and Henry Williamson. Henry's response to Galsworthy's introduction was to send a copy of *The Old Stag* to Edward Garnett, who was immediately supportive.

But in the middle of all the preparations for the publication of *Tarka*, while the actual printing was taking place, Henry Williamson decided to travel once again to the battlefields. So, at the beginning of June (his notes, some sixteen sparse pages in a small-paged pad, are headed 3–10 June 1927), in the company of his brother-in-law, Biddy's husband, William Busby, who had been in the Tank Corps in the war, he retraced the steps first taken in 1914. The catalyst for this was no doubt the '*Chyebassa* reunion' of the previous autumn, and it is obvious that Henry had a purpose in mind for a writing project. Expanded, these notes would form the basis for *The Wet Flanders Plain*, but first Henry wrote them up as articles to help pay for the trip. Some were accepted and published in the *Daily Express*, the first, 'And This Was Ypres', appearing on 20 July 1927. Some of the rest eventually appeared in the *Daily Telegraph* in June 1928, and one or two were sold elsewhere.

By the time he returned from this trip preparations for the publication of *Tarka* were well under way. Quite early on Henry had suggested to Putnam that the company commission maps from Thomas A. Falcon, an artist whose work Henry knew and who lived in nearby Braunton. These maps were to be used as end-papers for the book, and many letters about their detail passed between the two men.

T.M. Ragg of Putnam was responsible for the design of the book, with many suggestions from the author himself. In due course he sent a sample page for Henry to see. This was not at all what Henry had envisaged and he wrote on it: 'I do not like this at all. I would like to see the book printed in the type of the Essex Press Shakespeare's Sonnets, simply and austerely. . . . I would like a simple and beautiful binding, quiet and dignified.' (Document in HWLEA.) Ragg changed his design. For his part, he did not like the Falcon maps, saying they were too heavy and out of proportion to the design of the book, and at the very last minute they were not used. Henry was very embarrassed but Falcon seems to have taken it philosophically. Henry wrote in his bound copy of the *Tarka* proofs:

> There are also end-paper maps in 3 colours of
>   1) Estuary of Two Rivers
>   2) Last Hunt
>   I think they are lovely maps – so exact and faithful and original.
>   Done by a Braunton artist called Falcon.[14]

Apart from the difficulty of setting up the deal with Putnam, evident from the many letters from Constant Huntingdon of Putnam and from Andrew Dakers – complicated because Henry kept prevaricating and trying to add clauses to cover every eventuality and objecting to nearly every suggestion – Henry had decided to have a special deluxe limited edition of *Tarka the Otter* to be sold by private subscription, which made his own life even more difficult. He concerned himself very closely with the details and was personally responsible for selling the copies. He had a prospectus printed which he sent out to as many people as he could think of. This used up a great deal of his time and nervous energy.

The private edition printed at the prestigious Chiswick Press was limited to one hundred copies and was published in August 1927. It was a resplendent production in full vellum of pale creamy white, the only decoration a small rectangle of brown leather on the spine with the title and author's name in gold tooling. The hand-made pages are deckle-edged just as they came off their press and the sizes are slightly uneven – a true collector's piece which today commands a high price. Henry Williamson's price was 3 guineas. His list of sales shows that the first copy was presented to the Hon. Sir John Fortescue, the second he reserved for himself, the third was bought by his mother and the following three by John Galsworthy. The seventh went to Doline Rendle and the eighth to W.H. Rogers, MOH, to whom the book is dedicated in acknowledgement of all the help he had given. The twelfth was sold to Walter de la Mare, the thirteenth to S.P.B. Mais and the next to Edward Garnett. Various members of the Hibbert family bought copies, especially 'Grannie', Sarah Catherine Augusta Hibbert, with whom Henry had a very close rapport. Siegfried Sassoon bought copy twenty-two and Andrew Dakers the twenty-sixth. Siegfried Sassoon had written Henry a most charming little note saying that Walter de la Mare had introduced Henry's work to him, and that he sent a cheque with great pleasure 'for a book I intend to enjoy', and asking for some prospectuses so that he can do a little propaganda on Henry's behalf.

Around November 1927, en route to visit his uncle Henry Joseph in Bournemouth, Henry found himself in Dorchester. Stretching his legs he suddenly realized he was outside Max Gate, the home of Thomas Hardy, and with much trepidation he decided to call. On arrival at his uncle's home he sent an urgent letter to his wife relating how 'with much trembling' he had called on Hardy and found him 'olde, olde', and asking her to send the venerable author a special copy of *Tarka*. A letter arrived from Florence Hardy, wife of Thomas, dated 30 November 1927, apologising for the delay in thanking him for 'that most beautiful edition of Tarka the Otter'. Thomas Hardy wrote to Putnam to say that he thought *Tarka* 'a remarkable book'. This must have been almost one of the last things Hardy did. He died early in the new year, to the great sadness of his many friends and particularly to T.E. Lawrence, who had visited him just before leaving to serve in India, which must have been about the time of Henry's own visit.

Putnam published the first full trade edition of *Tarka the Otter* in October 1927, a lino-cut of an otter and river scene by Hester Sainsbury gracing the cover; a fairly ordinary looking book, its price was 7/6d. Henry wrote:

Tarka has been published 3 days & no reviews so far. I say I don't care what happens to it; what the critics say beyond the few reviews by personal friends & acquaintances such as Garnett, Mais, etc. But really I am alert as a falcon for appreciation.

Notebook in HWLEA, undated but October 1927

In fact reviews were favourable, but there was not the immediate outcry that Henry was hoping for. But when Dutton followed with publication in America early in 1928, the reviews there were very enthusiastic.

Edward Garnett had sent round copies to several people suggesting they review the book and unknown to Henry, he had also sent a copy to his friend T.E. Lawrence in India, where he was stationed at Karachi with the Royal Air Force. At the beginning of February 1928, Henry received a letter from Garnett enclosing Lawrence's reply, a long and detailed critique of the book. T.E. Lawrence mistakenly thought this was the author's first book and that he was encouraging a novice, whereas, of course, this was Henry's seventh, with others already in the pipeline. Lawrence's letter ends:

I shouldn't have written so much if the book was not, in my judgment, particularly worth writing about. . . .
'Very many thanks for sending it to me. It has kept me sizzling with joy for three weeks. The best thing I've met for ever so long. Fresh, hopeful, fecund, and so, so, careful. It is heartening to see a writer caring much for his words and chasing and chiselling them with such firmness. I hope he likes it well

enough to persevere, for I shall look forward to reading him again: – apart from Tarka which I'll read many times yet.[15]

Henry felt that at last he was in touch with a kindred spirit. He had read the serialization of Lawrence's book *Revolt in the Desert* in the *Daily Telegraph* in January 1927 and had been struck by the essential similarity in thought between a sentence of Lawrence's and a sentence from his own manuscript of *Tarka*. Henry had immediately felt that he *knew* Lawrence of Arabia, that he could be the friend he had always longed for 'with whom even words would be superfluous'.[16] Henry replied to Lawrence, calling him his 'twin psyche', explaining the background of his writing of *Tarka* and sending a copy of *The Old Stag*. The two men corresponded on a fairly regular basis from then on, and would later meet.

In mid-April Henry received an even more gratifying letter. It arrived in a small, grey ordinary-looking envelope, with a handwritten address, but the contents would change his life. The letter written by hand was dated 13 April 1928, and came from Bayman Manor, Chesham.

Dear Mr Williamson,
You don't know what pleasure it gives me to write this letter for it is to tell you that the Committee of the Hawthornden Prize have awarded the prize to you for your book 'Tarka the Otter'. The presentation will be made next month probably. I shall be able to tell you the date as soon as we have decided on who is to make the presentation.

I hope you have heard of the Hawthornden Prize. It was my idea to give one for what the committee consisting of Mr J.C. Squire, Mr E. [Edward] Marsh, Mr Laurence Binyon, Mr R. [Robert] Lynd, & myself consider to be the best imaginative work of the year and we are quite unanimous about 'Tarka'.

Please keep it a profound secret, only of course tell Mrs Williamson & swear her to secrecy till the day it is presented.

I cannot tell you what thrilling hours I have spent with 'Tarka'.
Believe me sincerely, Alice Warrender.[17]
Letter in HWLEA, dated 13 April 1928

Alice Warrender was a generous benefactor to many artistic enterprises and with the encouragement of J.C. Squire, the writer and critic involved in the Georgian Movement, and editor of various publications, particularly the *London Mercury* which had published several articles by Henry Williamson, had set up the Hawthornden Prize in 1919.

Henry wrote back immediately and must have sent Alice Warrender a copy of the limited edition of *Tarka*, for her next letter, dated 17 April 1928, thanks him for his 'wonderful gift, such a beautifully printed and bound book, and I do love the inscription.' She goes on to say that she had read *The Old Stag* the previous year and had wanted to award that the Hawthornden, but 'this is still better'. 'We are trying to get Mr Baldwin to make the presentation but he is difficult to catch.'

Henry forthwith wrote a postcard of restrained elation, enclosing Alice Warrender's letter, to 'Grannie', Sarah Augusta Hibbert, Loetitia's maternal grandmother.[18] She appears to have been unfailingly gracious to him and her experience as an artist's daughter and well-travelled woman no doubt gave Henry a sense of empathy. Her letters were always kind and encouraging and would have been soothing for Henry.

In the event Mr Baldwin proved *too* difficult to catch and it was John Galsworthy who made the presentation at the award ceremony which took place at the Aeolian Hall in London on 12 June 1928. This was a far more appropriate choice considering all the encouragement Galsworthy had already given Henry (indeed, Henry and Loetitia were staying overnight with him and his wife).

Several newspapers cuttings reported that in his speech John Galsworthy described *Tarka the Otter* as 'a truly remarkable creation. It was the result of stupendous imaginative concentration, fortified by endlessly patient and loving observation of nature. Henry Williamson had received as yet infinitely less credit as a writer than he deserved. He was the finest and most intimate living interpreter of the drama of wild life, and he was, at his best, a beautiful writer.' (Cuttings in HWLEA.)

Miss Warrender also made a delightful speech but the *Sunday Times* reported: 'The happy winner of the prize only emerged from the back of the hall to shake

John Galsworthy presents the Hawthornden Prize to Henry Williamson.

hands with Miss Warrender and Mr Galsworthy on the platform, and having done so again disappeared to a more retired spot. But he must be a proud man to deserve all that was said of *Tarka the Otter*.' (Cutting in HWLEA.) Other newspapers also reported that 'the shy young man retreated from the platform without making a speech'. It was surprising that Henry was not prepared for the occasion. He claimed there had been no rehearsal and he had not known what was expected of him; but surely he realized he would be expected to say at least a few words. He was apparently overwhelmed, his essential nervousness revealed.

The prize was £100 but, as Henry had written to Grannie Hibbert, more importantly it meant '. . . unlimited kudos and market rises for unsold stories etc. In fact, one arrives.' (Postcard in HWLEA, dated April 1928.)

One had indeed arrived. Publicity was instantaneous. One of the items in Henry's literary archive is a large scrapbook of cuttings and reviews, including a large section devoted to reports of the award. Constant Huntingdon at Putnam was most put out that Henry had omitted to tell them it was pending for they were totally unprepared for the rush of orders that was generated. When Henry pointed out that he had been asked to keep the event secret, Huntingdon retorted that he *had* told his agent.

A few days before the ceremony Alice Warrender had sent Henry some invitations 'for you will want your friends to be there'. A letter from Henry's old housemaster at Colfe's, R.A. Fitzaucher, shows that Henry had very kindly sent him one, but he was unable to attend (letter in HWLEA, dated June 1928). Henry had also invited Doline Rendle ('Spica Virginis'), and his old C.O. from Felixstowe days, Lord Ampthill. Initially unsure of his commitments at the House of Lords, Lord Ampthill did manage to attend, writing afterwards, 'Let me say again how glad I was to see you receive the Hawthornden Prize.'

Henry was now riding on the crest of a wave; 1928 continued to be a momentous year. He immediately applied or was put forward, to join the Savage Club, whose members were artists and literary men, and was admitted on 10 August. Once the Hawthornden award had been announced Henry's work was in demand, and he took the opportunity to publish several war articles. 'The Miracle I saw in France' appeared in the *Evening News* while the *Daily Express*, rather reticent about printing his war articles the previous year, published 'Fourteen Years After' on 8 August 1928: 'In this moving article Mr Williamson, one of the most notable of the new generation of writers, gives a sketch of the Western battlefield as it will appear to the 11,000 pilgrims of the British Legion now in France – just fourteen years after the outbreak of the great war.' They then published a series starting on 11 August 1928 called 'The Last 100 Days'. 'Mr Williamson, Winner of the Hawthornden Prize for 1928, who served as a soldier of the line, describes from time to time in these columns, the principal events of the last hundred days of the war.' On Armistice Day 1928 a long article appeared in the *Radio Times*, 'What we should Remember and What Forget',[19] while the *Daily Mirror* commissioned him to cover the Remembrance ceremony at the Cenotaph.

With sales of *Tarka* going well Henry sold his Norton and bought a second-hand 6 horse-power Peugeot. At the end of October he used it to drive his wife to the nursing home in Barnstaple where another baby was born, a second son, John Shapcote, on the very same day that *The Pathway*, the fourth volume of *The Flax of Dream* was published.

Henry had worked long and hard on *The Pathway*. The overall plan for the tetralogy had been laid down from the beginning, but it was now four years since the third volume had been published. One reason, of course, was the writing of *Tarka*, but Henry was also beginning to see things from a maturer viewpoint. Having met Loetitia he embodied her in the fictional Mary who becomes, after Willie, the central character in *The Pathway*. The book seems to have been worked on in fits and starts. The business letter file for 1928 shows a very complicated cat-and-mouse game being played in an effort to find a publisher. Richard de la Mare was by then a director at Faber and Gwyer, and was hoping that Henry would offer them *The Pathway*, or if not that, then a future title. Collins had, of course, published the first three volumes of the *Flax*, but Henry had already transferred allegiance to Putnam for *The Old Stag* and *Tarka*. In February 1928 Andrew Dakers wrote that Putnam would not agree to the £100 advance Henry was asking, thus freeing Henry from any suggestion of 'obligatory rights', but that Jonathan Cape were happy to do so. So eventually Cape won the day. The book got good reviews and sold well.

But it was again in the United States that *The Pathway* had its real success, with enthusiastic reviews right across the country. However, there was a tremendous outcry when the book failed to be chosen as 'Book of the Month'. John Macrae, President of Dutton, Henry's publisher and unfailing supporter, exposed the racket that surrounded this award, sending an open letter to the American press. He pointed out that the 'choice' was made only from those books whose publishers were giving a 70 per cent discount for circulation privileges and that he, as head of a reputable publishing company, refused to take part in such a 'ring'.[20] Henry Williamson's name and that of *The Pathway* were caught up in a blaze of publicity.

John Macrae made fairly frequent visits to Britain on business and Henry met him on several occasions in London to discuss various projects. On 1 January 1929 Henry wrote in his diary: 'Dined with John Macrae. He wants the early novels "as soon as I have them ready revised for him" & hopes to sell 50,000 of the Pathway in U.S.A. Perhaps!'

On this occasion Henry was passing through London en route for a ski-ing holiday in the Pyrenees. Arriving at Bagnères where he met up with his friend Kit Williams,[21] he 'bought skis, 140 fcs. Alternative was hiring same at 60fcs per week!!.' By Saturday he could 'more or less walk-glide, & keep balanced'. On the Sunday they went up the Monne where he saw among other birds, goldcrested wrens next to a sportsman's shelter with claypigeon traps. Monday's diary entry states: 'Goldcrested wrens for lunch! Refused them.' By Wednesday the 9th although complaining of pain in his lungs and coughing up blood-stained phlegm, he was 'ski-ing much better'. Next day he wrote 'the pain is gone. Very fit.

Climbed up sans vest or shirt in brilliant sunshine.' There are several notes to be used for stories, for example, 'very curious example of sheep that reasoned. Loved Shepherd's child & pined when it died. Pensioned off. – "The Sheep that was Pensioned".' Next to his return date he notes, 'Toys for Windles. Present for G.'

Once back home there are no diary entries as such but many 'Notes for Revision of Early Novels':

> *Beautiful Years* No chapter headings.
> Make more REAL & less intimate the Willie-Elsie episodes
> Great care with the Mary-bedroom scene in the penultimate chapter. . . .
>
> *Dandelion Days* . . . The exaggerations must be dealt with severely. There can still be plenty of fun. . . .
> Bring in more Mary. . . .
> Moderate and make more real, the English master's lesson; the Physic's lesson; the French lesson.

During this period correspondence with T.E. Lawrence continued. Lawrence returned to England early in 1929, due to the publicity and rumours that arose when his presence at the RAF station at Wharistan near the Afghanistan border was discovered. He was stationed at Plymouth in South Devon which although 80 miles away, was easily within striking distance on his powerful motorcycle, and Henry was soon urging him to cross the moors to visit him in Georgeham. Eventually a visit was planned for Sunday 30 June 1929 when Lawrence had a rare day off, but he did not appear as it poured with rain all day. The visit was reinstated for 28 July. Henry wrote in his book *Genius of Friendship* how he listened to the weather forecast on the wireless the night before which warned of a deep depression approaching and how, by midnight, the rain was driving against the window of his writing room and that in the morning it was still raining. But preparations went ahead.

> *Knowing that he did not smoke, I had hidden my pipe and tobacco jar; not because he might disapprove but because I was always wanting to give up smoking, knowing it was poison for my nature and temperament. I was glad to be able, with authority, to ask my wife to give my pipes and tobacco jar to the next tramp who might come along.*
>
> *For lunch Loetitia had prepared a salad of lettuce, tomato, onions, nuts, apples, and other fruit, with cheese, plums, figs, cream cake and chocolate. I had read in Robert Graves' book that T.E. disliked set meals and was happiest wandering about a room, taking an apple, and in short, pleasing himself. 'And quite right too,' said Loetitia. 'I think everyone should do just what they want to.' So apples were put on the shelf, the solitary book-case, the window ledges, and even in the washhouse. Our small son Windles, then three and a half years old, went round with us, approving this unusual distribution of apples. . . .*
>
> *Genius of Friendship*

Henry goes on to relate that as the church clock struck twelve so Lawrence appeared on his nickel-plated Brough Superior motor-cycle in the lane outside. After a wash and observation of the social niceties with Loetitia, the two men went up to Henry's writing room to talk. At one o'clock they ate the simple meal and then Lawrence departed for the three-hour journey back to Plymouth, where he had to report for duty. Henry summed up his feelings about this meeting by describing Lawrence thus: 'He was laughter, pure, sweet laughter.'

The books Henry published during 1929 were somewhat idiosyncratic, consisting mainly of limited editions which, although beautifully produced and superb examples of the short story genre, cannot have provided much income to feed the family. First came a limited edition of 225 copies printed by the Windsor Press of a short story, *The Ackymals*. This vignette tells how John Kift shoots the ackymals (marsh tits) because he thought, wrongly but determinedly, that they ate his peas; and how their deaths are echoed in the scenes surrounding that of a baby in the village; the two strands deftly complementing each other to show the unthinking futility in life. The story was later incorporated into *Village Life*.

Another limited edition was *The Linhay on the Downs*, 'being Number Twelve of the Woburn Books'. Of its two stories, the first, 'The Linhay on the Downs', tells how a man and his companion caught in a storm and seeking protection in a linhay, a hut for sheltering animals and fodder, find a vixen caught in a gin trap and manage to free her. The second, 'The Firing Gatherer', paints in words the scene of an old woman gathering up sticks for the fire along the tide line in an old pram. These again were later incorporated into a larger volume, *The Linhay on the Downs and Other Stories*.

Then, at last, Henry achieved publication of his first war book, *The Wet Flanders Plain*. Again, the book first appeared in a limited edition, in June, prepared by the Cyril Beaumont Press, and then Faber produced the trade edition at the end of the year, with Dutton publishing it in America. In the front of his personal limited edition copy Henry has written a page of notes, stating that the book is based on a mixture of his return visits to the battlefields during his honeymoon in 1925 and the second visit with his brother-in-law in 1927, and that although the companion of his trip, 'Four-Toes', was his brother-in-law William Busby, many of the sayings which he attributes to 'Four-Toes' were not actually spoken by William Busby himself. But Henry does say that he became 'very irritable with poor W.B.'; he ends with an entry copied from his 1925 diary:

Why have I a war-complex? Terrified by war, I now love to let my mind dwell on the immense destructive power and desolation of war. Is this a form of neurosis? I love to imagine guns flashing, and troops marching, and the vastness of our army's movements and operations. This is of course, in retrospect very different from the war that actually *was*. HW. 4 June 1929.

Apart from his own excursions into the war zones, Douglas Bell's *A Soldier's Diary of the Great War* with Henry's Introduction was also published at this time, and the revised version of *The Beautiful Years* appeared.

But Henry was restless and for some time had been hatching a plan. He now felt a little claustrophobic in Georgeham. At first it had been ideal, and he was no doubt still glad of the feeling of company and life around him, but as his status increased and his family began to grow he began to feel overlooked and hemmed in. Nor was Georgeham as quiet as it had been. For some time he had had his eye on a field above the village; a field which gave a vast panoramic view across the estuary of the two rivers, 'Tarka Country', and out to the craggy and wild Baggy Point, one of his favourite places; a field which, although still near and part of the village, was isolated and would give him back the freedom his spirit longed for. He had known of this field ever since that first visit to Georgeham before the war when he had walked several times up the steepish little hill on the road that wound up from the village, pausing at the top to lean over the field gate and admire the view of the distant estuary and then down again into the little wooded valley of Spreycombe where his young mind had been so excited by thoughts of 'the deserted tin mines (?silver)' as he wrote in his diary, and the finding of a buzzard's nest in a fir tree. He had visited it many times since, and he and Loetitia had walked up there over and over again, during their sojourn in the village. He now determined to buy this field.

Interestingly, as early as August 1927 there is a letter from his mother asking if Henry has heard from the farmer about her offer to buy 3 acres of land (for Henry) (letter in HWLEA, dated 10 August 1927). Gertrude's father, Thomas William Leaver, had died in November 1923 and left his house, No. 12 Eastern Road, to Gertrude, which she had sold, and also a trust fund (in favour of Henry and his two sisters) of stocks and shares of which she had the use of income as life tenant. Thus she had a little money of her own and had obviously decided to help her son, probably to offset his complaint that she had used some of these resources to take several holidays abroad accompanied by her eldest daughter, Kathie.

The land Henry Williamson now acquired was the open field plus the spinneys which lay across the two northern roads.[22] The crossroads was, and is, called officially 'Oxford Cross', a name which inflamed Henry's passions. He felt that the spot was so clearly originally a crossing place for oxen, thus Oxen's Cross – Ox's Cross. Never could there have been a 'ford' on top of that hill! Henry soon abandoned the names Down Close and Ox's Park; he always called the area simply 'The Field'.

He was soon happily at work engaged in building boundary banks and ditches and planting trees; Monterey pines to break the wind on the boundary, beeches as shelter. He drew a plan which shows complicated lines of predicted wind direction and swirls, all to be circumvented with planted windbreaks. Most important of all, he planned and built a hut – 'the Writing Hut'. He made several pages of careful notes and drawings which show the thought and detail he put into his preparations. Particular attention was paid to the fireplace, fire always being a point of great importance to him. This Writing Hut would provide Henry with a place of safety to which he could always retreat, a virtual hermit's cell where he could write in peace. It was also, significantly, a place which he had created out of

Henry's first son, William Hibbert Williamson (Windles), aged two years, striding out in Georgeham.

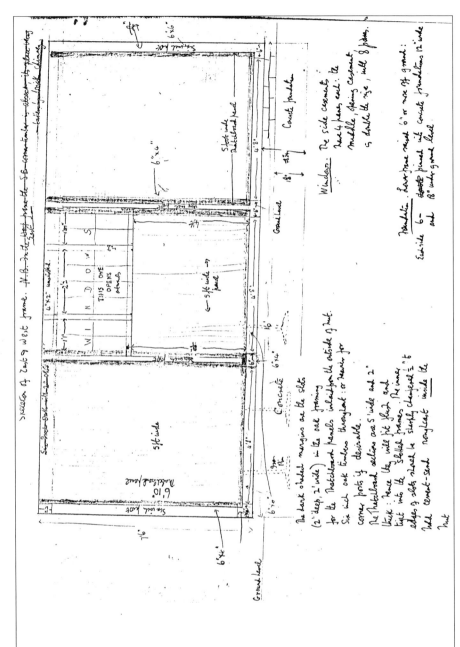

Two pages from Henry's notes and drawings showing his plans for the Writing Hut.

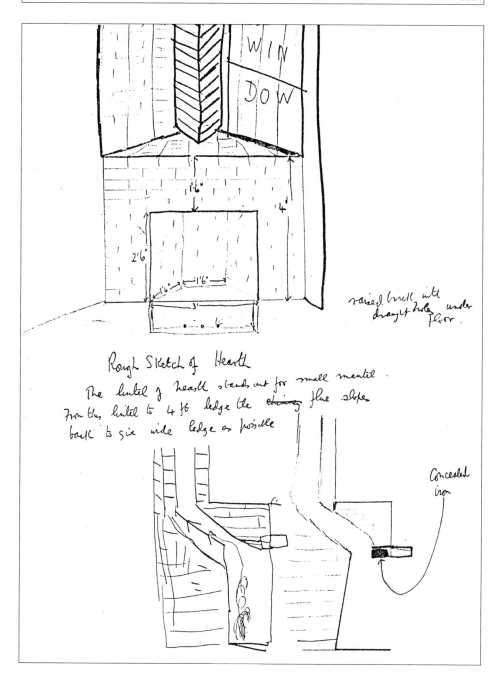

WIN DOW

1'6"

4'

2'6"

1'6"

1'6"

3'

raised brick with draught holes under floor.

Rough Sketch of Hearth

The lintel of hearth stands out for small mantel. From this lintel to 4 ft ledge the ~~chimney~~ flue slopes back to give wide ledge as possible

Concealed iron

Building the Writing Hut in the Field at Ox's Cross.

nothing. The Hut and the Field were, throughout his life, to be his refuge and his stronghold. Yet, almost perversely, while all this was going ahead, Henry Williamson had resolved to leave Georgeham altogether. Before he did so, however, he had one last 'Til Eulenspiegel'[23] trick to play on the village.

Henry had become friends with John Heygate, a journalist who was himself to write several books. He was quite a wild young man. Born in 1903 he was eight years younger than Henry and at this time was twenty-five. He had been educated at Eton, where his father was an assistant master for over thirty years until he retired in 1918, and at Balliol College, Oxford, where he had taken second class honours in History.[24]

There was an instant rapport between Henry and John Heygate. They had many things in common, including a great sense of outrageous fun and a down-to-earth attitude; and their friendship was to last throughout their lives, despite one quite monumental quarrel that was to occur in later years.

At this time, 1929, they were in the first flush of friendship, John was staying with Henry at Georgeham with another like-minded friend, Bobby Roberts (Cecil A. Roberts) and they were all enjoying themselves sailing Henry's dinghy *Pinta* in the estuary. This jollity extended itself to a jape which in other circumstances might well have been typical behaviour for three young undergraduates (which John Heygate had fairly recently been).

In August headlines appeared in several West Country newspapers and in September even made the national *Daily Express*.[25] The incident to which they referred had occurred earlier that year. Over the Whitsun weekend the three men had pasted over a newly erected village institute sign with pages from the local newspaper, although the later report in the *Daily Express*, from a 'Special Correspondent', who was of course Henry Williamson himself, stated that the pages were from *that* paper.

This jape naturally offended the local church and parochial worthies. The sign depicted St George slaying the Dragon, said in local lore to have lived in the cave at the foot of Baggy Point known as Baggy Hole (where it must have got awfully wet as the tide fills this cave twice a day!), which is supposedly why the village was called Georgeham. It had been painted by a local artist held in some esteem, Miss Kemp Welch.

On being officially reprimanded, Henry very properly wrote a letter to the secretary of the Georgeham Village Institute stating that he had humbly apologized to the rector, who was chairman of the institute, which was published in the paper. This would have been fine and no doubt the incident would soon have been forgotten, but Henry could not leave well alone, and gave an interview to the press explaining his motives for the prank. First, he pointed out the absurdity of the drama of St George and the dragon being played out locally, plus other historical discrepancies depicted on the reverse of the sign – which, naturally, was seen as a criticism of the artist and, by association, the local church and parish dignitaries. Second, he gave as his (very obviously trumped up) reason for the perpetration of this 'outrage' the excuse that he was going to ask his friend

Henry, John Heygate and Bobby Roberts toasting themselves with the set of pewter mugs after 'pasting up' the Georgeham Village sign.

the well-known artist C.R.W. Nevinson to paint a substitute sign, which after a short period of hanging for publicity, was to have been auctioned and the money used to provide a playing field for the village children. The description of the hypothetical sign showed Henry's tongue-in-cheek attitude: ' . . . a black pig grunting in a dark damp place, a rabbit in a trap; two men shouting at each other in argument over the ways of the Parish Council . . . a summer visitor with face and legs burnt red by the sun. . . . ' This produced a 'Vigorous Reply' from a Col. Elliott, DSO, who had lived at Pickwell Manor, very near Henry's field, for several years but had recently moved. He wrote on behalf of the 'inarticulate resentment' of the ordinary folk, who objected 'to an attitude of superiority that produces only a prank'. Henry's thoughts on the subject are revealed on the back of a photograph of the three malefactors, each holding up a different-sized pewter mug of beer: 'H.W.; J. Heygate & Bobby Roberts after "pasting up" unpleasant new village sign.'

John Heygate appears as Piers Tofield in the *Chronicle* novels[26] and we first meet him in *The Power of the Dead* where, in Chapter 4, 'Weest Weather', Piers and his friend Archie Plugge have paid a call on Phillip and Lucy, and Phillip takes them off to his writing room for a drink. 'There in the middle of a wall of logs, rested the pin of homebrew. A set of pewter mugs, ranging from quart pot to half-noggin, hung across the chimney piece.' Henry had stored the memory of those mugs and incorporated them felicitously into his novel.

In the summer of 1929 a new 'Barleybright' appeared on the scene. Henry describes her in his writing with a face 'like the rising sun, broad and strong, always laughing, her hair of saxon fairness cut short like a pageboy's of the fifteenth century, streaming back from her brow like sunrise, a Blakeian figure of joy'.[27] She was a young German girl called Barbara Krebs who was staying in Georgeham at the home of Miss Johnson, a redoubtable lady vegetarian and nudist, who also took in paying guests.

The small packet of Barbara Krebs's letters in the Henry Williamson literary archive prove her to have been a very mature young woman, with a grasp of Henry's character that is reminiscent of Doline Rendle's. Barbara was certainly in love with Henry, but she wanted to see him united with his wife and children. Due to her influence he briefly became a vegetarian, as he mentions in *The Children of Shallowford*. She believed that much of his irritability and general malaise was due to his smoking and consumption of meat, and wanted him to attend a health clinic in Switzerland which would revolutionize his life. Henry politely turned down the offer – he was not a person to be organized!

Barbara Krebs was attending lectures on English literature at King's College, London (where Henry travelled up frequently to visit her), also doing some translation, and planned to translate Henry's work into German. But she refused to be drawn into Henry's web and very determinedly returned to Germany in January 1930. There are only sporadic letters after that.

From early 1929 Henry employed Davey Jones, of North Buckland (a hamlet just below Ox's Cross), to do the labouring work up at the Field. Davey Jones kept a note of his schedule and payment in a small pocket notebook, 'Record of Work done at Oxes Park'. His first job on 22 February was 'Ditching coin & raising new bank'. For eight and a half days' work he received £2 12s, about 4 shillings a day. In March he was preparing the various hedges round the boundaries and fixing wire fencing for the same, and towards the end of the month he was 'cutting drive'. In April he spent some days (about eight or eight and a half hours each working day), 'breaking stones for concrete and preparing the site [for the Hut]'. The concrete foundation was laid on 30 April, and from 9 May onwards he was 'Erecting hut', work which continues until 16 June when he goes on to 'hanging gate', 'cutting grass', and 'making hay'. There then appears a little account sum: '352 hrs = £17 12s. 0d.', a rate of 1 shilling per hour. Documents show that Henry had also obtained planning permission to sink a well and that Jones was paid £20 for the work involved. But Henry had already resolved to leave Georgeham and the planned house, 'Down Close', which he marked on his original sketch map, was not to be built until his declining years.

CHAPTER 5

SHALLOWFORD DAYS

At about the time of the institute sign prank Henry Williamson had heard of a cottage to rent on the estate of Earl Fortescue (elder brother of Sir John) at Castle Hill, Filleigh, near South Molton, about 20 miles as the crow flies due east of Georgeham, a little further by what was then the main road from Barnstaple to Taunton. In the original edition of *The Children of Shallowford* published in 1939, Henry wrote that he heard about the cottage from his dentist as he was having a tooth filled, but he had also seen it advertised in the local newspaper. The cottage, called Shallowford, was described as decent-sized, with four bedrooms and four downstairs rooms, a pleasant garden, and as having once been three cottages in a row now knocked into one. Henry realized it would make an ideal place for the children to grow up (a third child was on the way), but what most attracted his attention was the information that included were 2 miles of fishing rights on the River Bray, which ran through the neighbouring meadow and the estate's deer park.

Shallowford, the cottage where the Williamson family lived in the 1930s.

Henry Williamson, 1933.

Henry drove out to Filleigh, at first on his own and later with Loetitia, obtained an order to view from the estate office, looked over the cottage still inhabited by the two elderly lady tenants, and then returned to the office and formally applied to take over the remainder of their lease. The application was duly accepted.

Apart from the *Chronicle* novels we can learn a great deal about the Shallowford days from various of Henry's autobiographical books. Family life, the children's sayings and doings, are movingly and amusingly portrayed in *The Children of Shallowford*, while *Goodbye West Country*, ostensibly a diary of his final year at Shallowford, actually ranges over a far wider span, and *A Clear Water Stream*, published much later, gives a very serene account of his work to improve the fishing on his stretch of the Bray.[1] However, the information in his literary archive shows that his Shallowford days also had a turbulent aspect.

From June 1929 onwards, although they did not actually move in until the autumn, Davey Jones, Henry's handyman, worked sometimes at the Field for 7 shillings a day, sometimes at Shallowford for 8 shillings a day, a distinct improvement in pay. To make it easier for Jones to get around between the two places Henry helped towards buying him a motorcycle.

Apart from Davey Jones, Henry also employed a most extraordinary character, one who appears in several of the books, particularly in *The Children of Shallowford*, as Coneybeare, and in the *Chronicle* novels as Rippingall. In *The Children of Shallowford* Henry relates how he came to acquire 'Coneybeare' or,

Henry sitting in front of the hearth he designed at Shallowford.

perhaps more accurately, how 'Coneybeare' came to acquire him. 'Coneybeare' had been employed sporadically by the rector of Georgeham. He was an 'old soldier, a man of deep feeling and understanding'. But he had a drink problem. The rector had finally come to the end of his patience when 'Coneybeare' turned up after a five-day binge – in which he had spent ten months' wages – and told him not to come back. And 'Coneybeare' promptly transferred his allegiance to Henry who, with the fellow-feeling of a comrade-in-arms, had been kind to him.

The Children of Shallowford reveals how Henry made 'Coneybeare' sign an agreement meant to ensure he had no money for drink as it contained the proviso: 'His wages being paid into a fund which he could only use at the age of sixty.' This would seem so extraordinary as to be one of those tales that Henry Williamson had made up to embellish his narrative, but hidden away in one of the packages in the archive there is indeed such a document, and it had been duly signed on 17 September 1929 by the man concerned, whose real name was Cecil Bacon. Henry's wife must have found the employment of such a character as general factotum something of a trial!

It was not long, however, before Cecil Bacon broke the terms of his 'employment agreement' by getting disastrously drunk yet again. Henry's diary entry for 16 January 1930, written while in London meeting his publishers, records: 'Damn, Return to sack the drunken Bacon.' This gives a slightly different view of the matter from that in *The Children of Shallowford*. There Henry details 'Coneybeare's' exit after a grand party which ended with the two men getting drunk together in the early hours when all the guests have gone. Henry salutes 'Coneybeare' for excelling himself, but the next day awakens to find 'his bedroom was empty. There was a scrawled note, and the words, "The artist dreads anti-climax. Will send for box later. Cheerio, and Goodbye". We never saw Coneybeare again' (*The Children of Shallowford*).

He may never have set eyes on him again, but a few months later Henry had to untangle the little problem that arose when Cecil Bacon accused him via a solicitor of having kept money that belonged to him. Henry had to explain about the special account and that all that was needed was their two signatures on a release document. It took several exchanges of letters before things were actually sorted out. It can be seen that the fictional character in the *Chronicle* played a far greater role than Bacon actually did in Henry's own life.

Cecil Bacon's place was taken by a person called Annie Rawle who was a stalwart over the next few years. She had once been housekeeper to Arthur Heinemann, a former Master of the Cheriton Otter Hounds (and related to Heinemann the publisher) and had herself been whipper-in to hounds during the First World War, when the men were at the front, which earned her the nick-name 'Galloping Annie'. Henry's eldest son Bill remembers her as 'wiry, with black hair, sharp, spare, and we liked her very much'. There was also a daily woman, Mrs Ridd, a cheerful and good soul, who lived in one of the nearby cottages, and a 'maid' who probably did the very rough work (the scullery maid), and various other people from time to time: a Miss Kirkman at one point, a German girl briefly at another.

'Humpy Bridge' over the River Bray at Shallowford.

Henry threw himself into plans to improve the fishing on the Bray. He bought rods and flies and took lessons in their use. His fishing rights ended at a little bridge across the river, an ornamental bridge of grey igneous rock, immediately known in the family as 'Humpy Bridge', which was to provide many happy scenes of family bathing and picnics over the years. The area of the deer park was dominated by the high and massive viaduct which carried the railway across the valley.[2]

In the spring of 1930, on 15 April, Henry and Loetitia set out from Shallowford to visit Georgeham. They planned to walk out to Baggy Point for Henry said he found it was 'a thought unbearable' that April should pass without visiting this 'open vastness of ocean and air' (*The Children of Shallowford*). It was possibly not a very sensible trip to have planned as the new baby was expected fairly soon and the walk would have been quite arduous for a woman in advanced pregnancy. They stopped in Barnstaple to buy some food for a picnic. Loetitia felt suddenly unwell with a pain which she brushed aside as indigestion from the rhubarb she had eaten the previous night. But as the baby's due date was not far off and as they were very near the Ebberley nursing home into which they were booked, Henry took Loetitia there as a precaution – luckily, as within half an hour of his leaving their third child was born, this time a daughter, to be named Margaret Mary. In *The Children of Shallowford* Henry describes her as having 'dark eyes, and much dark hair, like a japanese doll, on her head'.

Three weeks later a remarkable work, *The Patriot's Progress, Being the Vicissitudes of Pte. John Bullock*, was published by Geoffrey Bles, and was a striking combination of text and illustration.[3] The illustrations were stark linocuts by the Tasmanian born artist William Kermode. The words, almost equally stark, were by Henry Williamson. The subject was 'the war story of an ordinary man'; its hero 'John Bullock, a youth beloved by his parents, was a clerk in the City of London.' The plot is simple. A symbol for Every Soldier, John Bullock enlists, endures the war, is wounded, and returns home.

The idea for this book originated in the latter part of 1928 when J.C. Squire introduced the two men for this purpose. William Kermode had been born in the same year as Henry, but in Hobart, Tasmania. He had come to live in Britain before the First World War, had served in the British Army and been awarded the Military Cross for gallantry. He became an artist specializing in linocuts, of which those for *The Patriot's Progress* are probably his best known. Kermode also provided a cover design for a cheap edition of *Tarka*, published by Putnam in October 1929.

Kermode had shown his original drawings to Jack (Sir John) Squire who thought they could form the basis of a book with short captions written to flesh them out. Henry immediately had other ideas and decided to write a full-length book, rather relegating the linocuts to second place, and suggesting Kermode make several fresh drawings to fit his story. Kermode agreed to the latter but his letters show his patient tenacity to his original purpose. In February 1929 Henry sent him a postcard in which he suggested that the prose shouldn't describe the cuts, nor the cuts illustrate the prose. Kermode again insisted that Henry work closely to the linocuts and that there must be a relationship between the text and the cuts on each page. He wanted, rightly, the two to carry equal weight.

Kermode engaged A.D. Peters (who had taken over Daker's agency) as his agent to handle the whole book and thus facilitate matters, particularly for the foreign market. Peters then delicately negotiated the proportions of the two shares of royalties, which for the main rights were more or less two thirds to Henry and one third to Kermode. The *Evening Standard* agreed to serialize the book later in the year, for which they suggested payment of £350. Henry thought £300 of this should be his, but Peters said firmly that that was a little unfair to Kermode and suggested the split should be £250 for Henry and £100 for Kermode.

Despite the fact that *The Patriot's Progress* came at the tail-end of a surfeit of war books it was hailed as a true portrait and today is considered an important contribution to the literature of the First World War.

Arnold Bennett[4] gave the book a splendid review in his 'Books and Persons' column in the *Evening Standard* on 8 May 1930, which also appeared in the *Glasgow Evening Citizen*.

'THE WAR STORY OF THE ORDINARY MAN'

'Terrific Description and a Tremendous Overwhelming Indictment'
There have been so many war books, and so many good war books, and so many good English war books . . . [but] I must mention yet one more fine English war book.

The account is simple and awful, absolutely awful. Its power lies in the descriptions, which have not been surpassed in any other war book within my knowledge. . . .

A word as to Mr Kermode's pictures. At first I resented them, for they are very numerous and they cut into the text, distracting the reader's attention. But in the end they justified themselves to me. For they are very good, and just as much part of the book as the text itself.[5]

Henry was on friendly terms with Bennett, whom he greatly admired. They exchanged several letters, very politely phrased on the part of 'AB', as he signed himself with a neat calligraphic flourish. They met occasionally, probably sometimes at the Savage Club, but also privately – for instance, a telegram dated 5 November 1928 from Bennett requested Henry to dine with him that Saturday night. Henry wrote on this (he *had* only just 'arrived') – 'FAME'. Arnold Bennett recorded in his diary for Saturday 10 November 1928, 'Henry Williamson . . . came to dinner . . . seems to be very fond of his wife, and admires her. She is the original of "Mary" in *The Pathway*; so she must be fine.'[6] Later that month Arnold Bennett arranged for Henry to lunch with him at the Reform Club in Pall Mall.

His last letter to Henry, handwritten and difficult to decipher, was dated 13 December 1930. After discussing various small points he turned to writing technique, stating that although he liked to give language a 'poke', Henry had carried description 'a step further', and that they must meet soon to discuss this. But there was not to be another meeting. Arnold Bennett died on 27 March 1931.

Henry had sent a copy of *The Patriot's Progress* to T.E. Lawrence; possibly a proof ahead of publication, since Lawrence's letter on the subject spans the days from 18 to 21 March.[7] Lawrence wrote that he liked the book which he read at the same time as *Her Privates We*, and recited a longish list of particularly good phrases that he had noted with pleasure. Henry wrote back by return 'Your comments on P.P. are exact and valuable.' He goes on to criticise and complain about various aspects of the printing and publishing, and shows that he resented having to consider the theme of the linocuts and was afraid that he had used up his available material on the war.

Damn! I wanted 60,000 words recreating the Etaples mutiny; now I've popped it off in 600 words. I used all the stereotyped details of war books: reserving the fresh ones for my *real* war book, which has the war as background (often close background) and the human figures moving always just in front of it. 500,000 words – 1894–1924. *The Hopeful Life*. 3 volumes. I'm flinching from beginning.

Letter copy in HWLEA, dated 24 March 1930

He was referring here to what was to become *A Chronicle of Ancient Sunlight*, not actually begun for another twenty years. Henry went on to explain a little joke he had played. *Her Privates We* was originally published by Putnam anonymously as by 'Private 19022'. Henry makes John Bullock No. 19023 on the army list. In his letter to Lawrence Henry went on to explain that for a joke he had led Bles to believe that he was actually the author of *Her Privates We*, but then had got rather worried and had written to Bles 'to refer no more to my silly remarks about *Privates We*. My little joke went farther than intended.' Henry's 'little joke' could have caused serious problems for him if he had been thought to have masqueraded as the author (actually Frederic Manning).

In September 1930 *Woman's Journal* hailed Henry as 'The Author of the Month' as is shown by a cutting in the archive. This cutting has no name attached, but the author must have known Henry when he first started to write:

> I remember him, immediately after the war, at the Tomorrow Club, as an aggressive maker of speeches hurled at established and unassailable literary reputations, the owners of which, by the way, have been among the first to recognise Mr Williamson's worth as a writer. . . . [The writer goes on to enumerate and encapsulate all Henry's books to date ending] . . . the force, clarity, and unmistakable honesty of purpose of *The Patriot's Progress*. Honesty, indeed, is one of the outstanding qualities of Mr Williamson as a writer. To it is allied a vivid, exciting narrative style, a concern with the things that matter and a critically observant mind.

Then, as promised, from 8 to 28 November 1930 the *Evening Standard* serialized the book in its entirety. The series brought many letters from men who had been in the war, testifying to the book's authenticity; it was obviously a very popular item.

There are several references and hints from Henry at the time of the publication of *The Patriot's Progress* that he was seriously ill and an operation was pending. Letters from his agent and more than one publisher, and also one to T.E. Lawrence, refer to his health with anxious inquiry, but no operation occurred: apparently it was nothing more serious than a bad attack of piles which his doctor treated at home. Nor did it interfere with his social life as his diary is full of lunch and supper engagements.

For some time Henry had been working on a very different book, his stories of the people who lived in Georgeham. A note at the beginning of March in his 1929 diary states:

> Work in hand during March;
> 1. The Patriot's Progress
> 2. Village Book
> 3. Preface to Gamekeeper at Home
> 4. Read Jefferies & prepare Introduction to his selected essays

The work he did on Jefferies' books was a way of showing his respect and acknowledging his debt to his spiritual mentor. His own *The Village Book* was

Henry working at Shallowford. (On the wall is a self-portrait by Leicester Hibbert, grandfather of Henry's wife, Loetitia Hibbert.)

published by Jonathan Cape towards the end of July 1930. It is a collection of vignettes illustrating 'The Spirit of the Village' in Winter and Spring and 'Air and Light of the Fields and the Sea' at the same seasons. There is a charming innovation: it is illustrated by Henry Williamson himself with two little sketches. T.E. Lawrence wrote immediately to say that the book was 'the real thing' and that he loved it.

Soon after *The Village Book* was published, Henry Williamson was en route for Canada, where he had been invited to join a salmon-fishing trip with his American publisher, John Macrae, who was a member of the Mastigouche Fishing Club in Quebec Province. He sailed from Southampton on 6 September 1930 in a steamship of the Canadian Pacific Line, RMS *Empress of France*. Henry wrote a

Sketches by Henry for *The Village Book*, showing the printer's markings.

note to his wife from the boat as he left; this was his first crossing of the Atlantic, his first visit outside Europe. One senses a certain air of excitement:

> Here I am: 2 dobs of Mothersill in me belly . . . We sail in 2 hours. Nice bunk: but the whole 4-bunk space is about 'bedroom' size in the Cot at Ox's Park . . . Bubby would love it. The ship is white, 3 funnels. Rather fun . . . Now I'm off up to the deck to watch the first class passengers. Love Bill.
> I may winter in Ontario, work hard & ski hard while I'm there.
>
> Letter in HWLEA, dated 6 September 1930

Soon Henry was writing from the Mastigouche Club at St Gabriel le Brandon in Quebec Province to describe his adventure:

> We are just about to leave here – after one day in the home lakes – and go into the mountain lakes. It is a fairly big club – almost a hotel – but all wood built, the tools being mostly axes. Log cabins, etc. Walls of axe-smoothed balsam – a pine tree. The canoes are lovely, 60 lbs. The guides carry them from lake to lake. Balance a careful business. The lakes are all *stocked*. So far, only little fish of the kind we put back in the Bray! French Canadian guides – no english spoken. I wear mocassins. Boots too heavy. Wish I knew your size foot, I'd bring you some. Lovely things. Deer hide: feels like naked foot, & so silent & comfortable. My fishing coat much admired. Also jersey. Macrae very nice, also

son and son-in-law. J.M. shot a moose yesterday – great feat – each man allowed 1 a year by Government. Son-in-law didn't like the idea. Like many of us nowadays. Moose was drinking at edge of lake & J.M. shot from canoe. 600lbs weight – young 2 year old. There are big fish in the higher lakes – up to 6lbs. All put in from hatchery. Very little real wild stuff left in the world – except in Bray! This trip has already shown me what a lovely household I have, in every way, & the ideal life I *could* lead, if my belly were not so sensitive. J.M. wants you to come over next year. I'll arrange a lecture tour afterwards. You'll love it. Breeches. Red shirts. Just like pictures of the wild woods. The Canadians are charming – none of the English finesse, but so genuine & friendly. . . . I think a lot of our house, & field, & hut, & children. . . .

Letter in HWLEA, dated September 1930

Before he left England relations between Henry and Loetitia had become strained. As he writes in *The Children of Shallowford*, 'After a while I found Loetitia and I were not sitting any more before our fine new hearth. I sat alone, in the writing room upstairs. . . . Loetitia sat by the nursery fire, always knitting, sewing, or doing household accounts.' Loetitia's life was, had to be, given over to the children and domestic issues. Henry worked hard at his writing, led his own life, and was irritable in the home. Now he was away he immediately felt homesick for his home, wife, and family. And with the initial euphoria of his trip over, he quickly became bored and fed up, as a letter to his wife dated 24 September 1930 shows.

I have had nothing [i.e. no post] since I left home. At the moment am restless and melancholy, longing to be home. I am bored with this fishing. . . . Yesterday I was unwell – for the past three days I have been constipated, & took various medicines, they seemed all to out together. This place is closing down for the winter and everyone has left except John and myself. . . . Now I'm fed up. I don't want to fish. It bores me. . . . It's gone on too long. It's simply worn away my desire to fish. So I lie in a hammock all day . . . which is very ungrateful of me. . . .

Letter in HWLEA

Once letters had arrived from England, including one from T.E. Lawrence, and the diarrhoea had passed he cheered up again, sending an amusing (but extremely adult) letter to Windles with one of his cartoon drawings of the moose and a big fish he had caught. Henry frequently sent letters and postcards to his children on his trips away; they were not necessarily suitably worded for young children (for example, one explains a quarrel that is ongoing between himself and his wife), but they showed he was thinking of them. He included a simple and factual account of this fishing trip in *A Clear Water Stream*, published many years after the event, where he describes a little drinking cup carved for him by René, his French-Canadian guide, from the burr of a golden birch tree into the shape of an otter. This is still among his effects.

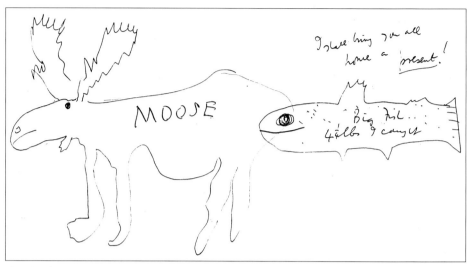

Sketch of a moose, sent in a letter from Henry while on holiday in Canada in 1931 to his son, Windles.

Henry wrote to T.E. Lawrence on 29 September describing his surroundings:

Your letter cheered me here in the land of coloured falling leaves and dark deep lakes, where the cries of the crickets in the woods tell sadly of the Ice and the Silence soon to bind a blank land. This country is spirit country; the air dreams of before the glaciers. For all its trees and blue skies, its grasses and its golden sun, it is a sad and ruinous tract, where the cry of the loon far across the water is a little insane, like the cry of one whose blue eyes are pierced by ice. It has suffered; it dreams of the sun everlasting; but the glaciers will grip hill and hollow again, scrape away life and all its seeds and cocoons, and leave it bare as the granite rocks rising from the edge of the dark lake. . . . I will come and fetch you [to Shallowford] when I come back. You will like our place. I must show you my cottage of one room (and tiniest bedroom in England [the Writing Hut]). . . . If I'd Shakespeare's skill I'd write a sonnet beginning

For / Of / With / the marriage of true minds etc

I must end. The lamps are alight. The great birch wood fire roars and thunders in the vast open chimney; the loon cries sadly in the star-shivering lake outside. Sirius glitters above the trees on the hills, where the arctic zones tremble and arise with wan light to the zenith. Sirius shakes his wondrous fires in the Ice Silence. . . .

Copy in HWLEA, dated 29 September 1930

The next day the fishing trip ended and Henry and John Macrae left for New York. The city drew Henry Williamson under its spell and he decided definitely to stay on over the winter and revise his novel *The Dream of Fair Women* for the new edition, a task he completed in three weeks. He arranged for a sum of money to be paid into an account for Gipsy to draw on and wrote urging her to get out and about in the 'Morris', a Morris Eight which had taken the place of the Peugeot. He was invited to speak to the 'Authors' Club' (this would seem to be an error for the 'Writers' Club') organized by Miss Emma Mills:

> So solemn, a la Dawson Scott – I ragged them – 'Take literature and wring its neck' etc – & was HISSED at conclusion of speech by a great fat poetess. . . . I thought it was fun until I realized she was serious! I'll tell you my speech when I return. . . .
>
> Letter in HWLEA, dated 17 October 1930

At the end of October he wrote to tell Loetitia that he had moved into an apartment at the top of a six-storey building:

> In Greenwich Village, the 'Art Centre' like the Latin Quarter in Paris or Chelsea in London, on a twelve month lease at 70$ a month. I shall furnish it and sublet when I want to quit. It is lovely . . . I've got 24 weeks cheap opera tickets, 2$ every Monday night. And many nice friends. One girl in particular is very nice.

Henry Williamson and his French-Canadian guide René on the fishing trip in the Canadian Lakes at Mastigouche.

... Buy *Decent Fellows* by John Heygate immediately, and send [papers] with adverts. They may quote me.

Letter HWLEA, dated 18 October 1930

John Heygate's novel, *Decent Fellows*, caused quite a furore in England. It relates the story, fictionalized but based on reality, of his schooldays at Eton in great detail and with honesty. It is dedicated to Henry Williamson, who had encouraged him, had introduced him to Cape, and would even write an introduction for the American edition where he reprinted the adverse reviews and attendant correspondence that had appeared in the English press.[8]

The 'one girl in particular' was a girl who worked at Duttons called Barbara Sincere. Henry had found a new 'Barleybright' and became very cheerful. In November he wrote to his wife to say that he was now in the new apartment, and that he had a secret – he was going to write a book called *Manfred in New York*. By 6 December this had become *The Gold Falcon – the Mystical Tale of Manfred in New York*.

On 22 November 1930 a very long article, with accompanying photograph, appeared in the Book Section of the *Boston Evening Transcript* written by J. Fletcher Smith and entitled 'Henry Williamson on the Literary Map'. In this interview, apart from giving some inaccurate biographical details, Henry paid tribute to those authors who had helped him; 'Galsworthy, Bennett. I love Arnold Bennett, over and over again he has gone out of his way to say a decent word on my behalf. Frank Swinnerton, Walter de la Mare, J.C. Squire, and T.E. Lawrence . . . ' and then he explained about Lawrence's 'Tarka' letter. By a strange coincidence, next to Henry's photograph is a (smaller) one of Colonel T.E. Lawrence 'wearing the Gold Sword of a Prince of Mecca' taken with Lowell Thomas and heading a review of *India, Land of the Black Pagoda* by the latter. Henry must have felt very gratified that his photograph was so much larger than that of his idol.

Another longish article had appeared in the *Worcester Sunday Telegraph* on 9 November 1930 written by 'E.O.P.'. A letter reveals him as Eugene O. Parsons, who had visited the Williamsons at Shallowford earlier in the year and was able to work into his piece all the domestic details he had observed, giving him, as he wrote to Henry, a distinct advantage over the longer and more prestigious article by Fletcher Smith.

Reviews of *The Village Book* appeared in newspapers all over America. Many quoted Frank Swinnerton[9] who wrote as 'Special Correspondent' in the Chicago *Tribune* on 20 September: '*The Village Book* gives a better picture of rural life than any other book of its kind to be published since W.H. Hudson died.' Duttons duly incorporated this phrase into their publicity material accompanying the photograph of Henry.

Barbara Sincere very soon found herself totally out of her depth in her friendship with Henry. It is apparent that she felt very deeply for him but, just before Christmas, decided to put a stop to the relationship and wrote a fine and moving letter to him on 19 December. This appears in full in *The Gold Falcon*, with Henry's own reply. The result of this rebuff was that Henry immediately sent for his wife (something he had anyway been vaguely considering).

> My dear Gipsy,
> I cabled you last night to come over here, if you want to, & if Annie [Rawle – the housekeeper/nannie] was trustworthy, & the baby parkable. . . . Bring your evening frocks, & your breeches, if you can wear them, for on Feb. 5 we go to New Hampshire to learn to ski. Also I lecture there. . . .
>
> Letter in HWLEA, dated 22 December 1930

She wrote back to say that she could not possibly come immediately as various arrangements would have to be made first. On 3 January 1931 Henry sent off another cable:

> WHY DON'T YOU SAIL OR INDICATE WHEN NO NEWS SINCE TWENTYTHIRD DECEMBER VERY UNHAPPY HOPE YOU WILL COME IMMEDIATELY. HENRY.

Barbara Sincere removed herself to work in a different city, but they remained friends for several years and there is quite a large file of her letters; later she would also help Henry over publication of the American edition of *The Gold Falcon*.

Loetitia eventually arrived and the trip proceeded according to plan. On the boat out from England Henry had met Professor W.K. Stewart who had invited him to Dartmouth College in Hanover, New Hampshire, for winter sports the following February; Henry and Gipsy duly travelled to Hanover. Here Henry met Herbert Faulkner West, Professor of Literature at Dartmouth, who described the visit, and Henry's lecture, in his book *The Dreamer of Devon*.[10]

> During his stay he gave a lecture at the college on the war and its effects on his generation. He had written out the lecture, and from my own experience of listening to lectures for ten years at Dartmouth Hall I never heard one so well written, or as sincere and moving. This is not faint praise, for there I had heard such English writers as Hugh Walpole, Rebecca West, Frank Swinnerton, Bertrand Russell and many others. He introduced to the audience some war literature quite unknown to most of them, as, for instance, the war poems of Wilfred Owen. I hope that this address, which he also gave at Harvard and Yale University . . .
>
> *The Dreamer of Devon*

Henry spoke on 'Hamlet and Modern Life'. The lecture equates *Hamlet* with the First World War drawing comparisons between Hamlet and Jesus, and with certain contemporary events.[11]

Henry was now working hard on his new book, *The Gold Falcon*, which describes in fictionalized form the story of his prolonged visit to America, transmuted into the visit of its hero, Manfred Cloudsley, ace pilot and hero of the First World War, war poet and war-neurotic, who flees to America to escape his own situation, his wife Ann, and family life, to seek a new life and new love. The character of Barbara Faithfull is a very thinly disguised Barbara Sincere, and the relationship that occurred in real life is explored in the novel. The story follows Henry's own adventures with some excellent scenes of authentic New York life in the early 1930s, including a visit to a speak-easy, its atmosphere heavy with a sense of potential trouble. In the final scene Manfred borrows an aeroplane and flies himself home to his dying wife – crashing into the Atlantic, suffused as he drowns by a great Romantic Wagnerian vision in which the 'Gold Falcon', his alter-ego, or soul, appears to him.

Henry and Loetitia returned home in the spring of 1931 to resume life at Shallowford, a life which proved eventful in many ways. During the previous autumn Henry had written to Gipsy to tell her that on his return, in order to facilitate visits to London, he was going to buy a fast car. In June 1931 he achieved his ambition, buying from Henly's Ltd of London 'One second hand ALVIS Tourer finished Black as seen, tried and approved . . . £335.0.0.' He was given £85 in part exchange for the Morris.

This beautiful and prestigious car was a model known as 'The Silver Eagle', first manufactured in 1929. This particular car, DR 6084, had been built in 1930. Its first owner had been Whitney Straight – racing driver, fighter pilot, quondam chairman of BOAC – who had used the car *very* hard. Henry equipped himself with leather flying helmet and coat, goggles and gauntlets, and, with the windscreen flat, would drive the Alvis as fast as possible. He kept this car until 1948 and it features in several of his books.[12]

In early June 1931 there was a tremendous storm with a cloudburst around Georgeham and the water running off the hills ran straight through the village, to devastating effect. Reports in the *North Devon Journal*[13] state that the centre of the storm seems to have been at Spreycombe some time between 7 and 8 a.m. on Friday 5 June – but for Georgeham to have been so badly flooded the cloudburst must surely have been on top of the hill at Ox's Cross. Henry must have been very concerned for his Writing Hut, Field and trees, but at this point he was in London negotiating the purchase of his Alvis. Under a subtitle 'Immense Damage at Georgeham' the *Journal* reporter states:

> . . . Probably the most pitiable sight of all [was] in the centre of Georgeham village [where] a number of cottages had been completely swamped, and the menfolk and womenfolk were setting about the seemingly impossible task of cleaning up the mire which remained. Here I met Mr W.H. Brown who showed me his home, 'Skur Cottage' [*sic*] so named by Mr Henry Williamson, who wrote some of his books there. The interior was an awful sight. . . .
>
> Miss Bessy Gammon, who lives in a cottage near the Rectory, also finding the water passing into her house, made an endeavour to open her door to let it pass

through, when she slipped and was immersed. Luckily her brother was at hand and managed to lift her on to the top of a table in the kitchen. Mr William Gammon, the occupant of another cottage, had a narrow escape from drowning . . .

The little culvert carrying the stream past Skirr Cottage was ripped away and the nearby wall with it. The Vicar of Georgeham opened a relief fund to which Henry donated 5 guineas, stating that he wished to remain anonymous. He received an interesting letter of thanks from the Secretary, W. Hodson, who related some amusing tales of 'the little subterfuges and petty deceits which are being practised by some in order to swell their claim'. On his receipt it states, 'N.B. Donor will appear as "Old Villager" in list of subscribers.' It is due to this flood that features at and around Skirr Cottage have altered, a fact which causes some confusion as there are thus discrepancies between early photographs in Henry's books and present details.

Henry used the account of Bessy's and Revvy's dramatic brushes with death by drowning towards the close of *The Labouring Life* in 'Surview and Farewell' where he also added in the little details from the letter above. It was all very understated – 'I meant to make a terrific description of the Great Flood of 1931, but the ambition, like the flood, is gone.'

The only book that Henry published in 1931 was *The Wild Red Deer of Exmoor* – 'A Digression on the Logic and Ethics and Economics of Stag Hunting in England', which came out first as a limited private edition of seventy-five copies and then, later, was published by Faber. The somewhat ponderous title is misleading since this is an interesting well-argued piece giving a balanced and at times amusing account of two opposing points of view.

In August Henry started a visitors' book at Shallowford. He used a dummy (a made-up but totally blank) copy of the limited edition of *The Pathway* for this purpose, so it has printed in gold titling on the front: '*The Flax of Dream*, Book 4, *The Pathway*'. There are not many entries, about ten pages in all. Henry wrote inside, 'Visitors Book for Recording of Appreciation, Veiled Sneers, Criticisms, Remarks Trenchant and graceful. Beginning 20 August 1931.' Three pages are taken up with cartoons drawn by C.F. Tunnicliffe. Herbert Faulkner West stayed from 7–14 March 1932, 'A week of peace! Fun and close harmony! . . . '; John Heygate wrote 'Clean and they seem decent people' (a pun on the title of his book); Francis Chichester, related to Loetitia by marriage (famous at this time as a long distance solo pilot and later as a round-the-world yachtsman) added after his name, 'at Shallowford July 4–9 1932 wishes his host and hostess a lifetime as pleasant as his visit'; Margot and Julia Renshaw (Loetitia's cousins, members of the Chichester family) restrained themselves to signing their names only; Henry's mother signed for herself and Michael Busby [Biddy's son], 'April 29th 1933 – May 1st.'; Bobby Roberts was 'deeply appreciative of a visit to this place of peace, the first made in the company of his wife'.

In the autumn of 1931 Henry took his wife for a holiday to the Hebrides, on the small island of Islay. They had been invited to join Loetitia's cousins, the

Henry and Loetitia on holiday at Islay in the Hebrides, September 1931.

Renshaw family, who had taken a homestead for the month of September (a visit recorded in *A Clear Water Stream*, Chapter 13, 'I Behold the Hebrides'). Henry took a route through Coventry so that he could stop at the Alvis works to have the timing on the Silver Eagle checked and the carburettors synchronized. They spent the night at Blackpool enjoying the fun of the fair, eating fish and chips for supper at 11 p.m. The next day they took the road for Scotland and, after a night camping out, the next morning, leaving the car on the mainland because Henry reckoned they could not afford the £5 fare for it, took the ferry across to Islay. The holiday was spent in walking on the hills and shoreline, a little shooting, and much talking and thinking – a happy interlude. On the very last day there was rain, which Henry had been longing for so he could fish, and with further overnight rain, he decided to stay on to fish the following afternoon, using a fly, 'a moth-spoiled Black Dog', from his grandfather's japanned circular iron case (the case is now in the archive). The extra day's fishing meant they had to take the journey back in one fell swoop, driving the 550 miles from dawn to virtually dawn the next day, stopping for Henry to have a sleep by the wayside near Hereford, but arriving home at Shallowford too exhausted to sleep. Henry likened his feelings to the trials endured by a salmon entering the estuary and fighting its way up river, to the place 'where the heart lay' – home.

In the spring of 1930 Henry had received a letter from the Honorary Treasurer of 'The Liverpool First Edition Club', I. Waveney Girvan, inquiring for details of first editions of the books to check if his set was complete. Waveney Girvan was very appreciative of Henry as a writer and was not just an astute collector of his first editions. Just as Henry returned from America Waveney Girvan sent him a copy of an article that he had written for the May issue of *Bookman* on the subject of Henry's books for their 'Collector' section. Henry liked this and thought it could be the basis for a book publication. The correspondence continued and by the middle of June 1931, Waveney Girvan had started on a bibliography of Henry Williamson's books to date.

The result of all this work was published by the Alcuin Press in December 1931 in a limited edition of 420, of which 400 were for sale, but it was not just a straightforward list of books. Entitled *A Bibliography and a Critical Survey of the Works of Henry Williamson* by I. Waveney Girvan, it has, apart from an introduction by the author, a subtitle: 'Together with authentic bibliographical annotations by ANOTHER HAND' (whose identity was an open secret, of course!). In Henry's own file copy under this he has written: '(this being Henry Williamson getting the itch out of a few old scars of his own seeking!).' The effect was very neatly summed up by the *London Mercury* in its March 1932 issue where, in gently ironic mode, the anonymous reviewer chides that 'other hand' for painting such a gloomy picture of Mr Williamson's career: 'Were no elder men of letters kindly, no editors encouraging?' Although no name is attached to this review, it must be remembered that the editor of the *London Mercury* was J.C. Squire, who might indeed have felt a little grieved to find past assistance from himself and other eminent literary names had not been publicly recognized.

While Henry and Loetitia were in London immediately after they had disembarked from their trip to America at the end of March, they had gone to Hampstead and paid a visit to Helen Thomas, the widow of writer and poet Edward Thomas,[14] whose work Henry very much admired. Helen Thomas had written a letter to Henry on reading *The Pathway* to thank him for writing it; stating that her dead husband sometimes felt very close and that reading *The Pathway* had given her that feeling. She compared *The Pathway* with *The Story of my Heart*, ranking it on a par with the works of Shakespeare, Dostoievsky and Cervantes – 'They utter truth so certainly that we are lifted up into heaven by them.'

In the summer their twenty-one-year-old daughter, Ann Thomas, wrote to say that she was on holiday near Barnstaple and asked if she might pay a visit. She took a bus out from Barnstaple to Shallowford[15] where she spent an enjoyable day being shown the various improvements and stages of Henry's trout fishing project; the pool netted against marauding otters where the young trout were fed on 'rank-smelling fish meal'; the watercress pool where water snails and freshwater shrimps thrived, 'very good for trout'; and 'the hatching-box, in which thousands of opalescent trout eggs lay'. At the end of the day – literally, it was midnight – Henry drove her back to her holiday lodgings in the Alvis, which she admired deeply, to which he replied, 'The engine is at last almost perfect. But I had a dreadful time to get it right.' When Henry had dropped her off at the end of a track leading to her lodgings, she stood and listened:

> As I walked back along the lonely path, the river dark and mysterious and rather sad, I thought of the poet I had left, and imagined that my father, killed under Vimy ridge a whole world of time ago, must have been like him: so alive, with such a sense of fun, so interested in everything, and yet, in moments of silence, changing so rapidly, as though the world of 1914–1918 were coming back upon the youth who survived where most of his friends perished. I thought of Richard Jefferies, Edward Thomas, and Wilfred Owen, and my heart grew chilled, for it seemd that he, like these other men, who felt things so deeply, was doomed, and that he himself was conscious of this doom. To adapt Edmund Blunden's phrase, something had flown between him and the sun.[16]

This empathy made a bond between them and it was not long before Ann Thomas left her job as a member of the typing pool at the BBC at their Savoy Hill premises (where John Heygate also worked for a time) and was permanently attached to the Williamson household as Henry's secretary, where she carried out her secretarial duties of answering letters and typing most efficiently, and accompanied Henry everywhere.

The second set of 'Village' tales, *The Labouring Life*, containing the summer and autumn sections of 'The Spirit of the Village' and 'Air and Light of the Fields and the Sea', thus making a pair with *The Village Book*, was published in early

Loetitia and Ann Thomas on the beach.

May 1932 to some very good reviews. There was no longer any pretence that the village was not actually Georgeham and the end papers contained a sketch map of the area drawn by Henry and had little phrases added as explanatory adornments. His 'Avoid this little cot, please' must have encouraged many visitors to go and look at his Writing Hut! In America the book carried the title *As the Sun Shines*.

The last two sections, 'Surview and Farewell' and 'Windwhistle Cross', are as innately valedictory as the grander-scaled *Goodbye West Country*. Here Henry is gently reflective, philosophically imbibing the essence of the village of 'Ham' and his life there. The surview is from the top of the church tower whose stone steps he has climbed and he indulges in a memorial mental view stirred up by the tranquillity imposed by the 'quiet grey tower', paying due tribute to his first acquaintance with the village in May 1914, and all that it has meant in his life.[17]

In late May 1932 Henry made an important contact – with a man who was beginning to gain a reputation for his etchings and wood engraving but who was, as yet, not generally well known. His name was Charles Tunnicliffe. He had read *Tarka the Otter*, which he liked and admired, and at his wife's suggestion had sent some aquatints of otters to Putnam. Putnam put the idea of a new edition of *Tarka* illustrated by Tunnicliffe to Henry, who agreed, and on 24 May Tunnicliffe arrived at Shallowford to meet Henry, to see Tarka country for himself and to start work on the project.

Ian Niall implies that Henry Williamson and Charles Tunnicliffe did not get on very well,[18] but the very large file of letters from Tunnicliffe in Henry's literary archive gives a rather contrary impression. Of a very different temperament from Henry Williamson, Charles Tunnicliffe's frequent letters over several years were matter-of-fact and to the point, concerned mostly with sorting out the many illustrations he was to do for half a dozen of Henry's books. Where answering on more personal matters he was again matter-of-fact and patient, and gently encouraging. Although he did not understand Henry's emotional entanglements – as he admitted in one of his letters, 'such torturings are foreign to my nature' – he just accepted that they were part of Henry's make-up. Many of the things he wrote were quite astute and frequently quite humorous; above all, their tone was unfailingly friendly.

Tunnicliffe's skill as a craftsman and his genius for portraying the countryside and all its creatures ensured his illustrations were the perfect complement to Henry's words, and it was this combination that made Tunnicliffe's early reputation as an illustrator. His talent and total dedication to his work were to make him one of the great artists in the genre of bird painting, but he certainly recognized that it was his work illustrating Henry's books that first brought him public recognition.

After spending a few days at Shallowford Tunnicliffe set off to obtain material for his present job, illustrating *Tarka the Otter*, and had returned back home to Macclesfield by 8 June, for he wrote to report his progress, enclosing prints of Rams Horn Pond with the swallows leaving and of the honorary whip probing the holt with his pole. He continued to work and wrote to report progress and to send

Cartoons by Charles Tunnicliffe from the Shallowford Visitors' Book. (Reproduced with the kind permission of the C.F. Tunnicliffe Estate)

prints of completed work for consideration, and the two men collaborated very closely over the finer points.

He planned to come down again on 15 July to Torrington to make one or two more detailed studies of various sections of the river, and Henry arranged to meet him so that they could go to Cranmere Pool together on Sunday 17 July. Unfortunately there are no details of this trip. Then a letter from Tunnicliffe dated 12 August 1932 shows that the illustrations for *Tarka* were finished and he was already working on those for *The Old Stag*, for which he enclosed six rough sketches.

Putnam published the new edition of *Tarka the Otter* with twenty-three full-page wood engravings and sixteen line-drawn vignettes by Charles F. Tunnicliffe later in the year. The next year they followed with uniform editions of *The Lone Swallows* and *The Old Stag*, and to complete the 'Tunny' new illustrated editions *The Peregrine's Saga* appeared in 1934. Later Tunnicliffe would illustrate two more of Henry's books.

Tunnicliffe was apparently having great difficulty with certain drawings of falcons, birds which he had not previously seen at close quarters; this is interesting as it was for his bird portraits that he was to become so famous. But, as Niall states, he did not make a detailed study of birds until the mid-1930s. In August

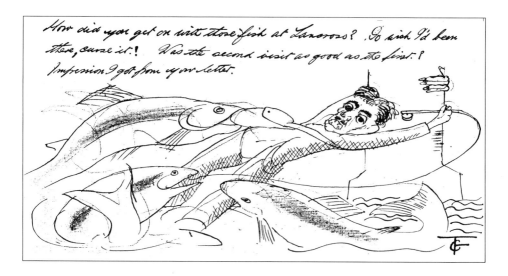

Drawings reproduced from letters from Charles Tunnicliffe to Henry Williamson. Top, 20 August 1932; middle, 21 February 1933; bottom, 25 February 1934, just before Henry left for America, hence content. (Reproduced with the kind permission of the C.F. Tunnicliffe Estate)

1932 he had obviously asked for, and Henry had sent him, information about where to see falcons at close hand with a professional falconer. It appears that Henry was very particular about having drawings done from real life, for Tunnicliffe wrote, tongue in cheek, 'I hope you don't expect me to go to the Cameroons to draw the baboons – will the local zoo do?' When he did finally get to see a falcon at close quarters in August 1933, he was completely overwhelmed, stating that he had never seen anything more beautiful. At the top of this letter he drew the head of a falcon, so fine that the bird looks almost alive. Another letter thanks Henry for pointing out that an owl only uses one talon to carry its prey.

Many of the entries in Henry's diary at this time are in Ann Thomas's handwriting and are jottings of business work completed with a few more personal notes by Henry himself, most frequently about oil put into the Alvis, speeds, and milometer readings! Then he noted on 2 July 'Pinta Major put in for repair to S. Pidler.' Sam Pidler was boatman to the North Devon Sailing Club at Instow, and Henry apparently actually owned two boats – a *Pinta Major* and a *Pinta Minor*. This occasioned its own little drama. 'Dear Sir, In answer to your letter re your Account, as you can guess the trouble I have had it is rather difficult to let you know exactly until I see you again.' *Pinta Minor* was apparently rented out for the summer, but letters about the repairs and delays, and Henry querying

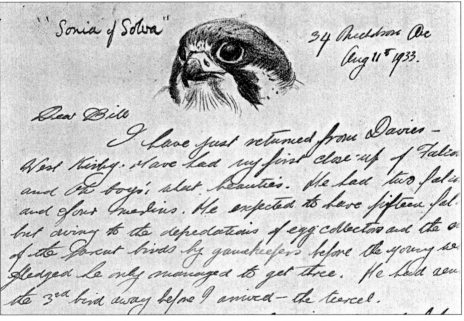

The falcon that completely overwhelmed Charles Tunnicliffe with its beauty, and which he drew at the head of a letter to Henry. (Reproduced with the kind permission of the C.F. Tunnicliffe Estate)

costs of same, were going backwards and forwards between Sam Pidler and himself all summer. Henry thought he had been overcharged originally by 8 shillings for 'launching two boats' and then proceeded to query every subsequent amount. Sam Pidler stuck to his guns and suggested Henry approach the club committee for corroboration of costs. The words 'solicitor' and 'libel' were used on both sides. Finally, on 10 November, Ann Thomas sent a letter with covering cheque for £3 4s to settle the account. Once again Henry had been his own worst enemy; it would have been so much easier to have paid the very small bill in the first place!

Henry's kindly elderly landlord, Hugh, Earl Fortescue, died in the autumn of 1932 and was buried in Filleigh churchyard on All Saints Day; Henry and his wife attended the ceremony, and the Order of Service is preserved in the archive.

Meanwhile writing work had proceeded apace. Reference has already been made to the book that was supposedly written by Willie Maddison in *The Pathway* when he abandoned 'A Policy of Reconstruction' and rewrites his material in the form of a 'celestial fantasy' which he called 'The Star-born'. On 8 August 1932 Ann Thomas entered in the diary 'Left Star-born T.S. at Faber'. (Faber as publishers of the revised editions of *The Flax of Dream* novels were due to receive this 'pendant volume'.)

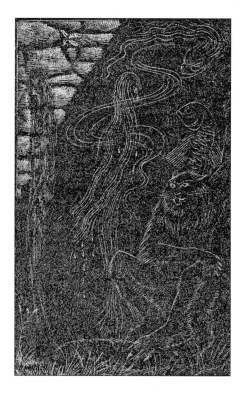

One of Charles Tunnicliffe's superb drawings for *The Star-born*.

On 17 October Tunnicliffe wrote to say that he would be happy to undertake the illustrations for *The Star-born*, but that he would want to visit Lydford where the book was set. Ann Thomas wrote back on Henry's behalf suggesting they visit Lydford together on 12 December and that Tunnicliffe should come to Shallowford first, so that he could travel in the comfort of the Alvis and not have to brave the cold weather on his motor-bike, which he had said he was dreading. Tunnicliffe then wrote back to say he would arrive on 10 December. (Incidentally, the Christmas cards sent out from Shallowford that year were a Tunnicliffe engraving of 'Staghounds at Cloutsham', an illustration from *The Old Stag*.) Then, on 28 December, Tunnicliffe's letter arrived enclosing a set of drawings for *The Star-born*. He had been very worried about his ability to capture the 'celestial fantasy' ideas behind the book: 'You know what an earthly mortal I am, heavy you know, takes a hell of a lot of lifting off the ground.' But Tunnicliffe rose superbly to the task, the wood engravings he supplied complementing and enhancing the text in a most exceptional manner.

The Star-born is very different from any other book that Henry Williamson wrote. It is indeed 'a celestial fantasy' and has a dimension of surrealism beside a core of truth that has never been truly recognized: Romantic in the true sense. Flaws the book undoubtedly has, but its mystical power far outweighs them. Henry had been greatly influenced by the Romantic, mystical writings of Richard Jefferies and Francis Thompson, and by the music of Wagner, its ethos too inspired by the myths of the gods. The story is on two planes: the one is a simple tale of a child born into a Lydford family whose father has been drowned in Lydford Gorge; the other is the story of the spirits that inhabit an unseen world and who steal the baby away so that he can inhabit that world and learn Truth, which he tries to impart to the real world when he returns as an adult. The chief spirit character, Wanhope, is a Christ-figure as is the Star-born, Sonnie, and the Truth that they try to impart to the world is, of course, rejected.

In his introduction Henry maintained the fiction that the book was written by Willie Maddison, but as the author's name on the cover is very firmly his own, it is not certain whom he thought he was going to fool. In the front of his own copy of *The Star-born* Henry has written out in red ink a poem by Francis Thompson, whose poetry his aunt Mary Leopoldina had sent to him in the trenches, and who was one of his main alter egos; it does much to explain what Henry's underlying idea really was.

> In all I work, my hand includeth thine;
> Thou rushest down in every stream
> Whose passion frets my spirit's deepening gorge;
> Unhoodst mine eyas-heart, and fliest my dream;
> As the innocent moon, that nothing does but shine,
> Moves all the labouring surges of the world.
> Pierce where thou wilt the springing thought in me
> And there thy pictured countenance lies enfurled,

As in the cut fern lies the imaged tree,
This poor song that sings of thee
This fragile song, is but a curled
Shell outgathered from the sea,
And murmurous still of its nativity.

Francis Thompson, who passed
to dream-tryst, 13 Nov. 1907[19]

Reviews of *The Star-born* in the files are almost non-existent and those few are not very complimentary. One, by Frank Kendon,[20] voiced grave misgivings; Hugh Walpole ended his review in the *Spectator* 'And Mr Williamson once upon a time wrote *Tarka the Otter*! *Can* such things be?'; while an anonymous reviewer in *Everyman* did not like it at all: 'This so-called "celestial fantasy" is the greatest pack of sentimental nonsense one reader has ever come across.' Henry Williamson himself said that the book was unsuccessful: its content and message were not understood. It is a work that is either immediately taken to the heart and soul, or totally rejected as nonsense, and 'sentimental nonsense' at that.

If *The Star-born* received little attention, then the other book that Henry published at this time certainly received plenty. Two days after Ann Thomas had left the typescript of *The Star-born* at the offices of Faber, on 10 August 1932, Henry wrote in his diary: 'Completed G.F. at 2.30 p.m.' G.F. is *The Gold Falcon* which had been started during his visit to America. At a very early stage Henry had decided that he was going to publish the book anonymously, possibly influenced by Douglas Bell's *A Soldier's Diary of the Great War* and Frederic Manning's *Her Privates We*, both published anonymously just as Henry conceived the idea for this book. The writing of it was made known to only a handful of close friends, and they only referred to it by the code-name 'Auriferous Bird'. All were sworn to secrecy. In order to maintain this cloak of secrecy, Henry chose two people to represent him and steer the book through the processes of publication; for the English market this was Frank Swinnerton and for the American market it was Barbara Sincere, herself a main participant in the story.

The typescript was sent to Frank Swinnerton ten days after that diary entry for he sent back a cryptic postcard, postmarked 20 August 1932 to say it had arrived, but what should he do with it once he had read it. He was instructed to send it to Victor Gollancz the publisher. Swinnerton wrote again when he had read the book saying he had found it personal, original, and that the climax was marvellous and that he had sent it to 'V.G.'.

However, Gollancz was worried that the book was libellous and turned it down. Certainly, a great many people, well-known writers and artists, were to recognize themselves from the very thinly disguised names used in the book, and many did not like what they read. Henry then suggested that Swinnerton should try Faber and on 10 December 1932 Swinnerton wrote that Richard de la Mare had offered good terms; an advance payment of £200, 15 per cent royalty on the first 3,000 copies and 20 per cent thereafter. Henry actually then tried to negotiate 25 per cent after 10,000 copies, but de la Mare drew the line at that. At some early point Richard de la Mare was told who the author actually was – Henry could hardly withhold the information from such an old friend – but he too was sworn to secrecy.

Most reviews tended to concentrate on the mystery of the authorship and in trying to decipher the various disguised characters, relegating the story itself to second place. Really, there were many clues that the discerning could work out and soon the authorship was an open secret. John Brophy recognized Henry's style and challenged Henry to sue him if he was wrong. L.P. Hartley wrote a critique in the *Weekend Review*, of 11 February 1933, in which he also discerns the author as Henry Williamson: 'the same awareness of beauty, the same appreciation of nobility, the same inclination to tear his heart out and wear it on his sleeve, and Manfred shares with Mr Williamson's Maddison the inability to make his life illustrate his ideals.' For his part, J.B. Priestley recognized the author, and himself, and did not like what he read. In the first appearance of his column 'Here and Now' in the *Weekend Review* on 4 March 1933, he wrote:

> Easily the worst book is that gigantic oozing slab of self-pity, that anonymous work carrying the wet trade mark of Henry Williamson, called *The Gold Falcon*. . . . What is one to say about a writer who will not put his name to a novel and yet introduces into it, under the thinnest disguises, a number of fellow writers? I figure in it as P.B. Bradford, 'a coarse, vulgar fellow, at best a second-rate imitation Arnold Bennett'.

Priestley could see no connection between himself and Arnold Bennett – he stated that he didn't even like him! In contrast, T.E. Lawrence, always a faithful friend, wrote that he was amused to be thought of as the author and that Henry's style exactly captured the jazzy subject and conveyed an astonishing sense of movement throughout.

When Barbara Sincere had received the typescript in America in early November 1932, she found herself very affected by what she read:

> It is too much a reliving of my own experience for me not to be absolutely personal in my reaction. Your remembrance and accuracy in retaining and putting down conversation, comments, sights, and sounds is uncanny. . . . I was fearfully startled when I saw my own letter to you, staring at me from page 386 and yours to me shortly following.[21]
>
> Letter in HWLEA, dated November 1932

Barbara, having abandoned Dutton to remove herself from Henry's presence at the end of 1930, was now running her own 'Knitting Shop' in Illinois. She was also writing a small column on poetry for a Woman's Club journal. There was no question of her offering the book to Dutton. John Macrae had already turned down *The Star-born*: originally, on a visit to London he had accepted it, offering $500 advance, but Henry demanded $1,500 and so Macrae refused. Their relationship, deteriorating anyway, turned sour. Henry thought he was getting very little actual monetary return from American sales and was very suspicious about it. Also his ideas about new editions of his books were very different from those of John Macrae.

Barbara first of all approached Longman, who turned the book down. While she was pursuing other lines of inquiry, in February 1933 she received a telegram from Harrison Smith asking if the rights for the book were available. Henry gave permission for her to proceed and it was the firm of Harrison Smith and Robert Haas who published the book in America.

As with previous books, American publication brought forth an amazing rash of enthusiastic and discerning reviews. Although interested in discovering the name of the author – for which the chief contenders were Robert Graves, T.E. Lawrence, Henry Williamson, and an American writer, Christopher Morley – they also, unlike any of the English counterparts, drew all the underlying Romantic inferences to be made by the use of the name 'Manfred' through its association with Lord Byron and investigated thoroughly the connection between the 'Hamlet' lecture to the character of Manfred, and thus to the author. In the *New York Tribune* a review by Eda Lou Walton was headed, 'The Byronic Egotist of the Post-War – A Terrifying and Fascinating, Annoying and Amusing anonymous Novel'; while one from the *New York Times Book Review*, 3 September 1933, by Edith Walton (these two must be the same person) stated 'The Fanciful and the Damned. In *The Gold Falcon* a More or Less Anonymous Author Writes a Byronic Allegory of the Literati of London and New York.'[22] Edith Walton opted for Robert Graves as the author. Graves was not amused and from his home on Mallorca, Spain, sent a 'Letter to the Editor' which the *New York Times* printed on 5 November 1933:

The Publishers know very well it is not me, and I resent their suggesting that it possibly may be. . . . When Miss Walton points definitely at me as the author she is being not only unsophisticated but completely wanting in literary judgement. Quite apart from there being no least resemblance between the 'Byronic' life of Manfred and my own, Miss Walton ought to know that I am incapable of writing such wretched stuff. . . .

The so-called parallels between my story and the one written by Mr Henry Williamson – for it is he – are not merely a 'prank' on his part but vulgar defamation. The only connection that I have had with Mr Williamson is that he once wrote a silly neurotic book about visiting the war areas and that I said in a signed review that it was silly and neurotic. . . .

Henry wrote Graves a conciliatory postcard pointing out it was not his fault the reviewer had named Graves as the author, but Graves refused to be placated and returned it, numbered down the side, each number annotated with succint one-word replies by himself. It was not until November 1957 that a letter from Robert

Graves indicates that Henry had just written to him, no doubt thinking it was time to heal the rift. Graves wrote back to thank Henry for his very decent letter and apologizing for his own initial bad-tempered reaction. The rift was healed – at least on the surface.

John Macrae took great offence at the portrait of himself in the book, which puzzled Henry somewhat, he could not see why, for he thought he had been quite sympathetic to 'Homer'. But the rift between the two men was complete, Henry only learning much later from Macrae's son that the final damage was due to his portraying 'Homer' as keeping liquor in his office – in Prohibition days this was forbidden. Macrae considered his reputation to be tarnished.

But to Henry's total surprise the person who really took mortal offence was C.R.W. Nevinson, whom Henry had met at the Cafe Royal several years earlier and who was the artist Henry mentioned in the 'St George of Georgeham' prank. Henry was on fairly friendly terms with Nevinson. He had dedicated *The Wet Flanders Plain* to him and in a letter he wrote to T.E. Lawrence on 12 December 1932, Henry mentioned that

> I have just spent a grand week here with Nevinson the painter, who has been damned ill with pneumonia, operation after twisted gut, etc. A sad but inspiring semi-wreck of a man. And what a gift for telling stories, always with his gargantuan laughter. Nothing petty, nothing mean, nothing unjust, as I in my niminy, pimminy way am inclined to be. . . .
>
> Letter copy in HWLEA

A few months later, however, the relationship deteriorated when Nevinson took offence at Henry's seemingly innocent portrayal of him as Channerson in *The Gold Falcon*. Henry had said little more than that Channerson was a struggling artist whose paintings sold for very little money. It does not seem like material to provoke such a strong outburst from Nevinson, who threatened libel action:

> *'What's New York like?' said Manfred to Channerson after a pause. Channerson's war pictures were immortal; they could still be bought at sales for a few guineas. They were powerful with the spirit of truth. Channerson had been persecuted during the War, called a defeatist, a little Englander, for his truthful pictures. . . .*
>
> *'O my God!' cried Channerson, at the question. He gave great bellows of laughter. There was no glee in his laughter. It was loud and hollow, and ceased suddenly.*
>
> *The Gold Falcon*

In a letter to Lawrence on 13 March 1933 Henry wrote:

> Keep this under your hat – C.R.W. Nevinson, who stayed a week here last December and who appeared to be a friend – may be suing for 'libel in trade' on

account of the alleged reference to himself in the book. He wrote me a most shocking letter, full of a most virulent contempt. I had been conscious only of benevolence towards him for years: puffing him when I could etc.: all of which is nothing and thankless: and then when he gets what he fancies is a slight, he just blows up. Phew! I'll avoid my own sort in future!

Letter copy in HWLEA

Although Nevinson's letter is not quite so shocking or virulently contemptuous as Henry made out to Lawrence, he *was* very annoyed and abrupt and Henry was very taken aback. Nevinson wrote that he never wished to hear from Henry again. But Henry felt he had to try and explain. On 12 March he wrote a letter to Mrs Nevinson telling her that he thought 'R. [C. Richard W. Nevinson] had got myself and the book wrong: that he was represented in book as a great artist whose reflectiveness was inevitably tragic: that it did not mean that he had lost power.' Two or three versions of Henry's answers are in the archive file, first to Nevinson's wife and then to Nevinson himself, plus roughs for a telegram of apology. At the end he has written 'Telegram & also letter were ignored'.

Another of Henry's close friends, Thomas Washington Metcalfe, known to Henry as Mecca, who lived near Barnstaple, features in *The Gold Falcon* as Thomas Volstead Wrink. (In real life Volstead Wrink was the man responsible for prohibition in the USA.) Metcalfe had had a distinguished record in the First World War. Now he wrote books, one of which, *Fare Thee Well*, was published by Faber in 1933. Henry's diary entry for 11 March 1933 records that he gave a party for Metcalfe that evening with champagne, to celebrate the publication of the book. The drink caused 'Mecca to rant against those who had neglected to see [his] genius'. Henry mentioned the party in a letter to Lawrence, 'As for 'Wrink' read the enclosed. As you say, it's a queer world. I gave a tiny party for him last Saturday.' Metcalfe does not appear to have been a very happy man. One letter is signed 'Mecca. D.F.C. (Distinguished Failure Cross)' – a joke but with an element of bitter truth in it; and one letter, dated 9 April 1933, ends with a postscript: 'I've sometimes wondered if it isn't a pity that Volstead Wrink didn't go on that last flight with Manfred. Nice final curtain for *both* of them!' On a newspaper cutting noting his death in 1953, Henry has written 'Poor sad Mecca'.

The other book with which Henry was involved during 1933 was *On Foot in Devon*. In July 1932 he had been approached by the publisher Alexander Maclehose who wrote to say that S.P.B. Mais had suggested Henry write a volume for his travel series 'On Foot In . . . '. Mais was himself contributing a volume on Sussex, and would Henry like to cover Devon, in about 50,000 words. Ann Thomas handled the ensuing correspondence stating that Mr Williamson stipulated that he could not write a 'normal' travel book but that he might write a personal book if that was agreeable. Maclehose agreed. The contract was signed and the typescript was to be delivered by 1 February 1933, so the book could catch the spring/Easter market. In December Maclehose wrote inquiring about progress and seeking details as he was preparing his spring catalogue. He also asked whether Mr Williamson had any particular wishes with regard to the jacket design. Ann Thomas sent back a stalling letter, but stated that Mr Williamson 'would very much like the book jacket to be done by Mr C.F. Tunnicliffe'. In mid-January Maclehose again enquired about progress and said Tunnicliffe had sent 'a delightful sketch for the cover'. Ann Thomas now sent the synopsis he needed for his catalogue. (This short description was not a synopsis for the book that was printed but was that for the book which was to be called *Devon Holiday*.) Ann warned that the typescript would not be ready by 1 February. That was hardly surprising: the date of her letter was 11 January 1933. On 14 January 1933 Ann and Henry walked part of the North Devon coastline to get material for the book. The following day 15 January 1933 Ann noted in the diary: 'HW Dictated 1000 words of On Foot in Devon'; for Monday 16th, 'Dictated about 4000 words'; on Tuesday 17th, 'Dictated 3000'; Sunday 29th, 'Finished dictating of ON FOOT IN DEVON'; then, on Tuesday 31st, 'John Galsworthy is dead this day'.

Henry and Gipsy left for London on 2 February, presumably to attend Galsworthy's funeral and leaving Ann to type out *On Foot in Devon*. Henry took the first two already typed chapters with him. In London he offered the book to Jonathan Cape and somewhat tactlessly telephoned Maclehose to tell him this fact. Having assimilated this information Maclehose wrote a letter the following day reminding Henry, very politely but very firmly, that he had signed a legal contract. It seems that Henry now decided that the book he had written must go to Cape as the terms of his contract with that firm demanded first options on a certain number of books, and that he would have to write a fresh book for Maclehose. While Maclehose 'understands his position', he nevertheless insisted that the book for his firm must be published first with a long gap before Cape could bring out their volume, to ensure his own sales.

In answer to an inquiry as to progress on 27 February Ann, on Henry's behalf, pleaded a bad dose of flu, which Henry certainly had, and 'congestion of the lungs' which could have been a bad cough residual from the flu or, more probably, a delaying tactic to gain more time. Soon Maclehose is again asking for a progress report. On 30 March Ann Thomas informed him that Henry was currently exploring South Devon for the purposes of the book. Henry's diary entry for 21 March states: 'Rec'd extended pass from S. Railway [he quite often asked for and obtained free passes!]. Set off today on my S. Coast walk, reluctantly and a little fearfully.' The following day he 'entrained to Sidmouth & walked to Exmouth', on 23 March he 'walked to Teignmouth, entrained Newton Abbott and Paignton, walked thence to Brixham.' On Friday the 24th he walked round to Kingsbeer and Dartmouth and then took the train to Plymouth where he: 'Went to Mount Batten to see T.E. Shaw, who had left 2 hours previously for Tidmouth for weekend, leaving valedictory note. He leaves the R.A.F. on Thursday next.'

Henry had written to 'Shaw' (T.E. Lawrence), who was currently stationed near Plymouth, on 13 March to say he would be making this trip and would come and see him the following week. Lawrence answered that he would probably not be able to meet him that week. Whether Henry deliberately delayed his trip in the hope that Lawrence would then be free is hard to tell, but he sent off a note with his new plans at the last moment, too late for contact, and found the note of apology awaiting his arrival at Mount Batten.

Henry made a further visit to the southern coast at the end of April; his diary entries recorded his progress: Exeter, Tor Cross, Kingsbridge, and on Tuesday 9 May: 'Finished the bloody book *On Foot in Hell* for Maclehose at 11.35 a.m. this day. Now for some real work – carpentry, dams, tomatoes, etc.'

In the late spring of 1933, Henry began to write regularly for the *Sunday Referee*. His diary entry for 29 April states: 'Wrote to Pinker accepting Sunday Referee offer of £3/3/- weekly for 52 articles of 300 words each. Good!' This would bring in a regular sum for the whole of the next year.

But now there were other, more personal problems to solve. Loetitia was pregnant with their fourth child, and almost at the same time Ann Thomas informed him that she too was pregnant. Ann left Shallowford at the end of May. Henry wrote to his mother telling her of the situation and that he had made arrangements for Ann to stay with his younger sister Biddy, who was living near their parents in Brockley and who by now had two children of her own, Michael, born in January 1928, and Brian, born in March 1930. Bill Busby had left her and she was bringing up the children on her own. Henry had been sending her sums of money from time to time to help her and he obviously thought this new arrangement would suit both women. Henry did not shirk his responsibilities and now regularly sent Ann sums of money, not large amounts but they would have enabled her to pay her bills, probably housekeeping to Biddy. Henry's mother was very upset by the news:

Dear Harry,
I can hardly tell you what horror & grief your letter has caused me, I cannot believe a son of mine would let his young wife & children down in this fashion. Also I cannot understand why you should want to bring her to Brockley. . . . What about Gipsy? I have always been very fond of her. What is she going to do? No wonder she has not written to me, & she has no Mother! . . . Well! Harry I have upon consideration decided to keep your secret but I hope it won't be for long. . . . Poor Gipsy, I should like to know how she is & if she is with you give her my love.   Your Mother.
                                    Letter in HWLEA, dated May 1933[23]

On 17 August Kathie wrote to tell him his mother had had a stroke and was paralysed; Henry wrote in the diary: 'I realise now the anguish that has eaten away that poor, sad, ruined little child, "Gertrude Leaver".' However, on 19 August he learnt that she was not actually paralysed but must be careful.

Loetitia with her innate dignity and gentle nature continued to be friends with Ann. Her life was undoubtedly difficult and turbulent but she did not blame Ann for its problems or, indeed, anyone else – not even Henry – fully realizing that he could not help his temperament. She was of a more enduring and stoical outlook.

However, this did not make the constant criticisms and friction any easier to bear, and Loetitia was not always submissive. There are many indications that the sparks did fly on occasion. But she had an inner strength that meant she could withdraw from conflict and submerge herself in her own affairs. Although frequently irritated with her at this time, in later life Henry appreciated her qualities and thanked her for giving him such wonderful children.

Their fourth child, a son, was born on 7 September 1933 – while Loetitia was still in her car en route to the nursing home, which annoyed Henry as if it were her fault, as he noted in his diary. The child was named Charles Robert, but he has always been known by his second name. On 14 September Ann Thomas gave birth to a daughter, Rosemary; Henry wrote in his diary, 'to the great joy of her mother, whose life is now, in her own words, "fulfilled"'. Loetitia wrote Ann a most generous letter after the birth, saying she was glad Ann had had what she wanted, a girl, and that although she had said earlier that she too wanted a daughter, it was better the two children were of different sex so no comparisons could be made.[24]

Despite the fact that they were so close in birth, the story found in *The Children of Shallowford*, that Robert did not thrive because Loetitia was unable to feed him properly (which was so) and that in May the following year he was virtually dying of starvation, so that Henry on return from his second trip to America suggested that Ann Thomas should feed him alongside her own thriving baby, is a fiction born, as Ann herself wrote, 'out of the more sentimental side of Henry's imagination'. Apart from anything else, these children were now just about ten months old, and weaned. Henry's diary records that Ann visited Shallowford from 2–10 June 1934. She came by train and there is no mention of Rosemary being present. In her letter to clarify this matter, dated 16 October 1992, Ann states: '[When I first met] Robbie [he] was a fine lively boy of about a year, when he had certainly outgrown a milk-diet and was obviously thriving like the green bay tree without any help from me.' Loetitia agrees with this statement, 'Henry's imagination really did run away with him sometimes.' Presumably Henry fondly imagined this would make a 'nice' story – and proceeded to believe it had actually occurred – as frequently happened.

When he found that Ann Thomas, like his wife, was pregnant and could no longer give him the total attention that his ego and spirit needed so desperately, Henry began to look for another 'Barleybright'. Several candidates appeared but were found wanting in the next few weeks, including a visit from Barbara Krebs then in England on holiday, with whom he now found friendship, rather than love, was the overriding emotion. But when he was walking the south coast of Devon for the 'wretched' guide book in April 1933, Henry had written in his diary on 26 April that while he was at Torcross watching the salmon netting he 'met a lovely young girl, Ann Edmonds'. He wrote to her that night but did not post it and wrote in his diary: 'Melancholy, oh damned lonely and loveless and death-haunted.'

On 11 September 1933 he wrote: 'Went to Torcross sometime about now and

renewed amity with 16½-year-old Ann of *On Foot in Devon*' and on Friday 15
September: 'Think myself to be in love with Ann of Torcross. Told her about my
domestic disharmony but I suspect her parents know nothing.' He had fallen
deeply and desperately in love with this young girl, his new 'Barleybright', and
visited her frequently at her home at Bickley in Kent. (The Torcross address was
the family holiday accomodation.) Her initials spell out the word ACE and that
summed up her character, for what Henry had not realized at this stage, although
he soon would, was that her sole passion in life was for flying, and she was drawn
towards that powerful magnet as single-mindedly as Henry was drawn towards
the powerful magnet of writing.

It was at this point that Henry wrote to Barbara Sincere explaining that he was
thinking of leaving his wife, but possibly either omitting to mention or not making
it clear, so that he could marry Ann Edmonds. Barbara Sincere presumed that the
content of this letter applied to her and she wrote, as Henry recorded in his diary,
that 'she is prepared to throw in her lot with me now that she knows G. and I are
definitely parting. Too late – the Bb [Barleybright] surrounds me. Dolor
descrescit.' About this time another entry recorded that he had begun to write his
'autobiography – Sun In Sands' (*sic*).

Towards the end of October 1933 Sir John Fortescue died. Henry wrote a short
obituary coupled with a review of his autobiography, *Author and Curator*, for the
Sunday Times of 29 October 1933: 'I have received much encouragement and help
from this man, my senior in letters . . . like the late Arnold Bennett, he was that
rare thing – a true sensitive.' (see *The Linhay On the Downs*, 'Stag Hunting').

Throughout this year he had seen a great deal of John Heygate, who was a
frequent visitor to Shallowford, and Henry stayed with him whenever he visited
London. In August 1930 John had married the Hon. Evelyn, youngest daughter of
the 1st Baron Burghclere and former wife of Evelyn Waugh, the author. The
Waughs are the models for Virginia and Anthony Croft in the *Chronicle*, and
Waugh mentioned Henry very briefly in his published *Diaries*:

> Sunday 11 Nov. 1928. On Thursday Bobby brought a man called Henry
> Williamson round to see us. He won a prize with a book called Tarka the Otter
> and has now had a great success with a novel. He is quite elderly – though I find
> him coupled with me in reviews as promising young writers – and wholly
> without culture. Very gauche and suddenly earnest-minded, but capable of fun.
> He stayed some time and took away a copy of Decline and Fall.[25]

Henry was actually only seven years older than Evelyn Waugh, who was born in
1902, and at this time the two men were respectively thirty-three and twenty-six
years old. *Decline and Fall* and *The Pathway* were both published in 1928. The
two men did not take to each other, jealousy probably being the root cause of the
antipathy on both sides. Henry was, however, on friendly terms with Evelyn's
brother, Alec Waugh, also a writer, who was of a more 'benign and unaggressive'
disposition than his younger brother.[26] 'Bobby' is Cecil (Bobby) Roberts, who

arrived to see Henry with John Heygate originally, was involved in the 'St George of Georgeham' prank, and who is one of those who contributed a line in the Shallowford visitors' book.

On the day in March 1933 that Henry Williamson left for the South Devon coast to gather material for *On Foot in Devon*, he received a letter from Victor Yeates, a friend from his days at Colfe's and a character in *Dandelion Days*, saying that he had written a novel and asking if Henry would give him his advice. The two had met from time to time during the First World War; once at the Cafe Royal, where they had dined and drank too much, and also on Blackheath Common in 1919. Yeates had been in the Royal Flying Corps, logging up 248 flying hours in Sopwith Camels, many on the Western Front. The typescript, at this stage entitled 'Adjustment', arrived shortly afterwards and Henry immediately sent a postcard:

> Your flying book is magnificent and will be a success. . . . Will send you a detailed constructive criticism & suggestions on minor additions, amplifications, excisions later on. Am certain I can get it published for you. Genuine congratulations. Yours, H. Williamson
>
> Letter copy in HWLEA, dated March 1933

But in his diary he wrote 'Yesterday Yeates sent the Tss of his novel "Adjustment". I read as far as the waitress in heaven, and then stopped, bleakly.' In his subsequent introduction to Yeates's published book, Henry likens this original typescript to *Ulysses* by James Joyce. 'It was formless but real.'[27]

Victor Yeates was ill, suffering from consumption, and his next letter, dated 27 April 1933, was from a ward in Colindale Hospital. Henry wrote back: 'Your book shows on every page that you have gifts as a writer . . . [but] you don't bother about transmuting those gifts into a medium . . . to hold the reader's interest. . . . Why not a novel of the old RFC [Royal Flying Corps]. They sell like hell . . . '

> Letter copy in HWLEA

Yeates was a little put out at this, after the first enthusiastic response he was expecting more of the same. His letter of 2 May 1933 shows that he was upset that Henry did not appear to have noticed the main theme of the book, and its moral tendency towards regeneration. But after grumbling that he 'doesn't want to write a novel, can't write a novel', Yeates added a postscript of capitulation, stating that he would write the suggested book and had indeed already completed the first chapter. In the meantime Henry had sent 'Adjustment' off to a publisher, but it received a polite rejection.

At the beginning of August, now out of the sanatorium and home, Yeates was working hard, had written over 70,000 words and was calling the book 'This Tassel Gentle', a quotation from *Romeo and Juliet*.[28] At the end of the month he wrote to warn Henry that 'Tassel Gentle' was nearly finished and, again, on

4 September, to say that he had posted 'G.T.' and that it was only the first part of a trilogy. Henry felt that it should be the first part of one single book.

From their correspondence it seems that Henry called in to see Yeates towards the end of September 1933 as he travelled to or from a visit to see Ann Edmonds at her home at nearby Bickley. There is however, no mention of the meeting in his diary entries, where Henry's only thought is the strength and tragedy of his feelings for his new 'Barleybright'. Yeates was very ill and found the physical effort of writing extremely difficult, but he continued to work with feverish intensity. On 10 November Henry wrote in his diary: 'Part II of Tassel Gentle is magnificent'. The next day he went to see Yeates and personally gave him £50 which he said was an advance on the book. (This was later reimbursed by Cape, with whom Henry had arranged publication.) Henry was very moved by Yeates's poor state of health and expended much time and energy writing him encouraging letters, and guiding him through the processes of publication.

Jonathan Cape wrote to Henry that he did not like 'Tassel Gentle' as a title suggesting instead 'High Adventure', but Yeates countered that it had already been used, and himself suggested 'Winged Victory'. In February 1934 Henry wrote to him, using a title not mentioned by either of them before, that he has read 'A TEST TO DESTRUCTION or whatever is your title. I have rewritten parts of part 3.' To which Yeates answered in anguish: 'NO NO NO NO NO NO NO I can't go on like this I must write my own stuff.' He continued to the effect that although he would accept Henry's judgement about when and where a piece needed revision, he must actually do it himself. Henry followed up with two long letters of explanation as to why he had done the corrections and sent back Yeates's typescript, begging him to let the corrections stand, and going on to expound his own miserable state of mind about life. A grand wordy argument about theory both in writing and in life developed over the next few letters – Yeates successfully holding his own. But, now diverted from his immediate anguish, Yeates went over the typescript again, making his own revisions and agreeing to let some of Henry's stand and the book was finished and sent off to Cape for setting. But the final effort had taken a lot out of Yeates and he had a relapse.

The year 1934 opened with Henry's emotions about Ann Edmonds in a state of turmoil. Every page of his diary records how he swung from elation to despair, the lows far outweighing the highs. His entry for 1 January included: 'She loves me. She will pursue her own ambitions to fly & enter the world of aeroplanes somehow. When she is older she will come to me. Suffered much last night, & wrote her a letter showing those feelings.' A long entry for Saturday 6 January 1934, written variously in red, brown, and green ink, contained a 'scheme for new anonymous book' which he had formulated in the early hours. This book was to be called 'WIT'S MISERY or THE WATERFRONT AT APPLEDORE'. The characters were to include 'Yeates, poet (H.W.); Winnie and John Mulock [Winnie was another of his admirers at this time]; Eme, Bb, and Major E. [Edmonds]; Joan Russell [a girl he had been drinking with the previous evening]; the Renshaws (Margot being cousin to Bb); John Heygate; Gipsy (vague: never appearing)'.[29] The theme was to be:

Poet's search. Bb has passion for salmon (equivalent of flying). She lives on S. Coast. Appearance of poet. Mother's wish to make him happy is hidden motive, or propulsive power, of all that follows. It is his poesy-spirit they are all stirred by: not the man himself. Therein lies the tragic theme. . . . Create feeling of Bb to Yeates almost like that of girl for her dream of Flying Dutchman. Contact with Bb must be tremendous in its restraint and suggestive power. Hero leaves, capture of maiden fish: determines to walk on, to the sunset. . . . There will be a scene of ice and snow, skiing, he with her (Bb) on the hills above where his hut is. . . . Heygate comes down after this: & hero believes all is to be found in a man's companionship: yet vaguely longing. They row in the quiet night: fish leaps: he dreams again, seeing the Bb.

I cannot see the end. Will it be the curve descending, even as it ascended in the first part. Will it be Bb and J.H. coming together in love? And Yeates going down in a storm? Or the fire on the hills? Or the return to his wife? Anyhow the bright salmon-dream between them is incommunicable, rather untranslatable into action. It will decide itself.

Diary entry, 6 January 1934

It is difficult to remember that in this plot 'Yeates' is actually Henry and not Victor Yeates. Other entries contain notes for his new book *Sun In Sands* (*sic*) of which he was writing several thousand words each day in early January. 'Bb is now one of the characters in the S in S. *That theme will make the poetic value of the book.*' On 10 January: '10 pm. Wrote about 800 words of Chapter 13 & finished, unexpectedly, Part I. It's grand.' The plot outlined above was incorporated, more or less, into the later stages of *The Sun in the Sands*.

While correspondence between Henry and Charles Tunnicliffe had been maintained in the background, it now assumed a particular importance. Henry had explained his situation *vis-à-vis* Ann Edmonds to Tunnicliffe, but no name had been mentioned: it was all described in mysterious tones and the hidden identity was certainly a mystery to the honest, straightforward Tunnicliffe. Henry now asked him if he would be willing to take Ann Edmonds as a pupil. Ann had left school at Christmas. Some cartoons she had drawn of her teachers had led everyone to think she might have artistic ability, and Henry had decided to try and organise an opening for her. Henry had also asked Tunnicliffe if he painted portraits, and if so, suggested some sittings for himself, to which Tunnicliffe tentatively agreed, and the arrangements were made. Thus on 21 January Henry recorded in his diary: 'Left at 11 a.m. for Macclesfield. Arrived about 5.30 p.m. 180 miles. Last 40 miles in fog & darkness.' The following day he 'sat 1½ hrs to CFT for my portrait with falcon'. But, more importantly for him, as soon as he had arrived he discussed and arranged with Tunnicliffe that he should take on Ann Edmonds as a pupil and Henry wrote immediately to her with the news.

On 24 January Henry received an answer from Ann's father; he recorded his reactions: 'letter from CHWE about Ann coming to study with Tunnicliffe. Somewhat hard and ferocious in tone . . . to the effect that it is his show etc.

Makes "condition" that I should not visit Bb while here.'[30] Ann's father had now realized what had been going on underneath his nose for some time, and he could see all too well what would happen to the girl's 'studying' of drawing and the technical production of work, if Henry had access. It would appear that while Ann's mother was sympathetic to Ann and Henry, even offering them encouragement, her father seems to have thought that it was his friendship that Henry had been seeking and had been totally oblivious to the reality. Henry had told Ann's mother, Edith Edmonds, that he intended to leave his wife and obtain a divorce, and in due course to marry Ann, but her father had been kept in the dark.

The day after he received Major Edmonds's letter Henry read *The Falcon*, a story by Scandinavian writer Per Hallstrom, and he recorded in his diary:

> Magnificent, as reality and symbolism. The Falcon = the boy's soul = Bb = aspiration. When it tears his breast it is unknowing . . . He [the boy] dreamed himself to death. Yes. Managed to write, against the heaviness of death-feeling, about 1000 words of comedy in the S in S. Tunnicliffe's portrait of me nearly finished.

The following day he noted that he had received a letter from 'an American woman Mrs Sheridan, here in London, asking me on behalf of a friend of hers in Georgia, U.S.A., to go and live on her estate and write and make my home there. A God-send, a miracle. I shall go, & never return: the falcon shall tear my breast no more.'

He was sent another letter from Ann's father, Major 'Monk' Edmonds, this time enclosing some sketches by Ann for Tunnicliffe to see. Tunnicliffe approved and everything was arranged. Ann was to come to Tunnicliffe and Henry had to keep away. Henry was in equal parts furious and heartbroken: furious with 'Monk' because of a remark the latter had made about Henry's writing – 'his damned dirty-stomach inspiration idea of my work'; heart-broken because he had to break with Ann, and he wrote in his diary:

> It is utterly cruel and wrong: but it is all in that magnificent story of the Iceland falcon. . . . [In America] I shall see B.S. [Barbara Sincere] and perhaps learn to accept second-best; although I feel I shall always have the feeling, in *all* of myself, that ACE was my soul, the lost part I have searched for since a tiny child: and indifferent as the falcon. . . . Guess I am boring the poor Tunnicliffe's horribly with my maunderings. . . . Went to bed and dreamed as I think, i.e. the subconscious mind is equal with the same mind as my talking mind – writing 10,000,000 words, as truly to reality as possible.

The dream was prophetic: *A Chronicle of Ancient Sunlight*, a novel as 'truly to reality as possible' was to run to over three million words, each of the fifteen volumes averaging two hundred thousand. But there were still nearly twenty years to go before he was to write them.

The portrait finished as far as Henry's part in it was necessary, he left for London and went on to the Edmonds' house at Bickley, knowing that he had to break with Ann. The decision made, he was relatively calm. The following day, 31 January 1934, he went into the City to see the American, Mrs Sheridan, and make the arrangements to go to America, fare paid, for two to three months. His hostess was to be an elderly rich benefactress of the arts, Mrs Robert (Louise) Reese from Augusta, Georgia, who liked to invite artistic people to stay at her home. On his return Henry recorded that he told Edith Edmonds: 'I was through, couldn't bear any more. She was sweet & realistic & sensible.'

Henry left and went to see Yeates and then on to stay with Ann Thomas, who was living with her sister 'Bronnie' (Bronwen, whose husband had died) in Tenterden, Kent and her young son Charles, who cried bitterly at night. 'I soothe the distraught Charles: soothe the haggard Bronnie: reassure the dumb Ann: and then go into another room to stare vacantly at the moon while tears drip from my worn eyes.'

Preparations were now put in hand for the trip to America. 'Monk' Edmonds arranging a cabin berth for him on the SS *Berengaria* to sail on 28 February. Ann had travelled to join Charles Tunnicliffe at Macclesfield on about 20 February. On his last day at Shallowford, Sunday 25 February, Henry stayed in bed all day with a bad throat, 'overcome with thoughts about getting ready. Gipsy patient and packed quietly'. He left for London the following day, laying up the Alvis in the County Garage in Barnstaple and travelling by train.

Just before Christmas 1933 Henry had written to T.E. Lawrence pouring out the details of his situation with Ann Edmonds, again without naming her: 'I'm wretchedly in love: she's young. . . . This girl cares only for flying. It's an obsession, a grand passion. . . . I'm reduced to sending telegrams to myself offering myself jobs in Hollywood.[31] . . . I am about to leave Shallowford for ever: but haven't heart to start, I don't know where to go, or what to do.' (This was before the offer from Mrs Reese.) Lawrence did not answer this letter. Henry realized he had made a mistake in confiding such intimate details and wrote again – 'My last awful letter must have put you off' – and goes on to say 'Please wait until you read THE SUN IN THE SANDS'. More importantly he went on to enthuse about Yeates's book.

> . . . What I must tell you is that one of the characters in an early novel, named Yeates, has written a MARVELLOUS novel about a group of characters, RFC and later RAF, in the war. . . . I rearranged the last parts of the book, etc, and rewrote the climax, merely suggesting and cutting and altering his stuff: it's really his. It's a great book, I swear . . .
>
> Letter copy in HWLEA, dated February 1934

There follows quite a long resumé of the book and Victor Yeates's situation and Henry asked, 'Will you read the book in proof, when ready, and give it a flip by a sentence Cape may quote? I hope this isn't a bad thing to do, to ask you thus; I'd shrink from asking it for myself, but for the BOOK itself. You'll see. I swear Yeates is a great poet.' He then tells him again that he knows a young girl 'with Puma's eyes, barleybright hair, who's run away from school to fly' who is now a pupil of Tunnicliffe. This letter included the information that he was sailing for America the following Wednesday, 28 February 1934 from Southampton, where Lawrence was now stationed. 'The boat sails at 11.30 a.m. which I suppose is in the morning. I wonder if you'll be about in a speedboat?' Lawrence replied in a letter sent to Shallowford but forwarded to the *Berengaria* that, duties permitting, he would try to be there. Also waiting for Henry at the *Berengaria* was a letter from Victor Yeates. 'Farewell, farewell, farewell. Thou goest to the warm south. O fortunate tu! I sit here and cough and cough and cough.'[32]

Henry had travelled down to Southampton by train. His diary records that the previous evening he had been to the pictures with 'Lucia Brownrigg, & supper at Rules. A nice girl.' There is no indication who Lucia Brownrigg was! On the train he 'thought of end of *Sun in the Sands*' – this 'autobiography' is now to have a thought-up end. This ending expands on his diary synopsis of 6 January and is a version of Barley's death, which he later refined for the eventual book. It was this emotional ending that caused tears to course down his face rather than his real situation. He boarded the *Berengaria*:

> T.E. Lawrence & J. Heygate to see me off. T. E. L. didn't recognise me – gave two sentences before exclaiming 'Is it you? You're fatter in the face, & not so tall.' He and J.H. got on well. T.E. liked John's book, 'Decent Fellows'. We agreed to meet at the hut in the summer. Very cheered by seeing TEL. Drank ¼ bottle champagne, ate good lunch. Telegrams from ACE, AT & Monk & Eme [Edith Edmonds]. Lovely passionate letter from AT. Also letter from Ace & the Tunnies. Much enjoyed the sight of S'ton Water, seaplanes etc.[33]

As the *Berengaria* crossed the Channel, somewhere 'near Cherbourg' Henry sent Lawrence a short letter enclosing one from Victor Yeates, 'author of the 200,000 *A Test to Destruction*. Merely for your interest.' He also enclosed an envelope so that Lawrence could send this letter back to Ann Thomas.

The SS *Berengaria* docked in New York at 2 p.m. on Tuesday 6 March 1934. Henry had suffered badly from sea-sickness the first day but had gradually improved, although his thoughts surged up and down in rhythm with the effect of the sea's surge on his physical body. He was met by his publisher, Harrison Smith, and handed him a proof copy of John Heygate's new book *Talking Picture*. Harrison Smith also agreed to take Yeates's book on Henry's recommendation. Henry took a room at the Brevoort and, after noting that he had dinner and went to the theatre with Harrison Smith, wrote: 'then met Waveney Girvan, champagne-swilling at Biltmore . . . drank beer all night – fatal.'[34]

He continued to see various people, some on business, some friends from the previous visit, including Macrae who gave him 'Cold draught over G.F.', and generally to have an interesting time, going to the theatres and seeing films.

Particularly he noted that he went to 'the Famous Hollywood Cabaret' restaurant and nightclub on Broadway where he met Rudi Vallee, and scores of 'extraordinarily beautiful girls'. He also 'bought several aviation papers for ACE; which she won't acknowledge – That's OK by me.'

An account of this visit appears in Part III of *The Linhay on the Downs and Other Adventures in England and America*, which was published later that year. Although fairly true to life, this does contain one notable 'flight of fancy' – literally, for Henry did not, as he states in the book, fly down the sea-coast of the Carolinas to the Savannahs of Georgia in an open-cockpit monoplane. In reality, as his diary records, on Tuesday 13 March at 3.30 p.m. Waveney Girvan saw him off 'on the *Empress* train to Washington and Augusta return fare 45$30 and the Pullman, one way, 6$75', where he arrived at 12.30 p.m. the following day, half an hour late. He was met by Mrs Reese who was 'reminiscent of Miss Emma Mills and Mrs Dawson-Scott. Like most American women, too verbose and too explicit.'[35] Her house, Le Manoir Fleuri, was one of many set among trees 'sort of Hampstead effect, only slower and quieter'. Immediately he was writing Chapter 21 of *Sun in the Sands*. Out for a walk he discovered a little airport nearby '& decided sometime to fly in the 40 h.p. little monoplane, 3$50 a lesson', obviously the source of his imaginary flight down – although he never records taking this proposed flight. The next day he wrote Chapter 22, played tennis, had his photograph taken and was 'Enjoying this famous writer stuff'. And he was writing regularly his pieces for the *Sunday Referee*, on the boat No. 42, 'Are Rooks Civilised', in New York No. 43, 'Ravens', now No. 44, 'North Atlantic' to No. 48, 'Southern Sun'. Readers of *The Linhay on the Downs* will recognize these titles, for apart from its title story and the strange interpolation of the critical pieces in the middle, *The Linhay on the Downs* is made up from a selection of the *Sunday Referee* articles.

Letters began to arrive, from Ann Thomas, Yeates, ACE, and also from the Tunnicliffes, whose correspondence, as he recorded in his diary, was

. . . chiefly about ACE. Mrs. T. says she doesn't think ACE cares a damn about anything except flying, merely regarding me as a friend; Tunny says she won't make good as an artist, being interested exclusively in aeroplanes; & she's an efficient 'go-getter' & even avaricious, whose ideal is to get money quickly to have a fast car & to do the things that people with money & sporting tastes do. He is sending her home on 23 March, at the end of her trial month.

From the outset Henry found Mrs Reese's constant talk irritating and when he 'pulled her up in a characteristic monologue & asked her to keep to the point' she took offence. But on the whole he was 'liking this life of work-play-sleep-eat very well & further & further recedes the image of Bb. But she's lovely, after the heart's desire, in my S. in S.'

Ann Thomas sent him a newspaper clipping which reported a disastrous fire at Castle Hill, the Fortescue's residence at Filleigh and he recorded in his diary:

'2 deaths of servants, what a tragedy'.[36] Henry wrote to Lord Fortescue (the 5th Earl, and heir of his original landlord who had died in 1932) expressing his sympathy and received a very friendly and appreciative letter in return.

In Henry's diary he invariably referred to his hostess as Mrs Reese although in the printed version she is 'Miss Louise'. Mrs Reese lived a very social life and Henry was taken the round of lunches, dinners, parties; and there were enough pretty and intelligent girls to soothe his ego. He became friendly with Count Giovanni Gregorina, an Italian, 'a nice young man who lives here part of the year & knew Appledore & many mutual acquaintances'. He was also working well. He wrote a long letter to Victor Yeates in which he outlined his 'novel-biography', where Part 3 is to be 'JULIA', and is to contain Pyrenean adventures where 'Julia' crashes to a forlorn foregone conclusion, and Part 4 is 'ALETHEA':[37]

who is my sweet but somewhat lost and neglected and sad and really beloved wife but she don't know it; is a lovely tribute or will be to her: Then the ultimate part 5, BARLEYBRIGHT . . . which will knock you flat with its loveliness and grace and reality . . . and she dies flying to me from the Pyrenees, to my hilltop field . . . crashes in equinoctal gales; and T.E. Lawrence tells me always to write . . . and I leave for the US and the book ends with me poised and an ARTIST . . .

Letter copy in HWLEA, dated March 1934

He also wrote to T.E. Lawrence on 19 March 1934:

Am writing my autobiography THE SUN IN THE SKY and making a novel of it, with imaginary and true-imaginary characters; the spirit of truth I hope but going anywhere for the letter. One of the characters is G.B. Everest . . . [he] is not mysterious; but he is a sort of deus ex azure, at the same time a very human built person; he comes in now and then, a sort of meteor and a presence, very queer, oh its a very queer and human and funny and sad and inevitable book, with a walloping crash at the end. I dreamed it welling-eyed between Brooklands and Southampton that 28 February 1934. It's true, but imaginary.

Letter copy in HWLEA, dated 19 March 1934

Not long after his arrival in Georgia, Henry met Edison Marshall, a writer who earned a lot of money selling short stories and serials in the highly lucrative American magazine market, and had written several books. Due to a mixture of his own jealous feelings and the man's brash American personality, Henry did not at first like Marshall, but they soon became friends and on 9 April they went together on a short fishing trip to Yenassee, 90 miles away in South Carolina. Henry enjoyed this trip, Marshall being good company, telling tales and singing songs accompanied by liberal applications from a bottle of whisky, which helped ease the pain of an abscess which flared up in one of Henry's teeth (and which on his return to Augusta was pulled out). Henry felt a bit claustrophobic at Le

Manoir Fleuri so he and Marshall arranged to go together to Florida on another, more extended fishing expedition. On his last evening in Georgia, Mrs Reese gave a party for him. That afternoon they had had rather a violent quarrel and both of them had somewhat flamboyantly burnt the other's letters, but Henry's diary entry, after detailing some of the insults they threw at each other, stated 'we parted on amiable and even affectionate terms'.

Henry travelled to the Marshalls' home at Valdosta in Florida by a bus crowded with local blacks, a journey which, despite the heat, he enjoyed very much – his short diary notes being exactly expanded for a *Sunday Referee* article, and thus in due course into *The Linhay on the Downs*.

The two men went off on a lengthy fishing trip for black bass and had a great time being men together. Henry felt very 'English and inhibited and almost over-hysterical with nervousness' at Marshall's efforts to procure two girls for 'tail'. To Henry's relief only one arrived and the three of them then sat drinking whisky and talking for a while until Henry tactfully went off to write letters. One of the places they stayed was the Hampton Springs Hotel 'semi-ruinous, edge of swamp, once a fashionable sulphur-cure place, now deserted. Poor food.' On 24 April Henry felt ill. He could not make up his mind whether it was the four ice-creams and hurried dinner (so he could go to the 'movies') the previous evening that were responsible *or* the sulphur water at Hampton Springs Hotel. To cure this he took 'several doses of salts' which, not surprisingly, made him feel 'sea-sick'!

The trip over, Henry returned very briefly to Georgia to take leave of Mrs Reese and to collect his remaining luggage. His large trunks had earlier been sent on to Barbara Sincere in Washington, who was now directed to forward them to New York. Barbara had been supposed to join him; several times it was arranged and each time Henry cabled to cancel at the last minute. Then he was to join her in Washington, but again he cancelled. Instead, on 26 April he travelled straight on to New York, where he found, contrary to his hopes and expectations, no mail, no trunks, and that the typescript which he was expecting from Ann Thomas had also failed to arrive. Henry was not amused!

The next day he talked to Rinehart Publishers about further books, but they were not very enthusiastic, thus depressing him further. He spent his last weekend in Harrison Smith's house in Connecticut, a large and ornate mansion left to him by his playwright uncle, Winchell Smith, full of photographs of stage beauties such as Mary Pickford and Marlene Dietrich, and of actors who had been frequent visitors. He tried to get Harrison Smith to discuss the publication of the 'autobiography' but 'Hal' would not be drawn, saying it must wait until they returned to the office. It was arranged that Henry went back to New York in someone else's car, Harrison Smith returning later. Obviously this was arranged deliberately to avoid a tête-à-tête, and Henry was getting edgy.

By now, he was very tired from the constant travelling and late hours and partying, and beginning to long to return to England. The final days appeared tedious to him. He dreaded packing, leaving it until the last minute and then his luggage was removed prematurely from his room while he had gone to get a sandwich lunch from the bar, which panicked him; he could not find his tickets, so he rushed down to the basement and unstrapped everything, which made him late (one feels deliberately) for his appointment with Harrison Smith. Here, inevitably, he was told that they would not take *Sun in the Sands*, and to get away from this disappointing situation he rushed off, saying he had to get to the bank before he left for Montreal where he was to pick up his boat.

His diary records that on the boat he read *The Sun Also Rises* by Ernest Hemingway, 'a very fine novel with two beautifully accurately drawn portraits of two English people after the war', to take his mind off his sea-sickness. (In his novel he reads this on the train going up to New York.) He also wrote: 'Am glad the autob. is scrapped: it was getting unwieldy.' Once again his thoughts rose and dropped with the sea's surge.

Whatever else had happened during this sojourn in the deep South, it had given Henry and Loetitia a breathing space. Henry's emotional anguish over Ann Edmonds had eased and more or less ceased; in writing up the 'Alethea' section in the 'autobiography' he had reminded himself of Gipsy's worth and he was ready to renew their life together, although he had some reservations.

He had sent a bag of pecan nuts to T.E. Lawrence from Florida and wrote afterwards: 'Hoped you liked the bag of nuts I sent you. Pecans. Florida. Gosh, the sun there is good and the breezes from the Gulf of Mexico fan away his silver-tiger-whiskers.' To which Lawrence replied, 'I eat one per week, ritually, as I visit my cottage where they are stored.' He had also bought four 'cotton pickers' cloth caps which the blacks wore while working in the fields picking cotton, and also six straw hats to take back as mementoes for the children, and some pecan nuts and oranges – 'I shall tip them all out on the lawn by the cypress tree, and cry to the children, "Help yourselves".' There is no record of this actually happening – one suspects the oranges went bad on the voyage.

On the boat home Henry wrote to Lawrence twice, the second a long letter ostensibly analysing Lawrence's character, but in reality very revealing about his own image of himself:

You have developed to the nth degree the art of diplomacy, tact, grace. . . . Awareness of self has made you aware of other men. . . . You have developed a sense of form that transcends the ordinary ideas of noblesse oblige. . . . I should think there are very few men with whom yourself is unlimited or even freed: so you must be a rather sad, or lonely, man at times. . . . I would say you see things almost as the sun sees them – the sun who has given them life, therefore knows them without the antagonisms of competition. Love is surely clarity, an almost secret sharing of the sun's vision among a very few people.

Letter copy in HWLEA, dated May 1934

The boat docked at Southampton in the early hours of 14 May, and Henry took the train to London where he was met by John Heygate, and then drank too much at the Cafe Royal and was overtired, not getting to bed until 3.30 a.m. The next day he went to see Ann Thomas; 'very nice. Daughter Rosemary charming', and two days later went on to Bickley to the Edmonds, and spent the Whitsun weekend there, although the visit was not altogether successful as everyone was a bit strained: 'ACE, on Saturday, turned up with a £5 second-hand motorcycle, which I thought was a dud but didn't thank God, say so.' Henry told her he had planned to buy her a Triumph (motorcycle) for her birthday, but could not afford it, to which she pertly replied that what she actually wanted was 'an MG Midget car'.

Henry returned to Shallowford on 22 May and once home his first entry in his diary states: 'Very quiet here in the Bray valley, nothing doing.' Waiting for him was a letter from Harrison Smith dated 4 May 1934 confirming his thoughts about the 'novel-biography' in the wake of their last brief conversation in New York. The publishers found the book 'sensitive, beautifully written, tragic'. But they could not see a sale for it unless it became all biography *or* all novel, which would sell better, but which would mean radical revision of the content to make the book more homogeneous. The letter is very sound in analysis and very carefully and delicately written. While Henry found the rejection of this book a tremendous blow, he does not seem to have considered altering it. Neither did he make any effort to get the 'novel-biography' published in England; possibly because he had written that immediate storm out of his system and was content to let it lie, and/or because he realized that the time was not yet ripe for such a book. When it was eventually published, Henry wrote in his Introduction that at this time the American publishers had thought the book was 'too English and too old fashioned' for the American market. This never did sound very convincing, and was not, of course, what the publishers had actually said. It was one of Henry's more awkward introductions, which would have been better left out.

Annie Rawle was back in residence at Shallowford after an absence elsewhere, 'with a badger cub in the kitchen', a story related in *The Children of Shallowford*. Gipsy went down with cystitis immediately on his return so the planned trip for the family to camp in the Field and Hut had to be postponed; this irritated Henry and, as he admitted in his diary, most of his fine resolutions were broken within hours. A further blow to his ego came when Tunnicliffe wrote to say that the portrait of Henry had been rejected by the Royal Academy. Henry was to take charge of it in due course, although there is no record of how much he paid for this portrait. To Tunnicliffe's horror Henry proposed collecting the painting in the open Alvis! 'Tunny' managed to persuade him that it should be sent, carefully packed, by rail. Meanwhile Henry employed his energies writing a short story, 'The Maiden Salmon', the idea for which had come to him while he was staying with Tunnicliffe having the portrait painted.

Towards the end of May 1934 T.E. Lawrence wrote to say that he had been reading a proof copy of *Winged Victory* which he found 'admirable, admirable, admirable'. Henry and Victor Yeates had been writing to each other regularly. All along Henry had called Yeates's book 'A Test To Destruction', while Yeates called it 'Winged Victory'. Henry was quite put out about this (but its non-use here meant he had it in reserve for his own title for volume eight of the *Chronicle* in due course). *Winged Victory* was published in June 1934; oddly there was no mention of the occasion or of Yeates in Henry's diary at this time at all. Yeates sent a copy; the printed dedication states:

> To Henry Williamson at whose suggestion this book was begun,
> with whose help it was written and ended.

Underneath Yeates wrote a manuscript about the genesis of the book.[38]

Letters between them show that a review by the poet G.W.M. Dunn upset Henry, though Yeates seems to have quite liked it, until Henry pointed out how damning it actually was. Yeates, who had read Dunn's poems with pleasure, quoted Dunn as saying 'Wholly praiseworthy'. Henry wrote back a fairly waspish letter: 'Who is Dunn? Why were those verses printed?' He outlined what he had wanted for the publication – a more or less anonymous book with a dedication to the anonymous author of *Gold Falcon*. Henry had intended that the reader should think it had been written by him and so buy it; it would thereby earn a lot of publicity and only *then* would the name of the author leak out. Henry did have enough grace to put at the end 'This is an awful letter. Don't react from it', but he still sent it. He urged Yeates to start writing again immediately, 'the novel about family life'. Yeates said he would as soon as he could summon up energy, and was soon doing 500 words daily. He now signed himself 'Wingless Victor'.

On 2 June Ann Thomas arrived for a holiday, seemingly without Rosemary, and he and Ann went to the Field at Ox's Cross. There they worked on the garden and bathed in the sea for a few days and then Henry drove her back to Tenterden via the New Forest, for a brief visit to Lymington where John Heygate was staying with his father who was very ill. Having delivered Ann to her home he then drove down to Southampton to meet Barbara Sincere who was arriving from America. The boat was delayed and he had to return to London, very tired after so much driving and the anti-climax, and thus irritable. However, the two met up eventually and after they had attended that year's Hawthornden ceremony, visited the Edmonds at Bickley, and then drove down to stay with Petre and Jill Mais in Brighton for a few days, Henry finally taking Barbara on to Shallowford on 14 June, where Gipsy was still ill in bed. Barbara stayed for a few days only; Henry's diary records that she was 'quiet and withdrawn', and she soon left for London.

Henry was overjoyed in June 1934 to receive a letter from the Poet Laureate, John Masefield, who wrote to say how much he had enjoyed *The Pathway*, that very few modern stories had such power and that he was thrilled to find himself mentioned and quoted. Henry pasted this letter into the front of his own copy of the limited edition of *The Pathway*, with a second letter received later (neither is dated). The latter states that Masefield had now read the previous volumes of the tetralogy and that the work is an 'astonishing achievement' and that although he had read *Tarka* and his other works, these novels are on a far greater scale and yet are 'so delicate'. Masefield wondered if they had possibly passed each other, or even met, in the war 'on the line of the Ancre'. There is a third letter in the archive, again undated, in which Masefield urged Henry to write some poetry as he felt he had more in him than could be uttered in prose.

Life, after the last feverishly hectic twelve months, had now become very quiet and Henry was rather bored, but once the holiday season got under way things livened up. In August Henry and Loetitia and the three older children went to live at the Field, leaving the baby, Robert, in the nursing home for a month. Petre Mais and his wife Jill arrived in Braunton with their eighteen-year-old daughter Priscilla, a lovely girl, who was recovering from a very unpleasant septic leg, the result of a post-operative infection. Henry was ready to fall, and did fall, for this new 'Barleybright', but Priscilla, to his chagrin, was more interested in the young men on the beach.

At the Field Henry and Loetitia did quite a lot of repair work, re-laying the floor in the room over the garage, known as the 'Loft'. Henry had arranged for the building of a garage complex at the end of 1932. He had specified his requirements and left the builders to get on with the job. On completion, when he went to inspect the building before paying the invoice, he did not find things to his liking. He wrote to the builders saying that 'apart from the fact that the window frame let in the driving rain where it failed to meet the window, that the door was two inches too small for its frame, that the walls were out of perpendicular . . . ' he was quite satisfied with the work!

This large garage with its overhead Loft was situated just inside the top gate[39] and was most substantial, more so than the Hut, with a set of steep, open barn stairs going up, and certainly liveable in. The present repairs were in preparation for a visit from the Edmonds family who were coming for the holidays. They arrived on 7 August 'at Morte Hoe station, I met them with trailer. They brought 17 boxes, trunks, grips etc with tennis rackets and golf clubs, Ann her motorcycle and John his ferret.'

On 10 August ACE joined the 'Barum Flying Club – spends much time there'. This was at nearby Chivenor; 'Barum' is an old word for Barnstaple. At the end of the month the Edmonds gave a big party to which Henry was, of course, invited but to which he decided not to turn up, going to bed in the Hut instead. Then, in the middle of the night, he got up and in the moonlight chucked turnips through the open window into the Loft where the Edmonds family were sleeping – and was surprised that Edith Edmonds did not find it funny!

Henry went to see ACE at the flying club and wrote in his diary that people said 'that she had more guts than anyone they've met, for flying. Knows no fear . . . I'm afraid of her.' Her parents went home leaving Ann in lodgings in the village so that she could continue her lessons and get her 'A' certificate – her pilot's licence to go solo. At some point Henry too decided to have flying lessons. When they landed after the first lesson the pilot walked rapidly away from the plane and, according to family folklore, exploded: 'I am never going to take that man up in a plane ever again. He can't take instruction and is a totally dangerous liability!'

Henry was doing rather less writing than usual. He prepared the material to go into *The Linhay on the Downs*, which included, apart from the title story previously printed in the 1929 limited edition, a selection of articles from the *Sunday Referee* series and a middle section, 'Essays on Books and Authors', which makes a very odd and uncomfortable addition. Jonathan Cape did not like this addition and also queried the fact that the book was not 'continuous prose'. This referred to the fact that Cape had contracted for three 'continuous prose' books, with advances of £250 for each. He also pointed out that most of the book had already appeared in the press and suggested that it should, therefore, have a separate contract with an advance of only £100. Henry's diary entry shows that he persuaded Cape 'that *Linhay* was a continuous prose work, but I would accept £200 advance instead of £250'.

At the beginning of September he began a new series for the *Sunday Referee*. Also during September he tried to persuade Victor Yeates to fill in an application form for a grant from the Royal Literary Fund which he was trying to organise on Yeates' behalf, but Yeates could hardly be bothered with it and kept putting it off. Henry now decided to write a play around *Winged Victory*. He wrote asking Yeates to sign a letter giving him a free hand and suggested they split any royalties equally.

Ann Thomas came for another visit for the last part of September and when she returned on 1 October, Henry began *Devon Holiday*, writing it over the skeleton pages relict from the original version of *On Foot in Devon*. By 6 October he had written 60,000 words and by 15 October noted, 'worked all day & at 11.30 p.m. wrote the last words. I am sad it is over. I feel it is lovely, light, full of fun & joie de vivre, & just the right touch everywhere.'

The walk undertaken by HW, Masterson Funicular Hengist Zeale (Petre Mais) and Scylla (always assumed to be Mais's wife Jill, but more probably Priscilla, their daughter – or a combination of both), the Assistant Professor of Comparative Literature (Herbert Faulkner West), and the Scribe, did not take place in quite the same way as it is recorded in *Devon Holiday*. The Mais family were frequently in the area and Henry certainly saw a great deal of them, and they did go for walks together. But it is not possible to place the American professor nor the Scribe there at the same time. Using the writer's licence to alter the facts to suit the medium, Henry had them all come together to provide a credible setting for a series of yarns which were, as he said, 'light, full of fun & joie de vivre' – not to be taken seriously.

The Scribe is a mixture of several scribes, including Barbara Krebs, and a young woman who had written to Henry in the summer of 1933, who had read his books and loved them, loved Jefferies' books and was an aspiring author herself. She was taken on as the modern version of the ancient 'scribe' and came to live at Shallowford, but almost immediately quarrelled with Henry and left precipitously.

In *Devon Holiday* the Scribe also disappears, to reappear later – ostensibly the same person in the book but a very different person in real life. For the Scribe to whom 'The Maiden Salmon' is dedicated was neither Barbara Krebs nor the young woman whose employment as scribe ended so abruptly. 'The Maiden Salmon' is Ann Edmonds who never was his scribe. 'The Maiden Salmon' is a symbolic tale even if one is unfamiliar with its background, and once more death proves the only cathartic end for an unrequited love.

Ann Edmonds would not appear to have been aware of the intensity of Henry Williamson's feelings for her. She did indeed become a pilot and in 1981, as Ann Welch, was awarded the Gold Air Medal of the Fédération Aeronautique Internationale in recognition of her distinguished career in aviation and for her devotion to the training and encouragement of young pilots.[40]

Ever since the family's move to Shallowford, Henry had had the idea for a book about a salmon at the back of his mind, a book whose story would parallel that of *Tarka the Otter*. Much of his time was spent in laying the groundwork for this, although it is not clear which came first: whether his cleaning and improving of the Bray and his experiments with trout rearing and the making of dams and so on were deliberate attempts to learn the background of his subject, or whether out of all this occupation the genesis of the book grew.

At the beginning of 1933, when he was in London for John Galsworthy's funeral, Henry had discussed a book about a salmon with Richard de la Mare at Faber. On 24 February 1933 de la Mare wrote to say that he had given considerable thought to 'your book on THE SALMON' and that he was very excited at the prospect of publishing it 'later on'. He had spoken to his fellow directors and they wanted to make a definite bid 'now', and offer 'an advance of £600 on account of a royalty of 20%'. But matters went no further at this stage, no contract was signed and no advance paid (as Henry tended to suggest). Presumably Henry would not commit himself as he was not ready to write the book. It was not until September 1934 that the topic was broached again. Henry visited London on 19 September and although he only recorded seeing Cape about *Linhay on the Downs*, he must also have seen Richard de la Mare and talked about the proposed salmon book, for a letter dated 24 September arrived from de la Mare with a definite offer: £750, £250 each on signing the contract, delivering the manuscript, and on publication, with a royalty of 20 per cent, and although he realized Henry did not want to commit himself to a delivery date, nevertheless they were 'thinking of the end of April with publication in the autumn'.

Henry himself now suggested a quite extraordinary move to insure Faber against loss: he handed over the manuscript of his novel-autobiography, *The Sun in the Sands*, as security. The contract was sent and duly signed and on 1 October Ann Thomas took it and the manuscript to London and personally handed them over. De la Mare wrote to Henry later that day sending the cheque for the first advance, 'The manuscript shall be put into our vaults at once, and it won't be disturbed until you give the word.' Henry received this on 3 October, referring to the new book in his diary as 'Atlantic Salmon'. On 7 October he went out to observe the River Taw from Umberleigh to Junction Pool on the Mole to get his salmon material started, taking, as he noted in his diary:

notes of various weirs and stretches. Watched peal & salmon ascending Head
Weir & Fullabrook. Got many valuable notes. Later went there with Windles &
stayed at Head Weir until dark. I handled several peal which leapt and slithered
on the weir face at the edge of the grass. Carried one small peal to the pool
above. These were spotted sea-trout and peal – two distinct species.

Diary entry, 7 October 1934

The following day he took Loetitia to the weir and recorded that later in the day he

spun with 4ft. steel rod & Pfleuzer reel in Bridge Pool in deer park, hooked &
played for ½hr. 8lb salmon, which I tailed eventually with help of all the
Shallowford folk. Didn't have a licence but didn't blow the gaff on myself. Had
a big yellow spinner & steel trace, 20lbs breaking strain. The fish took slowly
lazily under the alder on the other side of the pool. I've always fished wrongly
so far, I can see. Spinning from the wrong bank. This is the first salmon I've
taken in Devon. Telegraphed for Tunnicliffe to come down & sketch.

Tunnicliffe dutifully travelled all night and arrived on the 9.39 a.m. train on
Tuesday 9 October at Filleigh Station. 'He loved the sight of water, me fishing etc.,
& we went down to Head Weir & saw some grand views of fish jumping.' Tunny
left on Friday 12 October, 'having many terrific ideas and sketches'.

The Linhay on the Downs was published on 12 November 1934. A review in
The Times said that it might have taken its name from any of the forty essays in
the book and was unenthusiastic. Henry was devastated, as his diary entry shows:
'Oh God, when will people see that I can *write* better than anyone living today? A
generation to come I guess – when I am dead.'

On Sunday 18 November he recorded that he had finished the sixth revision of
Devon Holiday, 'a book which I had told myself during writing that I would *not*
revise it'. The same day he recorded that there were no reviews in the Sunday
papers of *Linhay* and that he had sent a synopsis of *Winged Victory* to
R. Humphries 'Screen Services Ltd'. On 29 November he went to London to see
Waveney Girvan and Humphries 'about the film producing company discussed at
Woolacombe last August'. On 1 December he recorded 'My birthday, 38 today'
(He was actually thirty-nine!)

During November he sent Victor Yeates a cheque for £25 – which he said was
return for a gift made by the Royal Literary Fund to help him when he started out
and which he was now reimbursing, not direct to the fund but indirectly to Yeates.
Yeates returned it immediately, but Henry sent it back again by return. Then, on
23 November, Henry received a note from Norah Yeates to say Victor was in the
Fairlight Sanatorium, Hastings.

Henry evidently wrote about his hurt over *Linhay* to T.E. Lawrence for on 11
December Lawrence wrote him a letter of good cheer, telling him that he was a
good writer, and not to vex himself over reviewers. Henry's answer of the next day
was typical; doom and gloom had disappeared and he was full of elation about his

scheme to form a film company and to make a film of *Tarka* and hoped Lawrence would involve himself in this. Also that he was trying to make a play out of *Winged Victory* and would be glad of Lawrence's help. He ended by inviting Lawrence for Christmas.

On 16 December Henry drove from Filleigh to see Ann Thomas at Tenterden, spending several hours en route with Petre and Jill Mais in Brighton, taking them to the cinema and out to supper. On the Monday morning he and Ann went back to Sussex. After lunch they went on to the Fairlight Sanatorium to see Victor Yeates to discuss the play version of *Winged Victory* only to learn that he had died at 7.30 a.m. the previous Saturday morning. Norah Yeates had written to him immediately, but of course Sunday held the post up, and he had already left anyway. Henry and Ann went on to Winchelsea, where they stopped for tea, and Henry wrote in his diary: 'Weak winter sunlight over the green distances of Romney Marsh; an aeroplane stunting over the houses, half rolls & flat spins and Immelmann turns. Thought of Yeates up there, free and happy in the sunlight; but no, the lad was lying dead in that chill sanatorium.'

The next day he called in at Yeates's home where he found his ten-year-old son alone eating a sandwich, and tried to offer him comfort by talking about the naturalness of death without grief – 'he a little dark-eyed boy with sensitive sweet face, his dear Daddy gone & no money left in the house'. He recorded that he wrote an obituary for *The Times* which was published on Christmas Eve. The following day he called again at 569 Sidcup Road and saw Norah Yeates 'whose conventional (although natural perhaps) attitude of grief I tried to dissolve'. After a short while, though, she grated on his nerves and he went off in some irritation.

Lawrence wrote to say that he felt the death of Yeates as a direct loss to himself although he had never met him. He also said that he could not manage Christmas as he was already engaged.

Henry sent £5 to the Yeates family to help with some Christmas cheer for the children. This friendly gesture, was, however, completely negated by a quarrel which subsequently arose over a tribute Henry had written for *John O'London's Weekly*. Norah objected to the emphasis laid on Victor's illness and wanted a more cheerful aspect presented. In his annoyance that she had dared question his judgement Henry wrote her a long letter which, rather unforgivably, included this wounding and uncalled-for comment: 'I have said nothing about V's homelife, altho' I suspected, from his general attitude to life and some of his letters, that he was not always cheerful and happy' (letter in HWLEA, dated January 1935).

Norah Yeates never really forgave him for this gibe, but she continued to cooperate with him, no doubt because she recognized that Henry was genuinely trying to do his best for Victor and his work. Henry persevered with the Royal Literary Fund grant and was able to procure some funds for the family. He also wanted her to hand over control of the play/film scripts for *Winged Victory*, the original typescript 'Adjustment', and the new unfinished manuscript fragment *Family Life*, which she did, but begged him to be absolutely certain to alter only what was really necessary, and to remember, for Victor's sake, his 'no, no, no, no'.

John O'London's Weekly published 'Henry Williamson's Personal Tribute to V.M. Yeates' on 26 January 1935, and this was later incorporated into an introduction Henry wrote for a second impression of *Winged Victory*.[41] Lawrence wrote again at the end of January thanking Henry for sending the *John O'London* article about Yeates, which he had read with a sense of shame that the man had been allowed to die. Henry then wrote a postcard telling him about the 50,000 word 'fragment' *Family Life* which he was hoping

> Faber will publish between an Introduction and an Epilogue by me, thus making its form. . . . In my next book, potboiler, there is a long account of a meeting on the Berengaria between me, a nameless friend, and G.B. Everest, an 'expert mechanic and authority on skycloclartactic impulses in supermarine craft.' Garnett reported that it seemed dragged in to the book. So it was. The whole book was dragged in, and dragged out also. . . . It is called DEVON HOLIDAY and I hope it will amuse 10% of readers, but doubt it.
>
> Postcard copy in HWLEA, dated February 1935

At the beginning of 1935 Henry managed to create one of his little 'joke' fiascos – he carved his owl symbol and initials on the bar at the Savage Club, and shortly after received a letter of reprimand from the secretary. His diary records that the day before a friend had mentioned to him that his owl actually looked like a phallic symbol with hairs, which had slightly shocked Henry, and now he put two and two together and realized that this was what the Savage Club thought he had drawn. He wrote a letter of apology and explanation – and resigned. The chairman of the committee wrote back saying that 'on his own responsibility' he had withdrawn the letter of resignation but repeating that he had been shocked to hear of the incident.

The situation between Henry and Loetitia was once again strained and to ease things, in the middle of the month it was arranged that she should go to Tenterden. It was felt that Ann's sister, who was then in a very nervous condition due to her personal circumstances, should not be left on her own there and Loetitia should go to look after things while Ann Thomas went to work at Shallowford.

On 23 January Henry 'started to write ATLANTIC SALMON at 7.15 p.m.' The next day 'wrote another 850 words of *Salar the Leaper*'. Ann Thomas was also writing a novel of her own, a fictionalized account of her life with Henry which was to be published as *Women Must Love* under the pseudonym Julia Hart Lyon by Faber in 1937. Interestingly, the character modelled on Loetitia is called Alethea in her book.

On Valentine's Day Loetitia informed Henry that she was once again 'with child', news he was not very pleased to hear. Prophetically, the forthcoming child was referred to with great certainty as 'young Master Richard'. Meanwhile Henry continued to work slowly on *Salar*. His spirits were lifted when, in the middle of March, he 'heard from Edward Weeks of Boston [USA] that he wants to be my

American publisher. Hurrah.' Edward Weeks was director of *Atlantic Monthly* Publishing Inc. In April further enthusiastic letters followed from Weeks and from his colleague, the editor of *Atlantic Monthly*, Ellery Sedgwick – 'They are keen on *Tales of My Children*', articles he was writing for serialization in their magazine. Henry captured the essence of childhood in these pieces, which were the basis for *The Children of Shallowford*. It is sometimes difficult to remember that ordinary family life continued in tandem with all the frenetic activity in Henry's own life. He was very fond of his children, as is evident from his very sympathetic treatment of them in the *Shallowford* book, which was to include 'John's Book', a journal which John kept at this time when he was off sick from school recovering from a perforated ear-drum. When Henry was in the mood he loved to play wild games with them which tended to get them over-excited, then he would walk away, leaving it to their mother to sort things out. But there is no doubt that he observed them very carefully for he was able to write with great precision and sympathy about their world.

In early May a further cable arrived from Weeks asking for 'Salmon Tss for serial. The first time someone has wanted my stuff in earnest.' He had of course written for the *Atlantic Monthly* right from the beginning but from time to time there was a flurry of rejections which led to a lull before he tried his material placed there again.

Towards the end of April Henry went fishing with John Heygate who was again visiting, and caught a 9 lb salmon in the pool between the waterfall and viaduct. This is the salmon in the photographs in *Goodbye West Country*. Henry seems to have forgotten the 8 pounder from the previous year, referring only to 'the other fish I caught in Islay 3 years ago'.

On 27 April 1935 a telegram arrived for Loetitia from her brother Frank Hibbert from Landcross (Frank had remained behind to look after his father when his brothers had emigrated to Australia): 'Father died suddenly last night.'

John Heygate was still staying with them and the Tunnicliffes had been invited for lunch. ('Tunny' was doing some work on the illustrations for *Salar* and staying in the area.) Henry withheld the sad news from his wife until after they had gone. Loetitia left for Landcross after tea and on 30 April Henry attended the funeral at the 'Church where I was married almost 10 years ago'. Loetitia told him sadly that 'Pa got out of bed & fell and hurt his head, poor darling, and I wasn't there to be with him at the end.' Charles Robert Calvert Hibbert would have been eighty-three on 9 May. He was buried beside his wife, Margaret Dora, in Landcross churchyard.

Henry wrote affectionately in his diary: '"Bill's an ass" remarked the old gentleman after finishing *The Pathway* in which he figures as Sufford Chichester [sic]. I was very fond of him, & admired him much; but he had no imagination. Perhaps he wouldn't have been so good & steady a gentleman if he had: but again, he might have been outstanding.'

A few days later, on 6 May, Henry noted in his diary that it was 'H.M. George 5'ths Jubilee, also 10 years ago I was married.' Henry, Loetitia, Ann and the older

The 9 lb salmon Henry caught in the Bray in April 1935: Henry (above, left);
John Heygate (above, right); Loetitia and Windles (left).

children (Robert and Rosemary were left behind) 'motored to field with flag-flying trailer and made bonfire of furze (etc). Fireworks. We had eggs and bacon in loft & saw at 10 p.m. 27 beacons breaking into small red points of flame in the darkness below and around us.' This party appears as a very happy incident in 'The Beacon on Ox's Cross' in *The Children of Shallowford*. But Henry did not relate there, as he did in his diary, how he nearly spoiled the whole thing by his extreme irritability when the beds in the Loft were not made up to his instructions.

Henry's diary entry for 11 May 1935 shows him busy with Windles who had found a dead salmon in a pool, a big one weighing about 20 lb, and which seemed to have been stabbed by a pitchfork. In the evening he 'wrote to T.E. Lawrence at his cottage near Bovington Camp, asking if I could stay with him on Tuesday next', saying that he was going to London 'and wonder if you will be home then?' moreover that he had been reading: '. . . through Yeates 60,000 fragment FAMILY LIFE. . . . I have the typescript here, and my pencilled alterations above the typing. Would it interest you to see it? I could leave it on Tuesday and pick it up on my return about Friday. . . . I'll call in anyway on Tuesday unless rainy day, probably 1–2 p.m. noon that is. Yours H.W. (Letter copy in HWLEA, dated 11 May 1935.)[42]

On the following day, Sunday, he was in bed with 'filthy influenza cold which has been enfeebling me for days'. He recorded that he had been 'for the past 4 days reading and revising Yeates' posthumous *Family Life*' and had altered about 20 per cent of it – 'keeping faithfully to the spirit of the scenes & book', but he was worried by Norah Yeates who was reluctant to 'entirely trust my judgement and taste'. His letter to Lawrence did not arrive until the Monday morning and Lawrence, realizing that a reply would not reach Henry in time, got out his motorcycle and rode to the nearby post office to send a telegram:

11.25 Bovington Camp   Williamson Shallowford Filleigh
Lunch Tuesday wet fine cottage 1 mile North Bovington Camp —— Shaw

But, as history records, as he returned to his cottage at Clouds Hill Lawrence had an accident, apparently swerving to avoid two young cyclists. Henry's diary entry for Tuesday 14 May 1935 reads:

Heard over the wireless that T.E. Shaw, just after leaving Bovington Camp yesterday morning on his motorcycle collided with a cyclist and now lies 'critically ill' in the military hospital there, with a fractured skull. About an hour after hearing this news I began to ache in the breast; while my thoughts before this were only of myself, of how in some future book I would have a picture of the telegram, the last thing he wrote. Not a dominant thought though: surprise, consternation: then later pity, pity for the thought of his lonely life, bare cottage, aloneness after the things he had dreamed and done and failed, and now, to be lying there with a cracked head. Perhaps Ida's thought of her father lying dead, with a bruised head after the old chap's fall, stirred this pity.

Lawrence was taken to the small military hospital at Bovington Camp where he remained unconscious, being turned and tilted every hour in an endeavour to control the fluid which developed in his lungs.

On Saturday Henry drove in his Alvis to stay with John Heygate who was at his father's house at Keyhaven, near Lymington in Hampshire. On the way he stopped off at Bovington. In the closing paragraph of *Genius of Friendship* he refers to 'the newcomer [i.e. himself]' who 'saw with a slight shock, faces known before only in *Seven Pillars of Wisdom*, but tempered by the years' thought and quietness, men who looked back through the desert of time to that which always shone brighter in lengthening memory. After greeting, it seemed fit that the newcomer, from another world, should travel on.'[43]

During that night a crisis occurred and by morning Lawrence was only just holding on to life: 'A few minutes after eight o'clock, on the 19th May 1935, there was a check in the struggle, the least fluttering sigh. So he died; and is immortal with the shining of the sun upon "plain men, his equals".'[44] From Heygate's house at Keyhaven, Henry wrote to Loetitia later that day:

> Lawrence died at 5 a.m. this morning. I lay with a headache until about then, I wonder –.
>
> I will tell you all about my meeting with his brother and others at Clouds Hill when I return. Sad; and now he will be a legend for ever. The one bright creature of our age *untarnished* by any rumour, failing, weakness. A young strong spirit; the Gods loved him. . . . O but I am sad about T.E. Lawrence. Such an aerial thing is lost. Love, Bill.
>
> P.S. I must be worthy of what he believed in me.
>
> Letter in HWLEA, dated 19 May 1935

Strangely, Henry's diary then becomes blank (apart from a few business details) for the rest of that year – as if his own life had stopped. Yet it was to contain an episode which was to be of grave import in his life. Almost immediately after Lawrence's death, according to a brief reference in his diary, Henry wrote and posted an article about Lawrence to the *Atlantic Monthly* in America.[45]

It was probably sometime now that the young Kenneth Allsop arrived at Shallowford to see his great literary hero. Henry rather palmed him off on Windles, who showed him around the area, to their mutual annoyance. It was Henry whom the young Allsop wanted to see.

But all of Henry's time and energy was directed towards writing the 'salmon' book. Faber wrote in early June to say that they had decided to publish it on 10 October and were advertising it in their autumn list. Therefore to get it written became a matter of extreme urgency and as he finished chapters or sections he sent them straight to Ann Thomas for typing and she in turn sent them straight off to the printers.[46] The last chapters went off at the beginning of August. Extracts were also sent to America where they were to be serialized in *Atlantic Monthly*.

But there was a problem that Henry had to overcome. His publishers were now actually Cape and he had sold this book to Faber. The situation between Henry and Cape had already become a little acrimonious over *Devon Holiday*, when Cape had taken the advice of a lawyer over the possibility of libel actions on several points in the original typescript; Jonathan Cape had enclosed details of a recent libel case as an example of what he meant. Henry had mentioned in his last letter to T.E. Lawrence that 'Mr. Rubinstein [the lawyer] found 15 possible libels in D. Holiday so the page proofs have been cut about awful, and will swallow up all profits if any I guess' (letter copy in HWLEA, dated 10 May 1935).

Henry added a postscript to *Devon Holiday* at the last moment before publication which was inserted on a four page collation at the beginning, giving an extra half-title page to try and fill the blank spaces: 'Since this book was written . . . the character called G.B. Everest has died. . .'. Enough clue was given to reveal the real identity of G.B. Everest!

Henry now seems to have decided to approach Cape obliquely about the matter of Faber publishing *Salar*, casually mentioning 'a new book' in a letter ostensibly about something else. Jonathan Cape put two and two together and wrote him an understandably very hurt and upset letter, dated 13 August 1935, stating that as his publishers they had supported Henry and been very sympathetic to his 'temperamental and financial difficulties' for seven years. Henry obviously did feel very guilty and wrote a long explanation which delved into the whole of his publishing history, most of which was totally irrelevant to the present situation. Jonathan Cape was not amused and sent a rather cold reply, which of course brought out the worst in Henry, who responded equally coldly and sarcastically. The publishing relationship between them was over. Jonathan Cape behaved in a very restrained and dignified manner over this episode, but he was undoubtedly very upset by it. A later letter concerning some reprint editions was sent via Henry's agent and refers to Henry in the third person only

In the meantime at Faber Richard de la Mare was organizing the printing of *Salar the Salmon*; proofs were arriving before the final chapters were written. He then became most alarmed when Henry announced that he was going off to Germany; 'What are you going to do about correcting the proofs of the remainder? Or was that threat to go away merely to frighten me!' (letter in HWLEA, dated August 1935).

There was never any time to rewrite *Salar* even once, unlike the mythical seventeen rewrites of *Tarka*, or even to do more than make the smallest corrections. One must admire the *tour de force* of the organization of his material which must have been in his head from the book's conception. He was often out for hours in all weathers walking the river banks, observing the details needed for an authentic rendering of his subject matter. *Salmon and Trout* magazines were thumbed through and perused with dogged determination. His health suffered and his irritability increased proportionately.[47]

During all this hustle and bustle the next child was born on 1 August; as predicted by Henry the previous February it was 'Master Richard'. Henry had by

The children of Shallowford. John and Windles are standing behind Rosemary, Robert and Margaret, who is holding Richard. Ann Thomas and Annie Rawle are in the background.

then taken himself off to the peace of his Writing Hut in the Field at Ox's Cross for
the hurdle of the last chapters of *Salar*. There is a description of him at this time
from an independent source. For the last year or two a young would-be writer had
attached himself to the periphery of Henry's magnetic sphere, paid visits on his
annual holidays in the area and wrote letters and sent articles and typescripts.
Henry offered him some encouragement. There were of course, many such young
men, and women, over the years. Henry referred to them as his 'staggarts'.[48] This
particular young man, Guy Priest, arrived in the Field towards the end of July, just
as Henry was writing the last chapter of *Salar*. He approached the Hut:

> Before me was the door of weathered oak, studded with hand-forged nails, in its
> centre a tiny lattice like a porthole. I hesitated in some trepidation, then raised
> my hand to knock. At that moment the door suddenly swung back, revealing in
> the opening an unshaven, wild-eyed creature whom I scarcely recognised. He
> studied me for a brief span through half-closed lids. Then he stepped back,
> bidding me enter. 'Come in, I can give you a few minutes. . . . Help yourself to
> lime-juice; it will keep away the scurvy.'[49]

Henry struggled on until the book was finally finished. By then he was involved
in a new venture. *Salar the Salmon* was published in mid-October, not far out,
despite all the problems, from the date of 10 October that Richard de la Mare had
hoped for in early June.

The car is loaded: Windles, John, Rosemary, Robert, Margaret.

CHAPTER 6

THE LAST ROMANTIC

On 1 August 1935 John Heygate wrote enthusiastically to Henry Williamson from Germany where he had a job with the Ufa film studios in Berlin. He had worked for them a year or two previously, writing the British version of film scripts, but had had to leave for health reasons. Heygate was plagued with persistent ill-health in the early 1930s, suffering from what seems to have been a twisted gut, and he had been in and out of clinics until an operation which he had undergone shortly before that meeting with Henry and T.E. Lawrence on the *Berengaria*, which finally sorted it out. For good measure, while he was under the anaesthetic his appendix was removed as well! In spite of such obviously painful interludes Heygate had now had several further books published.[1] His marriage to Evelyn was over and as soon as the divorce was made absolute he was to marry Gwyneth Lloyd, a British film star.

The letter from Germany invited Henry to join Heygate for a holiday in September which was to include a trip to the annual National Socialist Rally at Nürnberg (Nuremberg) – the 'Reichsparteitag'. Heygate had shown his newly published book *Motor Tramp* to the head of the Nazi Press in Berlin who was sufficiently impressed to issue him with the invitation to Nürnberg; Heygate wanted Henry to share in this excitement and so he had also shown the man an article by Henry and suggested that a ticket be issued to 'the finest descriptive pen in England.'[2] Heygate wrote that they were to be escorted by Chemnitzer, one of the heads of the Direction of German Writers. What this article by Henry was is not mentioned, but Chemnitzer told Heygate he would have it translated and published in Germany. Henry Williamson was certainly already known as a writer in Germany where translations of *Tarka* and other titles were available. Henry took a great deal of interest in what was happening in Germany at this time, understandably since he had German blood from his paternal grandmother, Adela Lühn; and his love for the Romantic music of Wagner gives the main clue to his inner being. His acceptance was also coloured by his cathartic experience of the Christmas Truce in 1914 when he had discovered that the ordinary German soldier thought, as the ordinary English soldier did, that he fought for the good of his country and that God was on his side – a revelation which was to be such a profound influence on Henry's life and beliefs. Of course he had an interest in what was happening in Germany! This is not an excuse for what he thought, merely an attempt to explain why he thought as he did, and to show why there was an innate tendency for him to think that way. Many others thought as Henry Williamson did at this time. Some of them had the sense to keep quiet, others have

The Last Romantic.

since recanted. Henry was not a man to do either. It was to cause him a great deal of trouble.

At that time the English newspapers were full of reports of the reforms that Adolf Hitler was instigating. In the mid-1930s much of what Hitler was doing in Germany was considered as exciting innovation, and he was certainly the focus of attention. Henry kept a large bundle of newspaper clippings reporting the circumstances of the death of T.E. Lawrence. Here, side by side with the long reports of Lawrence's accident, his hospitalization and subsequent death, funeral and inquest, are articles about Adolf Hitler. In these clippings headlines about both men appeared side by side: for example, in the *Daily Mail*, 20 May 1935 'LAWRENCE OF ARABIA'S SECRETS REVEALED : TRAGIC IRONY OF HIS DEATH' next to 'VITAL WEEK FOR EUROPE : HITLER'S SPEECH TOMORROW' and in that week's *Sunday Times* there was a short piece on Lawrence by 'Atticus' and on the reverse a long article HITLER AND AIR WAR' by 'Scrutator':

> A LIVING ISSUE OF HUMANITY – IF THERE IS BLUFF – CALL IT
> . . . A speech by Herr Hitler which everyone in the world might overhear has stimulated more hopeful discussion than anything he may have said in imperfectly reported private conversation and it was followed on the next day by a no less remarkable speech by Mr. Baldwin and a helpful debate in Parliament. . . . Herr Hitler says – that if we could end the inhumanity of bombing it would do more for peace and security than all the pacts of assistance and military conventions. . . . The nature of Herr Hitler's speech fully justifies – the Government's policy of persisting in negotiation.
> . . . Some may believe in Herr Hitler's sincerity; some may not.
> . . . History would accuse us with equal bitterness if Herr Hitler was indeed sincere and we had not examined with diligence and candour the proferred help in a great task. . . .
>
> *Sunday Times*, 26 May 1935, p. 17; cutting in HWLEA

Also reports of what was seen by everyone as a greatly exciting event, the 'GERMAN MOTOR ROAD OPENED BY HITLER', which was reported in all the papers, while a page from the *Daily Mail* for 4 June 1935, included a long article by Lord Rothermere which opened and closed thus:

> The most prominent figure in the world today is Adolf Hitler. His master-mind magnetises the whole field of foreign politics. . . .
> It is reassuring to see Herr Hitler's speech just over a week ago has greatly influenced his popularity in this country. I am profoundly convinced that the better he is known to the mass of the British Nation the higher its appreciation of him will be and the closer will become the relations between the two nations.

Multiply such news coverage over the weeks, months and even years, and it is clear that news of Hitler at this time tended to be optimistic rather than pessimistic. It is very easy with hindsight to condemn Hitler as a totally evil man who was responsible for some of the most appalling atrocities ever committed. In the mid-1930s this may not have been so straightforward. There were people who had doubts and were very worried by what they perceived of the situation, but there were also many others who took Hitler and his reforms at face value, on trust, having no inkling of the terrible pitfalls that lay ahead. Henry Williamson at this time was one of the latter. From letters in the archive it is obvious that Henry was already occasionally mentioning the name of Hitler in his letters to other people. For instance, a letter from the editor of the *Atlantic Monthly* dated 29 March 1935, mentions 'What you have to say of Hitler puts for me a new complexion on your thoughts, and I am greatly interested in your remarks.' It would be 'greatly interesting' to know what those remarks had been.

Henry's letter to his wife on learning of Lawrence's death is quite revealing about the way his psyche operated. He had set Lawrence up on a pedestal; 'the one bright creature of our age *untarnished* by any rumour, failing, weakness . . . the Gods loved him' (letter in HWLEA; see Chapter 5). Later, he was unable to accept that Lawrence might have had flaws. Now he put Hitler up on a pedestal in the same way. He could not, would not, accept that his idols had feet of clay. The juxtaposition of the names of Lawrence and Hitler in the newspapers at this very emotional moment for Henry Williamson – the death of two of his greatest friends, Victor Yeates and T.E. Lawrence, following one after the other – may well have given rise to his subsequent avowal that he had been going to see Lawrence on a matter connected with peace and later hinted that this was connected with Hitler. The thought occurred to Henry; he wanted it to be so; he imagined the scene; and he then believed it had happened. There are many instances of this fiction / fact transference in his life and writing and this is but another example. For it is not until the end of April 1936 that we find the first reference to what can only be called the 'myth' that Henry Williamson created about himself and T.E. Lawrence (a whole year after Lawrence's death) and a peace plan involving Adolf Hitler. It lies in a press cutting dated 23 April 1936 from the *Dorset County Chronicle* in which the reporter quotes an item from the current issue of *Radio Pictorial*. Headed 'Lawrence's Last Journey – Why He Made Fatal Ride' and states:

> The famous naturalist, Henry Williamson, now broadcasting regularly from West, has disclosed a hitherto closely kept secret about Lawrence of Arabia – a tragic secret, because it concerns his death. Henry had a big idea for a series of programmes for the support of world peace to be broadcast on a large scale from the Albert Hall. He wanted a partner to support his plan, and wrote suggesting it to Lawrence of Arabia. T.E. Shaw sprang at the idea with his full enthusiasm, rushed out of his cottage immediately, and jumped onto his motorcycle to go and wire Henry that he would support him. Returning from the post-office, T.E. Shaw was killed in the accident which shocked the world.

Henry has dropped the idea for the time being. 'There is not another man I can think of who would be so equal to it as he would have been,' he says.

Press cutting in HWLEA, dated 23 April 1936

It is not possible to decide what really made Henry embark on this path. We know it is a fabrication; his last letter to T.E. Lawrence contained nothing of the idea.

However, a most revealing letter came to light in the archive files which adds another dimension to the story. It was from Henry Williamson to Jan Mills Whitham, a writer friend who lived nearby, and had attached to it another letter. It has no date. (Henry was very particular about other people dating their letters but frequently lax on this point himself.) However, it was almost certainly written in the spring of 1934:

Dear Jan,
I thought this might interest you. The writer is John Heygate. . .

[P.S.] It may amuse you to learn what the balanced and charming young Heygate thinks of Nazism. I am for Hitler as a man; but I fear his Nazis may be, a few, awful blackguards. They would be so under any regime. But Heygate talks of the men he knows; the men in the street. He more perfectly knows the men in the street than anyone else I know. . . .

Letter in HWLEA, date est. as spring 1934

The letter from John Heygate was written from the Austrian Tyrol, 18 March (it mentions Henry's visit to USA thus the year is 1934, and indeed the next letter, also from Heygate, still in its envelope and from Prague, is postmarked April 1934). Heygate was on his own and had travelled to Austria from Germany. He wrote that Henry could have no idea how wracked and creaking Europe was, except for the Germans who were young, strong, inspired, and open-faced. But that the other countries were terrified, especially where, as in Austria, people were literally starving and were torn between supporting the German Nazi movement and the Roman Catholic Church.

He described his journey along the snow-bound roads at night – quite an exhilarating ride as he was a wild driver – through the Brenner Pass, where he could not find a single hotel that *had* a guest and so refused to stop. His journey was not without purpose. He was distributing a bundle of the forbidden (in Austria) Nazi paper *The Red Eagle* which the exiled head of the Austrian Nazi Party, Herr Hofer, had given him in Munich. Hence he needed other people in the guest houses – to cover his own movements. He explained how careful he had to be and how the transactions were carried out in the WC, and what a wonderfully interesting story this underground fight for Nazism in Austria was; that the whole country was organized in secret lodges; how daring runners crossed the mountain frontier every day from Germany to relay news by word of mouth; and how flaring swastikas suddenly appeared on the mountains hacked out of the snow, because the Nazis, who carried out this work, could climb better and higher than the others, who could not get to them to obliterate them. 'It is only a matter of time.'

This would have been part of the run-up to the annexation of the Austrian border country – where many of the population were of German origin – by Germany. The Anschluß proved the death blow of the Roman-Catholic dominated Austrian government, and disquieted the rest of Europe, but not so sufficiently at this point for them to be spurred to retaliate.

Heygate was actually on a 'recuperative' trip after his operation and must have left for Germany directly after seeing Henry off on the *Berengaria* with Lawrence. After Austria he went on to Prague, where he stayed for some time. Heygate obviously saw nothing wrong in what he was doing. Whether he was in earnest or whether it was just another 'St George of Georgeham' prank for him, it is not possible to tell. He was capable of the most extraordinarily wild behaviour.[3] And he was also dependent at this time on the German regime for his living.[4] The content of this letter appears in his book *Motor Tramp*[5] as a very long, hilarious tale; although portrayed as reading *The Red Eagle* he is not actually distributing it deliberately, rather by accident. There are very funny references to a code whereby scratching one's head denotes one to be a Nazi sympathizer. In the book he doesn't realize this and creates havoc by scratching his head but not going on to the next coded step. There are, also, photographs of Nazi leaders and the 'flaring swastikas' cut out of the mountain snow, exactly as described in his letter to Henry.

There is also a newspaper cutting in Henry's archive of a long article written by John Heygate in October 1931 of which the subject matter was 'pride of race': 'To have a real meaning the State must unite every member of the nation in one great fellowship. . . . If its people do *not* feel pride of race a nation is nothing but a geographical fact.' One paragraph states: 'In Germany Hitler seeks to bind youth and vigour in a political movement of blood-brotherhood; the Hitlerites see the gap between State and person.' It ends: 'There are innumerable young men like me who are waiting for a great leader.'[6] In view of this one cannot, therefore, entirely dismiss the Austrian trip as a jape.

Henry Williamson was very influenced by Heygate. He was extremely impressed by his aristocratic background and his Eton and university education. The correspondence between them was prolific and they saw each other frequently. Henry referred to Heygate several times in his letters to Lawrence in glowing terms, for example: 'Heygate's a fine blade of a man – the most graceful man I know' (letter in HWLEA, dated 29 March 1930). Henry would have taken on board unquestioningly the opinions expressed by Heygate on these matters, regardless of whether Heygate himself was actually being serious. For, although less obviously than T.E. Lawrence, Sir Oswald Mosley and Adolf Hitler, John Heygate was actually another of Henry's 'hero' figures.

Heygate insisted on paying Henry's passage on the *Bremen*, to leave Southampton on 5 September.[7] Henry needed a break after the mammoth exertions of writing *Salar* and he decided to take advantage of such a generous

A self-portrait in the mirror, Adlon Hotel,
Germany, 1935.

and interesting – exciting even – offer. He put Ann Thomas in charge of the final
processes of *Salar the Salmon* and sailed on the *Bremen* as planned. A full account
of this visit can be found in *Goodbye West Country*, where Henry shows that he
was very impressed with everything he saw and heard, all of which reinforced his
positive thoughts of Hitler as an ex-soldier of the First World War. He believed
Hitler to be a man with inspired ideas about afforestation, agricultural reform, a
youth movement akin to the great Boy Scout movement (of which Henry had been
a member as a boy) with a yearning to create order out of chaos – a principle that
was very close to Henry's own heart; and as an ex-soldier, incapable of wanting
the hell of another war.

Heygate also wrote about this visit in his book *These Germans* published at the
beginning of the Second World War.[8] This provides interesting and readable
background to the historical circumstances leading up to this war. It is significant
that towards the end of the book Heygate apparently changed his previously held
views and the book increasingly denounces Hitler and fascism.

Henry and his visit are introduced but Heygate decides that he is so well known
that he must be anonymous – so well known, in fact, that the description of him is
instantly recognizable:

Travelling to Nürnberg in John Heygate's MG.

From a blade of grass or the flash of a fish's tail he can evoke a whole philosophy. He is so well known that I shall not give his name. I shall call this third member of the Nürnberg Rally Expedition simply by his initials, H.W.

H.W., forty-one, ex-soldier from the Great War, was a man who was not only in search of a philosophy of *Nature*, . . . Like other writers who lived through that war . . . this soldier-poet was in search of the formula for lasting Peace. He believed that this formula must exist. . . . H.W. himself put his faith into his most serious book: the idea of the one-soldier who died for all. But the vision of a re-born Christianity soon faded. The Christmas candle of peace lighted on the parapet of the trenches was never seen again. Hundreds and thousands of these ex-soldiers, cheated of their dream, went about looking for a new hope, a new religion, a new Leader.

These Germans

While the passage is an incisive analysis of Henry Williamson's creed, it can hardly have preserved his anonymity! Heygate's description of the Nürnberg Rally which follows gives the impression that he was personally somewhat bored by it all and stayed aloof. Whether that was really so or not, we cannot know.

Interestingly, at the point at which Heygate starts to denounce Hitler his style changes radically, becoming very flamboyant and excessive. In his own copy of *These Germans* Henry has marked some passages here, and written in some somewhat petulant notes. Although they appear to reflect on Heygate's style rather than the content as such, e.g. 'come, come, my dear fellow', it is clearly the latter that is really irritating him. Heygate's *volte face* had pulled the rug from under Henry's feet. He influenced Henry's thinking about Hitler, now he had changed course. Henry was understandably annoyed. Under John Heygate's inscription, 'To my old friend Bill – Barnstaple to Nürnberg – Heil Friendship! John Heygate 1940', Henry has later added 'Note by HW. May 1963. I greatly regret my superficial comments on some of my old friend's writing in this book'. By then he had come to terms with the blow dealt by his great friend.

Although Henry did not publicly and definitely recant his ideas about Hitler he did actually modify them. He illustrated this by equating Hitler with Lucifer, the Fallen Angel, equal with Christ but who had chosen to be Satan, showing that he did recognize Hitler as a force of evil, a thesis that first appeared in an article he wrote for the *Adelphi* in 1943, entitled 'The Tragic Spirit'[9] where he contrasts the steadfastness of Christ who remained true to his ideals with the tragic fall of Hitler: '. . . when men of authentic genius change, the spirit of Man is wounded . . . thereafter the star burns sultry, then black. In my lifetime I have known such a tragedy.' He developed this theme in Volume 14 of the *Chronicle, Lucifer Before Sunrise*, but this was not published until the late 1960s, and even at that time his message was not truly understood (possibly deliberately misunderstood by some).

Henry's philosophy was to 'see things truly, as the sun sees them, without shadows'. This included being objective about events that are part of history. These things happened and this is how they happened. But in trying to be objective Henry managed to blind himself to what was really happening. Henry saw Hitler, like himself, as an ex-soldier of the First World War, and he transposed his own thoughts and feelings on to the Führer. He seized on the idealism that was possibly once the germ of Hitler's original philosophy, in the same way that the germ of the original philosophy of communism was idealistic and was meant to be a force for good. The origins of fascism arose in Italy in the First World War as an anti-communist movement, and as such was considered a power for good, relieving much oppression among the populace, and creating heroes out of its leaders. It was only later that fascism itself became oppressive and evil.

Despite all that has been ascribed to him, Henry Williamson was not a fascist in the normally understood sense of the word. He was not a political sophisticate, in fact everything points to the conclusion that he was politically naive. Seen in the context of his life and his life's work, any leanings he may have had towards particular aspects of the ideology of fascism can be seen to form but a small fraction of the whole. This small fraction has been seized upon and exaggerated on many occasions by those with their own axe to grind, particularly by the fascists themselves who have found in him a very useful mouthpiece, and equally by those who have wanted to see Henry Williamson denigrated, sometimes as a way of paying off old scores. Some of this has been entirely his own fault; because, unfortunately, he himself fuelled the fire which has all too easily been fanned into flames over the years. His naive analysis has puzzled and upset many people, who cannot equate his writings with his apparent political ideas: this was partly due to his own stubbornness, for he brooked no argument against his own ideas and opinions, but also, possibly because the wrong conclusions have been drawn.

Henry was interested in certain aspects of fascist ideals and he did become a member of the British Union of Fascists in due course, but he was not attracted to this for its political content. A detailed analysis of Henry Williamson's involvement with fascism can be found in J.W. Blench, 'Henry Williamson: The Romantic Appeal of Fascism', printed in the *Durham University Journal* in 1988.[10] In this article Dr Blench goes a certain way along the road of analysing elements of Romanticism in the fascist movement, but it is possible to pursue this further. For study of the roots of fascism reveals a very interesting aspect. It may be said that they really lie in the Romantic movement of the nineteenth century. Lay the parameters of the Romantic movement and fascism side by side and you will find that they are almost identical. Henry Williamson actually was, in fact, a twentieth-century Romantic – the last Romantic. Viewed in this light there surfaces a far truer picture of the underlying force that governed Henry Williamson's life and work. Within its framework we can assimilate his leaning towards fascism, but we can see that fascism itself was not his guiding light.[11]

In the autumn of 1994, BBC Radio 3 broadcast a series of programmes to coincide with and enhance *Deutsche Romantik*, a major exhibition at the Hayward Gallery. These programmes and the exhibition catalogue[12] thoroughly analysed the tenets of German Romanticism and demonstrated the very close connection that fascism came to have with the Romantic movement. Apparently even today it is considered impossible to stage any exhibition concerning Romanticism in Germany itself because of its intrinsic connection with fascism. But there is a fundamental difference between these two concepts: fascism ascribes to authoritarianism and a closed feudal order; while Romanticism is essentially a concept of freedom, an opening of horizons. This season of *Deutsche Romantik* laid out in erudite and unmistakable terms the proof of the thesis that Henry Williamson's innate nature was Romantic. Examination of his character, his behaviour and his whole life's work has the stamp of Romanticism in it through and through.

John Heygate inadvertently points to this perception of the Romantic in *These Germans* while writing about the south Germans – the Bavarians. He quotes a passage from D.H. Lawrence's 'The Crucifix Across the Mountains' in *Twilight in Italy*, written in 1916:

It is a race that moves on the poles of mystic, sensual delight. Every gesture is a gesture from the blood, every expression a symbolic utterance. For learning there is sensuous experience, for thought there is myth and drama and dancing and singing. Everything is of the blood, of the senses. There is no mind. The mind is a suffusion of physical heat, it is not separated, it is kept submerged.

Quoted in *These Germans*

Heygate uses this quotation to illustrate the fascist type. Hitler was a south German (he was born in Austria) and D.H. Lawrence was writing about the Bavarians, south Germans, 'with their strange brutal beautiful life of instinctive artistry'. But Lawrence was also describing, and therefore Heygate, unintentionally, the Romantic type, and in so doing gives, coincidentally, a superb analysis of Henry Williamson's character.

This view is reinforced when we look to the main influences that shaped Henry's destiny; first and foremost he had south German, Bavarian, blood in his veins. He felt his soul's greatest affinity to be with Wagner, himself the very core of the Romantic movement. It is the Romantic and mystical work of Francis Thompson and Shelley that he held foremost, while Richard Jefferies, Henry's great mentor, displays much that may be termed Romantic in his writings. Henry Williamson uses all the symbols connected with the Romantics over and over again: death, darkness, wild scenery, the search for idyllic love, a surreal presence of the other world. All are central themes of Romanticism: all are central themes of Henry Williamson's writings.

This was no deliberate assumption of a pose or a mask. The man was innately Romantic. His genes are the genes of Romanticism. In England we think of the Romantics mainly in terms of the Lake Poets – Coleridge, Wordsworth, Byron, Keats and Shelley – and we accept without question the fact that Wordsworth involved himself in the French Revolution, that Byron went off to fight in the Greek wars; both manifestations of the Romantic involvement in politics, the opposition to established order. Thus Henry Williamson's adoption of a political stance would seem totally in keeping with the Romantic ethos.

Henry wrote in the front of his own copy of *The Wet Flanders Plain*: 'It would seem that my imaginative life is full only in reaction to the mass ideas.' He was referring to the fact that his compulsive interest in the First World War had waned at the very time that the world's interest had waxed full; extrapolated, it can be seen as a statement about his whole life, as it is also a statement about Romanticism. If it had not been for the historical fact of fascism, which clouded so many issues, including the life and work of Henry Williamson, there would be no difficulty in seeing him as a great writer in the Romantic tradition. It is easy to view much of Henry Williamson's writing in this light: *Tarka*; *Salar*; *The Gold Falcon* with its Byronic connections; *The Star-born*; the later *The Phasian Bird*; and no doubt the thesis could be applied to the whole of his oeuvre.

If one had set out to create a twentieth-century Romantic, that man would have had to be Henry Williamson. George Painter recognized this, calling him 'the last Romantic', and so did Herbert Faulkner West. In describing Henry Williamson's life and character West did not actually use the word Romantic; his word was 'Dreamer' – but he *was* describing a Romantic.

The Last Romantic: on Braunton burrows in Devon (left); in his Writing Hut at the Field (right).

Williamson was Maddison and Maddison was a dreamer, a lover of beauty, of birds and animals, and a sensitive youth longing for a time when Christ's simple tenets would govern the world. His mind, turned too long upon itself, enjoying in its own solitude the inner landscape of the soul, the prey to imagined fears, dreaming of some Utopia which would give it adequate and complete compensation, soaring to a belief in an impossible and unearthly love, had woven for itself a set of ideals which clashed inevitably with the compromises the world of experience forces upon all men.

The Dreamer of Devon

The interlude of the short but catalytic German visit over, Henry returned to England, and *Salar the Salmon* was published in mid-October 1935. This first edition was not illustrated and only had a cover painting by Tunnicliffe, but it did have delightful sketch maps of 'Salar Country' on the end papers. It was dedicated jointly to T.E. Lawrence and Victor Yeates in tribute to his two great friends. Reviews were prolific and enthusiastic, but tended to be short. The edition illustrated by Charles Tunnicliffe did not appear until the following year; this is odd as Tunny's drawings were certainly prepared well in time to appear in the first edition. The American publishers were Little, Brown & Co.[13] who were in association with the Atlantic Monthly Press, who had already serialized parts of *Salar* in their journal.

In his Writing Hut Henry kept a stuffed bream in a glass case, a very good example of its kind; Henry always said that this was presented to him by the Sitwells as a prize for the worst novel of the year for *Salar the Salmon*. With no evidence to support this in the archive, it must be presumed to be apocryphal (although the Sitwells may well have *said*, or perhaps written in a review, that it was the worst novel).[14] It would have amused Henry to make up such a story against himself.

In March 1936 Henry Williamson finally achieved his ambition to publish *The Flax of Dream* in a single-volume edition. It is dedicated 'to All who fought for Freedom in the World War, and who are still fighting.' It is this book that contains what has been referred to by his critics as the 'infamous Foreword'. Infamous because it contains the sentence: 'I salute the great man across the Rhine, whose life symbol is the happy child.' Poor Henry; of all the thousands of sentences that he wrote, this one marked him for life. For it is this sentence that has been used as the main evidence against him, as a supporter of Hitler and a fascist, with all its evil connotations.

Two things must be taken into account; first, that people should read the whole foreword. It is very easy to quote out of context and either exaggerate points or make them mean something totally different in so doing. Second, one must remember that Henry Williamson was obsessed with his vision of what the world could and should be – 'a new world', a Utopia – a Romantic vision of an ideal world with a perfect social and political system. His experience of the First World War had led him to believe that, metaphorically speaking, 'something was rotten in the State of Denmark'[15] (hence the appositeness of his 'Hamlet' lecture) – i.e. that something was rotten in the world of politics. He had just visited Germany where he had seen with his own eyes the great happiness of the young people of the German Youth Movement. Of course, that was what he was meant to see and only what he was allowed to see. Chemnitzer would have ensured that. It is possible that Henry Williamson represented a great catch to the Head of the Direction of German Writers, a feather in his cap, and was seen as a very useful appropriation. But Henry did not realize that, he *really* was that naive, he only saw what was actually before him, and this was what he was referring to in this sentence. It has no more sinister reference than that. Quite apart from the previous argument that Henry was a Romantic, all he was guilty of was naivety and honesty – and a great ability to open his mouth and put his foot in it. He continues:

> *This long novel, telling a story of one human unit in Europe immediately before and after the War, has for its theme the unhappiness of the child: the thwarting of the social instinct which can only be developed by imagination freed from mental fear.*

> The Flax of Dream, Foreword, 1936

His ideas were unusual, peculiar, possibly misguided; but they were very honest ideas and he genuinely thought he was working for the good of humanity. He was very puzzled to find that the rest of the world did not think as he did, did not see the great Truth that he saw, did not see his great Romantic vision.

There are only a few reviews of this one-volumed *Flax* in the archive, but they are of interest in giving a contemporaneous viewpoint. Particularly, Geoffrey West wrote in *Time and Tide* that:

the story of William Maddison . . . remains in every way his outstanding piece of writing. . . . It is an undoubtedly personal, even a self-regarding and self-exalting, book, yet has within it sufficient authenticity and enough of universality to give it a larger value. . . . [But] in the foreword to the present volume, Mr. Williamson delivers his jolt, saluting, in this book dedicated to 'all who fought for Freedom in the World War' the great man etc . . . Mr. Williamson's gullibility cannot disturb his past achievements, but his strange notion that Willie Maddison would have been happy in modern Germany does seem to set something of a query across his future.[16]

The *Methodist Times & Leader* stated that 'It is the contribution of a sensitive, observant, and un-conventional mind to a post-war literature not pre-eminent for spiritual insight.[17] Other reviews took the book at face value, ignoring the foreword: for example, the *Bristol Evening Post* called the tetralogy, 'an authentic spiritual history of our times', and the *News Review* hailed it as 'a fine, inspiring book'.[18]

Apart from this, in March 1936 Henry Williamson began to give talks on the radio in the West of England Home Service 'Out of Doors' series. He had been trying to gain employment as a broadcaster on and off since the Hawthornden Prize award had given him prominence – the first BBC memo about him is dated 25 October 1928, but no openings had arisen.[19] Finally, towards the end of 1935, Petre Mais had suggested him as a suitable person for school broadcasting; this did not really ever amount to anything, although Henry did make one schools' broadcast in November 1936. An immediate result was, however, that at the beginning of December 1935 he received a telegram asking him if he could broadcast in the 'Men Talking' series. An unexpected gap had arisen and Henry's name was on top of the file! He agreed, but nearly ruined everything there and them by wanting to talk about Germany. However, he was deflected from this by Moray McLaren, and Henry duly broadcast 'Recipe for a Country Life' on 16 December.

'Out of Doors' was broadcast from Bristol. Henry drove there in the Silver Eagle, a round trip of 170 miles. He states in *Goodbye West Country* that he could do the trip 'too fast, in just two hours' an average of 43 m.p.h., which was pretty fast allowing for the quality of the roads and the four towns and thirty villages that he had to negotiate. Ann Thomas, who was in residence at Shallowford again at this time, with Rosemary joining the other children in the family, used to go with him. Ann was always an efficient secretary, coping unflappably with mammoth typing sessions, while her neat writing records in the diaries precise notes of letters sent, appointments kept, and work done. These journeys to Bristol were very tiring for Henry, using up a great deal of nervous energy – beforehand in preparing his material, fitting in the normal day's affairs (answering letters, writing, etc.) making the journey, doing the actual broadcast, and then driving back again; notwithstanding 'the point of honour' of the open car in rain, wind, fog, frost or snow!

At the microphone for a BBC broadcast. (Copyright BBC)

Henry demonstrates a nice example of literary skill in his entry for 22 March in *Goodbye West Country* where he describes the journey to Bristol and goes on to talk about the Alvis and describes a past accident, then another. This is a build-up (it would be a motif in music and clearly seen) for his actual accident on 16 April, when he turned the car over on a bend when he was almost home, due to tiredness and his concentration being diverted by a barn owl flying across the windscreen. He was not alone as he has always maintained, but was accompanied by Ann Thomas. He was worried about adverse publicity if it became known, and she and Loetitia were sworn to secrecy. It is Ann's writing that records the incident in his diary: 'Both uninjured.' But it was Henry who recorded the fact that she got the blame for the accident, along with Loetitia, because between the two of them they had managed to forget the flask of cocoa which would have recharged his energy, and thus prevented the accident. While the Alvis was out of service Henry used the very ancient Crossley which had belonged to the Hibbert family and which had been left with him when the 'Boys' left for Australia.

On 18 April, two days after Henry's accident in the Alvis when the white owl, traditional harbinger of death (and used as such for the dramatic opening of his first novel, *The Beautiful Years*), had flown across his windscreen, his mother, Gertrude Eliza, died aged sixty-eight years. The cause of death on the certificate is given as 'Carcinoma of Vulvae', but from the details that are available, it would appear that the cancer was far more widespread.

Henry with his overturned Alvis Silver Eagle.

She had been in failing health for some years, apart from the stroke she sustained in 1933; the photographs of her show a shocking change quite early in her life. She had been in a nursing home in St John's Park since the beginning of the previous October. Henry's visits cannot have been much comfort to her, as from the evidence available in the archive and from what Ann Thomas (who sometimes accompanied him) says, he tended to stride about the room worrying about his own affairs and problems. Like the earlier occasion when he was leaving for the war, this venting of angst may well have been due to his inner fears, then about the possibility of his own approaching death, and now about the imminence of his mother's. Nevertheless, as on that earlier occasion, it cannot have been very easy for her to bear. But he did feel remorse later for the impatience he had felt towards her during her lifetime.

Henry writes in the *Chronicle* that Phillip paid £50 into his mother's bank account to cover her overdraft, apparently incurred from losses from horse-race betting. In real life, Henry certainly did give his mother something, for a letter from her thanks him 'for your most generous & acceptable gift, dear, it is most kind of you dear & I shall never forget it.' However, it was William Leopold who actually paid in this sum of money, and he was annoyed to find after Gertie's death that she had immediately paid his £50 on to Biddy – who no doubt needed money quite desperately to cover her family's living expenses – and he made a caustic little note on his accounts to this effect. It might well be that Gertrude asked both of them, and then finding she had two sums of money decided to pass one on to her youngest daughter.

In the archive there is a letter of commiseration to his father which Henry wrote towards the end of March, but which he did not actually send, carefully filing it instead with the business letters for posterity. It is, as he would have realized, very revealing about himself and his ideas:

Dear Father,
I hardly know what to say. . . . Poor mother – she had had 'an awful time – an awful time' as she said to me. And now the poor little dear is soon to slip away from that over-tired body. She has always seemed to me to be such a strange person. In her essential self, I mean – the part of her that was *fey*, other worldly. If only she could have learned to develop that self, what misunderstandings and conflicts our house might have avoided. For the truth is she was never strong enough, confident enough, to bring up children to be men and women, or to be a companion to her husband. She was always fearful: and that feeling upset others. But then she didn't have the chances I have had since August 1914 – to unlearn, unlearn, unlearn, scrutinize myself and rebuild myself. Does this seem all rot to you? Anyhow, it is only one person's view – my own one. All is trial and error, finding a new way by looking at the old. Perhaps my children will benefit by what has been learned. They are confident, well-planted little creatures. . . . [Here he relates briefly the story of John saving Robert from drowning retold in *The Children of Shallowford*.] You must be feeling very sad and strange and rather lost just now. Perhaps – if it suits you – you might like to spend some time with us when we leave Devon for a new home (undecided yet). I am keener than ever on farming; and land is now so cheap; and the new European order (good and firm) will not be long in coming. We grope towards a new way, painfully, by looking at the wrongness of the past. When that new order comes, England will be, *must* be, a great family with a balanced living for the people – and farming will be a first class thing again. So I am hoping to get my land very soon. I can see the price of it back again in a book about the adventure of it.
    Meanwhile keep as serene as possible. And do remember that you have a son who feels, now that he is a man, in sympathy for you as a husband, a father, and a man.
    With love   [unsigned]
                                        Letter in HWLEA, dated 23 March 1936

A week later Gertrude fractured her left thigh while levering herself higher up the bed on to her pillow, a complication which weakened her further and although she sent a little note to Henry on 3 April it was actually written by her nurse. After that she deteriorated quickly and William Leopold was sending Henry almost daily letters apprising him of her approaching demise. On 13 April he warned that although the doctors were marvelling at the way Gertrude was holding on, the end must be very near. 'Poor mother is now living in a world of her own, she can't talk or write, & her sight is going rapidly, & her mind is giving way. She can't eat without being sick, & she lives on plain water. The end cannot be very far off now.' (Letter in HWLEA, dated 13 April 1936.)

Henry had apparently inquired about his share in trust from the will of his grandfather, Thomas William Leaver, which would come into operation on the death of Gertrude who was the life tenant, for William Leopold continued that he knew 'nothing at all about it, have never been allowed even to see it, so can give you no information. Anyway, the surviving trustee bids fair to be Percy Leaver, tho' one never knows' (letter in HWLEA, dated 13 April 1936).

On 18 April William Leopold wrote: 'My dear Harry, Deeply regret to inform you that your dear Mother died at about 1.30 p.m. this afternoon.' And on 20 April: 'The funeral is fixed for Thursday the 23rd of this month at 11 a.m. Ladywell Cemetery & leaves this house at 10.45 a.m. You will need to come up the day before. Please let me know if you are not coming, otherwise I shall expect you.' (Letter in HWLEA, dated 20 April 1936.)

Henry with his children in the garden at Shallowford just before migration to Norfolk. From left to right: Henry, John, Bill, Richard, Robert, Rosemary, Margaret.

Henry did not mention his mother's illness, death or funeral in any of three diaries for that year nor at the appropriate place in *Goodbye West Country*. He did incorporate it into *The Phoenix Generation* (volume 12 of the *Chronicle*) where he quotes the little flurry of letters generated by these events but he moved the occasion to the November of 1936 so he could couple it with the 'Götterdämmerung' effect of the disastrous fire that ravaged the Crystal Palace; the physical end of that great glass edifice epitomizing the end of the life of one tiny frail woman – a Wagnerian scene in true Romantic style.

Henry claims in the *Chronicle* that Gertrude's illness had cost nearly £1,000 but William Leopold's exact computations showed the true total to be £431 19*s* 7*d*, all of which he paid himself, only claiming back from her estate the £50 'loan', obviously feeling that as this money had gone to Biddy, he could do so with a clear conscience; his feelings about his youngest daughter ran very deep.

With Gertrude's death, Thomas Leaver's small trust was gradually wound up and resolved. Percy Leaver was indeed the remaining trustee. The residue was to be shared between Henry and his two sisters, Kathie and Biddy. It consisted of share holdings (Gertrude had already sold the house that had been made over to her at the time of her father's death, which had been a matter of contention with her brother Percy) for Gertrude had been the life tenant of the income generated by these shares, which would seem, from the accounts produced when the trust was wound up, to have been about £750 a year, a good sum in those days and one which would have given her a nice independence – hence the holidays on the continent. By the time estate duties had been paid on the trust and legal fees subtracted, the residue for each of the three beneficiaries was about £100 0*s*. 0*d*. cash with the shares being divided between them. Henry received his portion when probate was granted.

It was the end of an era for Henry. The events of his years at Shallowford are recorded in *Goodbye West Country*, published in September 1937, which is ostensibly one long diary entry for 1936 but coupled with myriad attendant associated thoughts – a detailed portrait of the life of Henry Williamson at that time. It was goodbye, indeed, for Henry had made the decision to leave Shallowford and the West Country. Apart from sensing the portents of war and the important role agriculture would play in the immediate future, he felt that the area had nothing left with which to stimulate his writing. Restless once again, he uprooted the family – 'The Migrants'[20] – travelling 350 miles due north-east to the coast of north Norfolk, to become owner of Old Hall Farm – the Norfolk farm.

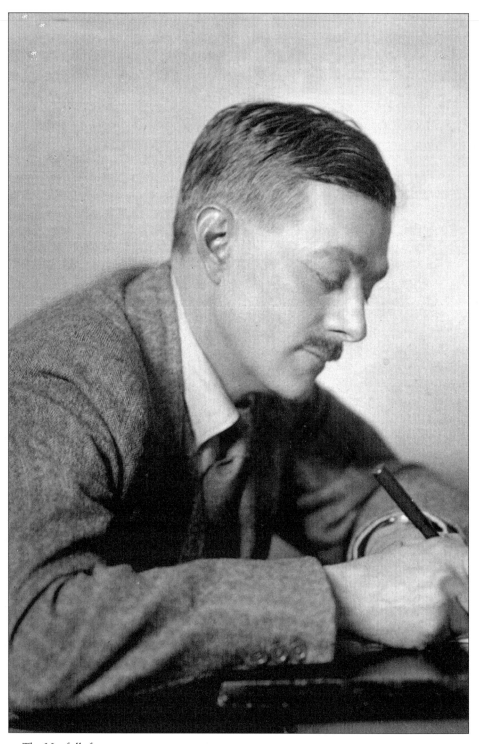

The Norfolk farmer.

CHAPTER 7

THE NORFOLK FARM

As Henry Williamson relates in the opening chapter of *The Story of a Norfolk Farm*,[1] at the end of 1935 (possibly after Christmas and over the New Year) feeling bored and stale he drove to London in the Silver Eagle to stay at the Savage Club. Here he was telephoned by Richard de la Mare who invited him to dine that night and then to join him for a few days at their family cottage at East Runton near Cromer on the north Norfolk coast.[2] Driving along the road out of London to north Norfolk Henry was reminded of his previous journey along that road some twenty-four years earlier, when in 1912, aged nearly seventeen, he had cycled to Norfolk for a holiday. He wrote and told his mother about this present trip to Norfolk, for a letter from her shortly after this referred to 'that awful summer we had in E. Runton. The tent buried etc. & the streets running with water.'[3]

Once ensconced in the warmth of the de la Mares' cottage, Henry unburdened his feeling of stagnation and frustration and fears for the future. Richard de la Mare's wife apparently suggested that perhaps the answer to his problems would be to come and live in Norfolk, adding that they knew of a place for sale nearby. The next day they drove the few miles along the coast to look at this property, the Old Hall at Stiffkey and its attendant 235 acres. Henry relates in *The Story of a Norfolk Farm* that he immediately took a dislike to the rather gloomy house, and further that he was told most honestly by the agent that the land was in bad condition. He also relates that the tenant farmer, Stratton, had let the fields go over to a massive crop of thistles. Yet he found himself making inquiries and, almost against his will, certainly without true volition, he ascertained that the house could be sold separately and was in fact under offer, and tentative arrangements were put in hand for the purchase of the land.

He returned to Devon to discuss the project with his wife. Loetitia offered the use of her inheritance from the family trust, which had become hers on the death of her father. Henry knew he would inherit money from his grandfather's trust on the death of his mother, which was now near. They thought they could just about manage to raise the amount needed for the purchase and decided to go ahead, and by 9 March 1936 Henry was committed to the farm project, for Ann Thomas recorded in the diary, 'Stiffkey agreement returned to Dewing.' Andrews and Dewing were the estate agents who handled the property.

Henry realized that he would need some help with this new undertaking and the idea came to him to enlist the help of Loetitia's younger brother, Robin, presently working in Australia. Loetitia had grave doubts about the wisdom of this and so, apparently, did Ann,[4] but Henry persisted. At the end of April he composed and dictated a letter to Ann which was sent to Robin with a copy kept for the archive files, telling him that 'I am dictating this letter in the presence of Ida' and that he has bought 'Old Hall Farm, Stiffkey, and two nice cottages adjoining for £2,250. . . . I am buying this property with money lent on mortgage to me by Ida [Loetitia's brother always called her by her first christian name] at 4%.' Henry went on to explain that he was expecting to inherit money from his grandfather's trust, his mother having died the previous week, and also that his aunt (Mary Leopoldina) 'who likes me and is like me, may leave me anything between £1000 and £4000.'[5] He proposed sending Robin on a course to learn farming when he arrived in England. This invitation to Robin really does seem to have been a rather extraordinary move, and Henry must have known at the time that it was fraught with pitfalls. He and the 'Boys' had not been able to get on before, their temperaments were too different. Why he should have thought that things would have changed is puzzling.

On 13 July Henry was broadcasting from Bristol and from there he again set off for Norfolk, stopping at Stephen Renshaw's for the night (the Renshaws had a house in north Norfolk as well as their Instow property) and meeting Edward Hawkins, valuer, at the farm at noon on 15 July, recording that it was 'Raining but cleared later. Simply loved the whole place in sunlight.' The following day, Thursday 16 July, travelling on, he stopped near Thetford where he 'shot rabbits with Miss Reeve' and then continued on to Tenterden to see Ann Thomas, and on again to stay for the weekend with John Heygate and his new wife (John and Gwyneth Lloyd had been married on 28 February) at their home in Sussex. There he met 'The Daily Express Editor, John Rayner, and Duncan Sandys & his wife (Winston Churchill's daughter) & an Oxford Movement youth – all nice. Dick Wyndham artist, came over in evening. Good supper.' He then returned to Tenterden for a few days before going back to Devon.

The legal background to the purchase of the farm was fairly complicated and is well documented in Chapter 8 of *The Story of a Norfolk Farm*. Eventually it was sorted out as is prosaically recorded by Ann in the business diary. 'Deeds & mortgage of Stiffkey Hall Farm signed, witnessed & returned to Wolfe Garrard [of the firm Garrard, Wolfe, Gaze and Clarke].' Henry described these final stages in *The Story of a Norfolk Farm* thus:

> *Loetitia and I and the children were in the hut in the hilltop field, camping out and having a free time in the sunshine, when the Conveyance and Mortgage arrived, in a large envelope sealed and crossed with blue lines. I called all the children to the hut to witness the opening of the envelope. These, I said, are our title to the farm. . . . Outside a young man hovered – the usual staggart who was writing a book and had come to see the author of the books he hoped one day to surpass – and he was called to witness the signature.*
>
> *The Story of a Norfolk Farm*

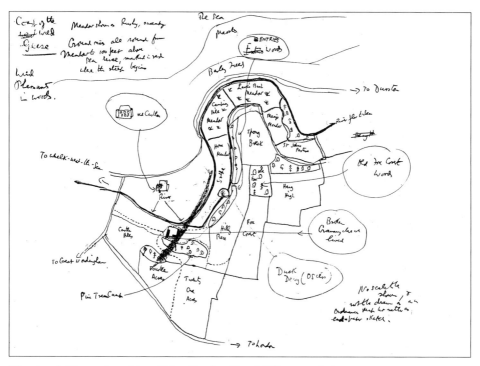

The sketch Henry drew himself for Charles Tunnicliffe to work from.

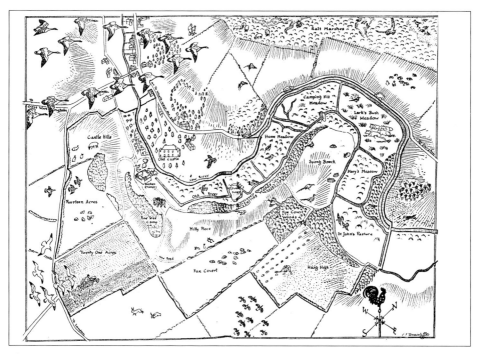

The map drawn by Charles Tunnicliffe for the endpapers of *The Story of a Norfolk Farm*.

The staggart was Guy Priest, once again in the area, having given up his job and camping for the summer while he finished a novel.[6]

As part of the many preparations that Henry made that year, reading books and magazines on farming (which he sent on to Robin in Australia) and generally trying to acquaint himself with some background for the task ahead, he had joined the Country Gentleman's Association. This entitled him to the annual little black tome 'The Estate Book and Diary'. Containing much legal and practical advice either side of the diary section, these black volumes dominate the Norfolk farm years. The first entry that Henry made was on the same day as the signing of the farm documents.

Saturday 22 August
Left Ox's Cross, where family is on holiday, for Stiffkey. Windles, Gipsy, and I, in Alvis with small green tent & flea-bags. We stopped at Shallowford and bathed the next day.

Sunday 23 August
Left finally at 2.30 p.m. after my usual sort of 'het-up' nerve storm. Due to derelict garden & no winter greens out, & repairs to car, greasing etc. We had tea near Yeovil and got to Aspley Guise, Beds, about 10.30 p.m., visiting the Boones after a 17-year interval. Found them all exactly the same. Talked about Mother's death & wretched end in expensive nursing home etc. Illness cost £600–£700. Camped at midnight near Ampthill.

In the *Norfolk Farm* book Henry recalled the progress to Norfolk as 'one of the happiest journeys of our joint lives: travelling with windscreen flat, in helmet and goggles, while the warm air of the harvest fields of Bedfordshire became hotter: then the midday ease of eating a fruit and brown-bread lunch under the hedge. . . . In the afternoon we drove slowly along the top lane to the farm.' The diary record shows that on Tuesday 25 August they 'wandered all over the farm, loving it all. Then over the saltings and to lovely yellow sands, where we bathed.' Again the following day:

Wandered over farm & river all morning. Tried to visit the cottages but were driven off with curses by Mrs. Francis, wife of age-old gardener to Old Hall. Called us cheeky devils, 'no right here' etc. Poked toy gun out of window & pretended to fire as we examined the well. Windles ran like a hare.

They left on Thursday 27 August, calling again on the Boones late in the evening, and continuing the following day via Swindon where they had tea and then bathed in Jefferies' lake at Coate – 'modernised and now very popular'. This happy interlude was the lull before a very long storm which rumbled on throughout the following years in the life of the family and in the life of a nation at war.

Business arrangements continued; taking over a farm was a complicated affair – notices to quit to be served, distress levies to be organized, disturbance money to be taken into account, dilapidations, drainage rates to be assessed, etc. etc. Eventually the solicitor's bill arrived. Henry thought the total, £71 6s 10d, reasonable for the amount of work involved. On the bottom he added, as extra expense involved, 'several journeys to Norfolk which, however, I regard as stimulation & relaxation'.

Towards the end of September he noted that he dined with Lady Fortescue at Castle Hill, Filleigh, and that one of the other guests was 'A.J. Munnings, painter, guest – painting her portrait. Nice chap; Knows Stiffkey well; and Stratton's

Surveying the land at Old Hall Farm.

thistles; once offered £6,500 for Hall & Farm.' Perhaps he had been invited to meet Munnings because of the Stiffkey connection. The two men took to each other and a friendship developed, which continued for some years.

Robin Hibbert was due to arrive from Australia during the first week of December. He too had been studying farming methods, taking a correspondence course for several months. On the voyage he had time to read the *Farmer's Weekly* magazines which Henry had sent him. He carefully cut out all the articles of interest and, as they were approaching England, decided to dump the bulk of heavy paper over the side as a simple means to be rid of it. It was a wet and windy night. The next morning the captain, at whose table Robin had the honour to sit, was decidedly 'frosty'. When Robin went for his morning constitutional round the deck he discovered why: the rigging was covered with hundreds of pieces of soggy

Henry and Loetitia make a start on the thistles and weeds. (Photograph copyright John Fursdon)

The original dilapidated state of Old Hall Farm.

paper. Unbeknown to Robin, the wind had blown all his *Farmer's Weekly* copies not into the sea, where they would have disintegrated, but back on to the deck where a disgruntled crew were laboriously clearing them up! Robin told Henry this story on his arrival and it was of course incorporated into *The Story of a Norfolk Farm*.

On 2 December Henry was once again at the farm in Norfolk with Mr Hawkins, sorting out the dilapidations, when he saw three condemned cottages in the village. Because he had not bought the Old Hall itself and because the two cottages on the farm were occupied, Henry had been worried about accommodation for himself and the family. If he could buy these three extra cottages and do them up the problem would be solved. He went into Norwich to arrange with Dewing that he try and purchase them on his behalf. While in Norwich Henry heard that Robin was due to arrive at Liverpool the next day, and sent a telegram to tell him that they could meet at Taunton as Henry would be returning home on the Saturday. The reply was to be sent to Marlborough for Henry to collect on his way home. But Robin's reply said that he could make it to Taunton either on Sunday or Monday, at 5.45 p.m. Henry sent a further wire to say that Robin should wait until the Monday. Then he continued on his way and eventually got home at 12.15 a.m., very cold and tired.

The next day, as his diary records, he organized a 'ceremony of greeting for Robin tomorrow, at approximately 6 p.m. Rehearsed children. Arranged for fireworks & champagne the moment he arrived, with great fire in hearth.' Such complicated arrangements were doomed to failure. The following morning a wire from Robin stated he was arriving at noon; he had got to Taunton the previous day, Sunday, after all. Henry's elaborate plans were overturned; it was an ill-omen as far as he was concerned. 'This is annoying: my energies & money in telegraphing all wasted by this substituting another plan for an agreed plan. Result, my day's work interrupted. Hope this isn't to be a symbol of our relationship.' Robin, arriving in a wet and windy Liverpool naturally could see no point in hanging around feeling miserably cold and uncomfortable when he could be on his way home. He had no idea that Henry was arranging such a grand ceremony of welcome or that his action was going to create problems. The two men formed an uneasy relationship; as before they were opposite ends of a pole and would never find common ground, and there would be much friction between them.

At the beginning of January 1937 Henry attended a mechanization conference at Oxford which was a jolly affair and he noted that he was quite optimistic about being 'a good farmer'. From here he went to London to meet Ann Thomas, which was disastrous because she greeted him with the news that she had had a proposal of marriage. He had to leave straight away as he was broadcasting from Bristol, and from there he went back to Shallowford. Two days later, having received a letter from Ann confirming this news, he set off back to Tenterden, taking his wife 'for companionship', but leaving her with Petre and Jill Mais while he continued to Tenterden, where he persuaded Ann to change her mind. Henry then went on to

Early days: Windles and his mother outside the barn (above); Windles finding out what farming was all about (below).

see John Heygate and Gwyneth at Warbleton, and the following day he went back to the Mais household; thence returning with Loetitia to Devon via Swindon, where he took photographs at Coate of Jefferies' home and lake for the book he was editing on Jefferies' work.

Meanwhile the complicated computations of taxes and schedules to do with the farm continued. The Old Hall itself had been bought by a Mr Cafferata and certain costs had to be apportioned between them. Then, on 9 February, Henry was finally able to sign the contract for the three derelict cottages, for which he paid £190, which had been agreed at the end of December. He wrote in his diary that 'there has been a lot of correspondence and I suppose cost over the abstract of title in the contract. . . . Many letters . . . weeks of delay.' Another problem arose over tithes which had recently passed from the jurisdiction of the Church to that of the government and the rules and regulations surrounding possible reductions in the rate levied were legion, with time-limits fixed to all the various stages. Every transaction was fraught with delays, conflicting advice, and general inefficiency. Henry's volatile temperament did not help matters.

In the middle of March he signed the contract with Putnam for *Goodbye West Country*, which he stated he was working on 'about 10 hrs. a day excluding stops – hard writing and rewriting. Dead beat.' In the middle of April he made another visit to Stiffkey, this time to meet the sanitary inspector and an architect at the 'Three Dilapidated Cottages – all damp, dark & awfully depressing'. So depressing that a day or so later he sent for Loetitia to come up by train, meeting her at Norwich. They dined with the Cafferatas, the new owners of the Old Hall, enjoying themselves, and equilibrium was restored again. He resolved that he and Robin would spend the summer months prior to taking over the farm at Michaelmas in renovating these cottages to make them habitable for the family and in building up the very poor farm tracks into firm roads, so that it would all be made good before he had to be involved in actual farming. For this purpose, he arranged to rent a gravel pit for use as raw material for the roads.

Soon after their return to Devon, on 2 May, he recorded that he had bought a lorry: 'a reconditioned 1932 Morris 2-tonner from More of S. Molton today for £66/10/- – Tipper, hoops & hood, engine, all new – rest made 100%. We have a 2-ton trailer (£21) this lorry, a £9 trailer, & caravan for our summer road building campaign. Lorry tax will be about £15, trailer £7, Insurance (3rd Party) £7 – £29 in all (approximately).' This prosaic entry was merely the precursor to a catalogue of woe. Robin was set the task of overseeing the completion of the deal for the lorry and trailer, and obtaining licences which were supposed to be ready for 11 May. They were not. Henry blamed Robin; by Friday 14 May the two men had a flaming row and Henry stormed off to see to things himself. It was the old story of two very different ways of getting things done – the tortoise and the hare. Henry could not tolerate the slower, easier mind. His was the quick, instant grasp and solution of a problem, and he did not have the patience to stand back and let others do things their way. That said, it would, of course, have been very frustrating to have planned his complicated itinerary and then have been baulked.

Henry was very tense at this time. He must have been very conscious that he had committed himself and the family to an enormous task, which he was not at all sure was going to succeed, or that he was fitted for.

Eventually the lorry was ready, arriving at Shallowford on 19 May, but at 2.30 p.m. instead of 9 a.m. Matters were not helped by the fact that Loetitia had at this time taken the family to friends at Westward Ho! for a holiday and there had been no one to cook for the men, which Henry remarked on several times in his diary (although one wonders why food could not have been cooked by the housekeeper or one of the maids). The two men now proceeded to the Field at Georgeham, stopping to wire to Loetitia to return to cook food at this important time, where they were to load up the yew wood planks, lathes etc, finally collecting *Pinta* from Branton Pill at 11.15 p.m. Henry drove back to Shallowford in the Alvis, arriving at midnight, to find his wife waiting, for which he was very grateful; Robin following behind with lorry and trailer at 12.30 a.m. He had found a problem with the lorry's brakes, which would have to be sorted out before the long journey – another source of irritation. Henry left the following day.

Packed badly, all scattered & het-up. Much stuff left in Field, tent poles etc. No organisation: I incapable of doing it, Robin not competent to take charge. Set out at 2.30 p.m. with caravan – leaving Robin in More's garage, all hands working on it, relining brakes etc. He leaves tomorrow, joining me at Chippenham, where I arrived at 8 p.m. to be met by Ann and Helen Thomas. [Helen was renting part of a farmhouse here at this time.]

Robin duly arrived, 'averaging 8 m.p.h. 8 m.p.g. Awful!' On the Saturday they set off at 2.30 p.m. for Norfolk, arriving at 7 p.m. on Sunday. It was a dreadful journey and is well recorded in *The Story of a Norfolk Farm*. Henry's diary entry for the day ends: 'Felt awful – dud lorry – failure, failure, failure.'

On Tuesday they commenced to cart loads of gravel from the pit and spread it on the lower road. 'Result was apparently negligible.' They continued to work. On Friday they were joined by 'one-eyed Jarvis' who had once worked on the farm but was currently unemployed. The work rate increased. On the following Monday they were joined by another man, 'young, red-haired [Norman] Jordan'. The ratio of work again increased. By 4 June they had made 400 yards of road – 3,000 yards remained to be laid.

Henry had planned to collect Ann Thomas from Tenterden on 7 June and bring her to the farm so that she could help and cook them decent food, but on that very day he had a letter to say that her sister Bronwen and her son Charles had mumps and that she, Ann, was therefore in quarantine for a month. Ignoring this fact Henry went to fetch her on 16 June and they returned together two days later. On 23 June Ann actually developed mumps, and was promptly blamed for ignoring the rules. Understandably Henry was worried about himself and Robin becoming infected; apart from the actual fact of being ill, it would have devastated the plan of work, although the situation was entirely of his own making. Ann was

Looking towards the Old Hall and Stiffkey Church – Henry's chalk roads are prominent.

banished to a tent yards away and all her food was pushed to her with a pole, the utensils collected in a like manner and disinfected. Luckily the two men did not catch the mumps – but there was still no one to do the cooking for a week or two. But not for as long as is indicated in *The Story of a Norfolk Farm*, for Henry's diary note for 19 July includes the fact that Ann and he went to Merton (Stephen Renshaw's residence nearby) for a very enjoyable party of champagne and lobsters.

At this point, Henry became worried about the high costs of the estimates for the rebuilding of the derelict cottages. Robin suggested that their own men could do the work far more cheaply. Henry was worried that this would take the men off the road building and so slow down the overall plan, but nevertheless agreed, although later on this was an item he used against Robin. The work did not go smoothly, and was a constant source of friction. Robin also remonstrated with Henry about the situation he now saw existed with Ann. Henry merely attributed his views to an out-of-date attitude.

In August Henry set off with Ann in the lorry to bring back a load of furniture and other items, returning with Windles who was on holiday from school. It was a difficult, tiring and frustrating journey. Henry grew exhausted loading the lorry and the difficult drive back was not helped when a puncture at Walsingham very late at night prompted the discovery that the only jack he had was for an Austin Seven. His shouts and oaths drew a man from his bed from a cottage some distance away. When the man appeared in pyjamas and dressing gown, Henry thought he had kindly come to help; but after remonstrating with Henry about the noise and foul language, the man went back to his cottage, while Ann and Windles walked to a nearby garage for help.

In the second week of September another journey to Devon in the lorry with Ann and Windles was made which was even more fraught than the previous one. Coupled to which the rebuilding of the cottages seemed to be accompanied by every difficulty imaginable. Bricks did not arrive; wood did not arrive; more work was necessary than was at first thought; men did not work, or did the work wrongly so that it had to be re-done. It really was a horrendous scenario and Henry's exhausted rantings are very understandable, although they did nothing to help the situation. The publication of *Goodbye West Country* went unremarked in his diary. At the end of September a third removals trip was planned. A furniture pantechnicon had been ordered to Shallowford to be prepacked and ready for collection. This time Henry made the journey in his Alvis and although loading the furniture into the pantechnicon hired from a haulier from Wells called Perkins was not easy, the trip went relatively smoothly. The children at this time were lodged with Annie Rawle at South Molton and so spared the upheaval.

Henry then sent the trailer on to Swindon by rail to be picked up later, while he left Shallowford to drive to Petersfield to attend a ceremony on 2 October to unveil a memorial sarsen stone to Edward Thomas on the Shoulder of Mutton Hill at Steep near Petersfield in Hampshire, near to where the family had lived.[7] Henry's diary records that at the ceremony he spoke to John Masefield, Walter de la Mare, and H.W. Nevinson, and gave 'a jolly lunch' for Ann and her sister Bronwen and their brother Merfyn. He and Ann then returned to Swindon to pick up the trailer and thence drove back to Stiffkey. Work on the cottages did not seem to have progressed much in his absence, and he was increasingly critical of everything Robin did, or did not do. The problem was that time was running out. However, a short note in his diary indicated that on 5 October he received £1,760 as his share of his mother's estate, which must surely have helped.

Michaelmas is the traditional time for property to change hands. On Monday 11 October his diary recorded: 'The farm is mine as occupier, noon today.' On 21 October: 'Valuation day – Ed. Hawkins for me, G. Dewing for Stratton. . . . Tomorrow I begin, Bob S. [Sutton] as head-man.'

All this month he was attending various auctions and buying up equipment; he also bought two horses, Blossom and Gilbert. In November work continued apace, with a man called Wordingham topping mangels while Bob Sutton, Jarvis and Jordan, Robin and Henry were doing the concreting in the yards and still struggling with the cottages. On 11 November Henry wrote: 'We finished the concrete slab by bullock yards today. I set my owl & initials in red brick on the junction slab.' The owl is still in place, fifty-five years later.

By now Robin had had enough and informed Henry that he would be leaving for a job in an electrical factory in Bedford by the end of the month, but promised to finish wiring the cottages first. The same week Henry bought his Ferguson

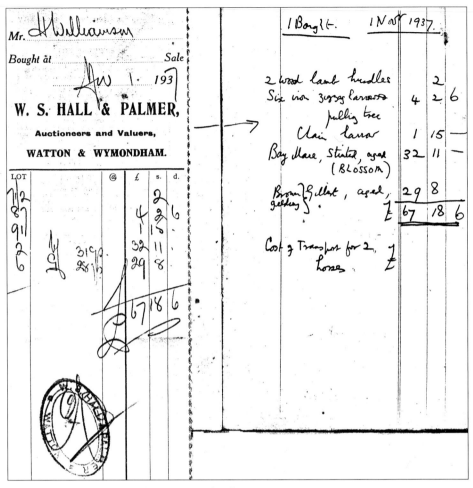

Receipts for the purchase of Blossom and Gilbert.

tractor, for £224, plus £26 extra each for spud wheels and plough. For once something went right and Henry was very pleased with his 'little grey donkey' (except that he immediately worried about the spud wheels ruining his concrete yard). Despite the protestations of Bob Sutton, the very light tractor was just what was needed for ploughing the difficult land.

It is not clear exactly how Henry Williamson came into contact with Lady Dorothy, the Dowager Viscountess Downe, who was a prominent member of the British Union. There is no entry recording their meeting in his diary, but it can be deduced that it was at the beginning of October 1937. In *The Story of a Norfolk Farm* 'Lady Sunne' stopped her car by the granary, introducing herself, and saying that she had read his articles, and 'found the spirit of them so creatively in accord with what she and her friends believed', that she had come to beg him to join their

'I set my owl and initials in red brick.'

Henry Williamson and the 'little grey donkey'. (Photograph copyright John Fursdon)

movement. Henry had returned from Devon on 4 October and the first actual evidence is a letter from Lady Downe dated 7 October which states that 'it was wonderful to meet someone who sees what fineness there really is in the Movement'. Apparently she enclosed 'some of our papers and propaganda', and a membership form 'on the chance that you might wish to become a member'. Lady Downe further mentioned that Jorian Jenks was coming to speak at three meetings at Holt and Fakenham at the end of October. Henry sent back the enrolment form, for Lady Downe's next letter, dated 18 October 1937, enclosed a receipt for his subscription. At the beginning of November another letter arrived from her from the Ladies Automobile Club in London, inviting Henry to lunch with her at the Criterion on Friday 26 November to hear 'the Leader' (Sir Oswald Mosley) speak. Henry travelled up to London on 25 November, staying with John and Gwyneth Heygate overnight, going with them to 'the disgustingly hot and decadent Cafe Royal'. The next day he attended the lunch as guest of Lady Downe and recorded in his diary: 'Mosley is a nice chap, & gives impression of much vitality in a solid sort of way.' He went straight back to Stiffkey and the next day's entry shows him involved with farm affairs, particularly Stratton's 'preposterous claim' for disturbance. On 14 December Lady Downe invited him to her home at Hillington, King's Lynn, to meet Mosley who was staying with her, and he noted: 'A fine fellow: strong, determined, integrated, staying-power. Very cold, freezing. We dined at the Hall home of the Dawnays. O.M. looks tired. I was tired, drawn, feeling 20 years on my age. But I get like this. When the cottages are ready, I'll feel great relief.'

Henry had found a new hero. He admired Mosley, who also had a strong and magnetic personality, and whose views on agricultural policy reflected exactly what Henry himself felt about farming being the backbone of British life and economy. But although associated with the British Union of Fascists and openly admiring its leader, to label Henry a political fascist is to grossly misrepresent him. The articles he wrote for *Action*, the organ of Mosley's party, show how little he really fitted into the political side of the party. During 1938 and 1939, until it was banned when war broke out, Henry wrote eight general articles, and had thirteen extracts reprinted from his book *The Patriot's Progress*. Even most of the other eight pieces had been previously published elsewhere and his overriding themes were the need to avoid a second world war and the need to revitalize farming, which was his life's work at this time. Alan Dilnot has examined these articles in depth, and concludes that they are not political writings in the sense of furthering the fascist cause, nor do they have a 'fascist' content.[8]

The day following this second meeting with Mosley, 16 December, Loetitia and the family eventually arrived from Devon, having had to delay their migration due to the lack of accommodation. (Loetitia had joined the children at Annie Rawle's when the lease on Shallowford had expired at Michaelmas.) They travelled from Devon by train, John Heygate meeting them at Paddington, taking them home for refreshments, and transferring them to Liverpool Street Station. The cottages still not being quite ready, Ann had got a good fire glowing in the stove in the granary and had aired blankets and sleeping bags in front of it. Henry took the Alvis to meet them at the station in Wells, recording an emotional and symbolic reunion in *The Story of a Norfolk Farm*.

His diary entry was somewhat more prosaic. It had been several months since Henry had had his family around him. He was not used to the hurly-burly of family life: 'Cottage not ready, so all come in this granary. Rather a noise & chaos.' On 21 December Loetitia moved into 'Cottage No. 3. Damp, poor kitchen range, floors and walls look as though leaking.' Henry tried unsuccessfully to alter the stove, feeling very depressed that 'all the cottage work is in vain & silly & much too costly'. On Christmas Eve the shelves fell down. Henry put them up again and also found that with a different type of fuel the stove worked. But the family remembers very clearly how kind Mrs Cafferata at the Old Hall saved the day by taking them in and providing baths and giving them Christmas lunch.

With the New Year the hard work on the farm continued, with very little let up. At this time Henry employed four workmen: Bob Sutton, as steward or manager; Jimmy Sutton, his father; Norman Jordan; and Jarvis as the yard-man. They had always farmed in the old way and found Henry's new ideas difficult to assimilate. They tended to listen to what Henry had to say but to go away and carry on as they always had. Of course, this irritated Henry and as time went on without any change in their ways eventually infuriated him. Much nervous energy was to be expended.

At the beginning of March he bought a 'good black mare, Gipsy, at Bircham Tofts, in foal, lovely beast, for 54 guineas'. The foal was born on 16 April, a red letter day and he made a little joke in his diary about it being the mare and not his wife that had given birth! By contrast 27 May was a black day, the day of the hearing between incoming and outgoing farmers about the dilapidations on the farm – Arbitration Day – at the Crown Hotel, Fakenham, where Stratton and Dewing managed to wriggle out of all their obligations, putting the responsibility for payments on to Henry. He felt he hadn't a chance. His depression was reinforced when, a few days later, he received a letter from Ann, who was away at Chippenham, to say she was not coming back. He seemed to be half-expecting this, and was actually more surprised and upset when Loetitia told him very plainly that it was his own fault. On 3 June he left for a holiday at the Field where Guy Priest and his wife were camping once again.

For some time Henry had been receiving letters from a man called John Coast, who had read the *Flax* and, according to Henry's diary entry, considered Henry to be 'the prophet of the Idea of a new order in Britain & Empire'. Henry met John Coast in London on 6 July. Coast stated that he was giving up his job in Rothschild's Bank in London, which he hated, and was coming to the farm, where he arrived on 31 July, 'a young man to take Robin's place'. (Coast is Hurst in the farm episode in the *Chronicle*.) Meanwhile Ann had returned briefly to supervise the removal of her furniture. Henry seemed quite calm about this, merely entering in the diary that they had walked on the marshes and had a lovely bathe and parted sweetly.

At the beginning of August, an Ipswich firm made an offer to buy the use of his chalk quarry for £750. Henry felt this was a godsend and would 'save the farm & probably me. I am feeling very near the rocks.' Thinking it 'the decent thing to do' he wrote to Cafferata to inform him of this. Cafferata immediately asked to see him, and on doing so begged Henry not to despoil the farm in this way. Henry explained his financial position, and Cafferata said he would help him, and as he looked frail and ill Henry gave in about the chalk quarry, although he noted that he could not imagine how help would be forthcoming. Loetitia was somewhat cross that he had decided to turn down this offer, which would have been useful income.

Throughout August he and the men were hard at work on the farm getting in the first harvest. In the middle of this the *Daily Express* informed him that they had lost that week's article, on kestrels, and could he send a copy. He did not have one and 'Tried to remember & recall & recreate article on kestrels. Spent three hours of hell and frustration.' As the days went by he began to realize that Ann had passed out of his life and began to grieve: 'I can't think or imagine life with her gone from me.' At the end of August Cafferata kept his word and, as Henry recorded in his diary, sent 'a cheque for £500 – on loan, at 2%, without security'. This was a great help, and Henry would regularly note that he had paid the interest due.

On 12 September he left for London with Windles, first calling at Bedford to leave a trailer load of things for Robin (the Alvis had been converted into a 'farm-waggon' with a pick-up body by Mr Ebbage, a carpenter in Stiffkey), and then going into London for a broadcast, staying the night with Loetitia's cousin Mary and continuing down to Devon where he took Windles back to his school at West Buckland, then on to Georgeham and the Field. Once there, alone and without the discipline of farm work, reaction to Ann's loss set in and the entries in his diary were full of despair. This was not helped by the news of the looming Czechoslovakian crisis and several entries reiterate his belief that Hitler would *not* cause a war. His world was crumbling around him and he was beginning to have doubts about everything.

Henry rushed up to Chippenham but found only Helen Thomas and the young Rosemary there. However, he discovered that Ann had her own cottage nearby, but when he managed to see her she told him that she was to be married. On 21 September he spent the night with his new friend Alfred Munnings, at his house at Withypool on Exmoor, and the next day although 'very unhappy', he walked with Munnings and his friend on the moor, and recorded that Munnings was 'a sweet man'. Returning to the Field, anguish overcame him. Night time was the worst: 'The hours were black monarchs that ruled by torture.' On the night of 24 September, he seemed to reach crisis point: 'At night I was in agony again, & thought of Edward Thomas, & wished I could die in war near him, & a voice said to me, WAIT! and again, Wait!, & I slept. I believed he had come to me.' And he noted that all the newspapers predicted that war would come.

I say, no, it will not come. I trust Hitler; but at night the anguish begins. I see myself as possessed by the war dead, their imperfect and faltering spokesman. I see Hitler as the same, yet strong in will determined to do & create what is Right. He is fighting evil. He is fighting for the Truth, not mentally and impotently as I have, but in a material world. Is his disillusion coming? I am filled with a parallel anguish.

On 27 September he went to Bristol with a loaded trailer to stay the night with 'young John Fursdon' whose father had been his platoon officer in 1914, and whose young children wanted to meet him. He heard Chamberlain's broadcast – 'sad, restrained, almost hopeless. Everyone says war is coming. I say Hitler will not make war. I know him. But my heart bleeds for the parallel & twin situation. Am I hopelessly wrong? Am I, after all, inspired by the Devil?'

There seem to be two things to take into account here. One is that his anguish over Ann had become irrevocably intertwined with his equally powerful feelings about the coming war and Hitler so that the two wounds merged into one longer, deeper wound. The second is his personal identification with Hitler, and herein may lay a vital clue to an understanding of the situation. Henry himself did not want war; he considered himself the 'imperfect and faltering spokesman' of the dead of the last war. Hitler was a soldier from the First World War, he must therefore have these same thoughts; *ergo* he could not want war either. To Henry it was all very clear. Again, his inherent Romanticism was blinding him to reality.

At this point he travelled back to Norfolk, first to Bedford where he spent a night with Robin, then on to London, staying with John Heygate and finally returning to Stiffkey on 1 October. By then he was putting the blame for the rift between himself and Ann on to Helen Thomas, who, he stated, had written him a 'fierce' letter. Helen was, naturally, concerned about her daughter's future.

Henry left Stiffkey again on 8 October, travelling to Bedford, and this time he also went on 11 October to see Marjorie Turney at Aspley Guise, 'The old old haunts! Marjorie was my first love, she was sweet to me, a shell-shocked youth, in February 1915. . . . But I was too raw & unbuilt to appreciate it. . . .' From there he travelled to Ipswich where he gave a lecture, 'Enjoyable. I read bits of *Salar*', but 'At night the black monarchs bring me before them. . . .' Once back at Stiffkey the diary entries were still extremely anguished. Farm work occupied him by day, 'But at night – let's have some more fun, cry the dark & terrible monarchs of the slow, slow, hours.' He refers several times to hearing Edward Thomas's voice crying 'WAIT!', the last entry to do so being on 26 October. 'Edward is dead, yet he lives: he cried *wait* to me: it was not imagined: it was true & sudden & instantly accepted.'

After this he seemed easier and the entries returned to a more even keel. On 11 November, Armistice Day, he stayed at Hillington with Lady Downe and spoke at the ex-serviceman's dinner there, in the great hall. 'A nice gathering. Perhaps the last in the pre-war idiom in England.'

A week later was the occasion of the famous Norfolk farm housewarming party:

Friday 18 November
John Heygate & Mary Hewitt arrived in evening for our party. Coast & I went
to Norwich at 9.15. p.m. to fetch John Rayner, Features Editor of D. Express . . .

Saturday 19 November
In morning Gipsy & Mary fetched Munnings from Brancaster while we others
went rough-shooting. In afternoon we all walked around the farm. Robert
Donat, film actor, arrived at 2.30 p.m. In evening a grand party in the Granary.
Algerian wine, nicely warmed. Strange hats – Florida, Texan etc etc. Munnings
was fine, Ballad of Cafe Royal, & other songs. John & Margie were there &
much enjoyed it. Candles in bottles. Donat left regretfully at 9.30 pm to motor
back 160 miles to Buckingham. [He was about to film *Mr. Chips*, having to be
at the studio early on Monday.]

Sunday 20 November
In evening we all went to Fakenham & heard Mosley. A grand speech &
afterwards in the hotel for coffee & sandwiches. I thought I'd make this the
climax of my Norfolk Farm book.

Henry describes this party towards the end of *The Story of a Norfolk Farm*
fleshing out the sparse details from his diary entry:

*So let us eat, drink, and be merry. Here is the granary, lit by fifty candles, and the
refectory table, polished by Loetitia, Mary, and Stella the maid, laden with all
sorts of good things. There at one end sits a famous painter of horses, waving a
chicken-bone and shouting about the iniquities of the art dealers and their
brothers, sons, cousins – 'our rulers', he calls them. Beside him is daughter
Margaret, wearing a cowboy's hat, her dark eyes sparkling and her dusky cheeks
flushed with excitement; and then my friend John . . . here's to you John, gosh
this Algerian wine, warming all day in the granary snugly heated by the stove,
makes one feel fine. There's little John, my John, wearing his grandfather's old
grey otter-hunting hat, which sits well down over his ears . . . When the last
bottle had been drained, the last guttering candle snuffed, when the* Ballad of the
Cafe Cosmopolia, *with the encores of* The Chef *and* The Pork Sandwiches, *had
been declaimed by the artist, and the last song ended; we went home arm in arm,
and found our way to various beds, couches, and palliasses . . .*
                    The Story of a Norfolk Farm, Chapter 44, 'Farmhouse Party'

Sir Alfred Munnings, had a large personality and was well known for his
rumbustuous behaviour and for being the life and soul of a party,[9] when he would
sing bawdy songs, of which *The Ballad of the Cafe Royal* was a prize example.
Munnings features briefly in the *Chronicle* as Frederick Riversmill. Windles does
not appear in this scene of family frivolity as term had not finished and he was at
his school in Devon. But he was to have his own involvement with Munnings later

on. Painting in the area, Munnings was visiting Henry, when he suddenly found the light and the scene before him exactly right for painting, and in his enthusiasm had seized the first thing from the Granary that approximated a canvas. It happened to be Henry's trouser press, and he set to work to capture the scene before the light faded. Windles, to whom Munnings was a stranger, came across him hard at work and seeing the ruined trouser press challenged the artist, who told him to clear off and not to watch him working. Windles stood his ground, stoutly defending his father's property.[10]

As the year drew to its end the weather turned very cold. On Christmas Day Henry went ski-ing on the Hall Hills. The kind Cafferatas again invited them to lunch in the Old Hall, and on 28 December he 'Went shooting with Windles, who carried, pleased & proud the .410 gun with sawn-off barrel'. His closing diary entry for the year was sad and resigned:

So the year closes. I have kept my own faith this year . . . I can honestly say I have tried never to let down a friend. . . . There are many people who dislike me, some hate me. It is very sad. I think of Ann sometimes, & feel the old wound ache, but am still.

From Henry's diary and papers it is evident he found 1939 a very dreary year. On 13 March he wrote in his diary, which was blank up to this point:

I must record that I have neglected this book the past few months. As I have neglected my literary work, my own life, the farm & everything. I am very tired. The crisis in Europe, the struggle of my mind for a new world, the misery of AT's inevitable departure – all wear my inharmonious nature.

In early May he sold *The Children of Shallowford* to Faber for £200 advance and 20 per cent royalty, and he also arranged for a series of his articles to be published in the *Evening Standard* over three months at a fee of £40 per month. *The Children of Shallowford* recorded intimate and happy scenes of the life in the family and was very well received.

The news continued to be ominous, and Henry was very affected by it. On 1 July he recorded, 'Lots of poppies have appeared in the fields this year. I must write an article about it. Another crop of Flanders poppies on the way?' His nerves were constantly frayed and he and Loetitia seemed to be arguing constantly, 'I am a drain on her & the poor dear is very tired, just as I am.'

He went to London for a broadcast on 21 July, returning the next day in the Alvis 'slowly at 30 m.p.h. (new big ends) with Alison S. & John Heygate & Mary Hibbert & John Rayner in the car.' He had brought them up for another 'house-warming' party which was also attended by Stephen Renshaw and his daughter Margot. Then at the end of the month he set out for Devon collecting John en route (seemingly from a short holiday with John Heygate) and picking up Windles from his school at West Buckland. He went over to Instow where the Renshaw family had a house and where Margot Renshaw was now staying and he admitted he was 'much affected by this 22 year old beauty'. They saw quite a bit of each other during the next few days, and on his return to Stiffkey Henry wrote to her hinting at marriage. Her reply was couched in very diplomatic terms, saying that although she would have loved to look after him, there was her family to consider and she also preferred to remain a free spirit. (Margot is portrayed as Melissa in the *Chronicle* novels.)

Henry was greatly disturbed by the daily worsening news. He could not believe that Hitler really intended to wage war. In desperation he apparently wrote to Oswald Mosley suggesting that he (and/or Mosley?) should fly to Germany as a last-ditch attempt to persuade Hitler, as ex-soldier to ex-soldier, not to proceed. Henry went to London on 26 August and while there he saw Oswald Mosley 'about my letter, which offered to fly to Germany to see Hitler & get him to put over a speech defining clearly for the ordinary man the fundamental causes of the present crisis. Mosley [realizing the futility, even the absurdity of this Quixotic gesture], said "I'm afraid it is too late – the curtain is down."' Too late it certainly was, for on 3 September Henry recorded simply: 'Today at 11 a.m. Gt. Britain declared war on Germany.'

When the summer holidays were over John returned to his choir school, now evacuated to Sevenoaks under the headmastership of Eddie Pine, while Margaret returned to her school at Weasenham, Norfolk. However, it had been decided between Henry and Loetitia that Windles, whose school reports were apparently showing a lack of application, should not return to school but should instead start work on the farm.[11] As he stated on several occasions, one of Henry Williamson's main ideas about the farm was to create a viable unit that would support the family, and he genuinely thought that to train Windles as a farmer was the way to go about it. It was to put an enormous burden on Windles that was far beyond his years and experience – he was then only thirteen and a half – mainly because whatever he did was considered by his father to be wrong.

So with war declared work on the farm continued apace; the diary entries record all the details of muck carting, calves being born and the buying of many items of farm machinery. There was a heavy workload, with the added rules and regulations of wartime to be adjusted to as well. Tiredness and depression frayed Henry's nerves continuously and the situation between husband and wife deteriorated. It was decided that Loetitia would take the two younger children and go and live with her brother Robin in Bedford, while the 'Tranters' came to live and work on the farm. The Tranters were in fact Freddy Tranter and Mrs Hurt (they feature in the *Chronicle* as Teddy Pinnegar and 'Yipps' Carfax, where their sojourn at the farm is well documented in *A Solitary War*). Tranter had served in the First World War with Henry, had recently read an article of his about the farm, and had written to offer his services, saying that he was selling his business and would have some capital to invest, and those of his partner, Mrs Hurt, whom Tranter said was a good organizer and housekeeper. They arrived on 26 October, a day or two before they were actually due, and were instantly critical of the state of the cottage that they were to live in within Loetitia's hearing. As she was not expecting them so early the work of clearing up prior to leaving had not been done, but her main concern anyway was that they should look after the turkeys which were her particular responsiblity and involved a great deal of work.

On 2 November Henry noted, 'Took Gipsy & Robt & Richard to Bedford today, with a trailer load of things & some hens & ¼ sack corn. This looks to be the end. I felt extremely sad.' Henry went on to Wiltshire staying for a day or two with Ann Thomas which restored him somewhat, returning to Bedford for an overnight stay before going back to Stiffkey on 9 November, 'feeling empty & ill. Found the place clean & altered & the Tranters most kind & cheering. Brought a land girl with me.'

This cheerful state of affairs did not last long. The land girl had only come to look at Henry and the farm set-up and left after the weekend, while Henry soon discovered that the Tranters were not what they had seemed. Freddy Tranter apparently did not have money from the sale of his business to invest in the farm, as he had intimated. 'I don't like Mrs. Hurt & Tranter. It is awful.'

About this time a visitor arrived, Henry's boyhood friend Terence Tetley. Henry did not record this at the time, but referred to it in his diary entry for 29 January 1940: 'Before Christmas Terence Tetley (Jack Temperley, of a sort, in my *Flax*) turned up from Africa. I didn't like him. He borrowed £2 on leaving & omitted to pay a poor cottage woman for his washing – 1/10*d*. etc.' These bare details are fleshed out in Chapter 11 of *A Solitary War* where Desmond Neville, returned home from a time in Africa, has read Phillip's articles about life on the farm in the *Daily Crusader* and contacts him through the newspaper. Also in this chapter, Henry introduces the extraordinary 'Laura Wissilcraft', a somewhat neurotic would-be writer with whom he had a short acquaintance in real life. Henry seemed to draw to himself some very extraordinary people, and they were all to be used in some form or other in the *Chronicle* novels, although certain of the details were changed.

On 15 December Henry again set forth for Bedford, this time to take Margaret and Windles to stay with their mother and the rest of the family for Christmas. Again he continued on, having lunch with Robert Donat at Wendover on 17 December, en route to stay with Ann Thomas, from whom he recorded he received a 'grand welcome', and the next day was hard at work on the farm book. He returned to Stiffkey in time for Christmas, but had a dreadful journey back towing the trailer in fog. On Christmas Day he 'couldn't stick depression within & had lunch alone in Townshead Arms. Can't bear Tranter or Mrs. Hurt. She calls me "Little ray of sunshine".' One can imagine the effect of such a cheerfully sarcastic phrase on Henry's psyche!

By 11 January 1940 the 'Tranters' had left, to Henry's great relief, leaving a trail of woe behind them, as none of the arrangements that Henry thought existed were honoured. According to his diary entries, they did not pay any of their share of the household expenses and left everything in a muddle. Of particular annoyance to Henry was the fact that through their own fault the cylinder block on their car was cracked by frost and Henry had paid for its repair, for which he received no thanks whatsoever. They went to stay with Mrs North[12] and the tale they told made her turn against Henry, until at the end of February he recorded that they had blotted their copybook with her over some misdemeanour – 'She has found them out but I doubt if she will admit she was wrong.' With the departure of Mrs Hurt there was no one to look after Henry and Windles and he arranged that they should take their meals with Mrs Sutton in her cottage.

Towards the end of January 1940 Henry pasted several newspaper cuttings into his diary about the unusually cold weather over Christmas and the New Year, which particularly mentioned the plight of bitterns and swans. This weather information had not been previously reported due to censorship regulations, in case it fell into enemy hands. Again Henry makes good use of this material in the *Chronicle*, combining his own observations with those from the newspapers (see *A Solitary War*, Chapter 17, 'At Mrs. Hammett's').

At the beginning of February Windles was in bed with a temperature. On 7 February Henry recorded 'Trying to work on "Story of a Norfolk Farm". Windles still ill. Poor little devil, has to listen to my wretched tirades. Thawing, thank God.' A week later Windles is still in bed, his temperature varying between 100 and 102 degrees. On 16 February there is an entry which shows Henry's state of mind at this time; not the wild outpourings of some of his emotional crises but a resigned statement.

It is very lonely here now. I live in my upstairs room, which has only bed, chair & chest of drawers: not even a sack on the floor. I walk to Mrs. Sutton's for meals, sitting at the table, reading or just sitting. I should have died, I think, if she hadn't taken us in. . . . How lonely it all is: how cold & blank. To what end? Gipsy is very happy with the little ones in Bedford & Robin has an ideal housekeeper. I am truly getting my deserts. I think of Ann much.

Windles was still ill on the 26 February. 'He is patience itself, poor little boy, lies in his day clothes, at least he is warm. He lies all day in his bed & I minister to him in a half-helpless, rough sort of way.' Henry wrote of this illness in Chapter 17 of *A Solitary War*, but there he ended the episode with a joke that 'Billy' had not been ill at all, it was just that the thermometer had been broken and the gauge stuck at 100 degrees. In fact Henry had been quite worried about the lad and had done the best he could to look after him. On 4 March Henry recorded that Windles was better and out of bed. Two days later he took him to Bedford to stay with his mother, and after a few days, Henry continued on to stay with Ann. 'It was lovely in her cottage in the dear little room with warm fire, black beams, and nice rush-mat, table & little armchair. . . . I felt almost normal – if one can feel normal in this bloody war.' Two days later his mood was further enhanced by an interview in London with a man called 'Soskin, film producer, re film with farming as background. Wants to see Mss of *Norfolk Farm*.'

By the end of the month, however, he was back at the farm, and found the situation was very poor. His calves had constant diarrhoea and many were dying, and he discovered the cows were being fed poor quality food. Windles was already back at work and Henry warned him to keep away from the men with their forgetful, careless, and easy-going minds, as he was growing like them. By the end of March things had improved a little. The farm work was going better and he recorded that he sold '4 fat bullocks for £104/13/11d. Best beast weighed 10 cwt, was graded A-, . . . This is satisfying & should offset the dead calves.'

At the beginning of April Henry went, again via Bedford, to stay with Ann Thomas to work on a synopsis of the proposed farm film, leaving Windles to

Windles at work at Old Hall Farm, Norfolk.

plough and drill with the men. He recorded 'Wrote scenario synopsis. Good stuff. Ann agrees.' On 6 April he went to see Robert Donat and read him 'synopsis of IMMORTAL CORN. He thought it very good.' The following day he went back to Bedford, collecting the family and they all returned to Stiffkey. 'Gipsy looks very fresh after her rest. The children did not want to return. "That dirty old rat hole" (Robt).' A week later, on 15 April, Henry once again travelled to London, having 'worked all night (ill and overset) on the synopsis (expanded). I sold it in the afternoon to Soskin for £1500, including work on scenario with another man called Dalrymple.'

On his return to Stiffkey he telegraphed Ann to come up to start work on the scenario. They had apparently made such an arrangement. But Ann prevaricated, to Henry's annoyance, saying that Bronwen was staying with her and had measles as did other children in the family. (Rosemary was at boarding school.) Henry went to London, where Ann again failed to meet him, to attend a Mosley luncheon at the Criterion on 26 April; afterwards he went on to stay with Petre Mais for the weekend, finally meeting up with Ann back in London. On 1 May he went to the office of the film company, but 'Something seems to be wrong with film, think I am going to be swindled.' He and Ann went back down to Shoreham to stay with Petre Mais again where he recorded that they had a 'Lovely walk in Arundel woods with Petre & Jill – Ann & I went off alone & it was lovely.'

They returned to Stiffkey on 7 May and almost immediately the diary entries are about the state of the war, for on 10 May, 'The (to me) unexpected & scoffed at BLITZKRIEG in France started today against Holland and Belgium. Parachute troops drop in clouds. I feel I was wrong, entirely, about "the only true pacifist in Europe" . . . I am heavy hearted.' On 11 May he wrote, 'Grave news. Holland appears to be scuppered. I sent off £750 cheque to Bank – sale of Drake Driver Leaver shares. Ann making up my accounts says that when all bills are paid I shall still owe to bank & others, about £400.' On 23 May he recorded 'Mosley taken to prison. Tom Driberg of the D. Express rang up & asked me to comment, while I was at the British Legion Meeting in the Village Institute. I didn't. The meeting treated me rather roughly. . . .' This was the meeting where Henry was accused of 'repeatedly blaspheming against King, Country, & the poor lads out in France'. Afterwards Henry complained to Major Hammond, the Chairman, and said that it was a lie. His diary records that Hammond's reply was 'I don't care a damn if its a lie or not. I believe it.' Major Hammond did not like Henry and was apparently glad of a chance to publicly denounce him.

On 28 May Henry travelled down to Sevenoaks to collect John from his school since even that location was no longer considered safe. He lunched with Rayner and Driberg of the *Express*, and said that he could write an article about the possible defeat of France by Hitler. The next day Henry returned to Stiffkey and two days later recorded the Dunkirk rescue: 'Most of the BEF rescued at Dunkirk, by hundreds of little English boats. Bravo! I wished I had been there with little Pinta Major, sailing across.'

On 9 June he and Loetitia lunched with Lady Downe and later in the day went to see Capt. Goodliffe (who is portrayed as Capt. Runnymeade in the *Chronicle* novels) at Brancaster. 'He had a Polish woman friend staying with him.' It was this lady, an ex-ballerina, who greeted him with hisses and spitting: 'Traitor, Spy, Liar, Fascist'. The following day he discovered that she had painted white swastikas on the Silver Eagle, which he immediately blacked out, thankful that they had not been seen on his return journey the previous evening.

For some weeks past someone in the village had been spying on Henry. His diary entry for 12 May recorded that 'the local rag & bone merchant went to Norman Jordan, my man, today seeking information or "evidence" to have me put in prison. . . .' Henry must have known that it was almost inevitable that he would be questioned at some point, for his views were very well known, and they alone, at such a time, made him suspect. The village people viewed his behaviour with total suspicion. They considered that he had made the concrete roads on the farm for the German invasion (what else could they possibly be for? – farmers didn't need such well-built roads); that the clear fanlight inserted to provide light on the stairway was a device for signalling to the Germans, and of course the fact that he painted the Mosley BUF device (a single lightning flash within a circle), on his cottage wall was the proverbial red rag to a bull, but that *was* his own fault. The younger children suffered many insults from their peers at the village school. But Henry's conscience was clear; he had done nothing against his country. On the contrary, in his own opinion, his every thought was *for* his country. On Friday 14 June his fears were realized and his diary recorded:

Today at 2.45 pm four plain-clothed detectives, armed, came to the house & arrested me under the Defence Act, Section 18B. They took me to Wells whilst others searched the cottages, the granary, & all my boxes. I was locked in a little white-washed cell. I spent a curious afternoon in the cell. . . . In evening Gipsy & Ann came & cheered me up. We sat in the yard behind.

He was kept at Wells Police Station over the weekend. 'The police at Wells were very kind. I wrote the farm story, sitting on my narrow bed.' On the Monday morning he was taken out to a car which set off, although he was not told where they were going. He was rather afraid that it might be Brixton Prison and was relieved when he found that their destination was actually Norwich Police Station, 'where the Chief Constable, Capt. van Neck, said I was to be released, as nothing found against me.' The chief constable apparently apologized, stating that they had had to act on the complaints received.

Henry returned to the farm and the next day simply recorded 'Making hay'. At the end of the month he noted that he had read in the papers that Lady Mosley was arrested, and Mosley had his examination. 'I go about with heavy heart.' Apart from the very depressing news, he was worried about the children's safety in the event of an invasion. He arranged to join the local ARP and was allocated the Friday night watch, but almost immediately received a letter saying his services were not required. He may not have been imprisoned, but suspicions were not so easily appeased. Their opinions about Loetitia were very different. She was involved in the village activities, the Women's Institute and the Red Cross, and everyone felt sorry for her and was very fond of her. However, Henry did have two very good friends in Major and Mrs Hollingsworth, 'Holly and Mossy'. Yet he never mentioned them in his diary at all until after he had left the farm, when he went back to see them several times and referred to them with great affection.

Problems continued to be rife on the farm; in particular one of the cows went down with contagious abortion and Bob Sutton neglected to report the resultant dead calf for 36 hours. Henry was despondent. 'This household is exactly a miniature of the world situation. The same ideas are in conflict. And the farm too.'

On 2 August he and Ann, together with John, left for a holiday in the Field in the Alvis drawing the trailer with food, luggage and 10 gallons of petrol, collecting Rosemary en route. For the first few days all went well and he recorded that they were having a lovely time, but on 9 August Loetitia wrote to tell him that the pigs were sick and that the vet said poor food was to blame. At the same time Ann told

A happy afternoon on the saltings at Stiffkey. From left to right: Margaret, Richard, Robert, John.

him that she did not want to return to the farm. Henry suggested that she and Rosemary should live in the Hut and Field, but Ann also turned this down and so Henry let most of the land at Ox's Cross to a market gardener called Pinn, for £3 a year for four years. Ann was seeing a great deal of some friends, a couple called Service, and their cousins the Thompsons, and they all – somewhat to Henry's annoyance, for he felt left-out and jealous – spent their time in the Georgeham Rock Inn at night singing songs. Henry returned home to the farm on the 23 August having taken Ann and Rosemary to Helen and Bronwen in Chippenham en route. Soon afterwards Ann wrote to say that she would go and live in the Hut after all. Henry then wrote to invite her back to the farm as a partner, which must have unnerved her for towards the end of September Henry noted that 'Ann's new idea is to work for Pat Thompson as housekeeper'. This disturbed him greatly.

On the 27 September he took Loetitia to visit Robin and continued on down to the Field, to find it all locked up, empty and no fire lit. Ann had spent two days in the Hut and had then left to stay with Pat Thompson in a cottage in the village. In the evening Pat and Ann came up to see him, acting very nervously, and Pat said she and Ann did not want to see Henry. He felt very bitter and for two or three days plunged back into ranting despair, 'pacing the darkened Hut, declaiming & struggling'. He then went to Instow and saw Mary Renshaw and Maurice and Margot. But it was not a very cheerful household as 'Mary's loved brother, Sir Edward Chichester, had been buried that day'.

He returned to the Hut on 4 October to find a note from Ann about the future, saying that she did not want any contact with him for six months, which caused him to hurl himself about the hut screaming 'It isn't fair, it isn't fair'. Then he calmed down and accepted the situation. The following day Ann went to see him 'looking neat & pretty . . . we talked & hugged & kissed & laughed. I felt young again & hung upside down from the hut beams.' The next day 'Ann & Rosie came to tea. I wrote AT 6 cheques for 6 months allowances & put them in the little secret wall-safe.' The next day he made black-out curtains and a saw bench for use when wanted, and then left for Stiffkey, picking up Loetitia en route.

Back at the farm things were as difficult as ever. On 15 October he recorded 'two shocks'; first, that the ploughing on Fox Covert was a mess and that when he ranted at Windles, Loetitia took the boy's part. Secondly, that the contract price for sugar beet carting had been arranged without his knowledge, a fact about which he felt he had been deceived. As he was so frequently absent it was hardly surprising that things were not done as he wanted. The problems on the farm continued and his diary entries are full of complaints about the men, especially Bob Sutton, until on 18 November Bob told him that he was giving up the 'teamsman' job as he was fed up with the sneers, although he would continue to work on the farm. On 23 November Henry got up to feed the horses at 3 a.m. and continued to do so for the time being. By 6 December he noted that he was by then too exhausted to groom them: 'I am almost to the roots of my nerves for nourishment & feel all disintegrated and black inside. Worry and overwork producing inability to work & thereby piling up more worry & exhaustion.'

However, they had a happy Christmas, lunching traditionally at the Cafferatas. 'It was a completely happy Christmas, which is unusual in our family – owing to my uncertain moods – the children made it, & it is for the children, bless their little hearts.' But this interlude of sentimental optimism lasted only a few hours, and as the year drew to its end he was once more deeply depressed; about the situation with Ann, although she had sent him greetings for his birthday and for Christmas, and also because 'we are threatened with invasion in 1941, & I fear we shall be terribly mauled, perhaps mortally'.

The mood of depression continued into January with much agonizing over Ann; the letters that did pass between them were antagonistic and involved Ann's mother at some point, creating a very tense situation. (Ann is still bitter about Henry's treatment of her mother.) This was not helped by the fact that on 18 January Henry went to Norwich market and, being cold and not bothering to eat properly, he caught a chill. He was ill in bed for several days, worrying and miserable on and off, but he got up several times to go and shout at the men, whom he could see from his studio bedroom window, in rage because they were not working. However, he was cheered by the fact that two girls had applied for jobs. The first one, eighteen years old, was employed as secretary from 8 January but she lasted barely a month. The second one, Miss Kathleen Thornton was older, aged twenty-eight and was already an experienced landgirl and ex-typist, and liked Delius. She was to become known in the family as 'Muffet'. Henry noted that 'the possibility of finding a decent girl for a help and a friend made me feel better. I'm desperately lonely & the segregated fretting male.'

On 12 February he was feeling better; 'Weak but walked around farm with Gipsy.' A few days later he noted that he had 'bought a desk & fish-spear & [also] leather watch guard for Windles' birthday'. *The Story of a Norfolk Farm* was published on 23 January and on 18 February, after noting that it was Windles' birthday, his diary stated: '*Norfolk Farm* has surprisingly long & good reviews. Punch, Times all praise it. Wonders seem to have begun.' The book was written in a calm objective style and is the literary equivalent to a great country scene painted by Constable. Henry takes his reader through all the processes that he and all those connected with the farm had been through, and the reader experiences it all with him. The file of reviews does indeed show them to be long and nearly all enthusiastic. The *Punch* reviewer ended by stating 'In *The Story of a Norfolk Farm* you have, documented up the the hilt, one of the shrewdest blows struck in the war that underlies all wars – the war of the country against the town' (*Punch*, 12 February 1941). The *Times Literary Supplement* (15 February 1941) stated: 'It [becoming a farmer] was the reaction of a generous-minded man, who had fought in the last war and had established himself as a writer, against the sense of aimlessness and frustration that has pervaded English life for the twenty years since the hollow peace had been declared.' By 4 April the book had sold 4,000 copies and a 2,000 reprint was in hand.

But on the farm matters were actually as difficult as ever. The work had fallen behind and on 28 February Henry asked the men to work on the Saturday

Taken from the Frontispiece in Henry's own copy of *The Story of a Norfolk Farm*. The scarecrow's message reads: 'I died in Flanders – I am the unknown soldier – I died for ideals which were not of the market place – my voice is gone, but not my ghost ——'.

afternoon which they normally had off, to spread muck on Spong Beck. Led by Bob Sutton, they refused. On March 1 Wright, the maimed old soldier whose job was to feed the bullocks, fell ill. Asked by Henry to help with the extra load, Bob refused, saying he was not going to have anything whatsoever to do with the livestock ever again. So 'Windles, Muffet & I fed the bullocks & littered them & I enjoyed it.'

On 12 May Loetitia and Margaret went to London to stay with her cousin Mary in order to attend Robin's wedding to Beatrice (Betty) Stirling on 17 May. The occasion caused Henry to reminisce and after some musings about Robin and Loetitia he continued:

Nowadays I feel myself growing less & less of use, to myself or others. I find that the *malaise* is now deep-rooted. Reason: I've never written the Phillip Maddison books. I know by past experience that freedom comes only by that partial new-world revelation-creation. Neither Salar nor Tarka nor the farm book really mattered to the interior urgency; only the stifled cries of my daemon or geist.

Like all creative spirits, he was already craving for the next step forward. His other books were in the past; they no longer mattered. Once written and published they were no longer of import to him. It was those books that he had yet to write that mattered.

On 17 May Henry took John to Bungay to see the writer on country affairs and farmer, Adrian Bell, whom he recorded as being most unwell, looking frail and suffering from very bad migraines. Although not close, the two men were friends and a family connection was maintained until the death of Mrs Bell in the 1990s.

One of the biggest problems on the farm was caused by the acquisition of land by the War Ministry for training soldiers, and for defence purposes. Officers were supposed to have permits issued and compensation was supposed to be paid for any damage caused. Both measures were lax almost to the point of non-existence. Henry was frequently very upset about the considerable amount of damage and chaos the soldiers were causing. His diary entry for 1 June 1941 is typical:

> The [armoured] cars are cutting the lower road, made with such patience & exasperation in 1937–38. The top road is ruined by the searchlight camp. The grass by the Entries Wood, bushed & rolled in the winter & spring, is all spoiled by the wheels. No compensation. No payment. . . . Soldiers all over the farm. I feel almost at the end of myself.

The problems with the soldiers were constant, a running sore throughout the war years, and the details can be read in the *Chronicle*. Henry's hard work and planning were undermined. His spirits lifted with the arrival of the Leicestershire Yeomanry to camp at the Entries Wood on 30 May and a week later he entertained the officers to dinner, to which Adrian Bell also came, 'nice fellow, understands almost everything', and they had an enjoyable evening with Algerian wine followed by 'elderberry wine'.

A few days later Henry went to London to lunch with Major Francis Yeats-Brown, who had written a letter of appreciation to him about *The Story of a Norfolk Farm*. Francis Yeats-Brown was the author of several books of which the best known was *The Bengal Lancer*, the story of his life in the Indian Cavalry. The two men got on very well indeed. When Henry returned to Stiffkey about a week later it was to find that Muffet had left in his absence. She had not turned out to be the new 'Barleybright' that he had hoped for. More importantly, a letter awaited him from the solicitors controlling T.E. Lawrence's estate; he was at last granted permission to use the long quotations from Lawrence's letters in his essay written soon after Lawrence's death. Henry immediately alerted Richard de la Mare at Faber to go ahead with publication, and *Genius of Friendship* came out later in the year.

At the beginning of June Henry had resolved to go with Eric Perkins, the Wells lorry owner-driver who had helped him with the removal of the Shallowford furniture, 'to Devon, with tractor & saw & cut & haul & carry oak-wood from my plot in the Ilfracombe valley. Live in the field & work all day. Selling some & storing others. Perkins can wield an axe and work a saw . . .'. Possibly he formulated this plan as a legitimate excuse to visit the Field and thus to see Ann, who was now living in the Hut, her job with Pat Thompson having very quickly fallen through. The area of woodland that Henry leased was one and a half acres of Stoneyard Wood at Heddon Mill.

But first there was the hay to harvest. It was a very good crop and all went well except that Bob and Jimmy objected to various things Henry wanted done and he exploded. But after venting his feelings to his diary he ended, 'But I don't want this to be all rant: both Jimmy and Bob have done a great deal of solid, patient work & I'd not have got on as I have without them.' Loetitia reported that an old man in the village, 'looking at our meadow hay said he hadn't seen the meadow looking like that since Farmer Buck's time, forty years ago.' This was very gratifying. However, the next day his entry estimates that his overdraft at the bank still stood at £857, with only £100 to come from drainage grant, £100 for the T.E. Lawrence essay, and about £200 in royalties still due on the farm book to be set against it.

Perkins helped with the hay harvest while he waited for the trip to Devon. Henry was very impressed with him: 'Perkins is a very sound fellow & all the work he has done for me, on car, tractor, etc, has been first-class. He is very careful & attends to the tiniest detail; & is quick.' Eventually on 14 July, late at night, they were able to pack the lorry with the Ferguson, saw, and gear for Devon. Accompanied by Bert's girlfriend, Kathleen, who was going to cook and generally help, they left at 5 a.m. the next morning, arriving at the Field at 2 a.m. the following morning. So as not to disturb Ann at that hour, Henry's diary records that he slept in the hedge, despite the fact that it was pouring with rain!

Henry had placed an advertisement in the local paper prior to his arrival, hoping to attract customers for his sawn wood. The little advertisement is pasted into his diary and is exactly the same as that to be found at the beginning of Chapter 7, 'Eclipse', of *Lucifer Before Sunrise* (except that the place 'Turnstone-Malandine' was really Croyde-Braunton). They worked hard each day, moving about 2 tons of wood daily. Ann left each morning for the Evacuated Local Government Officers' Camp at Croyde where she had a secretarial job. Henry was for once happy, and wrote in his diary:

It is lovely in the woods, the dappled sunlight, the fire for the tea billy-can at midday. Kathleen is an admirable girl – efficient, quiet, intelligent, most helpful.

I am enjoying the work & time more than any other for years. Perkins is a splendid fellow. Ann is also very sweet.

The advertisement did not generate any wood sales. Henry sold 6 tons to Ann's friends in the village for £13 and a further £3 worth to someone else. There were 20 tons of wood left in the Field, value £45.[13] They stayed until 12 August although work itself ceased a few days before, and accompanied by a young lady who was to work on the farm, Mary de la Casas (a relation of the Renshaws) returned via Oxford, when they spent the night with Petre and Jill Mais.

The arrival back at Stiffkey was not auspicious. The telegram announcing their return had not been delivered. There were the inevitable recriminations, further exacerbated by the fact that he found that in his absence the hay had not been properly covered and thus had been spoiled. The next day wet weather set in and the harvest was gathered in under difficult conditions. However, he recorded on 8 September that there were 'Four good stacks', and also that Mary de la Casas was working well, keeping the stables very clean despite discouragement from Jimmy and Bob Sutton. The harvest over, the crop had to be threshed and Henry enlisted the help of three soldiers from the camp, paying them 7 shillings per day, although they were not very good at the work. 'Perkins the faithful came and helped again.' The problems with Bob increased, culminating in him giving in his notice and departing on 3 October, leaving Norman Jordan to build the straw stacks, of which he had no experience and so made many mistakes.

Trouble with the soldiers flared up again. Towards the end of October a fresh contingent arrived to camp on the Hall Hills without permit. Henry tried to stop them, without success. They said the permit was being processed. Their lorries tore up the roads, making deep ruts and potholes. The men removed anything that they could find for their own use, including a door from a shed which they used by the river for washing and then let float away. Later, when Henry tried to claim for the damage caused, he found that the men had not had a requisition order and so had lied to him; and later still, when the claims officer finally came out, instead of the £100 Henry estimated was due, it was knocked down to £15. The entries that Henry made in his diary at this time were, for the most part, short and terse. The long entries that are to be found in the *Chronicle* do not exist. They are part of Henry Williamson's technique as a writer creating his story.

On 12 November he went to London to see Donald McCollagh about the proposed film *Immortal Corn*. Although described as 'First class', it had been shelved, so Henry, who had suspected as much, lost another source of income. He did not remark on the disappointment he must have felt, but continued down to Ox's Cross. There he started work on 'A Norfolk Farm in War-Time', a sequel to *The Story of a Norfolk Farm* which was never actually published but became incorporated into *The Phasian Bird* and eventually also into the *Chronicle*.

He returned to Stiffkey on his birthday: 'A nice tea and all the children to greet me, a tidy & nice house, a warm fire & good electric light – the house looks like home. Ida is very kind to work so hard for me.' But as always the happy mood was short-lived. The next day's entry stated 'Reaction. Felt farm too much for me. Feeling ill.' A few days later he had an argument with Windles which he recorded thus: 'Rather wretched incident with poor Windles, he ran away swearing. In evening Windles & I apologised to each other. He did so first. I thought well of him for this. But it was my fault.' Then just before Christmas Mary de la Casas left, to Henry's relief as they had not in the end got on, mainly because she had told him off for being so continuously irritable. On Christmas Eve he was glad, he noted, 'to be without strangers. . . . Our little family dined on pheasant. The long oak table was as usual a gay place at supper.' The following day they all went to church and then had lunch as usual at the Old Hall but with only Mrs Cafferata and her cousin, as Louis Cafferata had recently died. Robert and Richard had actually seen him collapse while he was out for a walk, and had told the family at lunch with schoolboy relish, oblivious to the awfulness of the occasion.

On New Year's Eve Henry wrote a long entry summing up the state of the war, for the news had been bad with the bombing of Pearl Harbour earlier in the month; 'I feel as always, it is such a tragedy that the war came. . . .'

The new year of 1942 opened with further gloomy entries in the diary; 'Another year dragging itself in, which means I am dragging myself into another solar cycle. I hardly have heart to write anything.' He was pessimistic about the state of the war and noted that Japanese invaders were racing through the jungles of Malaya towards Singapore. On 12 February he left for London by train where he went to see Tranter, who was working in the War Ministry and living in an hotel off the Strand. The following day he entrained down to Devon and caught a bus from Barnstaple, walking the last part. He wrote a few pages of *A Norfolk Farm in Wartime* – but referred to it as 'poisonous stuff, indicative of a poisoned age'. On 24 February he returned to London, dining with Francis Yeats-Brown and attending Maurice Renshaw's wedding the following day, and dining that night, and the next also, with Sir Herbert Morgan and Lady Annaly (there is no indication of the connection with these two) and others at Oddeminos where 'Gilly Potter talked in continuous monologue'. He returned to Devon for the weekend and had a pleasant and happy time with Ann, and then back to London on 2 March where he saw Robert Donat, returning to Stiffkey on 3 March 'somewhat dolefully. During my absence the farm has been going all right.'

On 5 March he stayed in bed with a cold, feeling tired, but the following week he helped with the threshing. On 13 March the artist Edward Seago, whom Henry had met when Seago was out sketching in the locality of the farm, came to tea and Henry returned with him to his home at Brook Lodge, the other side of Norwich for the night, the following day going into Norwich to take a grain sample for the market. The Seagos drove him home on 15 March. It was probably on this occasion that Edward Seago painted Henry's portrait. Although Henry does not mention this at all, it *was* during one of Seago's leaves in 1942, and this occasion fits the known facts.[14]

The following day they began the ploughing, but in the evening Henry felt ill and went to bed with a temperature and a filthy cold which lasted two or three days, during which he did a little writing but mainly composed letters to Ann asking her to come and join the farm 'Board'. Once up, he recorded 'continual tirades, shouting, upsets'. He was worried that the work on the farm, ploughing and drilling, was late and was very irritable with Windles all the time. The climax of this spate of mishaps came on 2 May when, he wrote in his diary, 'Bullock fell in grupp for 3rd time & was found dead at 9.30. Jimmy told Windles 3 hours later, who told HW Sunday morning, 22 hours later. Meanwhile it had become carrion [whereas Sat. it could have been sold as good meat].' He had also been to Norwich and found that his Alvis engine, which had been taken to a Norwich garage for repair, had been burnt out in the very heavy air-raid on Norwich the previous week. For this he blamed Perkins, who had been supposed to take it some time previously, when the repair would have been done and the car safely home.

On 3 May he was in such a state that he decided to kill himself, 'unable to bear any more. This has been my mood for several weeks. Always mental suffering and complete indifference to it in those around me.' There had been a bad quarrel between himself and Loetitia,[15] who had not supported him about Windles not reporting the death of the bullock. He was, indeed, quite desperate afterwards for on a separate page pasted into the opening of the 1942 diary is his farewell letter, a rather bitter document, signed and dated, with a later note added explaining that 'On this day I sat for 3 hours in my cottage room, by the bed, a pail and a razor blade by me, & my left arm bared. It was one of many such moods 1939–1945.' Also pasted into the front of this diary is another long note written at about the same time as this suicidal mood, addressed to no one – the recipient, to whom he intended sending his diaries for safety, is referred to only as 'you are my best friend' – in which he states that he does not want his diaries suppressed or burned, 'I want the truth to be told. . . . I am at odds with them & the odds are them & the odds are too great & like the Starborn I wish to go beyond.'

The next day he recorded that he felt very ill and utterly miserable. After two days when his temperature was found to be 102 degrees Dr Acheson was called. Henry had cystitis, and was given Prontosil, but the doctor also apparently advised, 'as I knew, that I should see a psychiatrist-soul-doctor'. That afternoon he played with the boys by the river and once in bed felt 'extraordinarily serene'. The build-up of electricity in his being had been diffused and earthed once the storm in his mind had played itself out.

On 13 May he got up for two hours and wandered around the farm, and a few days later bought a 1938 Ford for £145. On 21 May he went to London, staying at the Savage Club and seeing Reggie Pound,[16] with whom he was very friendly, going on to Devon and Ann at the Field the next day. Here he met Negley Farson, 'American "star" journalist, just back from Russia. Ann and I had dinner with them. I liked him much.' A few days later he and Ann walked to Woolacombe across the Downs and bathed with Negley Farson on the sands. 'It was a brilliant day, a lovely day – perfect companionship.' So began a relationship between these two tempestuous characters which was to be characterized by fireworks, some humorous times and some bitter arguments, a relationship which included Negley's son, Dan.[17]

Leaving on 2 June, Henry travelled as far as Salisbury to stay with Edward Seago, a camouflage officer on the staff of Southern Command, who was sharing a cottage nearby with his friend Flying Officer Clegg and a batman, returning to Stiffkey after a few days. Loetitia then went to stay with her brother Robin now living at Swaythling, near Southampton – Henry referred to having only 'tinned herrings for food'. On 19 June he drove down to Swaythling in the little new Ford 8, and was greeted with pleasure by Robin and found Betty, whom he had not previously met, 'young, graceful & clear'. Two days later they all drove to Parkstone to visit Henry's father, from whom he stated that he had not had a letter for six years. The visit was very successful.[18]

A few days after his return he drove down to see Middleton Murry's Community Farm centre near Stratford St Mary, the other side of Ipswich. He arrived late, but at 11.30 p.m. it was still light – 'double summer time' gave very light evenings during the war. He slept well and declared Middleton Murry to be a 'dear man, I was sorry I'd followed the mob in 1933 & sneered at him in the *Gold Falcon*.' One of Murry's 'Adelphi Centre' young men went back to the farm with him, but on his return to Stiffkey depression set in again about the farm situation. Everything was wrong; dead rats lying about, dead hens also, haycocks and cauliflowers overblown, only 26 out of 83 duck's eggs hatched; and although the gloom was alleviated by a 'walk and swim on the marshes with Windles, Margie, Rikky and Robert', plus the 'Adelphi Centre' young man on 5 July, a few days later he recorded 'Crisis here'. Windles, fed up, had applied for a job working with tractors in Cambridge, which Henry immediately cancelled.

On 17 July, 'weary of the hopeless struggle here' Henry loaded up the little Ford with food and petrol and set off for Devon yet again. Walking happily on the sands at the weekend with Ann, on the Monday he slept all day in the Hut, and then having regained his energy set about the maintenance jobs needed at the Field, cleaning the gutters on the Hut, and topping the pines, beech and ash by the Hut to make a thick hedge. Unfortunately, after a week or so he was smitten with enteritis which he put down to the water in the underground tank being contaminated 'with the year's accumulation of dead beetles, worms etc'. He also found all the food in Ann's tin storage boxes, figs, flour etc., was mouldy and stinking, which was very likely to have been the source of his diarrhoea. This instance of apparent mismanagement once again dented his optimism about any life with Ann, whom he frequently complained in his diary entries was chronically untidy. Three days later, still feeling weak, he heard from Loetitia that Jimmy Sutton, the cowman-shepherd, had handed in his notice. His mood was not improved when he telephoned the farm only to hear, as he recorded, 'that the Hang High roots are still unhoe'd. Awful time those 4 acres are taking! . . . Of course I should be there to manage the farm, & see that everything is right, but I'm an absentee. . . .'

He left to return to Stiffkey on 4 August, stopping at Moreton to visit T.E. Lawrence's grave, where he met two girls with whom he enjoyed tea at 'Tess of Durbervilles'' farm. He then continued on to Swaythling to spend the night with Robin and Betty, and the following morning on to Berkhampstead to Major Francis Yeats-Brown's home, where he may have stayed a few days as the next entry, about the farm, was on 11 August, complaining that the past sixteen days had been wasted, as it had been wet and the land should have been ploughed and wasn't, which seemed to imply that he had not been there all that time.

The threshing machine.

The farm work continued with the harvest which was a good one and gave rise to an optimistic entry on 17 September: 'Today we finished a long harvest, extending over one month. We have gathered in fine crops, and in all have 7 stacks. It has been hard work, and much worry and strain for me (I worked as a labourer all the time) but I would not have missed it.'

There are then only very sporadic entries: 9 November, 'Too tired to write. I am at odds with Windles'; 12 November, 'News stimulates us all that at last we are doing a decent show in Africa. Rommel is beaten & the Americans move into French Africa to cut him off. Hitler seems to be out-Hitlered. It's weeks now since we heard a German bomber'; 17 November, 'Blossom old mare died last night. Gipsy is away with Robin and Betty'; 1 December, 'My birthday 47 today'; 2 December, 'I am 46 not 47, being born on 1 Dec. 1896' (obviously he suddenly remembered his own fiction of being born a year later than he actually was!); 3 December, 'Haven't been able to write anything or do anything for weeks. Sunk in slough of despond.' He then went to London, to attend a protest meeting at Holborn Hall on behalf of those forcibly interned under Section 18B. There are several letters and documents in the archive files from the special committee set up by ex-officials of the British Union of Fascists (which had itself been banned at the outbreak of war) asking for his support in this matter.[19]

There was no further entry until New Year's Eve, when his usual despondency at this time overcame him. 'Did I ever write *The Flax of Dream*? All in vain, all is forgotten; I am a complete failure. I sit here alone by the fire & can't write further.' (As he was right at the bottom corner of the very last page, it wasn't actually possible for him to write any further anyway!)

So another year began. On 1 January 1943 Richard Perry, who had been the cowman for several months, left – to Henry's relief; another promising 'staggart' had proved a disaster. (Perry is portrayed as 'The Inquiline' in the *Chronicle*.) Norman Jordan took over the cows and the stock temporarily. A day or so later his seventeen-year-old nephew, Douglas Jordan, came to ask for a job, and he started work as a cowman on 16 January. Henry was relieved and overwhelmed to find that Douglas was a good worker and soon had the cow-house cleaned out and whitewashed.

The farm work was unremitting: ploughing, drilling, planting, hoeing, muck spreading, harvesting, all the details recorded. The main diaries for the rest of the war are missing,[20] but the 'work' diary for 1943 recorded all the actual farm work in detail, and Bill Williamson (Windles) very generously loaned his work records for 1944 and 1945. It is clear that throughout the war years the brunt of the work was borne by the young Windles. Henry had the worry of the responsibility and planning of the workload, but his actual physical input tended to be sporadic. When in the mood he would rush out and work like a dervish for an hour or so and then stop, leaving Windles and the men to continue with the sheer plod. This is not to belittle Henry's contribution to the running of the farm, for he did achieve the very difficult feat of turning it round from a C category to an A category,[21] but to try and put it into perspective. He was frequently away, and there were also the hours that went into writing; but it is very obvious that he was not, as he tended to claim, working on the farm *and* writing continuously.

John and Margaret were now away at school, although John was expected to work in his holidays and Margaret was given tasks at times, as we can see from the photograph of her leading in the horses in *The Story of a Norfolk Farm*, while Robert and Richard were still too young to do more than odd jobs. But Windles was there constantly, and he had no escape either from the work itself or from Henry's continuous criticism. Unlike the men who went home at the end of the day and were free of it all for a few hours, Windles still had to cope with his father at every moment of his life. He also, on occasion, took the blame for the problems caused by the men. Now seventeen years old, he had done a man's work since the outbreak of the war and his life was limited in the extreme. Later that year he joined the Air Training Corps, which got him out for two evenings each week – a relief and something he very much enjoyed; and which he thought would give him an advantage when he applied to join the RAF. However, unlike Billy in the *Chronicle*, Windles did not join the RAF, for by the time he was old enough to do so the nature of the war had changed, and quite a number of those joining up were being sent down the coal mines to work as 'Bevan Boys'. So it was decided that Windles was best off staying on the farm.

Early in 1943 Henry corrected the proofs of *Norfolk Life*,[22] the book he had edited which was made up from articles written in the *Eastern Daily Press* by Lilias Rider Haggard. He had started reading these anonymous articles in about 1939 and had contacted the editor to find out who the author was. He had then written to Miss Haggard suggesting that, well edited, they would make a good book and offered his services to do this, to which she willingly agreed as is shown in her letter of 15 July 1941. Daughter of Sir Henry Rider Haggard,[23] Lilias had previously published *I Walked by Night* and *The Rabbit Skin Cap*, both stories from life told to her by their subjects, local characters of the district around Bungay on the Norfolk/Suffolk border where the Haggard family home was. Lilias Rider Haggard was herself quite a character, and had accompanied her father on his travels when she was a young girl. Her letters show that she was very appreciative of the work that Henry put in, for at that time she could not undertake it herself. When it was published later in 1943 it proved very popular, and went through several impressions in the next few years. However, when Henry approached Lilias the following year about a sequel, she first of all diplomatically sidestepped the issue then, when Henry persisted, she very forthrightly told him, in a letter dated 5 December 1944, that she had had such a drubbing both from friends and strangers about the editing of *Norfolk Life* that never again would she allow anyone to touch a book of hers. Henry did not take kindly to this criticism, for he felt that the book would never have been published without his help, and got his own back by grumbling about Lilias to others. Henry himself started writing regularly in the *Eastern Daily Press* in April 1943, at first under a pseudonym 'Jacob Tonson' and later the column 'Green Fields and Pavements'.[24]

On 10 July 1943 Henry was taken into Cromer hospital to have his appendix removed. Not a pleasant experience for anyone, but particularly for a man of Henry's temperament. Letters written to Ann Thomas in the archive show that his imagination was working overtime, plaguing him with thoughts of imminent death and the conviction that he really had cancer. From what he wrote to Ann it seems that he was very irritable with his wife when she visited him, but no doubt Loetitia accepted that for what it was. He was also very bitter towards Ann herself, who did not go to see him. It was a repetition of the scene in which he had lashed out at his mother when he was frightened of going to war and facing death in 1914. The words which open Chapter 22 of 'Dream' of *Lucifer Before Sunrise* – 'Butterflies with tiger's teeth' – first appeared in a letter which Henry wrote to Ann the day after this abdominal operation: 'nerves are like butterflies set with the teeth of tigers . . . I sank far down into an oriental-mythical night.'

In *Lucifer Before Sunrise* Henry translates this hospital episode into the shooting of Phillip by soldiers on the farm. The soldiers were indeed very trigger-happy and did shoot a cow through the udder – but not until 3 September 1943 when Henry recorded in his diary 'Best heifer shot by 6th. Northamptons'.

Back from hospital, Henry was soon directing the farm work again but in September he went to stay in his Field for a holiday. Ann had left before he arrived and he now wrote a long and bitter letter to her. She took great offence at his tone and for the first time rounded on him and told him so. In answer Henry wrote a long 'apologia pro vita mea' which is dated '1931–1943' on Skirr Cottage headed notepaper. 'I cannot allow this to end on a harsh note. Nor on a sentimental or sad note.' Its gist was that the road to hell was paved with good intentions; but it is more than that – it states the *raison d'être* of his life and being (and was probably kept for this reason).

> I honestly & truly believe that God is order and scrupulous economy, and the Devil is disorder, carelessness, and waste. I use these ancient terms because they have been static through many centuries and are the common denominator of life. . . .
>
> I knew my little success from nothing was due solely to belief in such things: & I wanted to share with all I met: and finding disorder and waste, put personal feelings under and set to tackle the fundamental problems.
>
> And like all such men & women, created an opposition equal to the power or effort I put into the work.
>
> Poets know this; they are this; they live by this; it is their mission.

The missive, for it is more missive than letter, goes on to state that the pinnacle is now achieved, 'The farm is saved . . . I have £2000 in the bank' and he further relates details of future income, new editions of five nature books just contracted, £550 for the last of the barley, £800 due in January for sugar-beet . . . the children at decent schools' and he reiterates a point referred to on several previous occasions, that he wanted 'Rosie' to take her place with her brothers and sister, to be part of the 'family'. From this time on, although they remained friends after a fashion, the close relationship between Henry and Ann was over.

A highlight remembered by the family from this time was the arrival and friendship of the young pilot who is portrayed as Ginger in Chapter 23 of *Lucifer Before Sunrise*. George Mackie became a hero to the boys. Stationed nearby, he was from 214 Squadron flying B17s, the so-called Flying Fortress, whose job it was to accompany the bomber stream over Germany, carrying counter-radar measures, including a German-speaking member of crew. He used to turn up at the farm whenever possible in his open Singer sports car. Frequently when flying he would 'beat-up' the farm – fly very low over it, a dangerous and totally unauthorized act – which thrilled the boys. When Mackie had not been seen for a while, Henry intimated in one of his articles in the *Evening Standard*[25] that the young airman had been killed on a mission. When, a short time later, Mackie did arrive, Henry went through a pantomime of acute remorse. Mackie was, understandably, a little apprehensive that Henry had perhaps foreseen his death. But his article had not been prophetic; Mackie later had a successful career as a book designer and artist.

Involved in traditional country and farming activities, there are frequent references to shooting days throughout Henry's diaries. He shared the shooting with Major Cyril Case, owner of the adjoining farm, who is depicted as Charles Box in the *Chronicle*. Major Case had the greater acreage of land and he organized the shooting, which suited Henry, and the two men split the expenses and income. On one occasion, described in Chapter 20 of *Lucifer Before Sunrise*, the journalist Macdonald Hastings (gloriously translated at 'Bannock MacWhippett) came up from London as Henry's guest to write a piece on the shoot for *Picture Post*.[26]

Mrs Cafferata had sold the Old Hall and moved to Yorkshire to live with relations who owned a sizeable estate. The place had been bought by Bruno Scott James, a Catholic priest, who originally came to the Norfolk coast to convalesce and he and Henry became quite friendly. As Scott James got better he took to going out with a gun and apparently he shot at everything he saw, usually missing. One day on the marshes a doodle-bug flew over him; Scott James fired at it, no doubt in impotent and frustrated rage at this monstrous instrument of death. Henry heard about the incident and wrote it up in one of his articles.[27] Unfortunately, he rather implied that Scott James, who was not named, had thought he could actually bring down the doodle-bug with his wild-popping shot-gun. It was further unfortunate that several of Scott James's friends read the article

The farm shoot: Henry is mid-scene in the background facing the camera.

and recognized the anonymous figure and wrote to ask him why he let that 'cad Williamson' make fun of him. Bruno Scott James wrote Henry a very angry and hurt letter, complaining that he had trusted Henry, had had no idea that Henry would use this story for an article, and, in effect, never wanted to speak to Henry again. The article was really quite harmless and it is difficult to see why it should have caused such offence. Henry must have felt that he could do nothing right!

The situation on the farm and within the family had now reached an impasse. Loetitia took Richard, the only one of her children still not at boarding school, with her to stay with Mrs Cafferata near Selby in Yorkshire. Mrs Cafferata was Richard's godmother and he remembers this as a very happy time spent roaming the beautiful grounds and visiting the stables where there was a pony for him to ride. From here Loetitia wrote to inform Henry that she was once again pregnant.

Their sixth child, a daughter who was named Sarah, was born on 5 February 1945, a day after Loetitia's own birthday, in the hospital at Cromer. Soon after this the domestic situation came to a head, and Loetitia found she could no longer cope with Henry or the farm. A final scene was the last straw and she fled once again to Mrs Cafferata at Selby, and decided that the best and only course left was to instigate divorce proceedings. Robin, very protective of his sister, took up the struggle with Henry on her behalf. The letters between Robin and Henry were understandably somewhat heated. Robin was too blunt for Henry's psyche, and Henry predictably retaliated with a flurry of recriminations.

Henry was once again in a state of acute nervous disability due to the stress and strain of the years on the farm and the fact that Loetitia really intended to divorce him. He went down to the Field at Ox's Cross about the middle of June in a very bad state. While there he met on the beach a friendly couple, Desmond and Lois Sutcliffe, on holiday from their home in Wakefield, Yorkshire. Henry wrote later that he didn't know what would have happened to him if it hadn't been for their presence and kindness.

But with the decision to divorce made, Henry could see his own way forward clearly. The war was rapidly coming to an end. The farm could be honourably sold and he could become a full-time writer again.[28] The farm years could be put behind him. It had been an extraordinarily difficult time, but at least he could be proud of the 'A' status the farm had achieved.[29]

In July 1945, on his way back to Stiffkey from this visit to Devon, the Alvis broke down in the village of Botesdale on the Suffolk/Norfolk border near Diss. Henry's diary records that while he was trying to get the car going, he noticed that a large house across the road was for sale. It was relatively cheap, the purchase price only £1,700. The time was 4 o'clock. He decided on the spot to buy this property for the family. His diary records that by 6 o'clock he had made the necessary preliminary arrangements. He obviously considered that it would solve all his immediate problems.

His desperate need and intent at this time was that the divorce should be carried out as decently as possible with the least possible harm to all, and with minimal adverse publicity, which could affect his reputation and his future earning power and thus the future well-being of the family. He had seen the results of several messy divorces and also knew exactly how it could be sorted out with the least fuss. He now wrote to Loetitia (letter in HWLEA, dated 15 July 1945) a long and most reasonable letter (this version does not appear to have been sent but no doubt another version was), telling her about the purchase of the house, 'a nice house, a happy house' which is to be for her and the family; that for the sake of the family he wanted the divorce to be as amicable as possible and that they should sort out the farm together first, move to Botesdale, and then he could quietly remove himself to Devon and everything could be arranged in the most suitable manner possible. He made it very clear that he was very fond of his children and hoped that he would be allowed to have access to them. And, apart from the fact that Loetitia did not return to the farm, that was what happened.

Three books were published during these final months: firstly in June 1945 the novel-biography *The Sun In the Sands* finally saw the light of day from Faber's vaults where it had been imprisoned for ten years. Henry wrote in his short preface that he thought 'his story of a young man from the [First World] war, aspiring to the vision of a new world, and seeking clarity beyond the confusions of human emotions may be timely.' Then later in the year, at the beginning of October, Faber 'in complete conformity with the authorised economy standards' also published the companion volumes *Life in a Devon Village* and *Tales of a Devon Village*, which were rearrangements of those stories he had written in his earliest days and which were originally published in *The Village Book* and *The Labouring Life*. They were easy books for Henry to put together at this difficult time. None of them attracted much attention.

On the farm the last months were very difficult. There was much work to do before the farm was finally sold. Windles' diary shows how hard he was working up to the very end. If certain things could be accomplished before the final date it would be money in hand instead of wasted time and effort. Henry made many journeys down to the house on the southern border of Norfolk in order to prepare it for the new family home. The farm was eventually sold to Walter F. Roch for just over £9,000 (with interest due Roch actually paid over £9,500). Henry recorded on Friday 21 September, 'Farm sold this day. I was deeply shaken. "The very stones cry out".' The actual tenancy was taken over by Tom Pearson, and both these agreements were signed on 9 October.

The final scene took place on Wednesday 24 October 1945 when the 'Entire Live and Dead Farming Stock' was auctioned. The catalogue ran to nine pages and the total price raised was £2,227 12s 6d. Two days later Windles left to take up a farming job in Cambridgeshire, where he discovered to his surprise that farming was actually relatively easy!

The other children had returned to their boarding schools after the summer vacation: Margaret to her mother's old school of St Mary's in Wantage. John was at Paston Grammar School where Robert also went at this time. Only Richard was still young enough to remain at home and he and his father now became very close. From his earliest years Richard loved to roam alone through the country

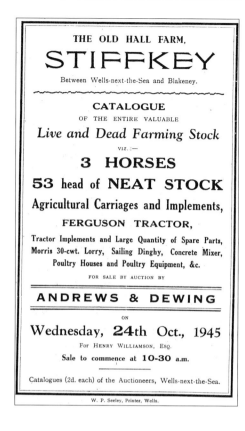

The farm auction.

lanes and fields and took a keen interest in nature, far more so than any of the others, and Henry obviously recognized his own boyhood in this lonely, wandering son.

At the close of *Lucifer Before Sunrise* Henry wrote of Phillip and Johnny (who is Richard) going for a last walk and bathe on the marshes, where they meet a young couple having a picnic, and see a butterfly struggling to get into an air current to take it eastwards across the sea, before getting into the Alvis and driving off. Richard remembers the occasion well: it was all as Henry wrote, except that as they drove off to go to the new house in Botesdale, Henry put his foot down to catch up the young couple on their motorbike to tell them that they would feature in his article in the next week's *Evening Standard*, but Richard's cap blew off in the fierce rush of wind occasioned by the speed of the car, and the ten-year-old had to endure Henry's irritable exclamations as he hared back after it, while the motor-bike tore away into the distance.

CHAPTER 8

INTERLUDE

The nucleus of the family took up residence in Bank House, Botesdale, at the end of October 1945. Almost immediately Henry went to London where he attended the annual *Chyebassa* reunion of his old 1914 comrades, on 3 November, returning to Botesdale but apparently going again to London for over two weeks at the beginning of December. Soon the rest of the children were home for the Christmas holidays, very excited about the new roomy house with its hidden doorways and passages built in the days when it really had been used as a bank. It was the perfect place for the grand game of hide and seek that Henry played with the children over Christmas. The old stables made good garaging space and the extensive garden had paths edged with miniature box, relic of Victorian taste.

Henry set himself up in what had once been the servants' quarters, approached by the back stairs, where he knocked the glass out of a window pane in his

Bank House in Botesdale, where the Williamson family went to live after the farm was sold. (Photograph courtesy of John Gregory, 1991)

Henry in his Writing Hut, 1946.

bedroom so that he could have a continuous supply of air. Above this was a large room that he made his writing room, and it was here that he began to work in earnest on the book about life on the Norfolk farm during the war. He posted off the manuscript, at this stage called *Norfolk Farmer*, on 15 and 17 July, to be typed up by a young lady in Beaconsfield. Between February and October he was also writing a series of articles for *Woman's Illustrated and Eve's Own* which were entitled 'Quest'[1] and which relate the story of the break-up of his farm and marriage, and the new beginning in the house at Botesdale.

Henry quickly made friends with a man living nearby, St John (Jock) Horsfall, who owned a 2 litre 'Ulster' Aston Martin which he raced and was preparing for the Belgian Grand Prix.[2] Horsfall and his car provided such a glamorous image that when Henry saw a 1938 2 litre Aston Martin, DYY 764, advertised for sale nearby by a Dr Vicenzi for £800 he decided to buy it. This car, like the Silver Eagle Alvis, always caused problems and cost a small fortune in repairs. Henry even decided to sue the previous owner at one point. But it was an exciting car to own. However, this period of euphoria during the first months at Botesdale was only a lull, an interlude.

For several years Henry had been friends with another writer, Malcolm Elwin, and the family had visited and stayed at the Elwins' house, Underborough,[3] situated at the end of a long track which led to the sea dunes at Northam Burrows, Westward Ho!, in North Devon. Now in 1946 Elwin took on the editorship of a new periodical, the *West Country Magazine*, which had been set up by another of Henry's friends and admirers, Waveney Girvan, who now ran Westaway Press specializing in books about the West Country. Henry provided two items for the first issue, which appeared in summer 1946. One was his story 'Yellow Boots', already published, but the second 'A Reverie of Exmoor' was new,[4] being an account of his walk on Exmoor with Alfred Munnings in September 1938 in the middle of his anguish over Ann Thomas.

In renewing this contact with Malcolm Elwin, Henry met his step-daughter Susan Connely, whom he immediately decided was another 'Barleybright'. Susan was still at school in Bristol at this time and was sixteen in May 1946. It was an almost exact repeat of the scenario surrounding Ann Edmonds twelve years previously.

Henry's diary for this year is virtually empty but he and Susan must have met in the Easter holidays for a correspondence commenced in early April when she returned to school. Her letters were unformed and immature; Henry as always poured out every thought and emotion he had ever experienced. Most of his letters were written on the backs of galley-proofs of *The Gold Falcon*. This idyllic 'Midsummer Night's Dream' romance continued throughout the year. Henry described their situation in some pages of an 'open letter' (not sent but written with biographical intent), which he entitled 'May and September'.

In May Henry went fishing on the Don in Scotland (so he wrote to Susan), possibly with Desmond Sutcliffe, although he may just have stopped off at the Sutcliffe's home in Wakefield on the way up and back. He certainly went to stay several times with Desmond Sutcliffe, including at the end of September when he had been invited to lecture in Bradford by John Braine.[5] On Sunday 29 September he gave his talk 'Hamlet and Modern Life' in the Bradford Civic Centre and the following Wednesday 'The Mind of the artist in relation to WORLD. Hopes and Fears. To Bradford English Society'.

By this time Henry was having grave doubts about his relationship with Susan, knowing that her mother, and Malcolm himself, were very anxious about the situation and also deciding that Susan could not possibly feel for him what he felt about her. Commencing on 1 October at Wakefield in between the two lectures above, he kept a special 'Journal' in an exercise book to record this emotional crisis.

He now returned to Botesdale to sort out his own affairs. Robin and Betty and their two children had been living there with Loetitia for two or three months, Robin's war job having ended, and they were waiting to return to Australia. Loetitia also let part of the house to an RAF officer and his wife. Henry recorded that he was very tetchy on this visit, dreading leaving his possessions behind for others to look after or, as he considered, not to look after. On 12 October he noted that he collected the Ford from Ipswich where it had been reconditioned, the Aston being out of commission, its engine and bodywork being rebuilt; he also noted that his father was dying, that he had made a will, and that he had instigated divorce proceedings. He thus had to remove himself from Botesdale to give legal credence to his case in the courts. He had arranged the previous year to take back the Field from Pinn at Michaelmas, so he had to solve the problem of temporary accommodation.

He further noted, almost casually among the above items, that 'In four days time those who faithfully served their Führer are to hang as criminals . . . I should hang with them for I, though inactive, have believed in those vital spiritual values by which alone Europe can rise and shine again. But perhaps I am not a proper national socialist, only a phoenix-illusion of ancient barrages and crater-zones.' This was the end of Henry's dream of the brotherhood of European unity. His disillusion was complete. The Elysian Fields had been shattered. It was to be many years before the German poet Schiller's words transcribed by Beethoven in the triumphant 'Ode to Joy' of the Ninth Symphony were to symbolize the new Council of Europe.

Henry arranged to lodge with Mike and Margery Mitchell (long-standing friends) who had a cottage in Georgeham and he arrived there on Wednesday 11 October. He had been delayed by a day because on the Tuesday morning when he had planned to leave he had received (totally out of the blue it would seem) a letter from Ann Edmonds, now married to an RAF officer and with two children of her own, and the 'Glider Champion woman of Europe and I gave her the old Silver Eagle and she came up and on Wednesday we took it and the Ford to Redhill, Surrey.' Also on that Tuesday Windles and his girlfriend had arrived at Botesdale. Henry thought these two went well together – 'they clicked. We had cigars & wine & a party & I played Tristan in the dark-beamed room lit by the open hearth fire & it was calm & pleasant for my last night at home.'

On his way to Devon Henry went down to see his father, now aged eighty-one, who was in a nursing home in Bournemouth where he had undergone a prostate operation and was in a terrible state. 'He is a skeleton, with white beard, gaunt face, & blue eyes frustrated.' William Leopold complained that he was not being attended to properly, but when Henry saw the matron and doctors he was told that this was incorrect and that his father was imagining things:

> . . . not mentally right and had delusions. He was not mentally wrong; but lying there, feeling unwanted, neglected, he suffered. He was always most meticulous, even neurotically fastidious, and it hurts him to mess himself and wet the bed. He was always distraught, poor man; his father broke him as a small boy, he the eldest son of his mother whom his father hated. His father had a mistress in the house (just as I did with Ann Thomas) but in Victorian times it was grim & things were unrelieved. Later he married my mother who gave me her temperament & mystic nature & they did not click or fit and she suffered terribly and so did I. But now he has no faith and no comfort and is lost. . . . I begged him to be stoical. . . .

Henry felt that it was not a good nursing home but that none at that time were, and that when he left he had probably pressed his father's hand for the last time. Mainly he felt he could not inflict his own old age on to Susan. Feeling distraught he drove to Dorchester where he had 'a good tea with plenty of jam and sweet cake and felt better'.

The next morning he woke up in a comfortable bed in Margery Mitchell's cottage in Georgeham where breakfast was brought to him on a dainty tray with 'silver and white napery, tea, 2 herrings, toast and marmalade' and surveyed his life:

> John is in the RAF – he joined a week ago
> Windles is happy, neat, & secure
> Margaret is happy at St. Mary's Wantage
> Robert is at Paston School, preparing for Blundell's [near Taunton]
> Richard is at St. Michael's, Tenbury [since September; Eddie Pine now taught there]
> Sarah is loved by all & a very good & clear little person
> I gave Gipsy £500 for a present
> Robin & I parted on the best of terms
> Gipsy said we must meet & see each other when it was all over
> Ann Thomas has said she will be co-respondent . . .
> Rosemary is happy at a Quaker's school in Pontefract
> The Aston Martin is in dock & the body being renewed

He proceeded to formulate a plan of action. This included an exact daily timetable for visiting the Field and partaking of food. He noted that he had to provide evidence for the divorce and 'By Christmas I shall have cleaned up the *Journal of a Farmer* and be on with the Pheasant Book'. He stayed in bed until after noon on Friday 18 October (although he had presumably got up some time in between!) and had filled in twenty-nine pages of the exercise book 'Journal' with these autobiographical musings and finally: 'I have just sneezed & my bladder is full of water & I must really now get out & down & peeeeeeeeeeeeeeeeeeeeeeeeeeee.'

The next entry was not until 13 December 1946; by this time he was worked-up and fraught. Although he had realized that any relationship with Susan was not going to work, he was still desperate that it should, and the remaining thirty-seven pages of the exercise book are filled with his usual acute doubts, longings and soul-searchings. He was also longing for the Elwins to invite him for Christmas so that he could be with Susan, while at the same time rejecting such a possibility; suggesting in his gloom putting all his books and manuscripts into the Hut, and make an enormous pile of wood around it and setting fire to it – a very Wagnerian/Romantic funeral pyre – while he walked off into the sea. (This sort of threat was frequently made and was not meant to be taken seriously – he would never have set fire to his archive.) He explained his state of mind as his response to the approach of Christmas, when his thoughts always turned back to the Christmas of 1914 that he spent in the trenches:

Christmas time is always, as it approaches, a sensitive time for me, & I tend to immolate myself, turn towards death and darkness, & have a picture of myself eating nothing, keeping alone & perhaps walking to exhaustion point for several days without food, sleeping out in the rain & cold & so reducing myself to a ghost. While I mourn alone, I long, behind the dark iron barrier of my stubbornness, for love & sweetness and above all, tenderness.

Christmas Day 1914: the awful rain of the November month; the freezing in trenches 3 ft. deep in yellow clay & water; . . . I want to write the Phillip M. novels with all the details, every single detail, being the cause of a later effect, in all the characters. This has never been done in literature, & it is my dream & has been since 1919. Such a work, if produced, would be accepted by all human beings. . . . But, O God, it will take every ounce of my strength & will require years of calmness & serenity. . . . [followed by a long paragraph to the effect that he will need a good woman, and whether that woman would be Susan].

To resume: – Christmas Day 1914, the fear & dread of our Noman's Land wiring party, coming after the nightmare attack over the same ground on 19 December, when we were shot up & screamed in fear as we fell & hid in 4 ft. of greenish shell-hole water, & I raved in my mind for what Mummie would feel if I were killed – me DEAD, oh God save me, O Christ save me, I am lost, O Jesu help us, we all thought & wept – Christmas Day followed after a quiet moonlight Eve when the 'Huns' heard us but did not shoot. Not one shot went off from their trenches in the turnip field only 50 yards away – & we worked with a lightness & joy until 2 am & then filed back to the water dripping blockhouses . . . The next day the miracle was manifest. . . .

He goes on to tell of being hospitalized in January with frozen feet and dysentery, of being sent back to England and the dreadful nightmare fear of being posted back to the front again, and the strangeness and strain of the return to his family home; applying for and obtaining a commission, and the horrendous ragging he received from fellow officers because he put their backs up by being a 'know-all' and was put through '2 subalterns' courts martial & punishment' (all graphically described – stripped naked, water thrown, beaten with knotted wet towels, by his fellow officers as their own punishment). 'It was only later that the enormity of my conduct in all matters struck me.'

> Every Christmas has been awkward: I dreaded it: I saw Mother's face, ourselves as children: I saw the frozen battlefield: & the ghosts walked with me again. . . . Just as I saw a miracle in 1914, smashed 5 days later, so I need in my life a strong, warm, loving complement to reassure me & fill me & keep me (by her presence & faith, which must not be a strain or a duty, but an instinctive & involuntary action) to my natural self, which is light-hearted, faithful and devoted to work & love.

At the very last minute the Elwins did invite him for Christmas but what happened was not recorded for the exercise book was full and Henry dated the bottom of the last page '22 Dec. 1946, 8.30 p.m. The Hut'. Although he made a note later that he had intended to marry Susan, it is known that the Elwin's felt that Susan should concentrate on preparing for university and probably made their views quite clear at this point; and so the idyll in his mind dissolved.

Henry's father had died on 31 October and he had attended the cremation. Ever afterwards he was bitter against Kathie, whom he believed had persuaded their father to change his will at the last minute and leave his house in Parkstone, 'Constantine', to her in return for her having looked after him. He was convinced that she had not carried out her part of the bargain and delayed getting William Leopold out of the nursing home, and that when at last she had done so, he died two hours after getting home. William Leopold's will was dated 10 September 1946. He left £100 to his sister, Maude. Henry received a one third share, with his two sisters, of specifically mentioned stocks, which amounted to just over £400 each, while Kathie was left the house and the residue of his estate.

The 1947 diary is equally bare for most of the year. The divorce decree was made absolute on 19 July 1947. Henry made suitable financial arrangements to cover his commitments, agreeing to pay school fees, including Rosemary's, for all the children (except for Margaret, who had inherited money in trust from her great aunt Mary Leopoldina Williamson, who had died in 1946 and thus could pay her own fees), and made his ex-wife a monthly allowance. Loetitia and the family also had the use of Bank House, and Henry went backwards and forwards between Devon and the family home much as he had always done.

Later in the year Ann Thomas returned to work as Henry's secretary and her neat entries of work done once again fill in the details from October onwards. At some point Henry made a sales outlet for his books at the 'Higher House' in Georgeham as two homemade posters show. Apart from articles, Henry was now working on *The Phasian Bird*, in which he combined the story of life on the Norfolk farm, much fictionalized, and of Wilbo, an artist who takes over the near-derelict farm (and was imprisoned for his political beliefs, from which must stem in large part the idea held by many that Henry himself was imprisoned for his political beliefs), with that of an exotic species of pheasant, its plumage like beaten gold, its tail feathers over six feet long, a Reeves' pheasant, named Chee-kai. Henry depicts the wildlife living on and around the farm with great attention to detail, skilfully interweaving them with the human characters who live and work there, the farm labourers, local poachers, and the American soldiers billeted at nearby camps. The first two parts of the typescript were taken to Cyrus Brooks[6] at the end of January 1948 with a copy to Richard de la Mare at Faber. The third part went off on 13 February and the entry on 20 February stated: 'HW finished "The Phasian Bird".' The book ends with the symbolic death of both Wilbo and Chee-kai from the senseless greed and ignorance of both soldiers and poachers in what is one of Henry's classic descriptions of dramatic death at a time of severe

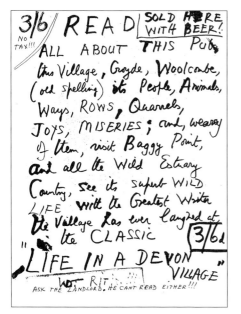
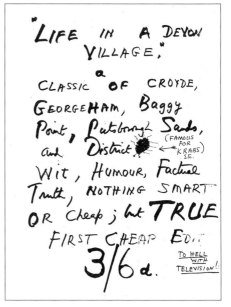

The two posters that Henry designed to help sell his book in the 'Higher House' (the Rock Inn) at Georgeham.

LAST SCENE., Xmas ~~reports~~ 1944

Phasis, dying, spread-eagled on the top of the
pine, lifts his head, as though to take a
last look at the golden eye of a god,
the god of the coloured birds of far
Colchis. He trembles, shudders, & lies still : the
spirit had departed.
The 8th O.S.S.A.F. bombardier who visits the new
farmer, helping, attending shoots, gets to
know Phasian, + falls on Christmas Day of the
Ardennes offensive, wounded, parachute, red flare
from the Flying Fortress, seeing the pheasant shot below
him.
Added 11·11·1947. Phasian shot by Syndicate – rich
½ drunks from building air-stations. Phasian pitches, dead,
in Pine Tree. Enamelled by ice. Aurora Borealis
glows with his colours in sky. Shall the Farmer, supposed
5th Columnist, be shot "accidentally on purpose"? Someone
in Norfolk, about this time, was shot by U.S. army poachers —
Sir Somebody. Phasian falls into top of tree. Dissolved.
As the battlefields would dissolve their dead.
End. Spring comes, Harina flies away over the sea,
and the geese cry under the stars, traditionally with the

Pages from a working notebook for *The Phasian Bird*.

39.

cries of dead soldiers.

<u>Death of Pheasant Mother</u>. To add sympathy for chick, loss,
seeking warmth & shelter. Seeks her, cheeping: finds old
boot washed over the bank in floods, tries to shelter
by it, but no warm wing comes for it to shelter him from
cold & fear.

<u>Bank of Stream in Summer</u>. Loose-strife, rose-bay,
meadowsweet, Kingcups. Sweet violets in woods,
pink centaury, white woodruff, purple bugle,
yellow wood-avens, who autumn fruits are looked for
fur of animals.

<u>Note</u>. Chestnut, or dark brown mark on partridge' breast
is not of horse-shoe as nettle, but bullock-shoe.

1942-43 Details nest on farm — collector of Yalt — next Sea
Spring migrant from Africa. Quail = Quailer, Quagmire the quail, calling
in the meadows, the voice of lost quail — runs fast — flies awhile & drops
suddenly to run-flies low, wings whirr. Secretes itself by day in grasses,
crying by itself, "wet of lips", "Quick - me - dick". This is Male cry: female is
softer and lower. Feeds early morning & towards evening. Pugnacious, fight often
(males). Lay 2nd half June 7 to 12 eggs. Eggs yellow - white, blotched &
spotted with dark brown. Buff, brown, black.

Kakkabis the red-legged partridge. Introd. East Anglia 1770. Less devoted to
cultivated land: prefers heaths, margins of woods, hedge-row moocher. Roosts
on a tree, wall, hedge. Alarmed, runs will seek out, before flying. Hedge-
hopper, skims, & alights: does it again, field to field. Can't run in soft snow:
flounders. Like quail, push early & late. Harsher note than Partries:
Chuck chuck chickor. Pairs Feb & fights. Yellow-buff eggs, spotted red-brown
thick shell. 23 days incubation: sits not so close as common partridge. Eats

and intense cold. Henry had asked Charles Tunnicliffe to do the illustrations, but he was too heavily committed to take it on. Henry also approached the famous bird artist Richard Richardson whom he had met at Cley during the Norfolk farm years, but he was also too busy. In the end it was Mildred Eldridge who provided the striking illustration of a Reeves' pheasant diving across the cover, of the edition published by Faber on 5 November 1948. That night Henry 'gave a party to 8 critics and fellow authors at Savoy. Dinner & dance.'

At this time Henry had a letter from Kenneth Allsop saying he had just finished a book, and Henry wrote to suggest he send it to Macdonald, although they did not actually publish it in the end. Allsop had been a reporter before the war, but had joined the RAF in 1940. The following year his plane had crashed during an aircrew training exercise and he had subsequently had to have his leg amputated. While recovering he had begun to write short stories, and eventually had returned to journalism. Now he had written a novel based on a true story of the little ringed plover establishing itself in Tring Reservoir, which was very well received.[7]

Several new editions of Henry's books were published during this period, including *Tarka*, *Salar*, *The Star-born*, and *The Gold Falcon*, and he wrote a large number of articles. He was also involved in several filmscript ideas, but they did not come to anything, and, as always, he wrote an enormous number of letters. Ann's precise notes tabulate a great deal of work.

Also Henry now took on yet another commitment, the editorship of the literary journal the *Adelphi*, previously edited, and indeed published, by John Middleton Murry. This was despite a very sharp quarrel that these two men had in 1947, when Henry made major alterations to an article for the *Adelphi* at proof stage, about which Murry had remonstrated – to receive one of Henry's fierce barrages in return. The July–September 1948 issue marked the twenty-fifth year of Murry's association with the journal and in a brief editorial he announced that he was giving up and that 'my friend, Henry Williamson, who was one of its earliest contributors . . . had expressed the desire to continue *The Adelphi*. I have therefore gladly made it over to him.' In this issue Henry had taken the opportunity to publish 'Birth of the Phasian Bird' (a useful advertisement).[8] Henry had indeed been one of the earliest contributors; in a copy of the September 1924 issue there is a very short piece by him, 'The Doom of the Peregrine Falcon'.[9]

The actual mechanics of editing the *Adelphi* were carried out by Ann Thomas from her Malvern address. Her entries in Henry's diary ceased in the middle of July and presumably she then went back to Malvern (where she had a cottage) from where she ran the business necessary to produce the journal. The idea was to provide her with paid employment so that she could earn her living. Their first issue was Volume 25, No. 1, October–December 1948, in which Henry opened with a long editorial, 'The Lost Legions'; first he paid tribute to John Middleton Murry, whose 'The Lost Legions' was the first essay of Murry's that Henry had read in a library copy of the *Athenaeum* in early 1920. He then introduced the work of a young airman, James Farrar, who had been killed in active service and whose mother had sent Henry some of his poems. Farrar's work seemed to Henry to be of outstanding worth and beauty, and in due course he gathered all that existed together and arranged for its publication as *The Unreturning Spring*.[10]

Also in this issue was an essay and a selection of 'Three Poems' by Charles Causley, the Cornish poet, with whom Henry had a longstanding friendship, although not a close one. There was, too, a small selection of poems by a young Australian poet, Alister Kershaw. Kershaw had emigrated to England with the express intent of meeting some English writers, particularly Henry Williamson, Roy Campbell and Richard Aldington and he was to be instrumental in making contact between Henry and Richard Aldington, who lived on the south coast of France.[11] Aldington had written a very complimentary letter to Henry when *The Wet Flanders Plain* was published in 1929, and Aldington's own war book, *Death of a Hero*, was published soon after, but there had been no contact since. At Kershaw's suggestion Henry asked Aldington for a piece for the *Adelphi*, which resulted in 'The Squire gets Married' a chapter out of Aldington's forthcoming biography of the eccentric naturalist Charles Waterton. Henry and Aldington now began to correspond and a friendship developed.

Henry only kept the *Adelphi* for three issues. In the two remaining issues his editorials, 'Words on the West Wind', contained many thoughts and biographical details.[12] For various reasons, not the least being that his personal circumstances changed, he then sold the *Adelphi*, which was taken over and edited by George Godwin. Middleton Murry was very upset at this abrupt disposal without any previous consultation with himself, for he had entrusted the journal to Henry thinking that it would be continued in the same spirit that he himself had so carefully nurtured for the previous twenty-five years. But Murry did not allow this upset to cloud his critical appreciation of the *Chronicle* in due course.

But this interlude in Henry's life was over. There was a final break with Ann Thomas, who thought after Henry's divorce from Loetitia that she and Henry would finally be married. But Henry had now met someone else, the girl who was to be his second wife, and with her at his side he was able to settle down at last to write those Phillip Maddison books that had been gnawing at his psyche since 1919: a task which was to be even greater than he at this time envisaged – the fifteen-volume *A Chronicle of Ancient Sunlight*. Although to use the term 'settle down' in relation to Henry Williamson is rather inappropriate.

CHAPTER 9

ANCIENT SUNLIGHT

In the summer of 1948 two young people, a brother and sister, turned up at the Field at Ox's Cross and asked for a drink of water to quench their thirst on a hot day. They were on a walking tour of the area. That is how Henry Williamson met Christine Mary Duffield, a young Yorkshire woman who was teaching at a school in nearby Bideford. Christine was a pleasant, good looking, open-air young woman with long corn-coloured hair, tanned arms and legs; a Saxon type. Despite having an apparently outgoing and strong personality, she actually tended to be nervous.

The first mention of her is in the opening entry of Henry's 1949 diary which states: 'I went to Yorkshire to see Christine Duffield with whom I had lived happily as my wife since October 1948. We were to be married soon. At York station I realised the marriage might not take place.'

Christine had gone home to her mother's for Christmas, and Henry had planned to go up for the New Year, and they were going to broach the question of marriage together. But Christine decided to tell her mother before Henry arrived. Mrs Duffield objected to this alliance and, according to Henry, used the excuse of her bad heart to put pressure on Christine, in fact 'forbade the marriage'. She probably found it all very sudden, especially as she had not even met Henry. Christine was very upset, saying that she could not 'kill her mother'. Henry fled to the Sutcliffes at nearby Wakefield, where 'I occupied my wasted hours in forcing myself to write *Scribbling Lark*, a child's story of an old horse'. He then went down to Botesdale where he noted that he was 'distraught'. He had already obtained a marriage licence at Oxford (where Petre and Jill Mais lived) and the ceremony had been planned for Friday 7 January at Oxford Registry Office. It did not take place. Henry continued to write *Scribbling Lark* at Botesdale. He received a letter from Christine saying that she loved him but could not marry him 'yet' – not because of her mother but because Henry 'was too self-involved'. Henry took heart from this and returned to the Field on 21 January, staying a night on the way with Petre Mais at Oxford where he received 'a lovely welcome'. Christine had already returned to her teaching job in Bideford. They met up that evening; Christine spent the weekend up at the Field and on Sunday 23 January Henry recorded: 'Happy! All's well! I proposed again, was accepted again.'

A fortnight later they went to Exeter to look at caravans and bought a model named 'Adelphi', which coincidence obviously appealed to Henry. Large and luxurious, this caravan was installed at Ox's Cross; more a mobile home, it provided comfortable living quarters for the rest of Henry's life, for themselves at

A fresh start. Henry at the time he returned to live in Georgeham, 1946.

this time, and later for visitors.[1]

Christine gradually won her mother (reluctantly) round. The marriage was re-arranged, and took place in the presence of Mrs Duffield on Wednesday 13 April 1949 at Knaresborough Registry Office, Yorkshire. Margaret travelled from London (where now almost nineteen years old – her birthday was two days after this wedding – she was doing a Cordon Bleu course); also present were Desmond Sutcliffe and Christine's brother. Henry and Christine then drove to Botesdale where Henry exchanged the Ford 8 for the newly refurbished Aston Martin, travelling the next day to the Hollingsworths in Langham near Stiffkey, and after two days going on to Ted Seago's for the Easter weekend. The occasion was only marred in Henry's mind when he discovered that Christine's mother had sent a notice of the marriage to *The Times* on 16 April, although he had expressly wanted to keep it all quiet – even to the extent of putting 'Retired Agricultural Merchant' as his occupation on the marriage certificate, at which Mrs Duffield had exclaimed loudly, thus (according to Henry) exciting the interest of the registrar. Henry never had a good word to say for Mrs Duffield; having crossed him, she joined his black list of 'over-powering women'.

It had been arranged that their real honeymoon was to be in France. Alister Kershaw was now living with Richard Aldington and his wife and daughter at Le Lavandou on the south coast of France. Kershaw wanted the two to meet and so it had been arranged that Henry and Christine would go there during their honeymoon and stay at a small inn next to the nearby beach. Also, Henry's agent, Cyrus Brooks, had suggested that it would be useful if Henry called on interested publishers during this trip, in France, Italy, and Holland, as a personal visit would help clinch deals for translation rights.

Finally, after a delay due to problems with the Aston, on Saturday 23 April they crossed from Dover to Calais, where there was much evidence of damage from the Second World War, and went immediately to visit the battlefields at Arras, as Henry had done on his first honeymoon in 1925, although this visit was not traumatic and was only recorded in passing. The following day they continued to Cambrai and 'all over the Hindenburg country' and then started for the south. At Bologne the 'car magneto conked out', and they were towed to a garage where a coil was fitted 'expertly en route at 6 p.m. Christine behaved wonderfully. Cost 2750 fcs'. The next morning they went on, but the 'engine conked at once . . . expertly mended, 120 fcs. Car ran well thereafter.'

They arrived at Le Lavandou very late on Wednesday 27 April where, although Richard Aldington was about to retire to bed, he gave them supper, and then they proceeded to the auberge Les Sables D'Or. This was a happy time: Henry and Richard Aldington got on well, and Henry enjoyed the 'wine, sun, love, and food' – and Chopin on the gramophone of the patron of Les Sables D'Or.[2] Later in the night when it was quiet, the nightingales sang.

They stayed for about a month, and towards the end of May left to visit Henry's Italian publishers, Bompiani, in Milan. This meant taking the Aston over the Alps, a daunting prospect, with the highly strung car matching its owner for

Henry and his second wife, Christine
Duffield, on honeymoon in the south of
France.

unpredictability. However, they achieved Milan without *too* much difficulty, where
Henry discovered to his total surprise that *Il Falco d'Oro (The Gold Falcon)* had
been a best seller for years; but inflation had reduced his due royalties to almost
nothing, so his success was almost meaningless. On the contrary, *Tarka la Lontra*
'hibernated'.[3] From Milan the Aston had to tackle the higher alps in the north, to
cross the Simplon Pass into Switzerland. Eventually they were over, the Aston did
not actually break down, although it threatened to continuously, and from then on
the journey was relatively easy. In Paris Henry found no one really wanting
translation rights, and so they soon went on to Calais, crossing back to England
on Friday 3 June 1949. The honeymoon was over.

The previous autumn Henry had settled down to write the first volume in *A
Chronicle of Ancient Sunlight*, to be entitled *The Dark Lantern*. This had been
literally decades fermenting in his mind. But the process was not to be so
straightforward as he had supposed. Henry was also working on and trying to
place with a publisher the sequel to *The Story of a Norfolk Farm* (variously
entitled over the years 'Wit's Misery', 'Straw in the Wind', 'Lucifer', 'A Chronicle
Writ in Darkness').

In August 1949 Henry and Christine had a week's holiday in Ireland at the
invitation of Evelyn Hardy who had a farm at Bantry, which it appears she was
hoping to sell to Henry, and this holiday was for him to investigate it. Although he

noted that it was lovely there, he found 'the house a disappointment, no trout stream (only a rocky beck overgrown with furze & bramble & unfishable) and the bedrooms have tiny original windows'. It would have been Shallowford and the Norfolk farm all over again, and Henry wisely decided against it.

On 9 September 1949 Malcolm Elwin wrote to tell him to leave the book on the Norfolk farm (i.e. the sequel) alone and to get on with the Philip (*sic*) Maddison books: 'Your job is the saga of Philip Maddison . . . [which] would lift you into the top rank of big novelists.' This had its effect and a few weeks later, at the end of November, he wrote again, 'great news that you are now 24000 words down the road to the Mecca of your career. Aye, indeed will I be honoured by the dedication of your first volume'. (Letters in HWLEA.)

The publication of *The Dark Lantern* had a curious history, for Henry had arranged a contract with Collins for this book before it was written and so it is obvious that there had been a rift with Richard de la Mare of Faber, Henry's publisher at that time. The clue lies in a manuscript letter from Henry to de la Mare dated 24 December 1949 (this version unsent) in which Henry wrote: 'If I offered a full explanation it would take many pages.' (He then proceeded to write many pages!) The gist was that he had come to a full stop, and needed a change and a new challenge and owed it to Collins who had backed him in his early years. This is exactly the same sort of letter as the one he had written to Jonathan Cape when he had defected to Richard de la Mare at the time of the publication of *Salar the Salmon*, and almost certainly was a smoke-screen. This letter suggests that he had previously asked for an advance from Faber for the unwritten book, which had been refused, but that Collins had agreed to take it on, which had given him back his faith in himself.

Another version of this letter is possibly nearer the real truth. Much shorter and undated, but pinned to the longer one above, Henry here refers to 'a painful scene for us both in your office. When I left I felt so bad that I had to ask Christine to meet me somewhere later.' This 'scene' was connected with Henry's 'obsession' with the political matter to be found in his original typescript 'The Norfolk Farmer at War'. Richard de la Mare did not agree with – probably at this point openly objected to[4] – Henry's views, and presumably refused outright to publish that book. It was to his agent Cyrus Brooks that Henry went 'somewhere later', who advised him to look for another publisher. So he took the typescript to Collins and also offered them the 'unwritten book' (books), i.e. the *Chronicle*. However, Henry did try to leave the door open to Richard de la Mare by suggesting that he would be writing many books in the future, including nature books, and he saw no reason why he should not share them around more than one publisher, and that if something suitable became available he would show it to Faber.

At the end of November Faber published *The Scribbling Lark*, to which they were already committed. This is the strange little fantasy of two talented monkeys, Zig and Zag, who escape from a dreadful zoo taking with them the old, condemned carthorse, Prince. After some hilarious adventures, Prince is disguised with indelible pencil scribblings (the markings look like those on the egg of a yellow hammer, called scribbling lark by country people – hence the title) and the three win the Derby, to the consternation and confusion of the entire racing world. The book did not excite much attention (it would probably have been better received if illustrated), and most considered it simply a story for children. *Horse and Hound* thought it 'clever, amusing, excellently written and likely to appeal to readers of almost any age';[5] the *Scotsman*, 'a lark, a flight of the most inconsequential nonsense that ever amused or bemused an innocent reader'.[6] But Janet Wilson in a long review printed in the *Socialist Leader* found far more in it:

> This book can be regarded in three lights; as a story for children, as a story for adults who are able to appreciate a simple imaginative tale and as a very clever, deceptively innocent satire. . . . Henry Williamson takes the mickey out of the Press, that cultural arbiter the B.B.C., the race-track spivs and the racing betting crowd. And he does it without malice, with a gentle humour which is much more persuasive. . . . The crowds of people mostly believing they were witnessing some kind of miracle decided to live better lives in the future.
>
> But Scribbling Lark had won the Derby, had turned a social and economic occasion upside down. So isolated a revolt, so brave, humorous and tragic, ends like all lesser revolutionary gestures by the poor and oppressed in "Anti-climax, Chapter 33".
>
> Allegory, satire, story and language, make this a most commendable literary achievement. Take your socialist understanding to it and make it warm in the sun of Henry Williamson's humour and his sympathy for those beings supposed to be the lowest of the low, the captive, the outcast, the decrepit, and the evil-doer.[7]
>
> Review cutting in the HWLEA

On 8 December 1949 Henry attended the wedding of his daughter Margaret to William (Bill) Thomson[8] in London and noted that he held a small party for twelve people in the evening at Chez Auguste. It was probably on this visit that he signed the contract with Collins to publish *The Dark Lantern*, for which he received a £500 advance, with an equal sum payable when the typescript was delivered. A few months later he attended a sad occasion, the funeral of his friend Desmond Sutcliffe, who died of cancer on 22 March 1950.

Christine was now pregnant and their son was born in an Ilfracombe nursing home on 12 May 1950 after a fairly long labour and a forceps delivery, not surprising as the baby weighed 10½ lb. Henry had wandered the fields and lanes all the previous night 'in anguish lest she die, I'd be lost without this darling golden girl. Went to see the Elwins at Putsborough[9] & had breakfast with them.' The boy was named Michael Harry,[10] but was always called 'Poody' as a child. After the birth Henry's sporadic entries in his diary read only: 'Writing', 'Writing – day after day', 'Still always writing.'

Then in September they went on another holiday to France; first on Tuesday 19th, with Poody, going to visit Loetitia who had moved recently into a cottage in

Bungay (where they may have left the baby while they were away as he was not mentioned again). The house at Botesdale was being advertised for sale. On the way to Bungay the Aston had burst an oil pipe and broken a rear spring and was being repaired while Henry went on to London by train to see his agent and publisher, where he was rather shocked to find that Collins did not like *The Dark Lantern*. He went straight round to offer it to Richard de la Mare, but 'Dick was a bit snooty over my creep-back to Faber'. However, he agreed to look at the book.

Henry returned to Bungay and on the Saturday the mended Aston was delivered and he and Christine left for Folkestone on Sunday 24 September. They crossed to Boulogne the following day and gradually made their way down to Le Lavandou where they arrived on Friday 29th, and found Aldington and Kershaw 'drinking absinthe in the square'. They took a 'room and kitchen' very cheaply. Henry bathed, noting that he was fatter than the previous year and 'a walk of 2 miles on loose sand made my calf muscles ache, so unfit am I'.

He was worrying about the book. Collins' chief criticism was that they thought the character of its hero, Richard Maddison, was too unsympathetic. Henry noted that he *wanted* Richard to appear unsympathetic so that he could show how all the ills that were to follow stemmed from this fact. It is difficult to put oneself in the place of Collins who did not know how Henry intended to develop the series, especially that Richard was *not* to be the 'hero' of the *Chronicle*, only the leading character in the early books. Richard de la Mare now wrote to say Faber would not take the book as he (also) found the 'hero' unattractive. After a day or two of bathing and walking and relaxing in congenial company, Henry resolved to rewrite parts of the book. A letter arrived from Loetitia to say that Bank House had been sold for £2,600, indicating that she was worried that Henry would be annoyed about this (they had obviously discussed a higher price when they had met at Bungay), and he wrote back to reassure her that all was well.[11]

Cyrus Brooks had told Bompiani that Henry was going to France and they now wrote to Le Lavandou to say they would like to see him, so as in the previous year, they decided to go on to Milan. The steep climb over the Alps was a nightmare as Henry had earlier over-revved the Aston causing damage to the plugs, but they made it without undue mishap, other than Henry losing his temper. The visit to Bompiani was very enjoyable and also successful which cheered Henry considerably, but he dreaded the return journey over the Simplon Pass. The car just made it, with frequent stops to bring it down from boiling point. They arrived back in England on 17 October, where Henry soon settled down to work on the book taking the fifth revision to Collins on 19 December, when he now expected to receive the second instalment of his advance, but it was not forthcoming.

On 18 January 1951 he received a letter from Malcolm Elwin, now editor at Macdonald, stating that the firm were willing to publish *The Dark Lantern*. Henry sent a series of telegrams to Cyrus Brooks to arrange the cancellation of his agreement with Collins, and to pay back a proportion of the advance. Collins were agreeable and only asked that £150 of the advance should be repaid, which seems extraordinarily generous. Henry was elated and he and Christine opened a bottle of champagne, which promptly disagreed with him and plummeted him into depression. Now, having at last found a publisher willing to take the book he worried that this was the wrong decision. He was not too sure about either Macdonald's or Malcolm Elwin's judgement, so he decided to collect the typescript and take it to an independent critic who liked his work, 'George Painter of the British Museum',[12] and ask him to report on it 'without tact or politeness'. This had a successful outcome and Henry signed the contract with Macdonald on 15 February 1951, with £500 advance on signature, and the same again on delivery of the typescript.

The stage was now set for the very long cycle of novels that comprise *A Chronicle of Ancient Sunlight*. Malcolm Elwin was to prove a tower of strength as Henry's editor, although Henry became increasingly irritated with his suggestions when Elwin made criticisms with which he didn't agree. Over the next nineteen years Henry wrote and Macdonald published one volume almost every year. It was a gargantuan task and was, and is, an enormous achievement. George Painter in his 1959 essay 'The Two Maddisons' wrote that:

> Here is an unrolling map of the labyrinth of three generations, our fathers, ourselves and our children, and the thread leading to the mystery – monster or divinity? – at the centre. . . . The whole cycle will ultimately be recognised as the great historical novel of our time, its subject as the total experience of twentieth century man.[13]

In the 1990s the historian Alan Clark has referred to the *Chronicle* as 'still far the best illustration of history as fiction that I have ever encountered'.[14]

As soon as the typescript of *The Dark Lantern* had been sent off to the publisher Henry started work on the second volume, recording that he began this on 13 June 1951, had written twenty-five thousand words by 3 July and abandoned it at the end of part 1 on 13 July, feeling 'extremely weary'. This had resulted in he and Christine having 'constant rows, all on the same pattern divergence of what she says and does'. He listed several items which had been annoying him. The wheel had turned full circle and was grinding away once again. He was, of course, under enormous pressure for he had reached possibly the most important water-shed in his life, after *Tarka*, and every fibre of his being was concentrated on getting it right.

The Dark Lantern was published towards the end of 1951. Henry was very anxious to know how it was going to be received: whether the beginning of his most ambitious work would vindicate him. There is a large file of review cuttings in the archive, but Henry was disappointed with them. He had possibly not come to terms with the postwar type of review; the old-fashioned, leisurely and analytic 'critical' reviews were, in the main, no longer viable. Henry's works now often had to share a short column with several other titles. However, he was greatly cheered to see that on 13 January 1952 the *Sunday Times* had a large advertisement for the book, very well displayed. 'It made me so happy: the book, after all the chill from Collins, Faber etc., & people not bothering to even acknowledge the inscribed copies I sent them . . . [he lists one or two names of prominent reviewers].' Here he also noted that he had been surprised to find that Petre Mais had liked the book and had given it a good review: '. . . Infused throughout by a passionate sincerity this novel has all the quality of greatness in it and as an interpretation of life rings true in every line.'[15]

But Henry was already steeped in the next volume, *Donkey Boy*, as further diary entries reveal: 'working generally from about 10 a.m. – 10 p.m., and, on 21 January, 'Working. Sometimes depressed. Book goes on & on writing itself. Any plan I make simply is written off by this pen wandering where it listeth.'

In February he caught a very bad cold, and he reverted to grumbling in his diary, against his first wife, against his son Richard whom he wanted to collaborate with him on a book,[16] and against Christine. On Wednesday 6 February he was in bed (in the Hut) listening to the radio while he worked on *Donkey Boy* when he was alerted by a long hissing pause: 'Then announcer spoke in a slow grave voice & I knew at once it was the King's death. So it turned out. . . . Poor King, one's tears fell. He was my age to within a week or so.'

On Tuesday 26 February he wrote that he was, 'Writing hard. The last lap. Wrote all day & afternoon & evening & night [and the entry continued on the next day] And finished *Donkey Boy* at 3.30 a.m. this morning. Slept ill but felt nicely empty & got up about 3 p.m. Christine very kind and understanding.' Of course, he did some rewriting, in particular of Chapter 29, and when it came back from typing he spent a whole week revising it: 'the first draft must be exploratory'. Macdonald took it for £750 advance and they also took *Tales of Moorland and Estuary* for £250 advance, 'so I feel secure'.

He had received a wedding invitation from Windles, now in Canada, who was getting married on 15 March. 'I often think of him, chiefly as a small child (tenderly) and as a youth on the farm (poignantly). But I was never *easy* with him. Our minds are unalike.' He did not travel to Canada for the ceremony but sent a copy of *The Phasian Bird* for a wedding present. Henry could be very generous on occasion. He could also be very mean. Mostly presents to his family for coming of age or marriage were copies of books he had reviewed.

On 23 March he recorded that he had a 'row' with Christine in the evening – he had been irritable and bad-tempered for several days, 'Hyperactive' – and stated that he had behaved very badly and hit her. 'Very sad – having just written Donkey Boy. . . . Poody must not suffer because Mummy and Daddy quarrel. I must try to be less argumentative & more tolerant.'

On April 9 he went in his Aston Martin to Exeter to an Authors' Society meeting, where he met Malcolm Elwin, E.W. Martin, Charles Causley, Morchard Bishop, and a man who was a writer and naturalist on Dartmoor, 'all pleasant people & we had an amiable gathering afterwards in the beamy, armour-filled bar of the old hostelry opposite cathedral.'

Then on 1 May he and Christine went to Bungay for a few days, calling at Aspley Guise to see his Aunt Lil (Marjorie Boone's mother, Margaret), now eighty-seven and 'bright as ever, surrounded by Marjorie's numerous children and grandchildren – & Frank Turney (Marjorie's husband), the ne'er do well.' They arrived at Bungay at 8 p.m. where he found 'Rikky with a half-grown vixen, Sarah & Gipsy'. They all went to Snetterton motor races on the Saturday, and when he returned to Devon on 6 May he noted that he was 'feeling less tired'. He then started on the third volume of the *Chronicle*: 'tentatively titled The Windflower – "Not I, but the wind" (?) quote from D.H. Lawrence',[17] but at the end of May he stopped writing 'The Wind's Will – Too weary. I shall continue in the autumn.'

On 3 June he went to Plymouth to attend the West Country Writers' Congress, which had been inaugurated the previous year, and had arisen out of Waveney Girvan's efforts with the Westaway Press and the *West Country Magazine*. The first President was Eden Philpotts, with Waveney Girvan as Chairman. Henry was one of the founder members, and when Eden Philpotts died in 1960, he was invited to take on the Presidency, which he accepted. Five years later he demoted himself to Vice-President (but continued to take a most active interest). On this occasion Henry travelled to Plymouth via Launceston where he had lunch with Charles Causley and then drove him to Plymouth, meeting up with E.W. (Ernie) Martin,[18] Denys Val Baker and others in the evening, and having a talk with Frank Swinnerton, 'a dear', and St Ervine, who gave a lecture on George Bernard Shaw.

From there he went on to stay the night with Ann Edmonds and her family in Surrey. She told him she had met 'Hanna' – Hanna Reitsch, the German test pilot who flew to Hitler in Berlin a few days before he died. On Thursday 5 June he drove the Aston to a specialist garage in Windsor and then he went on to Northolt, from where he flew to Ireland to holiday with John Heygate (now Sir John Heygate) and his third wife, Dora, Lady Heygate,[19] at their home at Bellarena. He found John 'rather like one of the ruins Cromwell knocked about a bit; rather glitter-eyed . . .' and Dora 'vital & sweet, reminding me of Rita Hayworth the film actress'. But the two men had moved apart and were wary and irritable with each other. John criticized a remark Henry made about Hanna Reitsch. Henry stated in his diary that he told Heygate (incorrectly) that he had met her personally (and noted that he will have Phillip do so in the novels). John called her 'tiresome' – and sparks flew.

The following day Dora tactfully suggested that Henry ask Christine to join them, no doubt thinking it would defuse a potentially explosive situation. Christine and Poody came over by boat late on the Thursday evening and indeed, the next day Henry wrote, 'Things much easier now between John & myself. Dora continues to be her unfailing cheerful and kindly self. I like Bellarena much.' But he had hoped to discuss with John how to handle the structure of his novels concerning Phillip and Germany and Hitler, and realized that this was not going to be possible. He wrote here that his plan was to have 'Phillip given a free pass from Hitler who believes him to be a great European artist. [Phillip] goes into Buchenwald & of course is sickened finally there, longs for death. He is Aeneas in Hades, a modern Virgil.' From this short entry we see how Henry now views Hitler and his deeds, although he did not actually develop this scenario into the

Henry, Christine and their son, 'Poody' (Michael Harry).

novels. Henry did not write any further about the holiday, merely noting that he flew back to London on 25 June and collected the Aston, and that Christine and Poody travelled back by boat and train on Friday 27th, and they all stayed overnight with Margaret in London.

The shortest of entries heralded the disastrous floods at Lynmouth on 15 August, and the fact that the next day he went to Lynmouth with Christine and Poody to see the results. They made a huge impression on him, however, for in the final volume of the *Chronicle*, *The Gale of the World*, the floods would provide the culminating scene that brings the long novel series to a close. A 'Götterdämmerung' scene with all the power of Richard Wagner's music described in words in a tremendous Romantic vision of the end of the world.

In the meantime he was working hard on 'The Wind's Will', even writing all through Christmas, and at the New Year he noted that he had done about 180,000 words of Book 3. At the beginning of 1953 he was correcting proofs of *Tales of Moorland and Estuary*, and worrying about the illustrations. Used to overseeing all the publishing processes himself, and to Charles Tunnicliffe's meticulous care in the preparation of the illustrations, he found postwar practice distressing; drawings were produced not only without reference to him, but also without observation of the actual subject. He was particularly upset about one drawing of the viaduct for the final story 'Where the Bright Waters Meet': 'The 'viaduct' is a few feet over the river – river with deep banks – with iron tubular supports etc. The Viaduct is described in the story, accurately, too.' He wrote and begged Eric Harvey of Macdonald to have that one exchanged for one of 'burning Bentley, 2 ghosts in it, instead'. This was attended to, but the resultant new sketch was not how Henry envisaged it should be (although it is actually very good). Richard remembers him as being scathing about it.

Tales of Moorland and Estuary, published on 16 March, was of particular importance to Henry. It contains twelve short stories, several of which have bizarre, even slightly macabre, plots – nature red in tooth and claw. Most stemmed from the earliest days of his writing career and he was perhaps hoping they would be recognized as on a par with *Tarka* and *Salar*. On the whole reviews were very ordinary, but some did recognize the book's worth. S.L. Bensusan wrote a long analytic and sympathetic piece in the *Fortnightly Review* (May 1953) stating: '. . . This collection of a dozen stories sums up the close and sympathetic observations of years and I cannot help thinking that most lovers and students of wild life will share my debt to a highly qualified naturalist, a writer of distinguished prose, and a poet.' Petre Mais wrote a good review in the *Oxford Mail*, while George Painter's review, 'The Ex-Soldier and the Otter', encapsulated Henry's life and work in one paragraph and focused on the *Tales* in the next: 'These stories move with their beauty and truth.' (Source not marked on cutting.)

Henry plodded doggedly on with the third volume of the *Chronicle*, noting on 16 January 1953, 'Dispirited at times. Christine helps much by affirming me to myself. I read every bit to her, for her reaction. She is very patient.' He complained frequently of his stupidity in spending his mornings writing long letters to friends instead of getting on with his book, for example on 20 February: 'I write & write, mostly letters to people – awful loose stuff, instead of disciplining myself to write my book. I start about 9.30 a.m. and get to the book about noon.' On Easter Monday he wrote that the book was getting very long and he was getting very tired. 'Am very stale. Beginning (?only beginning) to be afraid of the unmanageable length. Doubt just about equals my creative (if any) effort.' He also added on 15 April: 'N.B. I write in this journal only when rather upset; at night, or early morning, to escape lying still, impotent & anguished. There are pages of wonderful things I see & hear every day, about Poody, Christine etc. – but I devote all to my novel.' ('impotent' refers here to his writing rather than to his physical state.)

They left for a break at Bungay, arguing all the way there, Henry admitting in his diary that he had been very rude and unkind to Christine. She went on by train from Norwich to see her mother, referred to by Henry as 'Madame Duffield', in Yorkshire. Henry took Loetitia, John and Richard to Snetterton Motor Races, and afterwards on to the cinema in Norwich. Henry loved the cinema and often went to see films – and later in his life would watch television films for hours. While in the area he took the opportunity to drive up to Langham to see the Hollingsworths. 'Such a warm, sweet greeting . . . these people were such good friends to me in the war – probably saved my sanity, or life.' On the way back he picked up Christine from Norwich station and after a day or two, they returned to the Field on 28 April.

The third novel was finally finished and typed and taken to Malcolm Elwin on 15 June. It had a new title, *Young Phillip Maddison*, suggested by John Heygate for one of the parts, and Eric Harvey thought it would be good for the whole volume.

On 5 July there was a recording of a forty-five minute BBC Radio programme in Bristol in the arts series *Apollo in the West*, introduced by Charles Causley in which three critics, Morchard Bishop, Malcolm Elwin and D.S. Savage discussed Henry's writing, with readings of his work by Douglas Leach and ending with Henry himself reading a chapter from the as yet unpublished *Young Phillip Maddison*. Henry drove to the recording studio with Kenneth Allsop who was in the area researching an article for *Picture Post* for the Taw and Torridge Festival, convened by the poet Ronald Duncan. Charles Causley had prepared the material sensitively and thoroughly and the programme, broadcast on 7 July, presented an impressive resumée of Henry's work.[20] On the final day of the festival, Friday 17 July, Henry gave a lecture in the afternoon, 'The Two Rivers of my Youth' (ostensibly the writing of *Tarka*), attended a cocktail party at Ronald Duncan's house in the early evening, and a ball given by Lord and Lady Fortescue at Castle Hill later in the evening: 'Lady F. very sweet as always'. Although initially reluctant to attend, he and Christine finally left at 3 a.m. having had a lovely time with the festival cast of *Don Juan* who had arrived from Bideford in a bus.

Work continued until September when he had a short break to go to Bungay and to the Aston Martin races at Snetterton for the St John Horsfall Memorial Trophy. But he was living on the edge of his nerves; constantly tired, constantly irritable, constantly worried that the *Chronicle* was no good, and in constant fear that he would die before it was finished. The following spring Henry again went to Bungay on his own for a visit, arriving on 22 April, the Aston proving a total disaster the whole way. He stayed until the beginning of May when he went down to London and then on to take the car yet once more to Friary Motors in Windsor.

A trip had been planned with Eric Watkins, an editor on the *News Chronicle*, to go to the battlefields for a four-day walking tour and they left on Friday 7 May, first visiting Ypres and Loos. 'The place is still very sad, as though invested by the spirit of forgiveness.' By the end of the following day he had very bad blisters, it had been very hot, and their packs were heavy. 'I grew irritable and critical.' On Sunday they went by bus to Armentières and then walked to Ploegsteert and 'walked past the 1914 Christmas truce site (where was it exactly?) . . . .'. On Monday they 'hobbled' to Lillebeke and then back to Ypres, 'very weary', trained and bussed to Poperinghe and Hazebrouck, and then returned via Calais to Dover, arriving back at Victoria at 9 o'clock', 'said goodbye to Eric & hobbled to the Savage Club'. This trip served two purposes; firstly, to gather material for an article on the fortieth anniversary of the battle of Ypres later in the year; secondly, to refresh and bring to the surface of his mind the details of the war years, for he was now preparing to write the novels concerning that period.

However, he had another problem on his mind. Richard Aldington was engaged in writing a biography of T. E. Lawrence and in gathering his material he had discovered that things were not what they seemed, and because of Henry's first-hand knowledge of Lawrence, he had enlisted Henry's help to check the disputed circumstances surrounding Lawrence's birth. As the book progressed it had become obvious that it was going to be very controversial and Henry found himself caught up in a veritable whirlwind which, for once, was not of his own making. The establishment, led by the military historian B. H. Liddell Hart – Aldington referred to them as 'The Lawrence Bureau' – closed ranks against Aldington and, because they discovered that Henry had helped Aldington, against Henry also (although his part was very minor – virtually his contribution was only to check the source of entries in *Who's Who* and lend Aldington a selection of his Lawrence letters). Henry was very concerned about the outcome of Aldington's book. He was passionately pro-Lawrence and he urged Aldington to tone down the more controversial matters. But Aldington had discovered so many strange discrepancies in the material that he felt a big cover-up was going on and he determined to expose the truth.[21]

Henry decided to pre-empt Aldington's book[22] by publishing his own long essay in praise of Lawrence, which was printed in the *European* in two parts in May and June 1954.[23] This was the same material as that which appeared in *Genius of Friendship*, but with added passages explaining the Aldington connection and to give his own apologia for Lawrence's behaviour. It was also perhaps an apologia for his own behaviour. That he recognized that much of what was pertinent to Lawrence's story was also pertinent to his own is obvious from phrases he used in the article, especially the closing paragraph:

> Dear Lawrence of Arabia, 'world's imp' as the imaginative Arabs called you (and they knew) did your imagination fizz over at times? . . . Did you, in fear, instinctively use words to conceal your true self, which was of the quality of gold beaten so fine that it quivers in stillest air and is near transparent? Did you blurt out startling 'facts' to break a constriction with unclear people? Was it fun, Irish blarney, to embroider a tale you did not really want to tell, always because of the haunting need to conceal the 'reality' of Ned Lawrence. . . . Were your 'facts' flung out anyhow and anywhere, because in truth the whole thing to you was 'balls'? . . . God save us all from the truth that is not multi-lateral! . . . Shakespeare who created Hamlet as well as Prospero, Ariel, and Puck, would know what I try to explain. And you, I think, would be the last person to blame any biographer who accepted a contract job and then did his best to say what happened. . . . Let the critic who has never slurred or twisted in his own life throw the first stone.
>
> Threnos for T.E. Lawrence

By coincidence, at this time the Lawrence family now published a selection of letters from T.E. and his brothers, and Henry wrote long reviews of this book and gave a radio broadcast review.[24] He also recorded a talk about his friendship with Lawrence for *Signature*, a monthly magazine for the arts broadcast in the West Country.

At the end of September 1954, having been writing intensively for the past month on the Loos battle for the new novel – 'It has come with difficulty' – Henry went to London for an Authors' Society meeting. He had met Ruth Tomalin[25] the previous June at the West Country Writers' Congress ('charming girl, fey, Irish, large brown eyes') and spent all his leisure time on this London visit in her company, taking her to dinner at the Renaissance Club and the following evening to a family party at a Greek restaurant in Chelsea: 'present, Gipsy, John, Margaret, Robert, Joan Griffith his girl, Sarah, Bill Thomson, & myself [plus Ruth]'. On Saturday 2 October he wrote that he 'walked with Ruth T. & Eric Watkins over Hayes Common, to the Keston Fish Ponds & back. Carp, pike, rudd, roach, water-lilies still live in the pure water reflecting images of pines & birds as in my boyhood. A keeper told me that some people (visitors) wanted the "weeds" dragged out & the water chlorinated "for health's sake".'

On the following Monday and Tuesday he worked in the Imperial War Museum and on the Wednesday he 'Bought 12 volumes of the *Official History of the Great War*'. These were to prove invaluable to him for checking precise details of engagement and movements of troops etc., especially for those encounters in which he had not personally taken part. That evening he took Ruth to the Authors' Society dinner; but although he enjoyed it he felt Ruth had had enough of his company – she left immediately after dinner.

At this time Henry was having a new building erected in the Field. Known as 'The Studio' this consisted of two large rooms, one up and one down, connected by steep and narrow stairs. It was put up amid much controversy and difficulty. The builder would *not* use the water-proof cement that Henry wanted and neither would he impregnate the wooden beams with Cuprinol against rot. Henry gave vent to his feelings with much complaint in his diary.

The fourth volume of the *Chronicle*, *How Dear is Life*, was published on 25 October. 'Will it bring my name back as a serious writer?' But, as always, he was more interested in the current writing and wrote a long precis of that – 'a much better book'. Two days later Christine told him the rather startling news that she was deeply in love with someone he knew. Eventually, she admitted the name of an artist acquaintance. This revelation provoked one of Henry's now familiar long entries which lasted over several pages, although he was not totally distraught as he felt that at bottom everything was still all right between them, and that Christine would not have looked for love elsewhere if he had not been so irritable. He did set out once or twice to go and see this man and confront him, but thought better of it. After a few days they made it up, and decided on a 'new schedule' – soon broken by both of them. At this point the episode seemed no more than a bid for attention from Henry, but later on Henry did give it more significance. These diary entries are interspersed with entries of complaint about the building of the Studio: 'The builder, a local lad, tends to agree to do what I want & then to ignore

Henry inspects the newly built Studio in the Field at Ox's Cross.

what he has promised to do.' The situation was further exacerbated by the fact that on Sunday 7 November he went out especially to buy newspapers: 'I hoped for reviews of *Dear Life* in Sunday papers – none – hoped for 40th anniversary of Ypres 1914 would be noticed. None.'

Eventually the Studio was finished and Henry was able to get on with the next volume, *A Fox Under My Cloak*, which had been severely interrupted by the building work, which was the real source of his uneasiness.

In the spring of 1955 Henry bowed to the inevitable and went to London to buy a new car, noting on 9 April: 'Bought Austin A40 Countryman in morning, allowance £300 for Aston-Martin. Rather sad to see last of the motorcar which had caused so much trouble! Motored back slowly in fine weather, & arrived about 11.30 at Georgeham.'

On the last day of May, he and Christine and Poody set off for a holiday in the Austin, crossing to Ireland on 2 June. The first three weeks were to be spent on a fishing and camping trip, and Henry's entry for 2 June sets the tone: 'In bad temper. We carry too much clobber & I really don't look forward to the holiday – a camping hell I fear it will turn out.' He had five pints of beer before getting on the boat and was, naturally, very sick. They drove to Bantry 'to visit the sunny scenes of 2nd honeymoon with darling Chris in 1949 – that perfect holiday. . .'. This time it was pouring with rain and they quarrelled bitterly. Two days later the windscreen was shattered and they had to wait five days for a replacement – only to find when he telephoned to complain, that it had been at the local railway station since the first day.

He had been greatly cheered the previous November by a letter from John Middleton Murry who had written to say that he was upset that the critics had failed to see the fulness and beauty of the four new *Chronicle* novels and he wanted to write a long essay on them to include in his new book. Henry had been delighted. Now in Ireland, he received 'Rather a blow' in a letter from Eric Harvey (of Macdonald) to say that Cape had refused that particular portion of Murry's book, and that Murry had taken it to him asking him to do it as a pamphlet, but he felt as Henry's publisher, it would look sycophantic, and so had refused.[26] The weather was bad and this last straw was very depressing. However, the next day John Heygate contacted them to invite them to Bellarena as the weather was so rotten and they made their way north, arriving there on 18 June. To begin with, all went well until Henry decided that John was flirting (or worse) with Christine, and there was an unpleasant atmosphere for several days. Henry had bought two books about pigeon rearing before he left for Ireland to provide himself with the background facts for a book about a pigeon, which he now began to write, using his car as a writing station in order to gain peace and quiet, as the house tended to be full of noise and bustle. (This book, *The Scandaroon*, was then abandoned until the very end of his writing life). They returned to England on 20 July when, having eventually cheered up, Henry wrote: 'A wonderful visit: wish I'd kept a diary.'

The year 1956 was devoted to a long grind of writing; Henry noted at the beginning of March that he went to London 'tired and confused' to sort out the structure of the rest of the *Chronicle*. He had planned to publish *The Man Who Went Outside* (the latest title for the Norfolk Farm volume) at this point and then to track retrospectively from there. Middleton Murry had advised against this and the publishers (presumably through Elwin) were not happy either. They thought the political elements would detract from the series and from Henry's reputation. Strangely (or not!) it was a letter from his faithful typist at this time, Elizabeth Tippett,[27] writing from her home in Truro, accompanying a batch of typescript which actually decided him not to do this, as he noted in his diary on 8 March:

A letter from perceptive Tippett says, 'I agree . . . you should continue Phillip's story (i.e. from No. 6 onwards) . . . and not skip & fill-in later. As I've typed *Lucifer* & *Darkness* & see the 'I's' & the 'Loetitia' changed to Phillip & Alethea I find it especially difficult in fact impossible to look on him as anyone but yourself – and hard to associate Ph. with the Phillip of before – not knowing what has beaten against him in the years between & brought him to his present personality.' Admirable criticism! For the past week, intensively, I've been yea-naying. Now I say, NAY. Let it (No. 9) be put away & get on with No. 6.

In the end the Norfolk farm volume was to be a bit further along the line than 'No. 9'. But the principle had been established. So Henry settled down despite the fact that he 'had planned to rest this year & write the Bray Stream Book [i.e. *A Clearwater Stream*] for Faber, most of which is already done', and wrote the sixth volume, *The Golden Virgin* steadily through, finishing it on 11 October, and posted it to Middleton Murry; noting two weeks later that Murry's opinion was unfavourable, that the book was too long:

I read it [Murry's letter] dolefully in the churchyard . . . I recovered later and planted some oak trees in the west spinney. . . . I think I'll be grateful to Murry, because I shall condense & cut, & that hurts nothing, considering that I wrote the book rather vaguely & only found out things as I wrote . . . [the following day continuing] Jack is right & the severity (to me: it didn't seem like that to him) of his criticism was kill or cure. [I write this] after returning home from village at 9.15 a.m. – I walk down daily with the two dear ones, for their bus catch for Croyde school . . .'[28]

John Middleton Murry died the following March and Henry attended his funeral on 16 March 1957. He travelled to Diss in Norfolk by train and Loetitia met him at the station 'with luncheon basket, in the Ford. And a wreath. Splendid woman! How she has developed away from my suppressing influence, since 1946!' Henry returned to London by train that same afternoon and dined alone in the Studio Club as 'John, Robert, Richard, my sons, all in town, had other engagements. John to receive Gliding Club Trophy at Londonderry House from Ld. Brabazon, Robert with his girl (fiancée) & Richard also with a friend.' A month later Mary Murry sent him one of Murry's pens, which he valued greatly.

On 26 April Kenneth Allsop drove Richard down to the Field at Ox's Cross for a long weekend. Henry noted, 'Very glad to see them.' Richard has never forgotten the somewhat hair-raising drive – Ken was a fast and furious driver who tended to take corners on the wrong side of the road without a thought. The next day they all went up on to Exmoor, and on the Sunday they took a picnic lunch and walked to Baggy Point.

In June Henry was approached by Walt Disney Distributors Ltd who wanted to take up an option on rights preparatory to doing a film based on *Tarka the Otter*, and he went to London to discuss this with their representative, afterwards instructing Cyrus Brooks to act as his agent. On 19 July he instructed Brooks to say that he felt unable to sell the copyright, but would grant an eight-year lease for £1,000. He thought that Disney was actually going to make the film based on a very inferior American book which had already plagiarized *Tarka*.

On 22 June Richard arrived on leave for ten days from the RAF to write the last chapters of his first book, *The Dawn is my Brother*, the story of his young life at school and early RAF adventures; in fact, he revised what he had already written but found it impossible to actually create in Henry's presence. During this visit Henry asked him to be his literary executor.

One afternoon at this time Henry received a visit from Dan Farson who brought along his friend, Colin Wilson, who described the occasion in an article in an early issue of the Henry Williamson Society *Journal*.[29] In this Wilson stated that because Negley Farson and Henry had quarrelled some time previously and were not on speaking terms, Dan Farson and he set out secretly to go and see Henry,

Enjoying a pint at the Rock Inn, Georgeham, with Christine and 'characters' from his books.

pretending they were going for a walk along the beach. Henry did not record this event.

At the end of July Henry, with Christine and Harry (now too old to be called Poody) left after 'the usual tantrums' for a holiday in Ireland. (Preparing for a journey was always a nightmare where Henry was concerned, his quick temper and hysterical reactions always creating total chaos.) Again they were to camp and fish before going on to Bellarena. Details of the holiday were not recorded until 6 September when he wrote: '*The Golden Virgin* published today.' The following day Henry went out to buy newspapers knowing that Kenneth Allsop was doing a big piece on him in the *Daily Mail*.

> Ordered 6 copies of the *D. Mail* with Kenneth Allsop's eulogy. I read one in Limavady in the car, outside the newsagent's shop; & was apalled. K.A. said I was an M.C. (Military Cross) at 20 years of age. . . . he had assumed this from 1) Knowing *The Pathway* from his early days of consciousness 2) seeing my 21-year-old photograph in studio, where the Mons Star looks like a decoration. John Heygate asked me, 'Is it true' & I made a gesture of displeasure. I didn't want K.A. to be knocked as a bad reporter; nor myself to be widely known as a liar. Was worried & suppressed the six copies.

They left the next day making their way slowly, staying one or two nights with friends, and finally arriving home on 12 September. There he found a 'Letter from Allsop, saying that he was very sorry & should have checked. All is well. . . . But I wrote to John Heygate & others, saying the truth.' Unfortunately, however, many people took this to be a true fact stated by Henry, wrongly accusing him of lying – one more black mark against his name.

At the beginning of October 1957 Henry went to London where, on the 3rd, he was made a Fellow of the Royal Society of Literature: 'Very happy day for me.' The papers in the archive show that he had actually been elected at the end of 1954, nominated by William Kean Seymour and seconded by Kenneth Hopkins. Fellowship was an honour reserved for 'persons of distinguished literary achievement', and nominations were restricted to authors whose published work was of such literary value as to deserve this high recognition, and had to be ratified by the vote of the council in session. Two days later there was a cocktail party at the Savage Club, to which Henry invited Margaret and Bill Thomson, Richard, and a rather strained young lady Henry had met a fortnight previously, with whom he now quarrelled and sent home in a taxi. Henry was urging Richard to finish his book which was scheduled to be published the following spring. Robert was not present as he was currently working in Newfoundland, and was getting married there on 8 November.

A Clear Water Stream was sent off to Faber on 21 November. A week later he and Christine drove the 8 miles to Ilfracombe to view the cottage they were planning to buy – 8 Brittania Row or 4 Capstone Place – depending on whether one entered by the front or back door! The occasion caused an outbreak of irritability and bad-temper, Henry as always being overexcitable at such times. The house needed some structural refurbishment and the logistics of this became a running sore over the next year.

At the beginning of December Henry went to London for various business appointments and while there dined twice with Margaret and Bill Thomson. On the second occasion there was also another guest, Father Brocard Sewell, 'with whom I've exchanged letters about the G.V. [*The Golden Virgin*] & other books'. Father Brocard was editor of the *Aylesford Review*, a literary magazine published by the English Carmelite Fathers,[30] and had planned a special issue devoted to Henry Williamson, whom Brocard felt had not received the attention from the literary world that was his due, for the forthcoming winter issue. This was published at the end of January 1958. Henry noted in his diary: 'The copies of the H.W. number of Aylesford Review arrived. Splendid, kind, warm number.'[31] Father Brocard's editorial 'Henry Williamson' opened with an overview: 'We direct our readers' attention to the works of a great living writer, the maker of many beautiful books. . . .' It contained among other items, a posthumous essay by John Middleton Murry, and an essay by Malcolm Elwin to which Henry took exception because Elwin had used sources that Henry had shown him privately and confidentially, and which he had not wanted publicized at that time.

MARCH–APRIL, 1958—14th Week.

31 MONDAY [90-275]

APRIL 1 TUESDAY [91-274]

APRIL 2 WEDNESDAY [92-273]

APRIL, 1958—14th Week.

3 THURSDAY [93-272]
MAUNDY THURSDAY.

H.W.
THE TREMBLING OF A FLARE
COURAGE IS WILL POWER.
GREATER LOVE.
THE DONKS OF PASSCHENDAELE
TALE OF A TRANSPORT OFFICER
A TRANSPORT OFFICER'S TALE
THE CANDLE LIGHT
THE DEATHLESS ARMY
SALVATION
THE HIDDEN VICTORY.
COURAGE AND MYSTERY
HE THAT ENDURETH
ENDURANCE IS ALL
SIEGFRIED AND PASSCHENDAELE
THAT ENDURETH AND IS KIND

4 FRIDAY [94-271] GOOD FRIDAY.

ENDURANCE AND KINDNESS
ENDURE TO BE KIND
MANNERS MAKETH MAN.
SIGHT AND INSIGHT.

5 SATURDAY [95-270]

6 SUNDAY [96-269]
EASTER SUNDAY.

An extract from Henry's diary showing the titles suggested for the new novel for a £1 prize.

This year marked a turning point in the tide of Henry's literary career. With the public affirmation of the worth of his writing in the *Aylesford Review* and with the award of the FRSL he could not just be dismissed as a cranky eccentric with peculiar views. It must certainly have helped his faith in himself after the very difficult writing years since the war and given him the confidence he needed to proceed. It was the start of a firm friendship between Henry and Brocard Sewell. They corresponded prolifically and Henry was drawn into the very successful 'Literary Meetings' held at Spode House in Staffordshire. Henry found these friendly and interesting weekends relaxing and refreshing. He particularly enjoyed the attentions of the eager young writers, such as the poets Michael and Frances Horowitz, who tended to lionize him, and others such as the shy photographer Oswald Jones, who became a particular friend and took many excellent photographs of Henry in the ensuing years. It was Father 'Brocard who, after Henry's death, organized and edited a symposium of tributes and critical essays.[32]

Work on the *Chronicle* progressed with difficulty. There was much research needed for the war era. In March 1958 he suddenly changed the structure of the current volume which meant that his title *A Test to Destruction* no longer applied – so he offered £1 for a winning entry for a new title from Christine, Harry and himself! None of the entries was chosen; the novel was called *Love and the Loveless*.

In April 1958 Henry wrote his first article, 'From a Country Hilltop', for the *Co-operative Home Magazine*, the monthly magazine of the Co-operative Society and he contributed a regular piece for over three and a half years, and refers frequently in his diary to writing his 'Home' piece, for which he was paid £15

Henry Williamson by Oswald Jones.

monthly.[33] Also at this time Henry wrote an important article about his schooldays which appeared in the *Spectator* in their series 'John Bull's Schooldays'.[34]

Henry had been invited to give the prestigious Wedmore Memorial Lecture to the Fellows of the Royal Society of Literature on 9 October 1958.[35] Henry chose for his subject 'Some Nature Writers and Civilisation',[36] a discussion of the work of Richard Jefferies and W.H. Hudson, the two writers about whom he felt passionately and who had been such an influence on his own thoughts and writing.

Henry's diary during this time was one long tirade, extending over several days, of his view of Christine's general inefficiency and *laissez-faire* attitude. The repair work on the Ilfracombe cottage which he had bought was not progressing well; there was another problem over the use of water-proof cement which the builder (a cousin of the man who had built the Studio) would not or could not use. Christine apparently would not organize the domestic details (stoves, cookers, sinks, etc). Henry noted: 'I am desperately tired, I only want to be allowed to write but this seldom happens; there are so many outside things that come between me & the wish to work.' He admitted, 'This may be seen to be an utterly selfish declaration, but events speak for themselves.' One such was the fact that he had delegated to Christine the task of organizing the purchase of a plot in the churchyard in Georgeham for his eventual grave, because he knew there were very few sites left. This dragged on for months and was the cause of much argument between them. Christine probably felt that whatever she did was bound to be wrong and therefore she could not bring herself to complete any task, which only exacerbated the situation.

Love and the Loveless was published on 22 October and a month later Henry recorded, 'Deep depression over Love and Loveless – unreviewed.' This was not so, there is a large pile of review cuttings for this volume but they were rather slow in coming out. He must surely have been cheered by one that Goronwy Rees wrote in *The Listener* in mid-December:

The description of the fighting itself is so vivid as to make one wonder once again how the human body ever endured such intolerable hardships. . . . It is no ordinary achievement to write in a way that does even approximate justice to an immense human tragedy. . . . It is a feat of recollection that has something in it which is akin to genius. . . . it seems certain that when the story of Phillip Maddison is finally completed it will compose a chronicle which will be of permanent literary and historical value. There are not many works of fiction of which one can say that.[37]

In the spring of 1959 negotiations began over a proposed omnibus edition to be published by Macdonald of Henry's animal books. This was complicated because of the various rights involved and took quite a while to sort out, which worried Henry as he was relying on this to provide a source of income. On 11 March

Henry noted that he corrected the proofs of the revised *Children of Shallowford* book.[38] 'It looks good to me. Faber's catalogue gives pride of place to Richard's *Dawn* in their catalogue under the Autobiography sub-heading. I come next. Most satisfactory.' The Ilfracombe cottage continued to cause problems. Christine and Harry were now established at an Ilfracombe primary school but because they were not yet able to live in the cottage Henry was having to drive them in and out twice a day; whilst the saga of the grave-plot continued almost like a French farce. The plot that the sexton, Clibbit Thomas, had said was available turned out to have someone else buried in it; then Henry drew up a map for the position of another grave but Clibbit had got it all wrong again. Henry blamed Christine for not having organized the matter when he first asked her, when there were six plots still available; thereafter three people had died in quick succession, leaving only three plots, and now there was only the one remaining. Henry wrote to the vicar yet again offering a fresh map so that the necessary permission could be applied for. Then he recorded on 15 March:

Clibbit Thomas, sexton, died today, so even his poor faulty memory won't be available to remember the new site of the grave – by a CASTOR OIL TREE planted by Miss Hyde some years ago ('Miss Goff' of *The Pathway*). [and further on 1 April] I mooched about the Churchyard after posting 11 letters in the village & made a rough map of new Grave Site by the Castor Oil Tree – appropriately on All Fools' Day.

One reason for Henry's anxiety was the fact that Negley Farson was also after this last plot and the two quarrelled bitterly over who should get it. Henry won, but he was eventually to lie only feet from Negley who was buried just across the stream in the 'extension', where no doubt they continue to sharpen their wits one against the other in the ancient sunlight of eternity.

The cottage at Capstone Place was finally finished in mid-April 1959; there is no record of when Henry and Christine actually started living there, but it was probably soon after this. However, all was not yet smooth: there followed several further weeks of wrangling, of claim and counter-claim about who was responsible for the various delays at the different stages; this was finally settled by an independent arbiter, on 28 July, when Henry then took the builder and others for a drink in the Britannia (the Royal Britannia Hotel, which he later used to call the 'Brit'). This pub, just down the road from Capstone Place became his local. In his later years, Henry enjoyed pubs, for the companionship rather than the drink, and would attach himself to anyone who caught his attention, whether he knew them or not.

After a long stint on Volume 9 of the *Chronicle* (it had no title at this point), he noted at the end of April that he was ahead of his 'time-pressure schedule . . . & tension which has held me close (& affected poor Chris) since 1950 or even before', and went off on a visit to Bungay. He called to see John at Swindon on the way, and at Bungay saw Richard and went the next day with Loetitia to watch

Sarah (now fifteen years old) riding in a gymkhana. To provide adequate space for Sarah's horse Loetitia now arranged to rent an isolated cottage with a large garden and orchard area called Wood House at Bath Hills in the nearby village of Ditchingham on the estate of Lilias Rider Haggard (with whom the family were very friendly), renting out her own house. (Loetitia lived there until in 1980 she felt it was too isolated, especially in winter when she could easily be cut off in the snow, and moved back to her own cottage on the outskirts of Bungay.) After his visit Henry went down to London, dining with Margaret and Bill and the following day inviting Doline Rendle, Spica Virginis, the girl with whom he had been in love in the far-off Folkestone days, to dine at the Studio Club (a favourite place of his in these years), but he found her argumentative – by which it can be inferred that she did not agree with his views.

The following day, 4 May, Richard arrived in London and they went together to the Llewellyn Rhys Prize presentation for which Richard was runner up, with *The Dawn Is My Brother*. Henry returned to the Field the next day. On 12 May he and Christine drove Michael (Henry made a great point that Harry was to be called Michael henceforth, but the resolve was never kept) to the Choristers' School at Exeter where he had obtained a scholarship. A week later Henry went to Wales for a visit to see an old friend 'Captain' Bill Child (Henry noted here that he was 'Bill Kidd' and also a basis for 'Piston' in the *Chronicle*), who had moved from North Devon to Abergavenny. But they argued continuously, mainly because Child drank a great deal which made him aggressive, and Henry thankfully left and went on to see Father Brocard Sewell who was at that time with the Carmelite community at Llandeilo. Father Brocard had obtained permission for Henry to fish from the local squire, Richard Rhys, heir to the Dynevor barony, who lived with his wife Lucy in the grounds of Dynevor Castle. Henry liked the Dynevors, who were very interested in the arts, especially Welsh theatre, and they became friends. Henry left on 26 May with Father Brocard whom he was taking down to Devon as his guest for the West Country Writers' Conference being held at Barnstaple. Richard Williamson came down for this also. One of the events laid on for this meeting was a visit to Henry's Field. Dr W.G. Hoskins, the social geographer, wrote afterwards that it was the highlight of what was otherwise a rather dull conference.

Henry had bought a 1956 Morris Minor to replace Loetitia's rather ancient 1938 Ford, and Richard now drove this back to Bungay. Unfortunately, the new engine was faulty and sucked the water through and vaporized it – so Henry arranged for Richard to return it the following month for a replacement engine. There seems always to have been a gremlin where cars and Henry were concerned!

In August Christine went to visit her mother, and Richard arrived for a month. He and Henry were to go to Bellarena together where they were supposed to collaborate on a short book about a hybrid roseate tern, a book Henry had had in his mind ever since the Norfolk farm days (he had seen one there) but which he wanted Richard to actually write. Before they left on 9 August Richard cleared the garden and overgrown hedges at the Field. Henry found he could not work at

Bellarena: 'Simply cannot write here – too much "life". Am feeling tired, but relaxed & well.' He would not let Richard write either!

They returned from Dublin to Exeter in a small DH Heron aircraft. When they were airborne Henry suddenly disconcerted Richard by asking if he would be able to fly the aeroplane. Instantly irritated by Richard's hesitancy, he cut across his reply, exclaiming that he would therefore have to do it himself – he thought if he breathed deeply he could manage it! Apparently he had noticed there was no co-pilot and therefore immediately convinced himself that the pilot would have a heart attack and die in mid-flight.

On their return Richard continued to work in the garden at Ox's Cross and to help re-cement the walls of the Ilfracombe cottage until he left on 1 September, when Henry noted in his diary: 'Richard's last day. He has worked well. In J.H.'s garden at Bellarena & here. But the writing of the roseate tern? Practically nil!' Richard feels that there was never any real intention that the book should be written. It was an excuse to keep Richard with him.

Henry's own writing now continued at a prodigious rate. Long blank gaps in his diary show his absorption. He recorded on 3 May 1961: 'Working hard. 75 hrs a week. 7 days a week.' Most of the novels had several versions before he was finally satisfied with them. But such concentrated effort took its toll and he was

Work on the *Chronicle* novels continued at a prodigious rate.

increasingly irritable with Christine. He did realize how difficult he was to live with, recording many instances of his bad temper getting the better of him. He also from time to time paid tribute to Christine's patience and help in listening and allowing herself to be a sounding board.

At the end of August 1961 Henry recorded in his diary that Father Brocard Sewell had sent him a copy of an article by Colin Wilson on Henry and his work for the *Aylesford Review*'s autumn issue. This very over-assertive critical essay, in which Wilson expressed somewhat dogmatic views and conclusions, apparently contained at this stage several quite virulent remarks, including the fact that if Richard Aldington were to write Henry's biography on the lines of the T.E. Lawrence book, he would prove him a congenital liar. This was apropos the differences between the episodes concerning 'Barley' in *The Sun in the Sands* and the newly published *The Innocent Moon* which uses the same material; that she died in the former but lived in the latter. Wilson did not seem to have grasped the fact that one was fiction and the other 'a novel-biography'. This worried Henry as he realized that all that would be picked up was the 'congenital liar' phrase and he would be branded as such henceforth, thus damaging him dreadfully, especially with regard to the war volumes. Father Brocard was very reluctant to cut Wilson's work but Henry eventually persuaded him to do so, and the main problem was averted.

Christine's mother died during the last night of 1961. It was not unexpected, as she had been ill with lung cancer. Christine hinted to Henry that her relatives wished the funeral to be entirely private (i.e. that Henry's presence was unwelcome), so Henry did not attend the service in Yorkshire.

The year was devoted to writing. On 26 September he noted that he had made a contribution for a television film about T.E. Lawrence: 'Recorded at Ealing Studios BBC TV stuff for T.E.L. programme.' This was to go out on 27 November 1962. On 20 November Henry left for a visit to London. The following day he was 'Guest of R.J. Nicholson (childhood friend 1918) at Leathersellers Co. Manning of D.Days [*Dandelion Days*], the Master. Wonderful evening & atmosphere.' He went to Ditchingham for the weekend returning to London to be Alec Waugh's guest at a 'Sette of Odd Volumes' dinner. This was a very select little group whose chief rule was that members must be amusing. Henry became a member; he was 'Brother Lutra' and he attended several of their functions over his remaining years. Petre Mais was present on this occasion, in a very bad mood, brought on by the fact that Henry had gone as Alec Waugh's guest, while he had refused to go with Mais on some earlier occasion. Henry himself was also upset, worrying that he would not get away in time to see the television programme on T.E. Lawrence (with his own contribution) that went out that night.

The next day, on 28 November, Henry returned to Barnstaple where Christine met him, accompanied by John Fursdon. Henry was annoyed as he had picked up flu (he was probably just overtired from the party) and had to entertain Fursdon when he had wanted to get home to bed. When they did return he was appalled to find almost total chaos. In his absence Christine had moved the furniture from the

Hut and the Studio to Capstone Place, tipping out books and files of letters from bookcases and cupboards to facilitate matters. 'My Hut was a shattering sight.' Worst of all he had wanted to check something in his T.E. Lawrence letters arising from the television programme and they could not be found in the chaos.

It is very difficult to explain this action on Christine's part; she seemed to think she was genuinely trying to be helpful, but she must have known that the Hut was sacrosanct to Henry. It could have been a last, desperate attempt to get attention from Henry. Or perhaps she was trying to provoke him to some final showdown. It is obvious that he left her alone a great deal while he went off to enjoy himself, as he had Loetitia in earlier years, and she may have been very aware that he saw other women on his frequent trips away. The storm raged between them for several days and then after a violent last confrontation in the middle of the night when Henry could not sleep, they made it up. The next day the T.E.L. letters were found and Christine said she would put the furniture back. Henry got on with the revision of the last chapter of 'No. 11', at this point the title was to be 'A Drive to Perfection', 'i.e. a power-drive, of both Phillip and his Uncle Hilary, for 'the dead'.'

On 9 December he motored to Cornwall to finalize the revisions with Elizabeth Tippett, who had recently left her husband and had moved to St Mawes with her four children. He was to be away about a week. He telephoned Christine at 8 p.m. that night and 'she sounded cheerful, asked me how long I would be away, & said she had got the music room for Harry's Xmas present'. They were in touch by telephone again the following day, 10 December. Henry and Elizabeth Tippett worked well together; 'Working and writing happily. The children and I have great fun.' On 14 December he received a letter from Christine to say she had left him, and she had been to see Harry at his school and had told him. Henry drove straight to Exeter from Cornwall to see Harry's headmaster who confirmed that Christine had been there and told him and Harry of the divorce plans. He told Henry that Harry was very upset about it, crying out at night. Henry returned to Barnstaple and saw his own solicitor, and then back to Ilfracombe where he found Christine had left the cottage in beautiful order, tidy and clean, and some work he had left for her to do 'carefully laid out with explicit notes – so helpful, bless her – . . . (How sad to think that only on her last day here was such exemplary help given).' Henry was in deep shock, especially to receive a letter from Christine's solicitors to say they were filing a writ for persistent mental cruelty. He was particularly worried because he did not know where she was.

He gradually unravelled the elements that culminated in this débâcle, going to see Christine's close friend, Jill Cook, who told him that Christine was in love with John Fursdon, who had asked her to marry him. This added further to Henry's shock. A letter arrived from Christine to say she was staying at a hotel in Exeter. Henry went down and they met at her solicitors on 22 December, and it was arranged that she and John would call to collect her things that afternoon. The situation was very complicated. Christine went to see the Bishop of Exeter, leaving in tears because he was cross with her (according to Henry she had asked to be remarried in the cathedral, and the bishop was shocked as she was still not only married to Henry but had only left him days before); she had already been to see the vicar at Ilfracombe after evensong on the very day that Henry had originally gone down to stay with Elizabeth Tippett, and yet she had had two cheerful and seemingly normal conversations with Henry after that. Henry arranged to see Christine again on 26 December at the home of his friend Dr W.G. Hoskins in Exeter, and they both went to evensong (Harry would have been singing in the choir) in the cathedral, although they did not sit together. Afterwards they had a long talk but Christine said that her decision was irrevocable.

On 27 December he returned to Cornwall to give Elizabeth Tippett instructions about finishing the revisions of volume 11 and then went on to spend the night with Colin Wilson at Mevagissey. 'He was pleasant and understanding and generous. Played some beautiful *Tristan* records.' The following day on the way home he was caught in a blizzard and had to spend the night at Wadebridge, continuing the next day after obtaining some chains, and spending the next night with Ronald Duncan. 'He was very kind, also Rose Mary [*sic*] his wife & daughter Bryony.' His diary entry at the end of 1962 reads: 'A moment of heavy despair which is borne somehow. It is hard to realise, to accept, the fact that my wife has left me for ever and for ever. She is part of my life – the best part, the major part, I would say, the only part.'

He decided to take Harry to Bungay (by train – his doctor had prescribed barbitone and advised him against undertaking a long journey by car), but blizzards were raging and trains delayed. He did not feel able to cope with a difficult journey 'in this cold grey time'. Harry travelled up from Exeter on 5 January 1963, 'He looked well and bright.' Henry found he had analysed the situation and apparently come to terms with it. 'He did so with admirable clearness. He liked J.F.; he loved Mum; he loved me. Mum and Dad were not suited. So it was better to be apart.' They left for Ditchingham on 7 January, and there was 'a warm and friendly welcome, as always'. The following day he and Richard went to London for a party to launch a new magazine, *Animals*, at the Zoological Gardens Restaurant[39] returning on the last train. Over the next days Henry occupied himself in writing 'letters, letters, to all & sundry – John Heygate, Fr. Brocard Sewell, etc etc' to inform them of the situation. 'I cannot write, or begin, No. 12 . . . this unhappy fixation, – fear, dread, sudden appalling inner shock that one is *done for* . . . .' On 14 January he took Harry down to London and put him on the train for Exeter. He went to see Ruth Tomalin, hoping that she would become his companion, but Ruth had her own problems and was committed to work in London. After a day or so he returned to Ilfracombe, to find the severe frost had burst pipes in Capstone Place, and the house had been awash with water. His neighbours had broken in and cleaned up for him before he returned, for which he was very grateful.

He went to stay with Mike and Margery Mitchell, now living at Boode, who were again very kind, 'putting themselves out for a suffering lump of half-guilty humanity' as they had in 1946. This helped him immensely as he came to terms with the situation and by 12 February he felt strong enough to return to the Field and cottage. On 17 February 1963 he read in the newspaper 'with sadness of the death of Ted Hughes' wife, Sylvia Plath, today. I had met neither poet, but his grief was my grief, and I wrote to him c/o Faber & Faber.' Ted Hughes lived in the area and the two men were to get to know each other as time went on. Hughes recognized his debt to *Tarka* as a book which had moved him deeply as a child, and was a great influence on his own work.[40]

On 25 March he went to London but found it very lonely and so took the train to Beccles and on to Ditchingham for the weekend where he felt 'happy and at home with Gipsy, Sarah, and Richard'.[41] They went to Snetterton for a race meeting, and he and Richard went to see Middleton Murry's widow, Mary and her friend Ruth Baker, and he then returned to London the next day.

On 4 April he went to Westminster Abbey for the memorial service for General Sir Hubert Gough, of the 5th Army, who had died aged ninety-two on 18 March; 'most moving: my tears dripped. Vaughan-Williams music to Milton's verse. Trumpets of 5/16th Lancers.' Henry had had a letter from General Gough the previous January thanking him (in desperately shaky handwriting for he had recently been ill) for *A Test To Destruction*: 'The book is incredibly interesting and you can imagine how deeply it has moved me.' On the obituary cutting from *The Times* Henry wrote 'Goughie died X/Y Night 1918 (1963)'. He had been very upset a year or two previously when he discovered he had missed the unveiling of a window to the 5th Army in a City of London church, St Peter-upon-Cornhill, by General Gough because he had not known about it. He had felt hurt when a reviewer of one of his books at that time had said he must be a phony because he had not been in the 5th Army, i.e. he had not attended the ceremony. Henry had then written to Gen. Gough apologizing for not knowing about the association and asking if it was not too late to join, and this was probably when he had sent the book.

Christine gradually dropped her original idea of suing for mental cruelty and decided she would sue for adultery instead. Henry warned her that he had evidence of her own adultery as she had stayed unchaperoned at John Fursdon's immediately after leaving Henry, and also evidence with two other men (one of whom being the artist Christine had confessed to being in love with), which he had been told about since her departure and had witnesses willing to substantiate this. John Fursdon seemed to take fright at all the implications, which would affect his family's reputation, and distanced himself slightly. The situation drifted into an uneasy impasse. Despite all his inner turmoil, Henry now attempted to make a start on the twelfth volume of the *Chronicle*. But there was a great deal of rather frenetic driving around to see friends; he found the Field and Hut very lonely and although it was bearable when he was writing, he could hardly find the energy to write. He visited Richard and Lucy Rhys (now Lord and Lady Dynevor) and 'Bill Kidd' again briefly; his son Richard went to stay with him for a week and John for a weekend. In July he went down to Elizabeth Tippett to do the proof revisions on *The Power of the Dead*, staying ten days.

Then at the end July he took Harry and Sarah to Ireland to stay with John Heygate. Although the young people had a very enjoyable time with the young social set of the district, the two men quarrelled violently. Ostensibly this was because Henry failed to phone John from the airport (where he was seeing Sarah off on her return to England on 16 August) to inform him that he had delivered an important package to its destination; but in the ensuing squabble Henry referred to the previous holiday when John had made a pass at Christine, and voiced his jealousy and resentment. John took extreme offence and told Henry to leave the house; so he and Harry toured around until they were due to return on 23 August. There was a rift between the two men for a long time afterwards.

Henry had seen quite a lot of Ronald and Rose-Marie Duncan all through the year and he now met a friend who was staying with them, Kerstin Lewes, whom Henry noted as 'the ¼ Swedish beauty'. They all met with John and Ann Irving, BBC Television producers in Devon to make a film about Henry and Devon. This involved nearly three weeks' intensive filming, and Henry, not used to this medium, found the inevitable hanging around a little tedious. By the time the filming was finished it had been decided that Henry would join the Duncans on their holiday in Sicily the following week.[42] The day before leaving for Sicily, he saw Kerstin again in London at a wedding, and was ready to believe her the next 'Barley-bright'.[43]

Ronald Duncan related in his introduction to the *Symposium* that he and Henry 'squabbled mildly a good deal on this journey'. Henry's diary shows that he found it all rather tiring (they went from Sicily to Rome and then to Venice, with much tramping around as well as the travelling) and certainly very expensive, while the unaccustomed food and wine did nothing for his digestion. As soon as they returned he went to see Kerstin. At the front of his 1963 diary he inserted a note, dated 25 October 1963: 'I am in a position, possibly, to be destroyed by my ideal-woman-fixation – revealed in Lily Cornford, Helena Rolls, Barley, Melissa, & a living Galatea at the end of my life.'[44]

When he returned to Ilfracombe, Sarah went with him to help with some typing. Two days later Henry returned to London to persuade Kerstin to join them. Harry also came for a day or two before returning to school on 7 November. The two girls then rather ganged up on Henry, drank quite a lot of wine and went off to roam about Ilfracombe on their own. Henry left 'in a huff' and spent the night up at the Field. He returned the next day to find the two girls had made what they thought was a very funny tape-recording which ridiculed Henry somewhat, which did not go down well with Henry. Sarah left the next day, probably at Henry's suggestion so that he and Kerstin could get on with some work. But after a week with very little work achieved Henry decided he would go first to his Hut in the Field, and then walk over Dartmoor, from Belstone to Ivybridge. He said he would be away three weeks or more. The weather was appalling with gales and pouring rain. Without turning a hair, Kerstin went out and bought prodigious amounts of bread and cheese. Henry left around midday on Monday 18 November and went to the Hut, spending the night there. He got up at 3 a.m.:

Why am I doing this? To try and dissipate the trauma, always in my mind since Christine forsook me nearly a year ago, of the death-wish. . . . The hopelessness of my position now makes me acutely aware that I must face up to this feeling, & if I get through, – and why not? – I may have conquered it . . . I am afraid to leave the Hut & afraid to remain in it. . . . And now for the journey, which I hope will give me a sense of reality for the climax of my A.S. series, in the night of the storm when Lynmouth was washed away.

He drove down to Okehampton to walk from Belstone through the raging winter wind (he did not necessarily do this overnight as is implied; one suspects the night was spent comfortably in a hotel) and his diary entry for the next day reads:

I got through, great winds, rain, heavy ascents on springing legs, clad in nylon mackintosh under German 1944 cape, with otter staff. The Taw and Ockment dangerous white foaming and very swift and deep rushing rivers. Returned at 2 p.m. to Belstone & fled to Ilfracombe to find K had cleaned house, and typed some of the CMW-HW 1948 letters. [CMW = Christine]

Kerstin made him a good meal. Apparently she was a very good cook but did not eat herself as she was obsessed with the fear of putting on weight. Henry also recorded that she was very particular about the tidiness of her hair and did not like him disarranging it. The next day Henry went up to the Field on his own and got out the typescript of *The Scandaroon* (the 'pigeon book') and 'found the framework professional & enough'. On 24 November they motored to Black Torrington to have lunch with Ernie Martin to collect the mass of *Lucifer* material which Ernie had expertly analysed and indexed. At the beginning of December Kerstin typed some of the T.E. Lawrence letters but after a day or so told Henry that she wanted to return to London. She had previously had a rather unhappy love affair with a married man, and had fled to Henry to get away. Now she wanted to return to London and get on with her life. Henry drove her there on 13 December. The following day he went to see Eric and Kathleen Watkins (Eric now worked on *The Times*) who 'were as usual, gentle and kind'. He met Kerstin on and off during the following week, until returning to Devon on 20 December, where depression set in. On Christmas Eve he went down to Exeter, where he dined with Christine, and on Christmas Day they attended matins at the cathedral where Harry sang a solo. This was his last day as a chorister – he was to go to Millfield. The next day Henry took Harry back to Ilfracombe for a day or two; and at the New Year he went back up to London, taking Harry with him.

Henry had arranged to rent a room at the home of Mary Hewitt (Mary Hibbert, Loetitia's cousin and bridesmaid) and he installed himself there at the beginning of 1964. He returned to Devon on the 17 January to take Harry for his first term at Millfield. While in Devon he collected his notes for Volume 12 of the *Chronicle* and on returning to London he resumed work.

He settled into a regular pattern of 'writing in the morning, going by underground to the National Liberal Club for lunch,[45] retiring to the large smoking room to read papers and sleep; to the Author's Club thirty yards away for tea and back for drinks in bar of Savage [National Liberal] Club 6–7 p.m. & dine alone at the Studio or Renaissance Clubs [if not invited out, which was often].'

On 13 February he went to the Queen's Elm, a pub in Chelsea much frequented by artists and writers where Henry got talking to a young girl. By the evening he had decided he was in love with her, and immediately they were spending all their time together. This was Ann Quin, author of a book called *Berg*.[46] Ann was almost as temperamental as Henry, and although she was very loving and mostly bright and lively she was also neurotic. But for a time they were good for each other. At the end of February Henry went down to Devon for a few days working while there, and on Saturday 7 March he set off for Ditchingham, arriving on Sunday, where he found all his family (except Bill) gathered for the wedding of Richard and myself the following day. After the simple celebration he returned to London and Ann Quin, and they were continually together. He tended to refer to himself and Ann Quin as 'Prospero and Ariel' and from this time on he frequently used this expression with reference to his relationships.

It was arranged that Henry would visit the battlefields in May 1964 with an *Evening Standard* photographer for a series of articles for the paper to coincide with the fiftieth anniversary of the outbreak of the First World War. Henry suggested that Ann Quin should go as his official secretary. But at the beginning of May they had an argument about this and she refused to go, so Henry asked Kerstin Lewes to go instead. They left on 5 May and returned on the night ferry of 8/9 May. Kerstin gave an account of the visit in her contribution for the *Symposium*, op cit. Henry's diary notes were fairly short and prosaic but the articles when they appeared were very moving. For him it was another opportunity to pay tribute to his fallen comrades: 'The eyes drop their tribute salt.'

On his return Ann Quin was incommunicado and Henry was desolate once more. He asked Richard and myself if he could come to us for Whitsun and on 15 May he arrived at our tiny flat in Chichester in time for breakfast, and then went up to Kingley Vale, the National Nature Reserve of which Richard was warden. This place of ancient sunlight with its yew trees and tumuli exactly recreated Richard Jefferies essay: 'I came to feel the long-drawn life of the earth back into the dimmest past, while the sun of the moment was warm on me.' Henry slept in the sun on and off for two days and on the Sunday he and I drove over to nearby Lasham where the annual National Gliding Championships were in progress, seeing John (who was competing of course) and his wife Boel, and Loetitia, and Ann Edmonds (now Welch). John took him up in a glider and he was surprised to find, instead of the total silence he had envisaged, a battering of wind noise (they were in an open cockpit). After another visit to Kingley Vale on Bank Holiday Monday, he left for Ilfracombe on Tuesday morning.

The following weekend he went to the Pump Rooms in Bath for the West Country Writers' Association, of which he was still president at this time. The guest speakers

'Fallen Comrades'. Henry visits the battlefields in 1964 to commemmorate the fiftieth anniversary of the beginning of the First World War.

were J.B. Priestley and Jacquetta Hawkes. At the beginning of June he went to Rugeley for an *Aylesford Review* meeting where he gave his Jefferies and Hudson talk. Ann Quin was there and he took her back to Devon with him. On 16 June they drove to Chichester to stay two days with us before going up to London. Ann was going to Greece for the summer and Henry went to see her off. He was worried that he might have caught a venereal disease from her – and told her so just as her train pulled out. Naturally, she was very upset and thought he had acted to stop her from having any other relationship while she was away, and was very angry and bitter about it. As it was, all he had was a slight urinary infection.

Henry now flew to Oslo for a PEN meeting. On his return he worked hard on *Lucifer Before Sunrise*, bothered by having to find his way through many versions as he found a tiny mistake in Ernie Martin's indexing which caused him to lose confidence in all of it. He had a break towards the end of July in Cornwall where Loetitia, Margaret, and Sarah were staying in a rented cottage. Margaret had left Bill Thomson and when divorced was to marry Julian Bream, the lutanist and classical guitarist.

At the beginning of August Henry gave a lift to two girls he found hitching along the road, one of whom was Sue Gibson, an eighteen-year-old would-be writer. Afterwards she wrote to him and he responded, and he sent her some typing to do which she carried out well. On 21 September he noted that he attended the funeral of his friend from the very early days, Douglas Bell, Old Colfeian and author of *A Soldier's Diary of the Great War*. Soon after he went up to London and spent his energies worrying about his relationship with Ann Quin and vascillating about whether to contact her, and seeing Susan Gibson, who in a quieter way was equally difficult, in between.

He came to stay with us again towards the end of October to revise 'No. 12'. Ann Quin had told him his books needed a more 'modern' approach and had suggested quite a lot of extra material to be added in between Phillip and Felicity, which were very sexually explicit scenes, along the line of those in her own novel. He had gone through his typescript and just added these at random. It really jarred when read, as if two different books had been riffled together; the style was totally against Henry's usual way of dealing with such instances. I was typing out a clean revised version for him and I dared to tell him quite bluntly that it really should all come out again, and that I was not going to type it in. His diary recorded: 'Have to recast or rather true-up Felicity, . . . [she] has to be simplified & the A.Q tensions – mental nature, removed.'

Henry was always meticulous about handing over money for housekeeping when he stayed, especially if he had invited someone else as well. We were extremely hard up in the early days of our marriage, and by giving me work to do for him he could make payment for this, which was a big help to us. At this time I was heavily pregnant and seeing I could not afford to buy any maternity clothes, Henry very sweetly gave me the money to go and buy a dress. He was also very generous to other members of his family, giving John the money to buy a house, and helping Robert with a regular allowance while he was at teacher training college, and also to buy his house; Sarah was helped too in many ways. This is no more than any father would do, of course, but it is worth noting here because it has often been said that Henry had no contact with his family – which is completely untrue. He was a difficult man to have as a father, and his children all had to be wary of what they did and said at times, but they all were fond of him, and he was obviously fond of all of them. At his best he was superb; conversely, at his worst he was appalling. He was also very fond of all the grandchildren and loved playing with them. Unfortunately, he would tire of play before they did, and often left them in a state of wild excitement, which others then had to deal with – just as when he used to play with his own children, their parents.

On this occasion he stayed until 5 November by which time we had finished the work on 'No. 12 [*The Phoenix Generation*] – It is now *good*, and a novel. 120 pages of the original 700 have fallen by the way, & deserved to.' But as soon as he got back to Devon he started to revise it yet again!

Henry was sixty-nine years old on 1 December 1964. That night he took his daughter Sarah to the 'Skinner's Hall to hear Shakespeare poetry readings, in the

Lord Butler presents Henry Williamson to Her Majesty Queen Elizabeth the Queen Mother. Henry's daughter, Sarah, is standing behind him.

gracious presence of Her Majesty Queen Elizabeth the Queen Mother.' At the champagne buffet after the readings, Lord Butler ('Rab' Butler), President of the Royal Society of Literature, presented Henry to the Queen Mother, who asked him 'Did you like the readings?' To which he replied 'Yes, Ma'am', adding in his diary entry: '(but I didn't)'.

The following day he went to Buckingham Palace for a working luncheon with Prince Philip and others to discuss a forthcoming World Wildlife Conservation meeting. On 6 December he went to the studio of Anthony Gray 'to have my head sculped' [sic]. On 9 December, as President of the West Country Writers' Association he attended a committee meeting where one of the items on the agenda was the idea floated by Waveney Girvan of combining their congress in May 1965 to coincide with the presentation of a selection of his manuscripts by Henry to Exeter University. Henry had already taken down a selection of his manuscripts to Exeter University in May 1963, presumably for the faculty to approve the donation.

In February 1965, Henry met Patrick Garland who was making a film for the BBC Television programme *Monitor* in Ilfracombe, and this led to Garland making, in December, a television film of Henry in the West Country called *The Survivor*, broadcast the following year.[47]

As the important May presentation approached so Henry was involved in the
complicated flurry of organizing his own guests, their hotel rooms and dinner
arrangements. He had invited Loetitia and all their children (except for Windles in
Canada) plus Harry. His list comprised thirty-six, but when it came to the actual
dinner, he entertained about sixty people. For the presentation there was a large
audience of nearly three hundred people for, apart from his personal guests, there
were the university officials and the members of the West Country Writers'
Association. Speakers at the ceremony were Ted Hughes, E.W. Martin, and F.
Brocard Sewell. It was a good occasion but Henry was a little hurt that Exeter
University did not show their appreciation. He mentioned to close friends that he
had felt that the conferment of an honorary degree might have been appropriate
for the occasion. It is known that this was actually put forward more than once,
but blocked by the faculty concerned. At the end of the weekend family and close
friends repaired to the Field.

The cat and mouse game being played out by Henry and Sue Gibson continued.
Over and over again he arranged to meet her only for her to cancel at the last

Henry presents a selection of manuscripts to Exeter University in 1965 (the member of the
University is not known).

After the ceremony at Exeter University, family and close friends repaired to the Field at Ox's Cross. From left to right: Boel (John's wife), Henry, his son Robert, (hidden, Maurice Renshaw), Mary Hewitt (née Hibbert, later Lady Bagot), Christine, Michael Horowitz, Loetitia Williamson, Francis Horowitz, Harry Williamson, and Henry's daughter Sarah (seated).

minute. The girl that he described in his diary, and whom Richard and I met, is almost impossible to recognize as Sue Caron the 'Porn Queen' who was to publish some of his letters (against copyright rules) in one of the Sunday newspapers only a few days after his death, and who was later to describe their relationship in a book.[48] She was a nervous and introverted person at this time, and Henry noted several times in his diary that he had not had any actual sexual relationship with her (and he was only too happy to note when he had had sexual relationships with his girlfriends); in fact she had told him that she was having a relationship with her flatmate.

From this time on there was to be a series of similar scenarios with young girls, most of whom, through no fault of their own, were quite unsuited for the role he wanted them to play. Most of them treated him like a wise guru, thinking to have their own problems solved or magicked away. Henry was constantly searching for someone to relieve his loneliness but they were not of the métier to provide the almost mythical qualities that he was seeking. They, of course, were flattered by the attentions of this most extraordinary man and did provide him with temporary interest and diversion, and most of them tried for a while to live up to his expectations, but in the end they either could not, or would not give him total commitment. Henry was always very generous to his various girl-friends and over and over again there are notes of cheques he had made out to them, either in return for (almost nominal) typing done or just as a present. He was in the main happy to do this, but occasionally even he realized that the money had been angled for.

He did have an enduring friendship with Margot Renshaw (now Margot Wall), who returned from South Africa for a while, but he was wary of her involvement with Ron Hubbard and the Scientology movement, although it gave him interesting material for the *Chronicle*. Margot was an elegant and beautiful woman and Henry always held her in high regard. They came to stay with us once or twice at this time. Margot is Melissa in the *Chronicle*, although he attributes a larger role to her in the novels than she actually played in real life.

Henry had now become President of the Francis Thompson Society. In June 1966 there was a festival and exhibition at 47 Palace Court (the address where Thompson lived with the Meynells in London) to commemorate the seventy-fifth anniversary of the publication of Thompson's poem *The Hound of Heaven*. To celebrate this event a limited edition of *The Mistress of Vision*, first published in 1897, was brought out in May 1966. Henry noted on 17 March that he had to write '3000 words on F. Thompson & self in 1917'. This essay was 'A First Adventure with Francis Thompson'. It was almost fifty years since Henry had first read Francis Thompson, when his Aunt Mary Leopoldina had sent a volume of his work to him in the battlefields of Flanders. In his essay Henry wrote that Francis Thompson's words made

> . . . instant impact . . . I know now, that what drew me to Thompson was that we shared the same sense of sight, which with reflection becomes insight. . . . He, dreamed of love, which appeared always but to elude him. The lost mother-image – lost because he was no longer a child – was never replaced by the shared love of a woman.[49]

Henry then turned his thought towards Shelley, for it was Thompson's essay on Shelley that made most impact on Henry: 'So beset [the poet wrote in his Shelley essay] the child fled into the tower of his own soul, and raised the drawbridge.'

The following year another commemorative volume of Francis Thompson's work appeared, *The Hound of Heaven*, containing a further essay by Henry Williamson, 'In Darkest England',[50] a transcript of the presidential address delivered by Henry to the Francis Thompson Society on 21 January 1967. Although the two essays cover the same ground to some extent, both need to be read: for in them lies hidden a very clear view of Henry Williamson's own inner being, that of an essential Romantic.

Henry was also president of the Richard Jefferies Society from 1965 to 1975 and took a very active part in its affairs. He took on the Presidency on the death of Samuel J. Looker, the great protagonist of Jefferies. These two men did not always see eye to eye about Jefferies, each probably being a little jealous of the other as regards Jefferies. But it was a fitting role for Henry, who had been so profoundly influenced by Jefferies and who had championed the man and his writings all his life.

On Sunday 8 May 1966, Patrick Garland's BBC programme on Henry, *The Survivor*, was shown. This marked the fiftieth anniversary of the battle of the Somme. A further film was made, *No-Man's Land*, to mark the fiftieth anniversary of the end of the First World War. At the end of June the first part of Henry's long article 'The Somme – just Fifty Years After' appeared in the *Daily Express*. The three parts that constitute this major essay gave an immediacy and clarity to an event that was relegated to history in most people's minds. Recently there has been enormous coverage of both First and Second World Wars, but in 1966 the media were only just beginning to realize the potential of the material available.

Having returned to the *Daily Express* fold, Henry continued to write for them for several years.[51] One series of nature articles which appeared in 1968 were illustrated by Richard Richardson, whom Henry had met as a young artist on the Norfolk farm, as Richardson was closely connected with the nature reserve at Cley just along the coast.[52]

Henry and Christine had settled down into a fairly amicable relationship. Henry frequently went to see her at her cottage at Stuckeridge and Christine came over to the Field to work in the garden and sometimes gave the cottage in Ilfracombe a good clean. Harry was mainly at school but came and went between the two of them during his holidays. Nothing further had been done about the divorce and John Fursdon seemed to have faded into the background. Henry sometimes noted that he had thoughts of Christine returning to him, followed immediately by another note that he knew really that this would never happen.

In August Christine and Harry were camping near Instow, when on 27 August she was suddenly taken ill at a friend's cottage at Appledore. Harry telephoned Henry to say that his mother was ill and saying wild things. Henry went straight to Appledore where he found Christine prostrate, weeping, and in great distress. Henry noted that her mind was disturbed; she had said something to Harry about being Jesus Christ (although Henry was able to get her to admit that this could not be so) and she seemed to think that she had had a miscarriage (although Henry was not sure whether to believe this or not). Henry took her and Harry back to their cottage at Stuckeridge. After Henry left, Harry went off to spend the weekend with some of his own friends, so Christine was on her own. She apparently then became very distressed and was convinced that he had drowned. She telephoned Instow Yacht Club four times about Harry drowning in the estuary. On Tuesday 30 August she suffered a total breakdown and spent the night wandering about with a hurricane lantern looking for Harry whom she now thought was drowned in the River Exe. Henry had gone to her cottage where he found she had left all the lights on and had made shrines with red roses for her mother, her first lover who had left her after the war, and for Harry. Henry waited for her for some time and then went out to look around the immediate vicinity for her. He was told she had gone off wandering. In the morning, by telephoning around various friends he heard that she had been seen, and he drove slowly off in the direction of Barnstaple and eventually found her. Henry had already phoned Margaret, who now lived near Shaftesbury with her second husband, and she left straightaway to come and help Henry to cope with the situation and do what she could for Christine. Henry noted, 'Margie splendid, as always.'

Despite tranquillizers, Christine remained hyperactive and very disturbed, and Henry arranged for her to be taken into a hospital for the mentally ill near Exeter, where in due course she underwent electric shock treatment, the standard treatment at this time. She discharged herself on 5 October, but she was far from well, although she gradually improved. She and Henry now decided to proceed with the divorce, and Henry went to court in Exeter on 17 October 1967 to sue for desertion, taking Margery Mitchell as his witness, and was granted a decree nisi, made absolute in three months. Christine married John Fursdon at Easter 1968.

On 19 January 1968 Henry had an accident in his car, at this time a Triumph Herald. On his way out of Taunton on a dark wet night he hit an unlit kerb in an area of recent roadworks. Luckily he was unhurt. Margaret again came to the rescue, driving out to fetch him. (The car was repaired but it was to be totally wrecked later when Harry turned it over.) Henry had been on his way to London to take the typescript of *Lucifer Before Sunrise*, Volume 14 of the *Chronicle*, the Norfolk farm volume, at last finalized, to his publishers. He had finally been delivered of this gargantuan infant which had been about twenty years gestating, with several false labours along the way.

Soon after this he brought another car for Loetitia, a Morris Minor with 'good engine and no rust on the chassis', but the car gremlins were still on his trail. He drove it 180 miles and found it had used up three pints of oil and had various other faults, including holes in the chassis! He insisted on a replacement reconditioned engine and the chassis being welded up.

He now hated the thought of driving into London, and from this time on tended to arrive by car at either our house, or Margaret's (we were both convenient for main line trains to London) and then the next day go on by train, reversing the process when he was ready to go home again.

In August he went to tea with Dawyck Haig and his family who took one of the cottages on the Putsborough Beach for the summer, and all the Haig family went up to the Field for tea the following day. He liked them all immensely, and they invited him to stay sometime at the family seat at Bemersyde in Scotland. The earl, son of the First World War Field Marshal Earl Haig, was interested in artistic matters (he is a painter of landscapes and nature) and appreciated Henry on that level. He stated in a recent letter[53] that he had read the *Flax* novels and *Tarka* while he was at school at Stowe and that they had eased his homesickness for his beloved River Tweed. His letter reinforces the thesis about Romanticism as the creative root of Henry's literary imagination: 'The mood of Romanticism was very much part of those early 1930 days and part of the ethos of 1914–18 under whose shadow I grew up.' Earl Haig very much appreciated Henry's championship of his father when many others had criticized him. He also stated that Henry was a man of immense charm and kindness, and that he (Earl Haig) enjoyed every minute of the time he spent with him. They were to meet several times when the Haig family were on holiday at Putsborough in succeeding years, and on other occasions.

Henry's diary is crowded with appointments at this time; some for business but most with meetings and visits with family and friends. In early October 1967 he was to be found at the Cheltenham Festival of Literature, then the following week he was involved with the conferment of the Freedom of the City of Barnstaple on Francis Chichester, while the first half of November saw him in Dublin, for a PEN meeting, Swindon, to give a talk to the Jefferies Society, and London, for a 'Galsworthy' dinner at the Criterion.

On 7 December he went to Lime Grove in London to record a BBC programme in which he was interviewed live by Kenneth Allsop for the series *Personal Choice*. This was broadcast on 7 January 1968.[54] Allsop asked several questions of a personal and political nature, and when Henry tried to parry them, Ken Allsop pointed out very sharply that he *knew* Henry. This aggressive questioning is taken for granted in interviews today but then it was not so usual. The programme upset several of Henry's friends who felt that Allsop had been too rough and thrusting. His diary entry stated: 'Kenneth Allsop asking questions (which I hadn't seen) I thought he was just a little "near the knuckle" when he mentioned my "two marriages that hadn't worked out" and also a slightly snide remark about my (apparent) approval of "squires".' Henry dealt with all these questions, which might have floored a lesser man, extremely well and answered with great dignity. Several friends telephoned or wrote to say that he had been splendid. But it did leave a coolness between the two men, and although they remained friends Henry was a little wary of Allsop from then on.

Henry's mind was actually concerned with more important matters. He was writing the final scene of the last book of the *Chronicle*, *The Gale of the World*. On the morning of the Allsop programme he had driven to Lynmouth to 'look at the Barbrook area for the flood climax of "15". And on down to the valley road to site of caravans (Lucy among them) which was flooded on the Friday/Sat night of August 15, 1953.' On 11 January he wrote: 'Writing final scene, flood recession at Lynmouth. What will happen when I have finished the Chronicle? Writing in early 1918 after I was back from the war in France, became what today would be called therapy. I began to live an "idealised" life in writing a novel . . .'. On 5 February: 'After weeks of depression, & tenacity to the idea of the final scene, I came to it today, about 7 p.m. & was very happy.' On February 11: 'At 4.20 pm today I finished the *Chronicle* and got up, suddenly broken, from the table – or hysterical is a better word – my eyes streaming and my voice uttering lament, at the strangeness of *physical dissociation*. It felt like suddenly being born – or borne away from and old existence. I walked from empty room to empty room of this Ilfracombe cottage crying "It is finished – O my God, I have come to the end" – Then I sat down by my wood fire & remained still; before going upstairs to telephone in turn, Margaret, Richard, Robert.'

A week later he noted: 'Much to be done on/in *Gale*. Various versions – exploratory, building up the story, re-placing and fitting in new-discovered incidents, scenes, etc – to be jig-sawed into final draft.' *Finished* was a concept that was missing from Henry's psyche. So the work continued, but he had in spirit 'finished'; what he was doing then was honing and polishing. The actual form was in place.

In August he heard from John Mills (later Sir John), whom he had met once or twice previously over the years at the various clubs they both frequented, that he and his wife Mary (Hayley Bell) were making a film about a pony on Dartmoor, at Princetown, and inviting him along to watch. He had a very happy time with them and Sylvia Sims and Bernard Miles who were also in the film.

On the occasion of the fiftieth anniversary of the end of the First World War in September 1968 he was commissioned to write articles by the *Radio Times* and the *Daily Express*. He also participated in a BBC film about the Armistice broadcast on Sunday 10 November.

Earl Haig invited Henry to attend the unveiling of a .59 German howitzer as a memorial to his father at the end of September 1968. Originally presented to Field Marshal Earl Haig by the Army Council in recognition of the British capture of

In happy mood while watching John Mills (later Sir John) and his wife filming on Dartmoor.

the Hindenburg Line in 1918, the gun had recently been restored by the army. The unveiling was at the Infantry Depot at Glencorse Barracks in Edinburgh, to whom the Earl Haig had presented the gun. Henry travelled up to Scotland by train on 28 September and was met by the earl and his son, also Dawyck, and stayed for the weekend with them at the family home at Bemersyde. Henry thoroughly enjoyed the visit, and obviously appreciated the opportunity to be an 'old soldier', and the kindness shown to him by the Haig family. To show his gratitude Henry wanted to give them a pair of sixteenth-century firedogs, which he unearthed on his return and cleaned up, ready to dispatch. Earl Haig mentioned in his 1993 letter that the firedogs are still used almost daily, even in midsummer, in the drawing room fireplace: a sharing of 'ancient sunlight'.

On 5 October he flew to Geneva for a week for a PEN meeting. Then later in October he and his photographer friend Ossie Jones went to stay at Margaret's home near Shaftesbury to read the galley proofs of *The Gale of the World* – which he literally read aloud: 'Read galleys all day. Tired voice, rough, eyes smarting.' He then retyped some replacement passages. He also wrote an article for the *Daily Express*, 'embodying much of what Richard W. sent to me re fallow and roe deer'. He relied a great deal on Richard for natural history detail at this time. His knowledge of actual facts had always been minimal, and over the years even this had gone rusty, and by this time readers expected every detail to be correct. He could no longer rely just on the superb phrase.

In November he made a programme for ITV Westward which involved filming in the Valley of the Rocks near Lynton, and Exeter, and finally on 19 December at the Hut. He was also preparing the material for the volume which was to be published by Macdonald as *Collected Nature Stories* and noted that he was feeling 'less melancholy [he was in the throes of yet another difficult relationship], having started the Introduction & prefaces for the 3 phases. . . . It comes easier & fresh as one alters, rewrites, & finally — [last word indecipherable].

At the front of his 1969 diary Henry penned a quotation (taken from *Don Quixote* by Miguel de Cervantes) which he obviously felt applied to himself:

Don Quixote . . . rides forth, his head encircled by a halo – the patron saint of all lives spoiled or saved by the irresistible grace of imagination. But he was not a good citizen. (Bravo!!)

Quixotic is indeed an apt description to sum up very succinctly the life and character, and indeed the appearance, of Henry Williamson. Anyone who has seen illustrations showing Don Quixote's thin, gaunt, figure (not that Henry was particularly thin or gaunt – but the impression was such) with his shock of white hair, and read of his 'quixotic' adventures ('tilting at windmills' – a true Romantic) can feel this immediately; one might think that the book had been based on Henry Williamson.

Henry retained his magnetism almost to the very end and also the energy which attracted everyone's attention. When in the mood he was totally charming and a superb conversationalist. But he felt deeply, too deeply for his own comfort. After Henry's death, Colin Wilson wrote in an article for the Henry Williamson Society *Journal* that he thought Henry 'a man who lacked self-confidence. . . . He was always too tense, too nervous, too emotional, thin-skinned to the point of paranoia. . . . I felt an immense sympathy and pity for him. He was an "outsider" if ever there was one.'[55]

After the 'Don Quixote' entry, Henry summed up his feelings at that time – tired, lonely, and old. He was conscious of the kindness of family and friends but felt that he had 'declined more & more since February 1968 when I finished *A Chronicle of Ancient Sunlight*'. This was the problem: he had finished his great work and everything that followed was an anti-climax. It was inevitable. For nineteen years he had put into that work all his energy, all his emotions, all his creative thoughts. He wanted to start on the re-writing of *The Scandaroon* but could not summon up the energy. He was pursuing yet another young woman. He yearned continuously, and was disappointed continuously.

On 17 February he went up to London, by chance meeting Ted Hughes on the platform, 'who looked very big & healthy & glad to see me'. They travelled together, which cheered Henry greatly. He went round to Macdonald and collected an advance copy of *The Gale of the World* – his only comment: 'Poor cover. Saw several misprints.'

Two days later he travelled to Edinburgh to attend the inauguration of Kenneth Allsop as Rector of Edinburgh University, arriving in time for a champagne party at 4 p.m. The following day there was a dinner and a ball: 'Great fun (& scene) at Installation of Ken Allsop as Rector. Speech good, but too long I thought (but I was very tired). In evening was presented to Chancellor (Edinburgh, Duke of, Philip)'. He had taken with him the 1595 firedogs that he was presenting to Earl Haig, but does not mention actually handing them over. Presumably Earl Haig would have attended the ceremony too.

On his return he went to Robert's for a night to check *Gale* for mistakes: he found '54 misprints, slight changes necessary'. He complained that he hadn't been allowed page-proofs and therefore it was Macdonald's fault. As he had already made radical changes at galley stage Macdonald had been very wary of letting him have any further access. Now they had to scrap the copies already printed (about three thousand) and make the corrections for the new printing.

In April 1969 Bill Williamson came over from Canada. To ease what could have been a tense situation Margaret arranged for them to meet at her home: 'Margaret had invited "Windles" and his wife and me to meet. We all got on well: my eldest son is much different from his last meeting with me – assured, well-mannered & very able.' Henry returned to the Ilfracombe cottage and a day or two later Bill and his wife Diane drove down to stay at the Imperial Hotel in Barnstaple. Henry took them out to dinner, and he noted that Bill revisited 'Shallowford, Baggy Point, & all the places he knew as a boy'.

The Gale of the World was eventually published on 29 May. Henry dedicated it to Kenneth Allsop, who did not like the book at all and felt unable to review it.

Reviews were very mixed. Some, including those in the *Spectator* and the *Times Literary Supplement*, were outright in condemnation, feeling that the politics had once more got in the way; others saw beyond that and referred to the worth of the *Chronicle* as a whole. For example, Christopher Wordsworth in *The Guardian* (5 June 1969) wrote:

> As a repository of some of the despairing moods of the century, as a threnody to a dying generation and a dying countryside, as a painful, intricate description of the morbid creative process and the holiness of life, it may endure like a kind of rune-stone when defter and more fashionable works have blown away.

In July Henry met with his solicitor and his children to set up the terms of a settlement trust concerning his property, particularly that of the Field, in order to secure it after his demise. This was a very complicated undertaking and required many meetings before it was finally settled.

After the end of yet another somewhat difficult relationship which alternately elated and depressed him, Henry met a young girl who seemed more stable and gentle and he was once more feeling buoyant. In September he went to the PEN conference in Menton in the south of France for a week, but he did not really enjoy it and was glad, although very tired, to get back to England. He was met by Robert and Mary and went to stay with them for the weekend to recover before leaving for London to meet Roy Plomley to record a programme for *Desert Island Discs*. Henry's choice of records was typically Romantic, and included Delius, Debussy, Rachmaninov, and ended with the 'Liebestod' from Wagner's *Tristan und Isolde*. For his luxury item he wanted a cor anglais; his book was, of course, Richard Jefferies' *The Story of My Heart*. The programme was broadcast on 18 October 1969.

The weekend after the recording he came to stay with us at Chilgrove near Chichester and enjoyed a walk in Kingley Vale. During the following week, he returned to London, went back to Devon, then drove to Chepstow, and from there went to Margaret's near Shaftesbury! On Sunday 5 October, 'sunny-lovely', they went for a walk on Cranborne Chase where by chance he met a longstanding friend who lived nearby: 'Met Rolf Gardiner, dressed in silk shirt, scarlet braces, natty trousers & boots. He talked much, but all was delightful. "Henry, I have just planted my 4-millionth tree."'[56]

By the end of October the new relationship was over and Henry was desolate once more. The winter was ahead of him and he dreaded being alone in his cottage, feeling miserable and death-haunted. Usually these moods were dissipated by the consumption of a good meal. He had become adept at making hotpots and casseroles, which he could keep going for several days, adding bits in as necessary. He spent Christmas with Pat Chichester and family, which he enjoyed.

Towards the end of 1969 Henry had been contacted by David Cobham, a film producer, who wanted to discuss a filming project, *The Vanishing Hedgerows*, with him. They arranged to meet on 23 January. Henry accepted £250 to write a 'treatment' for the film, plus his expenses paid to write it at the National Liberal Club. He noted that he and Cobham 'got on splendidly'.

The next day it had been arranged that he should meet Dawyck Haig to discuss an introduction by Henry for a book of Field Marshal Earl Haig's 1919 speeches, to celebrate the fiftieth anniversary of the founding of the British Legion. He had been invited to Lord Cornwallis's home at Ashurst Park in Kent for the weekend where they were all to discuss the book and Henry's approach. Henry noted that several people were there and all had their own ideas about how it should be done. He began to feel mentally claustrophobic, but he enjoyed the ambiance of stately home living. They dined at Hever Castle where he met Lord and Lady Astor (she was the daughter of Field Marshal Earl Haig). He was rather tickled to 'see one's rags – shirt, vest, dressing gown, all neatly laid out for me'.

However, he found he was expected to toe the official line for the Haig introduction and David Cobham also gave him 'heavy data' re Pollution, Conservation, for the film treatment of *The Vanishing Hedgerows*: 'I was appalled; Haig & Hedgerow frantic, fearful, morbid. I simply can't work for such Officialese Data Govt. Department Prose!' At this same time he was approached by the Lords' Taverners to write a contribution for a book *The Twelfth Man*,[57] to celebrate Prince Philip's fiftieth birthday in July 1971. And also in February 1970 Kenneth Allsop was deputed by Victor Bonham Carter, secretary of the Royal Literary Fund, to suggest to Henry that he should be the recipient of a Civil List Pension. Henry turned this offer down; he felt a little insulted. He was not in need of what he felt was charity. He had expected that any approach would be to confer an honour of some sort. It may be that his outspoken refusal was taken as a total refusal of any offer, and this may have stopped future approaches of any kind.

After a few days struggling with his material, he got on with the 'treatment' for *The Vanishing Hedgerows* film and delivered it to David Cobham on 25 February, but it wasn't what Cobham wanted so he had to re-do it. 'I find it difficult. I am Henry Williamson and used to writing in response to what HW sees/feels/knows.'

Henry was also worried about the undertaking to write the 'Haig' introduction. He wrote to Dawyck, Earl Haig, to say that he thought that the introduction he would write would not be to his liking. In the middle of March he received an answer in which Earl Haig stated that he hoped that Henry would not be upset but that he felt that under the circumstances it would probably be better that John Terraine, who had been involved in his father's life for many years, should write the introduction. Henry should have felt relieved, but illogically, felt rejected and was upset. In the end the project apparently proved too expensive and did not materialize.

Henry's left eye was causing a problem, continuously dripping tears which made the eye very red and sore, and he went to see a specialist, Frank Law, a fellow 'Brother Savage'. It was arranged that he should have a small operation in 'King Edward the Seventh's Hospital for Officers' – a venue which Henry made a great point of noting. His war service was still of paramount importance to him. He rather dreaded the operation, imagining that as there was to be no anaesthetic he would have to lie still without blinking or moving for hours, and could not see how he could manage to do this. On 15 April 1970 the tear duct was cauterized by laser; all Henry noticed was one or two pricks on his eyelid. It was over in seconds. However, the eye continued to be sore and bothered him. He may have rubbed it at too early a stage (he admitted in his diary that he took the bandage off to look at it the next day although he had been told not to) and he certainly didn't rest it as he was no doubt requested to do.

In July he was contacted by Peter Scott and asked if he would write some articles to coincide with the World Wildlife Congress to be held in London that November. (Peter Scott was a great friend of John Williamson as they were fellow glider pilots and rivals in the National Championship competitions.) Henry was worried about these articles; yet again he was given a large amount of official papers on pollution and conservation to read and incorporate. Once again he turned to Richard for support and help, and Richard more or less wrote his material for him.

On 3 August the family arrived at the Field for 'The Working Week at Ox's Cross'; the work party comprised three sons, John, Robert, Richard, while Margaret went to cook for the first two days. Some of the trees needed taking down and were more than Henry could manage on his own, and so this working party had been arranged. His sons worked hard and on the final evening Henry celebrated with a massive bonfire at 10 p.m. to burn up all the unwanted rubbish. Henry was in his element with a bonfire and these were always a ritual at family gatherings. At 11.30 p.m. the Barnstaple Fire Brigade arrived! Someone had reported that Ox's Cross was on fire. Henry had meant to inform the fire service

'The Working Week At Ox's Cross': Henry and his sons, John, Robert and Richard, stacking wood.

that he intended to light a big fire but had forgotten to do so. A rather irate fire officer was pacified with the promise of a 10 guinea donation to the benevolent fund! However, Henry recorded, 'The entire job has been splendidly carried out.' He was very sorry to see his sons go.

Emotionally he ranged from happiness when he was with one of the circle of successive girl-friends, to misery as he yearned after one lost love after another. He gained much support at this time from local friends, particularly the McKinnells at Appledore (who had been Christine's friends) and Avril Vellacott, a sculptress, whom he visited frequently and who accompanied him to many local parties and occasions out of pure friendship.

On 12 November he went to London, staying overnight with us at Chilgrove beforehand, and there signed the Deed of Settlement which handed over all his property to the Trust to be administered by his children. 'I had long dreaded the legalese of the Clauses but now all seemed delightfully simple.' That evening he went to the Elephant House at London Zoo for a party to celebrate the publication of Peter Scott's book *The Living World of Animals*, which Henry had reviewed. Peter Scott presented Henry to Princess Anne, who was guest of honour: his diary noted 'She is beautiful' and that her press photographs did not do her justice. He returned to Sussex for a few days alternating between Richard and myself and John and his family, who lived nearby at this time, and then returned to London for the World Wildlife Conference, to which he had also invited Richard. His three supporting articles were in the *Daily Express* on 16, 17, 18 November under the overall title 'Save the Innocents':[58] the first about the killing of song-birds as they migrate across France, 'Singing their way to the sun – then death in the skies'; the second on the plight of whales; and the third on the deadliness of chemical sprays. Henry bought several copies of the paper and placed them on the breakfast tables of the congress delegates, but few noticed – they were mainly scientists. After the celebrations they returned to Sussex, Henry continuing on down to Devon via John's. There was sometimes a problem about him staying at Margaret's house; Julian Bream was necessarily totally absorbed in his music, practising for concerts and entertaining business associates and other musical colleagues. Also he and Henry had, in many ways, similar characters and the sparks tended to fly.

On 9 December Henry was once more in London, this time to see David Cobham about the forthcoming film for which he was to be paid a further £500. He discovered, as he had surmised from the start, that the film was to be about him rather than erosion and pollution. But he did not mind. What he did mind was that he was expected to write yet another 'treatment', and the worry of it all was stopping him from working on *The Scandaroon*.

Christmas was once more spent at Pat Chichester's home. He could have enjoyed the festivities with any one of his family – we always invited him and so I am sure did the others, but he preferred not to do so.

He now had an idea about how to publish his thoughts on the film *Oh, What a Lovely War*. He had attended the preview in April 1969 as the press representative

Henry had a powerful figure and a magnetic personality throughout his life.

for the *Daily Express*, for whom he was to write a review. To his chagrin his article was returned and someone else's used instead. Henry wrote: 'My first article ever rejected.' One reason might have been that it was practically illegible, with so many corrections typed in and crossings out made in blue and red pens that no compositor could have followed it! He obviously had had no time to make a clean copy. Also the angle Henry took was too personal for a review of a major film – he soon reverted to describing his own experiences. But early in January 1971 he decided to rewrite this, incorporating also some of the material from the aborted 'British Legion' piece for the Earl Haig book. He called it 'Reflections on a Brighton Rubbish Dump' (the film had been made on a Brighton rubbish dump!). Henry had been over to see the filming briefly as he was slightly friendly with Len Deighton, who was working on the film and had written the filmscript. In the end he decided that 'Reflections on the Death of a Field Marshal' would be a better title. The article was published in the *Contemporary Review* in June 1971,[59] although he wished he had placed it somewhere where it would have received a little more prominence.

The article completed, Henry felt the creative urge return and was able to turn at last to the final scenes of *The Scandaroon*. He took the finished typescript up to Mark Hamilton (his agent at A.M. Heath & Co.) on 2 March, who although he advised Henry that the book should not be offered to Macdonald, actually did take it to them.

At the end of February Henry noted: 'Disturbing news! The 20 acre field immediately north of Ox's Cross (Spinney) is under application to B'ple R.D. council, for a caravan site.' Henry soon had a letter composed to the rural district council and some publicity organized – television and newspaper reporters arrived for interviews. He pointed out that the area was designated as an Area of Outstanding Natural Beauty which gave it special protection against development (an argument pointed out to him by Richard). After a while he heard through the grapevine that permission to go ahead was highly unlikely, and he relaxed again.

On 19 March he left Devon to go to Norfolk for the filming of *The Vanishing Hedgerows*, leaving his car at Margaret's and taking the train as far as Robert's in Essex. On Sunday 21 Robert drove him up to Norfolk, calling briefly at the Hollingsworths 'where once, in my time in Norfolk, 1936–1946, Holly and Mossy grew the finest Cox's Orange Pippin apples. Now all had been ripped up, and the garden almost desolate.' Robert left him at the Black Lion Hotel in Walsingham where David Cobham and the film crew were ensconced. Henry was feeling very tired, and was rather dreading the fact that David Cobham had decided to film him on the Old Hall Farm, whither they went on the Tuesday morning. 'The road I made to the Corn Barn was still there, tho' covered with mud. . . . I met my old 'cowman', youth of 15 or so, 1945–6 – Douglas Jordan, now a mature man, & such a good one. He 'made my day'. Efficient & man of skill & honour, appreciating most of what I did in those years.'

Henry was not very happy with his own scenes, feeling he had not made a good job of them, forgetting his lines etc., but David Cobham was gently encouraging.

The following day he left, returning to Robert's and, the next day, to London, then going on to Margaret's to collect his car, and straight on home.

While in London he had seen Susan Hodgart at Macdonald, who told him there were problems with the flow of *Scandaroon* and it needed working on. Henry did not take very kindly to this criticism mainly, no doubt, because he was tired and had had enough of the book. Also his eye was bothering him again and on 31 March he saw an eye specialist in Barnstaple Infirmary, thinking that there was again a serious problem. This time the tear ducts were simply unblocked and he was shown how to care for them. Susan Hodgart came down for the weekend to help him with *Scandaroon*. He found it very tiring keeping up with her, and keeping track of the three foolscap pages of closely typed notes, and after a little work they spent the weekend walking around Morte Point and Baggy. After returning to London, Susan sent down a revised set of notes, but Henry could not bring himself to settle down to the book.

On 28 May 1971 he gave a talk at the Lobster Pot at Instow arranged by the committee of the Beaford Centre (part of the Dartington Trust). There were several such talks and readings and they were always well attended by a crowd of young people, who appreciated Henry's approach which tended at times to be a little eccentric. It is said that on one occasion he spent most of his talk arranging paperclips on first one ear and then the other! Another young lady had appeared at this time, so he was generally in an optimistic mood.

In June there were two more days' filming for *The Vanishing Hedgerows* at the Old Hall Farm, where Robert accompanied and supported him. He found all the waiting about and having to say particular lines at particular moments, very tiring. He returned to London, and worked on 'the FINAL draft' of *The Scandaroon* at his room in the National Liberal Club ('his' room was virtually correct – he always occupied Room 62, and on the rare occasion when he did not he was quite put out!). On 17 June he recorded: 'Finished *Scandaroon* 6.15–8.15 AM & felt relief.' He took the top copy round to Susan Hodgart at Macdonald that morning. In the evening he was on a BBC Radio 4 programme 'Something in Common – Flanders' (pre-recorded), but he made no comment about it in his diary. On his return to the Field at Ox's Cross on 19 June he was immediately involved in filming as he found David Cobham and his crew already there, although he had got up at 6.15 a.m. and left immediately after drinking the tea and sandwiches the porter at the club prepared for him. These scenes were completed by tea-time and the crew left. He was sorry to see them go but admitted to feeling very tired: 'My age has caught up on me.'

Henry Williamson in the doorway of his Writing Hut, *c.* 1970.

CHAPTER 10

EBB TIDE

In the summer of 1971, with no real writing project to hand, Henry set himself to fretting and worrying. He worried about the 'Settlement', thinking that none of his trustees (John, Margaret and Robert) would be able to administer it, so he decided to change it, and ask his long-term friend Eddie Pine to be trustee instead of Margaret; not realizing that now it was legally binding and he no longer could do as he wanted – he had to consult his trustees and it would be their decision. They decided against the change. He had not visualized this when he set up the Trust. Actually, after his death it was found that the trust part of his affairs was so complicated, every detail so hedged about with safeguards that it was impossible to administer, and steps were taken to legally terminate it, leaving the terms of his actual will paramount, for which his named executors were John, Robert and Richard. He also worried about the amount of work there was always to do up at the Field, finding he had little inclination or energy to tackle it all. Above all he constantly worried about his lack of female companionship, and constantly sought to rectify this. He was lonely and dreaded the thought of getting old.

The possibility of making a film of *Tarka* had been broached by David Cobham who wanted Henry to produce a 'treatment', a working synopsis of the film. Henry wrote to David to say he needed a break and would not begin until the autumn, as he wanted some exercise which he would get from cutting the grass and hedges in the Field. But, of course, he immediately started to think how he would approach the project. From the very beginning he thought to involve three books in his 'treatment', *Tarka the Otter*, *The Children of Shallowford*, and *It was the Nightingale*. He wrote in his diary on 27 June 1971:

> I dread the idea of the job. At the same time I must have something to do – yet I am so tired, indeed sick of, H.W. as author. [But the very next day he immediately got down to an outline draft.] Treatment of the Otter book, combined with extract – eldest son poorly as a baby, HW writing *Tarka* at night in Ham Cottage 1926–7 and Phillip & Barley (Bédelia, cycle-car) & bathing in Loire & finding a drowned & trapped otter, and her lost cubs in river bank. Thus to marriage with Barley, her death in childbirth; Lucy the compassionate – marriage with her & the Grasmere Prize for Literature 1928.

In August several of the family gathered for another work party at the Field: John, Robert, Robert's wife Mary and their daughter Sarah, Richard and myself and our two children, Brent and Bryony. Henry referred to 'the team [as above,

The Last Romantic, tired out after writing over fifty books.

except that Mary and Sarah went off riding elsewhere] moving the massive wood-pile by the western gate – 2–3 tons of beech thrown & sawn up 2 years ago – to the eastern eaves-wall of Studio.' The young grandchildren did their bit, staggering around with the smaller lumps of wood! Henry was in his element, directing operations in the grand manner. Tempers got a little frayed as he insisted that each piece of wood had to be a particular length and, when a good rhythm had been established, suddenly decided he wanted a different length and why was the wood too short or, again, later, too long? It was not too bad as there were several of us and we could joke among ourselves to relieve the tension! The week ended with the usual ritual bonfire, but there was a lot of wet grass from cutting and it would not burn properly, which disappointed Henry greatly.

In September he went to Dublin for a PEN meeting travelling with one of his friends, Parnell Bradbury and his wife and daughter. On his return he stayed in London and worked on the final version of *The Scandaroon*, going to see Eric and Kathy Watkins to read it and get their response, 'so very kind and *real* friends'.

David Cobham wrote that he wanted to film some extra scenes for *Vanishing Hedgerows* the following month and on 3 November Henry went by train to London and then on to Norwich. Richard and I were on holiday at Bungay (it was half-term and we had taken the children to see their grandmother, Loetitia, and my aunt). Richard had gone off to see a friend near Stiffkey for a day or two, and so I met Henry at Norwich Station in Richard's vintage Alvis and drove him up to rendezvous first with Richard and then with David Cobham at Walsingham. Henry did not enjoy the filming, finding it all very difficult and tiring and he felt he had made a mess of it, but David was as always kind and encouraging: and Henry always came over very well on film, and on the radio.

He spent Christmas with Pat Chichester and family, but although he enjoyed himself it was all too brief and his overall mood at this time was in constantly grieving for and yearning after lost, or unfound, love. It is noticeable that he was beginning to grow forgetful: the entries in his diary often repeated facts several times and he obviously sometimes forgot appointments to meet friends, but he was still busy and went up to London to do the voice-over for the *Hedgerows* film. In February 1972 he at last began work in earnest on the 'Otter Treatment' and went to stay in Cornwall at a cottage near Liz Tippett (now Liz Cummins). Then there was a further trip up to London for a preview of *Hedgerows* and to record some more voice-overs. While there he attended the memorial service for Rolf Gardiner at St James, Picadilly, which he found rather too long. He was still working on the 'Treatment' and now was beginning to add in much detail. On 18 March he received the galley proofs of *The Scandaroon*: 'I was surprised and delighted by my little book. It is in splendid order from all aspects – narrative flow; characterisation, action & progress to climax; and above all, humanity & kindness. . . . A tremendous weight off my mind – knowing that Scandaroon is all right – a burden 1955–1971. In 1971 a depression. Today – a triumph.'

About this time Margot Wall (Renshaw) came back from South Africa, and he saw her from time to time at the Instow Yacht Club and at her own home. Also after a break of some two or three years, one of his ex-girlfriends wrote to him out of the blue, saying she would like to see him, and he was additionally writing and phoning continuously another long-standing correspondent, who was married and had a young child, and obviously had no intention of leaving them, although Henry was always hoping that this would happen, yet knew that it would not. He longed for female companionship, and expended quite a lot of money in a continuous dribble of small sums in keeping these girls in attendance.

The film 'treatment' started to become very complicated as he continued to add in extra material, for instance, copying out long passages from *A Test to Destruction*, particularly that with Phillip at the Opera House at Covent Garden. By May he was up to 40,000 words and telephoned David Cobham to tell him he was half-way through, and it would be 80,000 words when finished. He realized that David was a little taken aback, but was not sure why.

The worrying and fretting began to increase. He worried about the amount of work to be got through at the Field, and wrote in his diary on 19 July 1972 'Ox's Cross grass is 3–4 ft high, & owing to the rains has yellow-brown rotting tangle about 9 inches off ground.' The family was due to visit at the end of the month and he was planning various repairs that need doing, 'removing west elmboards of Hut, fixing iron lattice, a new south window for Workshop [this was the original 'Loft' building]. Also to discuss cottage to be built, by whom – & estimate. . . . I'm alone and *long* for harmonious companionship – a wife indeed.'

Margot Wall came up from Instow and cleaned out the caravan in readiness for a family visit of John, Boel and their children and also Robert at the end of July. They were all due to attend the Hartland Festival, where Henry gave his talk 'Reflections on the Death of a Field Marshal'. Henry noted that 'The audience was 70% young people: the attention was "rivetted" and the applause sincere.' John and family lived in the caravan and feeling they had only a few days and were on holiday, mainly went off on their own. Robert stayed in the Ilfracombe cottage with his father; they went daily to the Field where Robert mended the window, repaired the Hut and helped with the other work Henry had detailed, in between times listening to Henry reading the 'treatment'. John and family soon left but Robert (who as a teacher had a long summer holiday) stayed until 10 August and then drove his father up to London, where the whole family, Loetitia included, gathered for a preview of *The Vanishing Hedgerows* at David Cobham's working studio. Henry was gratified that they liked it; his reaction was more muted; he had 'seen it all before'.

Afterwards everyone repaired to Margaret's house for tea,[1] the men going off later for a drink at the Chelsea Arts' Club, a favourite haunt of Henry's. *The Vanishing Hedgerows* was broadcast in the evening of 20 August. Henry was at the Ilfracombe cottage and some friends came over from Instow to watch it with him. Over the next several days he received many letters of appreciation.

On 21 August Richard and myself and our children arrived for a week in the caravan at the Field. 'We all get on well together . . . [they] are great fun.' A day or two later he noted that 'Brent *six years old* is reading and understanding *The*

Screwtape Letters by some Oxford don and understanding it [Brent was actually seven and a half at this time] . . . Bryony (four) [she was six] *thinks* what to say coherently and with truth.' He also noted 'More family honours. John Willie is leading in the Dunstable Gliding Championships. . . . Sarah is in Greece or Italy – writing articles which get printed in British Magazines.'

Towards the end of our stay we all drove up to Exmoor and took the path that leads to Pinkworthy (pronounced Pinkery) Pond. He was very nervous about us all losing the path and disappearing in a bog, despite the fact that a fairly solid track existed since a youth hostel had been established at the farm there. He was harking back to the early days when it had possibly been dangerous. He was equally nervous about the children and Richard going too near the cliff edge at Baggy, and nearly had a fit when they 'dared' to clamber down the steep path to the cave at the bottom, which can be explored at low tide.[2] Richard worked hard trimming the trees and cutting the grass. Henry noted that when we left the 'pall of loneliness' fell.

The Scandaroon was published on 19 October 1972. The book itself was not of the substance to attract major critical attention, although many reviewers noted that it was good that Henry Williamson had returned to the writing of an animal story. One of the better reviews was by Joseph McKierman in the *Evening Chronicle* : 'The Scandaroon is a splendid bird of the pigeon family from the Baltic. Around it Henry Williamson has woven one of his romantic nature novels. . . . The Williamson pen has lost none of its old magic.'[3] Another reviewer stated that its 'vivid prose brings out each telling detail. . . . There is a sense of sureness – not a word has been wasted and not a word is wrong.'[4] Maurice Wiggin called it 'a sunny, May-fresh story. . . . The old master's evening gift to us is luminous with his own poetic and piercing insights into the mysteries of the natural creation.'[5]

'The old master' sitting pensively in his Writing Hut.

Two long retrospective articles based on interviews with Henry also appeared. In *The Scotsman* Henry revealed to William Foster that the 'Thurby' in the book was his name for Durby, a suburb of Barnstaple; but on the whole in this article Henry was playing to the gallery, repeating several past myths.[6] Another one in *The Guardian*, by Alec Hamilton, was really the resumé of a conversation with Henry. It was as if Henry was speaking from the page. It is disjointed, confusing, but very immediate. Henry's cousin Marjorie Boone, his first love from those far off Bedford days, happened to be present at the time, and Henry bossed her about in a mild sort of way. One of the things Henry told Alec Hamilton was that he had been to see Hitler with Yeats-Brown (the Bengal Lancer), a totally new invention of his Hitler visit story. Whether Henry himself now believed that or was muddled, or whether he was just saying something to be a little sensational cannot be ascertained. In the last lines Hamilton quoted Henry as saying 'He didn't say he had done it [the writing], it was done through him. It was in the blood . . . he wrote in a dream . . . "The unseen world of the spirit", said Marjorie, chipping in her gloss for the first and only time.'[7] It is interesting that Henry felt himself to be 'The Dreamer of Devon'. Alec Hamilton had no idea of the ancient love story that was before him, that had once unfolded between Henry and Marjorie. She had been to see Henry several times in recent years; she had a large family, nine children and many grandchildren, and yet she was still drawn back to her first lover. When she initially reappeared in his life, Henry made a note in his diary concerning the fact that it was she who at the age of thirteen had given him his first experience of sex.[8]

From the time when he had first bought the Field, Henry had planned to build a house there; he drew a 'Down Close' on his original sketch of the Field with its complicated computation of windflows, and in his archive there is a plan for a large and imposing house drawn by G.A.G. Schwabe, Architect, of Braunton, amazingly dated June 1929. It was the one thing out of the many he had planned in his long life that he had not yet achieved. It is interesting to wonder why he *had* never done so. One suspects that he knew that the Field would never be the same wild, empty, spiritually peaceful place if he did. But with the end of his own life approaching, when it would not affect him in the same way, it had now been in his mind for some time to realize this last project. He wanted to build a house in which the family could all gather and hold large parties and dances. He had decided to resurrect plans already drawn up by a firm of architects in 1951. But on 15 October 1972 he went to Exford on a visit with a friend who was touring in the area, and in the hotel there where they stopped for lunch he 'saw a familiar face – it was Dennis, the Surveyor of B'ple [Barnstaple] R.D. Council in 1951, when he visited Ox's Cross about my caravan and plans for a cottage. I liked him . . . & arranged with him (he is now a builder at Braunton) to visit Ox's Cross at 11 a.m. tomorrow.' They got on well.

At the end of October he went to London, mainly to attend the memorial service for Sir Francis Chichester in Westminster Abbey, and sat with the family but felt he should not have been there and became very morose. 'Later Margaret and Gipsy found me.' They rescued him, and he took them off to lunch at his club. He had been asked to do a television programme about T.E. Lawrence and while in London he arranged with the lawyers concerned for his daughter Sarah to type out copies of his letters to T.E. Lawrence in readiness for this programme. He also saw Margot Wall and wanted to attach himself to her, but she rushed off to the Scientologists at East Grinstead. He returned to Devon and loneliness.

On 29 November he met Julia Cave, the BBC producer who was to make the Lawrence film, at Taunton and she drove him to Lawrence's cottage at Clouds Hill on a reconnaissance visit, 'the gloomy cottage of poor T.E. Lawrence in those far off days. . . . Talked to Mr. Knowles the once-friend (RAF ranks) of T.E. . . . The inside of the cottage is Gothic – all dark heavy wood, & the trees & small windows add to the dark brown gloom.' It was over thirty-seven years since the day he was supposed to have stopped off there for lunch to discuss Victor Yeates's 'Family Life' volume, and it was the first time he had ever been inside the cottage. He noted that Knowles showed signs of annoyance, worried that yet another person was going to denigrate his 'Master', and Henry hastened to reassure him. (It does not appear that Pat Knowles knew who Henry was.)

Two days later Henry wrote: 'I am the horrible age of 77.' The actual filming was on 15 December; it did not go well. Henry found he could not cope with the complications of the various takes and could not remember his lines direct to camera. When Julia Cave eventually 'closed down operations' Henry felt he had failed, 'and pretty awful I felt'. After a day or two he decided to go to London, as always driving to Taunton, as always taking the road over Exmoor:

> The main run to Blackmoor Gate – Simonsbath, always the slight heart-longing for memories of Pinkery Pond & the Chains from 1913 when I had left school & gone alone (7/6 return ticket Waterloo–Braunton) to that place of magic. Now I was old, tired, and heart-sick. And now the long straight road & downhill to Weddon [sic] Cross (always memories of Loetitia & me married – what a dreadfully idiotic creature I was!). . . .

For several years, whenever he had passed Wheddon Cross he had mentioned in his diary how it always brought back memories of his first honeymoon.

He returned to Devon in time for Christmas which he spent with Pat Chichester and family as always. On New Year's Eve he watched on television 'A splendid "Revue" of events at Royal Covent Garden – John Gielgud – Lawrence Olivier – the incomparable Schwarzkopf singing a poem by that great Jewish-German poet – I forget, forget, forget [presumably it was Goethe] – his verses set to music by the equally great Mahler. Such beauty, such grace – and produced by Patrick Garland, who has gone to the top – Patrick who produced the programmes of H.W. in the summers of long ago.'

In mid-January 1973 he was invited to contribute a foreword to a volume of *The Wipers Times*,[9] a complete facsimile of the famous First World War trenches newspaper. Early in 1916 a Captain Roberts of the Sherwood Foresters had discovered the remains of an old printing-house just off the square at Ypres – called 'Wipers' by the British soldiers. Captain Roberts had decided to use the press to publish a monthly newspaper and so the *Wipers Times* was born, and was to cheer many an unhappy, frightened and lonely soldier. In his foreword Henry described his first days as a soldier, turning in his last paragraph to 'the spirit of the Western Front in the pages of the *Wipers Times* . . . is a charity which links those who have passed through the estranging remoteness of battle . . . men who were broken, but reborn.' And finally he used an incident in the autobiography of Field Marshal Hindenburg to show the brotherhood of the soldiers of the opposing armies.

It is strange that over these last months he was involved in happenings and projects which encapsulated most of the major moments of his entire life; almost as if he were conjuring up episodes himself, when actually it was all due to outside forces.

In February 1973 he again met Arthur Dennis, who had discovered that Henry had actually been granted planning permission to build a house in 1951 and that this licence would soon run out, and with tighter regulations was not likely to be renewed so if he intended to build, time pressed. But his trustees were worried about this project, feeling he was undertaking something he could neither afford nor cope with (and one which was not really necessary, but they could not say that to him). However, Henry stubbornly intended to go ahead, causing dissension for a while. He wrote to me complaining about this non-cooperation on the part of his trustees (he probably wrote to several people about it); my reply in the files states: 'having created a Trust you should really take a wise and dignified pose of Patriarch – the grand old man – the figurehead . . . Edward James[10] is in this position, very much magnified, of course, but he keeps his "cool" and so gains respect from all for his dignity and manner of handling things.' This quite possibly only determined him all the more to do exactly what he wanted!

The hapless 'Tarka treatment' script was now about a hundred and eighty thousand words long. Henry was incorporating more and more material which had nothing to do with *Tarka*. It was not that he did not know how to adapt his always detailed style to the terse taut prose that is necessary for a 'treatment', where only the outline plot and scenario are required, but that his now very muddled mind could not cope. He was actually rewriting a novel which combined several of his previous books. It was all too much for him, and he was very sadly aware of it.

In May there was the appalling tragedy of Kenneth Allsop's death. Kenneth sadly could no longer cope with the constant pain he endured from his old wound and the stress of pushing himself to the limit in his profession and he took his own life. The two men had both been present at the annual West Country Writers' Congress in Exeter two weeks previously. Henry gave the address at the funeral of his friend at Powerstock Church on 29 May 1973, where he was supported by Margaret. In August he attended a charity performance of *Jesus Christ Superstar* in aid of the Kenneth Allsop Memorial Fund, of which he was a patron for a short

Reading one of his books out loud. This photograph was taken in his Hut, but this is how Henry would have looked at his readings at the Lobster Pot in Instow in the last years of his life.

while. Eventually, the money raised was used to purchase the island of Steep Holm in September 1975,[11] a bird sanctuary which remains a living memory to Allsop.

In October Henry gave a further reading at the Lobster Pot at Instow where he read some James Farrar which went down very well with the young people, while in November he was pleased when 'Richard sent his new novel *CAPREOL the story of a Roebuck*. Magnificent!'

He spent his seventy-eighth birthday in London: 'I spent the evening with Margie and Sarah & some of their friends in the Chelsea Arts Club . . . fooled about like a clown – a real show-off . . . [then they went on to the Queen's Elm] And there more fun – I was a super-show-off.'

Christmas was spent, as was the tradition now, with Pat Chichester and his family. But the New Year saw Henry downhearted and dejected. He was worried about the trustees' objections to the proposed cottage at Ox's Cross; and very downcast that when he was in London the previous month he had seen David Cobham who had firmly told him that his 'Tarka film treatment' was no good and that therefore he himself would take it on (in the event Gerald Durrell and Cobham collaborated). 'My preposterous 220 foolscap pp were quite out of key and volume.' He had also learned that one of the 'angels' (the term used for people who put up the money for film-making) was John Coast, who had come to him for a job when he was on the Norfolk farm, and felt that he had come full circle. He knew his powers were deserting him and that his memory was becoming totally unreliable, and he lived in a state of uneasy dejection. One of the symptoms

Building the new house at Ox's Cross in 1974. Henry is inspecting the work from the scaffolding with his grandson, Brent. The building in the background is the Studio.

of his loss of memory was the saga of the missing keys. He could not keep track of car-keys, house keys, or Hut and Studio keys, and spent many hours each day hunting for them. They were usually somewhere quite close to hand, and it seemed at the time as if he was deliberately losing them just to get attention. In retrospect, of course, it should have alerted everyone to his mental state. But in everyone's thoughts Henry was invincible. He still had the same energy and the same power to dominate with his powerful personality.

In May he went to the West Country Writers' Congress at Bristol where the Chairman was now Dr William Kean Seymour. The guest of honour was Bernard Price, the writer and broadcaster.[12] Henry gave two or three more talks at the Lobster Pot and on 8 August one at the Beaford Centre itself in a seminar 'By Devon People about Devon People': 'Total success.' He really loved these occasions, and many people still speak of them with great affection.

On 12 August we went down for our annual visit – 'Dear Richard comes to Ox's Cross tomorrow.' But he forgot to record what we were doing there. The house was in process of being built and he would make a daily inspection and give orders to the men about how he wanted things done, but he never mentioned it at all in his diary. The house that was built is very similar to the one on the 1929 plans, but with details like 'the maid's sitting room' omitted! Henry had had ever since the 1920s some huge wooden (teak) stanchions, that he said had once been part of an Elizabethan battleship, that he had bought at one of the many auctions he attended in those early days. He had always planned to incorporate them in the house, to support the first floor over one end of the main room, while the major part of the room soared right up to the roof with a huge cathedral-like window that went from top to bottom.[13] This was the area in which he envisaged the huge family barn-dances would be held. He also still had the planks of very beautiful yew wood which he had bought in the 1930s and had had sawn at the saw-mills at Shallowford when a yew tree had been felled. These had been transported to Norfolk, down to Botesdale, and back down to Devon again and had been stored in the workshop ever since. Henry never quite got round to incorporating them in the house. After his death, Harry made one or two items of furniture from a few of the planks and then sold the rest, a rather sad end to their saga.

Henry had planned his own quarters to be right out of the way at the top of the house, an eyrie with a look-out window from which he could gaze out across the so familiar countryside to his beloved Taw and Torridge estuary in the distance. He thought to have a fireman's pole down which he could slide in a dramatic entrance to join the family for breakfast! He also gave strict instructions for the building of the fireplace, still a point of great concern with him. Sadly, he never lived in this house. Despite the fact that it was the last of his ambitions, he must have found that it altered the character of his Field totally.

He told us how he never ate and had no friends whatsoever, but when we mentioned to the workmen how worried we were, they told us not to pay any attention as he went out to visit this friend and that friend for lunch or to the pub, and always came back very happy to sleep for a while in his Hut, only to awaken again feeling miserable. He was still desperately trying to find solace with the one remaining female to feature in his life. He recorded the five pound notes and chocolates and 'extras' being sent off to 'Mus' every week over and over again, knowing that he was buying her brief over-loving replies which assuaged his loneliness very temporarily, because he did not fool himself that there was any real feeling reciprocated. But it brightened his day when she did write, although he noted 'It's all money and tinsel.' However, locally, the McKinnells were still very faithful and kind friends and he went to see them and other loyal friends frequently.

Towards the end of November 1974 he received a letter from Harry who asked if he could come and work with the builders at Ox's Cross. Several projects in which Harry had been involved had come to nothing, such as the plan to manufacture wind turbines as part of an alternative energy project and he was in need of a job. Soon after this he arrived with his partner Carol, and his huge painted furniture pantechnicon took up residence at the Field, with several of his hippy friends who came and went.

The following summer, August 1975, we and our children again went down for the annual visitation, accompanied by Robert (one could not say 'holiday' because there was always a great deal of work to be done, but by being a little firm, work was always combined with pleasure, with visits to the beach for the children). The two men got on with the work and I helped wherever possible and kept them

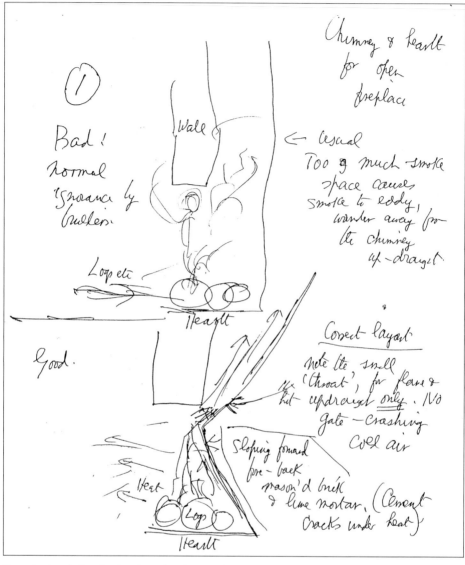

Henry's sketch for the fireplace for the new house at Ox's Cross. Always an important element in his life, you can almost feel his annoyance because it was not being done 'properly'.

The new house was finished in 1975. Henry is sitting outside the big window with our labrador, Flight. His granddaughter Bryony is sitting in the doorway while Harry meditates against the wall.

supplied with food and cups of tea and coffee, which meant a daily walk down to the village for milk and provisions. The house was finished but occupied by Harry and his friends. As usual our family slept in the Studio which was snug and comfortable as long as one did not mind the basic conditions, which we did not. Henry arrived daily from the Ilfracombe cottage at about 10.30 a.m., as he always had. By now he was very forgetful and somewhat irritable, but only a degree or so more than we were all used to. One morning he appeared about 7 a.m. while we were all still, naturally, in bed and stumped up the narrow Studio stairs, very annoyed that no one was up. He demanded that Robert and Richard got up and took him to get petrol because the garage would shut at 8 a.m. They protested but he became so agitated that they decided it was better to give in to him and go, and so off they all went. Henry was being difficult and it was best to humour him. They had, after all, been dealing with this phenomenon for forty-five years or so! None of us realized what was actually happening to him. In retrospect, he was being so illogical that we should have known, or guessed, that something was really very wrong. A few days later, the same scene was re-enacted; this time it was the middle of the night when there was a stomping up the stairs and the appearance of a wild figure through the trap-door like entrance. We all groaned and said 'Go away Henry, its still night-time.' 'It's not Henry, it's me, Harry', said the figure. 'I've just come back from the hospital. I'm a father. Carol's had her baby. It's a girl.' It hadn't been due for some time as far as we knew. Later in the day we drove over with flowers and fruit to welcome the new arrival, who was to be called Bee.

The family decided to go down to Devon for Henry's eightieth birthday on 1 December 1975 and take him out for a grand celebratory lunch at the Imperial Hotel in Barnstaple. John and his wife, and children, took Richard and our son Brent in their car (our Alvis coupé was never on the road in the winter). Bryony was upset that there was not enough room for her and me. Robert went down with his family, and Margaret also. Henry was in fine form; he threw little pellets of bread about the dining room, one of his favourite pranks, and even whole rolls, and took off his jacket and shirt and squared up to one of the waiters with his fists; the waiter wasn't quite sure how to deal with this! Henry thoroughly enjoyed himself.

That evening BBC 2 broadcast a film that had been made earlier in the year, *No Man's Land*. Dan Farson had made large and clear notes in Henry's diary in June to remind him that the filming would be taking place then. With that kind of help he could continue to operate. Dan Farson also wrote an excellent article, 'Recognising Henry Williamson', which appeared in the *Daily Telegraph* colour supplement on 28 November 1975. Although these two men had had a turbulent relationship, due mainly to the quarrels between Henry and Dan's father, Dan did on this occasion do his best for his old friend.

Christmas came and went and the year turned. In early January there was a panic call around the family. Henry had been found wandering and had been taken to hospital; what to do? Richard was away at the time, but I offered to have him to stay with us, understanding that he was just in need of some 'tender loving care' and thinking that he would enjoy the peace and quiet of our house in the middle of a wood. John, Margaret and Robert drove down to Devon and collected him and drove him to our house, one of them driving up his MG saloon. They left directly (they had to get home themselves). It was immediately obvious that there was more wrong than we had thought. Henry was behaving in the most extraordinarily wild manner. Richard, in response to the emergency, was travelling home but would not arrive until very late. It was the most frightening moment of my life. Henry had been given tranquillizers, but for some reason instead of calming him down these had made him hyperactive, and a hyperactive Henry with whom one had no means of communicating whatsoever. He was totally shut off from the real world. It was a terrifying prospect. He was enormously strong, and he proceeded to try and destroy my very large kitchen cooker, by wrenching out the coiled plate elements. He decided he wanted a wash and poured a pail of water into the wooden kitchen drawer, full of the paraphanalia one keeps in such drawers. The children were very frightened, they were still quite young, being eleven and nine-and-a-half respectively. Richard returned eventually and we were able to get Henry to bed. The next morning we asked for an emergency visit from our doctor, who examined and questioned him carefully. He then explained that Henry was in a very advanced stage of senile dementia and advised me not to cross him as he could fly into a dreadful rage (this is a symptom of senile dementia, not a reflection on Henry's temperament) with devastating results, and he changed the tranquillizers, which did help a little.

And so began a very difficult few weeks. All Henry wanted to do was walk. The weather was bitterly cold, but luckily fine and bright. With the comparative calm that the new prescription gave him, he was living in the 1920s, and he would continuously want to start off to go to Instow to 'catch the tide' so he could go sailing. Off we would set through the woods; after a while I would stop and manoeuvre him round so that we were facing the way we had come, and return, suggesting as we came back to the house, that we could call on 'these people' for coffee – and so indoors we would go, to sit for a while, and then the process would be repeated. Henry was incontinent and also seemed to have no idea of what a lavatory was for, so taking him in there and suggesting he used the facilities was useless. This entailed a great deal of washing (and I did not possess a washing machine).

He wanted to drive his car, but we hid the keys and told him he was not allowed to drive as he was ill. This conversation, of course, had to be repeated every hour or so. Occasionally I offered to drive him out for a little, which he seemed to enjoy, although I was very worried about what he might do, and dare venture no further than slowly round the local lanes. He took to trying to start the car with a paperclip, but as that kept him occupied we let him sit there and fiddle. One day Richard had been servicing the car and came in for coffee. Henry had been very busy all the morning trying to pull up a huge root attached to a large yew tree at the bottom of our garden. Again we let him do this, it gave him exercise and helped to tire him out. But as we sat drinking our coffee we heard the car engine start. Richard had forgotten to remove the keys. Luckily the car was facing into the wood. By the time we had dashed out and down to the track, Henry had managed to turn the car round, but in so doing he had luckily got it stuck across the track, and he could not get it out. Richard leant in and removed the keys. Henry could not understand why the car would no longer go. When the keys were there he knew what to do, now they were not he reverted to the paperclip. Sometimes we were convinced that he was playing some huge elaborate trick on us, and must surely merely be joking.

He talked continuously of the 'Crake'. It worried him and preyed on his mind, but he was not able to be really coherent about it. He would try and tell the story but it was all garbled and made no sense. 'The Crake' was the title of one of his earliest stories, and was a symbol of death.[14]

He had to be watched all the time. He was enormously strong and would walk off through the garden and when he came to the fence he would try and walk straight through it. The same with the hedges. Paths had no meaning, he would walk on and straight through the tangle of undergrowth, often getting stuck. One day the poor soul got into the middle of a bramble bush. Before Richard could get to him to try and extricate him he decided that it was his shoes that were hindering him and took them off, getting his feet into the most dreadful mess from the thorns. But it did not worry him.

One afternoon Richard was out at work as usual, and as Henry seemed to be resting, I went into the bathroom. I can hardly have been two minutes. When I came out there was no sign of him. I went outside and looked around. He had vanished. I ran down every path that led from the house, but could not see him anywhere. I kept on looking, casting a wider and wider net but to no avail. It was bitterly cold and it was now late afternoon. I decided to telephone the police and explain the situation. Soon van after van load of police men and women began to arrive. Some searched the house: apart from the fact that Henry might have hidden himself, it was obvious that they had to be sure that I had not done anything dreadful. Others went off through the woods. Most were in their normal uniform, especially the police women with black nylons and ordinary shoes. I found as many pairs of wellingtons as I could, and handed them out. Darkness fell, and no one had been successful. We knew he would not survive the night out in the open, but they had called off the search and were gathering back at the house. One of the policewomen, who had stayed by my side throughout, started to make cups of tea. Richard returned home from work and so did the children from school. Suddenly the field telephone buzzed. One of the officers had driven up a track and had got his vehicle stuck, and had got out to see how to extricate himself. As he did so he had seen something white ahead of him in the trees. It was Henry; his white hair gleaming. The policeman brought him back into the kitchen full of uniformed police. 'Oh, how lovely,' Henry said, 'a cocktail party just for me.' He had told the policeman that he was going shrimping.

The next morning our doctor arrived. He said the police were very concerned about the situation and felt that Henry should be transferred to the local hospital for the mentally ill, as they felt the responsibility for the safety of such a famous man was too great, and that it would be better if we did this voluntarily. We understood the implications. He made the arrangements and we drove down to Chichester. Henry walked into the locked ward to which he had been allocated for assessment, which was full of obviously disturbed people, without a murmur. Up to that moment I was still wondering if he could possibly have been joking all along. But no one could have walked into that place unless they really were living in a different world to the normal one. Henry said, 'Oh, how lovely, we are going on the boat to America.' And really, one could see how it could have looked like a large liner to him – the SS *Berengaria*.

We had to inform the family of the new development, explaining that we had had no choice. The doctor had made it very clear that if we had not taken him voluntarily then he would have had to commit him, in which case Henry's care would have passed out of his family's control. He was worried that Henry would turn violent and do some irreparable harm, for he was constantly on the verge of temper, and had to be handled very circumspectly; this symptom of senile dementia being exacerbated by his enormous physical strength. Besides which I was exhausted, and the situation was affecting the children. Margaret was, of course, very upset, and determined to find somewhere more suitable for him, which in due course she did, and Henry was transferred to the care of the Alexian monks at their hospice at Twyford Abbey, on the outskirts of London. Margaret, being nearby, bore the brunt of the visiting which she undertook gladly, and many of his friends also went to see him frequently. He liked to talk about the old days, especially the war. He had been stabilized with the use of drugs, and was allowed to walk around the grounds. He retained the urge to walk almost until the very end. Sometimes he would wander away, but some kind person would steer him back again. (The local people were used to the wanderers.)

Meanwhile David Cobham had begun to make the film of *Tarka the Otter*. In July and August 1977, all the hunt scenes were being shot down in Devon. Richard and I and the children went down partly out of interest but also to help with advice and to be extras. Loetitia went to stay with a friend who lived fairly locally and she came over most days to watch the filming, and again to advise on the finer points of etiquette and manners of the hunt. We could not afford a hotel, so took our tent and established ourselves on a camping site. Filming went on all day and every day and we found it all very interesting, hounds and otters never mixed – but you would never realize this from the film!

The scenes for the 'Last Hunt' and the final scene of Tarka's death were very carefully set up. David Cobham was meticulous about filming in the exact locations which Henry had described, although some manipulation had to be involved, such as pots of balsam plants for the river banks, and a realistic but plastic tree to provide Tarka's 'holt'. It took all day to film the last scene. The dead hound was prepared; one which had died naturally some time before and had been kept in a freezer until wanted, and was now made-up with the same markings as the dog that played Deadlock. Finally it was all over and David called a 'wrap', that is, the end for the day. We went out and got some food and returned to our very damp tent (it had rained a great deal and we had had a rather uncomfortable time). The site manager met us with a message: would Richard telephone Mrs Williamson.

Richard got through to his mother. She had had a message from Margaret to say Henry was approaching the end, and we should all stand by. The next morning, 13 August 1977, Richard telephoned his mother again and heard that Henry had died during the night. Margaret was with him until almost the very last moment. She told us afterwards that towards the end Henry crossed his hands on his breast, and indicated to her that he wanted to be alone. She left him, and he must have died soon afterwards. It really does seem to have been a most extraordinary point of fate, that it should have happened on the very day that the film crew were filming that particular scene: Henry and Tarka went out together on the ebb tide of the 'sea-going waters' of life.[15]

We had to tell David and the crew. Everyone was very upset. Filming that day was a difficult affair. Henry's death was broadcast on all the major news bulletins, and soon the papers were printing obituaries, all of which told of the tremendous opus of work he had written during his life.

The funeral was in Georgeham Church, as Henry had wished and planned for a long time. His pall-bearers were his five sons, Windles, John, Robert, Richard, Harry, and the sixth person was Bill Thomson, Margaret's first husband and one of Henry's great friends. The church was full of friends and well-wishers who came, as he used to say, 'to pay their tribute salt'. After the service was over, he was taken to the grave that he had bought with such a fuss some twenty-five years earlier – the last plot in the graveyard. It was a beautiful day; one might have said that 'the sun shone without reproach', those very first words Henry had written and about which he used to laugh at himself when he realized how naive they had been. As we all stood by the grave, a swarm of bees was busy around the church tower above our heads, murmuring away as they attended to their own affairs. Henry would have appreciated that. He would probably have written a story about it. There were many floral tributes; Richard and I and our two children had been out that morning and gathered him a bunch of heather from the moor that he loved. The Dreamer of Devon – the last Romantic – had joined the Ancient Sunlight. Later his headstone was to be the simple slate that he had requested.

Henry's gravestone in the Georgeham Churchyard. (Photograph courtesy of Peter Lewis)

On the day that would have been his eighty-second birthday a memorial service was held at the church of St Martin-in-the-Fields in London. Apart from the usual ceremony of such an occasion, readings of Henry's work were given by Mandy Allsop, Kenneth's daughter. The address was given by Ted Hughes, who related that he had read *Tarka the Otter* when he was eleven years old and for a year after had read little else:

> It entered into me and gave shape and words to my world, as no book has ever done since. I recognised even then, I suppose, that it was something of a holy book, a soul-book, written with the life blood of an unusual poet. . . . It is not usual to consider him as a poet. But I believe he was one of the two or three truest poets of his generation.[16]

Henry Williamson's owl colophon, which appeared at
the end of every one of his books.

NOTES

The following abbreviations are used throughout the notes:

The Henry Williamson Literary Estate Archive: HWLEA
The Henry Williamson Society *Journal* : HWSJ
The Henry Williamson Society: HWS

PREFACE

1. Herbert Faulkner West, *The Dreamer of Devon* (Ulysses Press, 1932). Herbert Faulkner West (1898–1974) was Professor of Comparative Literature at Dartmouth College, Hanover, New Hampshire, USA. Henry Williamson met West when in the USA in early 1931. West then visited Shallowford from 7–14 March 1932. He then went on to London where he wrote his essay on Henry Williamson. In his obituary in *Dartmouth Alumni Magazine* (Dec. 1974) written by 'C.E.W.' (copy kindly provided by Philip Cronenwelt, Curator of Manuscripts & Special Collections at Dartmouth College Library) Professor West is referred to as 'a favorite teacher of thousands of Dartmouth students over his 40-year teaching career'. He had had a distinguished academic career albeit as a non-conformist. The two courses most associated with him were 'Rebel Thought' and 'The Nature Writers', which gives us insight into his obvious interest in Henry Williamson. West befriended several writers, of whom Robert Frost was one. This essay is reprinted in the HWSJ, centenary edition, No. 31 (September 1995).

2. Edward Seago, *Peace in War* (Collins, 1943), 'Henry Williamson', pp. 49–52. Edward Seago, artist, lived in that same area of East Anglia as Henry Williamson's Norfolk farm (see Chapter 7). At this time, the Second World War, he was a major in the army serving as a camouflage officer. Seago's portrait and short accompanying essay is reprinted in HWSJ, centenary edition, No. 31 (September 1995).

3. Henry Williamson presented a selection of manuscripts and typescripts to Exeter University in 1965. The university then became the repository for the collection of MSS and TSS accepted by the nation under the National Heritage Scheme. These are available for study by bona fide research students. The university also houses the Henry Williamson Society Archive, some of which is not available for research at this time.

4. J. Quiddington West, *The Incalculable Hour*, (privately printed Hazell Watson & Viney, 1910). J. Quiddington West was the pseudonym of Mary Leopoldina Williamson. *The Incalculable Hour* will be printed in HWSJ, centenary edition, No. 31 (September 1995).

5. George Painter, 'The Two Maddisons', *Aylesford Review*, Vol. II, No. 6 (spring 1959). Reprinted in HWSJ, No. 5 (May 1982), pp. 30–3. George Painter (b. 1914) was employed as a specialist in fifteenth-century printing at the British Museum (retired 1974). In the late 1940s and early 1950s he wrote reviews for *The Listener* and the *New Statesman*, and was particularly an admirer of Henry

Williamson, John Cowper Powys, and Sylvia Townsend Warner. His books include biographies of *Marcel Proust*, (Chatto and Windus, Vol I, 1959, Vol 2, 1965) (the Duff Cooper Memorial Prize for 1965), and of Andre Gide, William Caxton, and Chateaubriand (the James Tait Memorial Prize 1977).

CHAPTER 1

1. I am grateful to the archivist at Girton College, Valerie Perry, for checking the university archive records on this matter. As there was no entry for Mary Leopoldina Williamson, Valerie Perry suggested that she may actually have attended the 'Lectures for Ladies' which were held at that time and were very well attended, but for which no records were kept.

2. See *Stratford-upon-Avon Herald*, 16 April 1886. I am grateful to the curator of The Shakespeare Birthplace Trust for providing a copy of this obituary from the trust's archive, and for other items concerning the Shapcote family. It is printed in full in HWSJ, No. 31 (September 1995), pp. 10–11.

3. See Anne Williamson, 'Roots: an Examination of Henry Williamson's Lineage', HWSJ, No. 31 (September 1995), for a more detailed examination of Henry Williamson's family tree with background information.

4. Letters from Maude Gregg (née Williamson) and Mary Leopoldina Williamson, sisters of Henry's father, are in HWLEA.

5. Ibid.

6. From a few pages of autobiographical notes written by Henry Williamson, probably in the mid-1960s, placed in an envelope with the letters mentioned above, in which he is giving his own explanation as to why his aunts called him 'unhappy'.

7. See Leland L. Duncan, DVO, FSA, *A History of Colfe's Grammar School* (1910). Leland Duncan was a distinguished former pupil of the school, and knew Henry Williamson. There are some letters from him in the HWLEA.

8. The Revd Thomas Bramley had been the previous headmaster and on retirement had inaugurated a series of prizes for divinity.

9. The convent still operates as a school, but they have not answered my letters of inquiry.

10. By piecing together various notes and hints found here and there in documents in Henry Williamson's archive, it appears that there was some homosexual activity in his early years. While this does not seem to have been any more than merely adolescent experimentation on his part, it is possible that it held deeper meaning for some of his friends. It is inevitable that Henry's deeply imaginative and magnetic personality drew towards him passionate admirers of both sexes throughout his life.

11. Henry Williamson, 'The Last Summer', *Sunday Times Magazine*, 2 August 1964, pp. 5–11.

CHAPTER 2

1. These volumes are: Vol. 4, *How Dear Is Life* (1954); Vol. 5, *A Fox Under My Cloak* (1955); Vol. 6, *The Golden Virgin* (1957); Vol. 7, *Love and the Loveless* (1958); Vol. 8, *A Test to Destruction* (1960). All the volumes of *A Chronicle of Ancient Sunlight* were first published by Macdonald & Co., and are currently being published in paperback by Alan Sutton Publishing.

2. Henry Williamson, *The Wet Flanders Plain* (Faber, 1928) and *The Patriot's Progress* (Geoffrey Bles, 1930).

3. Douglas Bell was to write his own book when the war was over, as did another school friend, Victor Yeates. Henry Williamson was to help them both to get their work published (see further references in Chapters 4 and 5).

4. This is possibly a reference to a painting by George Frederick Watts (1817–1907) entitled *Hope*. Painted in 1885, it shows a lonely blindfolded figure in blue seated on a brown-gold globe and holding a lyre with all except one string broken. The painting was presented to the nation in 1897.

5. *Short History of The London Rifle Brigade* (Aldershot, 1916).

6. This item plus a longer one covering much of the same ground appeared in *Colfensia*

'The Chronicles of Colfe Grammar School', No. 22, 1915.

7. Lady Ursula Redwood, *Trefusis Territory* (1987). I am grateful to the Cornish Studies librarian at Redruth for sending photocopies of material from this booklet, and for a copy of Henry M. Jeffery, FRS, 'On a Tudor Mansion at Trefusis in Mylor', *Journal of the Royal Institution of Cornwall*, Vol. 10, Pt 37 (1891), pp. 399–402; and also to Lady Redwood for her personal interest, and permission to use material from her pamphlet.

8. The notebooks containing this manuscript are part of the Henry Williamson Manuscript Collection at Exeter University, Devon. For a detailed analysis of HW's early work see: Dr J. Wheatley Blench, 'The Apprenticeship of a Novelist: the Early Unpublished Fiction of Henry Williamson', Pt I, HWSJ, No. 17 (March 1988), pp. 5–19; Part II, HWSJ, No. 18 (September 1988), pp. 39–49; Part III, HWSJ, No. 19 (March 1989), pp. 31–45.

CHAPTER 3

1. Henry Williamson, 'Confessions of a Fake Merchant' in *The Book of Fleet Street*, ed. T. Michael Pope (Cassell, 1930).

2. Richard Jefferies (1849–87). More generally known for his writings on the natural world and for his novels, particularly *Bevis: the Story of a Boy*, Jefferies also had a strange surreal side to his nature, which prompted his outpourings of mystical emotion.

3. This information is contained in a note by Henry Williamson in HWLEA.

4. Marjorie Watts, *Mrs Sappho, The Life of C.A. Dawson Scott* (Duckworth, 1987) and also *PEN The Early Years 1921–1926* (Archive Press, 1971). No reference is given for the letter from Henry Williamson. The area of Constantine referred to in the letter is on the North Cornwall coast where Mrs Dawson Scott owned a house.

5. For an examination of this unpublished work, see Dr J.W. Blench, 'The Apprenticeship of a Novelist', HWSJ, op. cit. (see Ch. 2, note 8). The manuscript is

part of the Henry Williamson Manuscript Collection at Exeter University.

6. Most of Henry Williamson's first journalistic writings have been gathered into a small book: *The Weekly Dispatch, Articles Contributed by Henry Williamson in the Years 1920–21*, ed. John Gregory (HWS, 1983). As it was printed in the London *Evening News*, 'My Owl' was not included in this collection.

7. Ibid.

8. In an article entitled 'A House of No Morals' published in the *Sunday Express* (18 December 1921), Henry Williamson claimed that he paid £1 per annum rent for this cottage, but usually references are to £5 annual rent.

9. Henry Williamson, *The Sun in the Sands* (Faber, 1945). Called a 'novel-biography', some of this book was based on autobiographical material, but as it progresses it becomes more and more fictional.

10. Letters from Walter de la Mare to Henry Williamson are reproduced with the kind permission of the trustees of the Walter de la Mare Literary Estate.

11. See 'The Otter' (broadcast 28 October 1936), reprinted in *Spring Days in Devon*, ed. John Gregory (HWS, 1992), pp. 58–64.

12. Henry Williamson, *Dandelion Days* (Collins, 1922) and also *The Lone Swallows* (Collins, 1922).

13. One of the wreaths at Henry Williamson's funeral was from 'Julian Warbeck', so this gentleman paid his last respects to his friend from those far-off days. Unfortunately, Richard and I did not think to follow this up at the time.

CHAPTER 4

1. See Preface, xiv, and Ch. 1, p. 5; also Dr J. Wheatley Blench, 'The Incalculable Hour', HWSJ, No. 8 (October 1983), p. 18. J. Quiddington West [Mary Leopoldina Williamson], *The Incalculable Hour* is reprinted in the HWSJ Vol. 31 (September 1995). See also Dr J. Wheatley Blench, 'The Flax of Dream, a Reappraisal', HWSJ, No. 20 (September 1989), pp. 5–27.

2. The letter mentions several family items and shows them to be on friendly and fairly close terms. 'Dolly' is a nick-name for Marjorie Boone's mother.

3. Henry Williamson, preface to a special Limited Edition of *The Pathway* (1931), recently reprinted in Henry Williamson, *Threnos for T.E. Lawrence and Other Writings* (HWS, 1994).

4. Charles Hibbert was the eldest son of Leicester Hibbert, a captain in the Queen's Bays Regiment and Arethusa Jane Calvert, who lived at Chalfont Lodge in Buckinghamshire, the family seat. (Chalfont House itself was inhabited by an older member of the family.) Charles had married his cousin, Margaret Dora, the youngest child of Leicester's eldest brother, Col. Hugh Robert Hibbert of Birtles Hall, Cheshire (another family property) and his wife Sarah Catherine Augusta, daughter of the artist, Frederick Lee. The Hibbert family tree can be traced directly back to Charles II and Nell Gwynn via the younger son of their son Charles, 1st Duke of St Albans and his wife Lady Diana de Vere. Soon after Margaret Dora's birth, their family had gone to live at Broadgate House in Barnstaple in North Devon, which was owned by her mother's family. Charles Hibbert visited the family there and eventually courted his young cousin. After their marriage in August 1896, Charles and Margaret Dora lived at the White House, Abbotsham on the coast near Bideford, where 'Pa' as he was known in the family, engaged in country pursuits and lived on his income, which gradually dwindled. There were four children: Francis (Frank) born in 1897; Charles Thomas (Tom), 1899; Ida Loetitia (Gipsy), 1901; and Robert (Robin) in 1902. The two elder boys spent about six years, including some war service, in the Merchant Navy as wireless operators. In 1915 the family moved to the nearby hamlet of Landcross, where the 'boys' engaged themselves in their own engineering business – the 'Works'.

5. Verses related from memory by Ida Loetitia Williamson (née Hibbert). See Richard Williamson, introduction to *Tarka the Otter*, (Bodley Head, 1964). This edition is illustrated with photographic stills from the Rank film directed by David Cobham.

6. J.C. Tregarthen, *The Life Story of an Otter* (1909).

7. William H. Rogers, *Records of the Cheriton Otter Hounds* (Taunton, 1925).

8. See Lois Lamplugh, *A Shadowed Man* (Wellspring, 1990; 2nd rev. edn Exmoor Press, 1991). A biography of Henry Williamson told mainly from the point of view of the friendship of the author's parents with Henry Williamson in the 1920s and 1930s, and with herself.

9. Sir John Fortescue, *The Story of a Red Deer* (Macmillan, 1897).

10. Letters from Sir John Fortescue to Henry Williamson are reproduced with the kind permission of the Fortescue estate.

11. Copy of entry in the visitor's book for Cranmere Pool for 1926 reproduced with the kind permission of Devon Library Services, Plymouth.

12. See note 10 above.

13. Printed in George Jefferson, *Edward Garnett: A Life in Literature* (Cape, 1982), p. 242: letter quoted from E. Garnett (ed.), *Letters from John Galsworthy*, 1900–1932 (Cape, 1931), p. 243.

14. These maps were reproduced in HWSJ No. 16, (September 1987) with the permission of the artist's son, accompanied by a short explanatory note by Anne Williamson.

15. The full text of the letter from T.E. Lawrence was published in *Men In Print: Essays in Literary Criticism* by T.E. Lawrence, ed. Prof. A.W. Lawrence (Golden Cockerel Press, 1940) and has been reprinted in Henry Williamson, *Threnos for T.E. Lawrence and Other Writings*, ed. John Gregory (HWS, 1994).

16. Henry Williamson, *Genius of Friendship: T.E. Lawrence* (Faber, 1941: reprinted HWS, 1988).

17. Letter reproduced with the kind permission of the trustees of Alice Warrender and the Hawthornden Trust.

18. Sarah Augusta Hibbert sent Henry's small packet of letters back to him before she died, thus this postcard is in HWLEA.

19. This article was reprinted in HWSJ, No. 27 (March 1993), pp. 40–1.

20. The text of John Macrae's letter can be found in Anne Williamson, 'The Amazing Storm that attended *The Pathway* in the USA', HWSJ, No. 20 (September 1989). This was a special issue devoted to *The Flax of Dream*.

21. Kit Williams is Becket Williams, composer, and writer on the Pyrenees. See Becket Williams, *The High Pyrenees in Summer & Winter* (Wishart, 1928).

22. The area concerned had a complicated history. The official deed documents are difficult to decipher, but from a document dated 24 June 1905 it appears that the whole area once belonged to the Fortescue estate and on that date a large area was sold to George Montague Style for £14,900, plus £720 for timber. This included farmlands and woods, Pickwell Barton, Saunton Fair and Pickwell Wood, Vyes Wood and part of Ossaborough Down. This is probably the area that was known as Pickwell Manor Estate. Style sold off 45 acres, 'area 1122', a large field north of the crossroads which included the woodland area, 'Nod. 1070', found in the V made by the roads, in March 1922. In June 1919 a mortgage for £80 for Arthur Bernard Thomas bought from William Gammon that 'parcel of land known as Ox's Park otherwise Down Close situate near Pickwell Down in the Parish of Georgeham numbered 1072 containing one acre three roods and thirtyfour perches'. On 1 December 1927 Thomas borrowed £30 using this land as security. This is countersigned as having been duly paid back on 25 October 1928, thus freeing the land for legal tender and is probably the point at which Henry Williamson concluded the sale.

23. 'Til Eulenspiegel', which interestingly translates as 'Owlglass', was the name of a German prankster who lived in Brunswick in the 1300s. Eulenspiegel was a peasant who outwitted the nobility, churchmen, and townspeople. A collection of tales relating his jests and tricks was printed in German in the 1500s. William Copland printed them in England in 1528 entitled 'Here beginneth a Merry Jest of a Man that was called Owlglass'. Probably the most famous exposition is the symphonic tonepoem 'Til Eulenspiegel' by Richard Strauss. The combination of German nationality, the translation of 'Owlglass' and the particular prank played here, make use of the phrase very apposite.

24. Burke's Peerage describes the Heygates as an ancient family emanating from Essex and Suffolk. John Heygate's uncle was Sir Frederick Gage Heygate, 3rd Baronet. He had no heir so John Heygate was to succeed to the baronetcy when his uncle died in 1940, and to inherit the family estate at Bellarena in Ireland. John Heygate's own entry reads 'Sir John Edward Nourse Heygate, 4th. Bt. of Southend.' (But of all the various addresses on many letters etc. there is not one for Southend.)

25. Cuttings in HWLEA include the *North Devon Journal*, 15 August 1929 and 29 August 1929; a Cornish newspaper, and the *Daily Express*, 12 September 1929. See also Lois Lamplugh, 'The Georgeham Village Hall Sign Incident', HWSJ, No. 29 (March 1994), p. 44.

26. Henry Williamson wrote an elaborate scenario to fit round the Tofield family in the *Chronicle* novels, which when compared with real life events can be seen to be entirely fictional, and its blending into those parts that are based on real events is a tour de force.

27. *The Gold Falcon* (Faber, 1933) where Barbara Krebs is translated into the character 'Marlene'.

CHAPTER 5

1. These three books were published as follows: (i) *The Children of Shallowford* (Faber, 1939), illustrated with photographs. The revised edition (Faber, 1959) had much of the original material deleted, which was then used in the *Chronicle* novels. A recent edition (Macdonald, 1980), has an introduction and additional material by Richard Williamson; (ii) *Goodbye West Country* (Putnam, 1937); (iii) *A Clear Water Stream*, (Faber, 1958).

2. After the railway was closed the viaduct gradually fell into disrepair, but recently the pillars were strengthened and now carry the

new main road which crosses the moors. It is now quite difficult to locate the site of Filleigh Station.

3. *The Patriot's Progress* (Geoffrey Bles, 1930) was due to be published on 29 April 1930, but a letter from A.D. Peters, Henry's literary agent who bought out Andrew Daker's firm, dated 14 April 1930 states, 'Bles has now postponed P.P. until May 6 "owing to the difficulty of obtaining supplies from the binders on account of the Easter holidays".'

4. Arnold Bennett (1867–1931), journalist, writer of over seventy books, playright, essayist, and critic, chiefly known for his novels set in the Potteries – *Anna of the Five Towns, The Clayhanger Trilogy,* and *The Old Wives' Tale* (inspired by his sojourn in Paris) – where he was born and grew up. A great friend of Lord Beaverbrook under whose influence he undertook the 'Books and Persons' series for the *Evening Standard* from 1926 until his death in 1931.

5. The full text of the review was printed in a preface written by Henry Williamson for a new edition of *The Patriot's Progress* (Macdonald, 1968), and in subsequent editions.

6. *The Journals of Arnold Bennett*, ed. Sir Newman Flower, Vol. III (Cassell, 1933), p. 280.

7. This letter is also included in the preface to *The Patriot's Progress*, op. cit. Lawrence signed the letter using his pseudonym, 'A/C Shaw'. A/C denotes aircraftman, the lowest rank in the air force.

8. This introduction was recently reprinted in Henry Williamson, *Threnos for T.E. Lawrence and Other Writings* (HWS, 1994). Heygate's book would stand comparison with Thomas Hughes, *Tom Brown's Schooldays* (1857).

9. Frank Swinnerton wrote some forty novels and twenty books of criticism. Originally a reader for Chatto & Windus, he was a highly respected critic for the *Evening News* and *The Observer*, and he was a great friend of Arnold Bennett. The small file of his letters to Henry Williamson in HWLEA, written in a small and carefully neat script, show him to be fine, fair, and friendly. He was quite able to laugh ruefully at himself

and the treatment a writer gets from critics, and had a very honest, down-to-earth view of his own work.

10. Op. cit. See Preface, note 1.

11. This is almost certainly the same lecture that he gave to the Authors' (an error for Writers') Club in New York, where he decided to enliven the proceedings by pretending to drink whisky (in the Prohibition era!) from a bottle – it was actually cold lemon tea, as he describes in *The Gold Falcon*. The basic idea behind this lecture may originate from an essay by John Middleton Murry, 'The Nature of Poetry' in his book *Discoveries* (Collins, 1924), where Murry states that 'The crucifixion of Christ is the archetype of all Shakespeare's tragedy [of which *Hamlet* is the prime example]'. Henry Williamson also used Murry's essay as source material for his 'Threnos for T.E. Lawrence', see editorial, HWSJ, No. 28, (September 1993).

That Henry Williamson also gave this lecture at Harvard is corroborated by a letter from Edward Weekes of the Atlantic Monthly Press dated April 1935, mentioning 'your visit to Boston when, following your memorable lecture at the Widener [Memorial] Library [Harvard] . . .'. I have been unable to ascertain the assignment at Yale University, but presumably Professor West would have been correct.

12. The Silver Eagle Alvis, DR 6084, celebrated its sixtieth birthday in 1990. See Richard Williamson, 'The Silver Eagle has Landed', HWSJ, No. 23, (March 1991), p. 40 and HWSJ, No. 30 (September 1994) p. 46.

13. Long accounts of this storm and its effects, and accompanying photographs appeared in the *North Devon Journal*, 11 June 1931. I am grateful to the librarian of Barnstaple Library, Ms Jamie Campbell, for providing photocopies of the accounts from the library files.

14. Edward Thomas was killed in the First World War at the battle of Arras on 19 April 1917, probably by a stray bullet fired by fleeing troops. See Edward Thomas Society newsletters for further information.

15. See Ann Thomas, 'A Visit to Henry Williamson', *John O' London's Weekly*, 25

June 1932, p. 427. Reprinted in HWSJ, No. 10 (October 1984), pp. 30–7.

16. Ibid.

17. The tower is very symbolic. It is the confessional. It is a place where only truth can be spoken. One is reminded of William Golding's *The Spire*.

18. Ian Niall, *Portrait of a Country Artist, C.F. Tunnicliffe, RA, 1901–1979*, (Gollancz, 1980), Ch. 4, 'The World of Henry Williamson'. This book was reviewed by Alan Dilnot in HWSJ, No. 2 (October 1980), p. 29.

19. From Francis Thompson, *Sister Songs* (1895). Francis Thompson (1859–1907), metaphysical poet, was addicted to opium. He was rescued from living rough on the South Bank of the Thames by Alice and Wilfred Meynell in 1888, and they supported his life and work until his health, weakened by the opium addiction, gave way to death by tuberculosis.

20. A review of *The Star-born* by Frank Kendon reprinted in HWSJ, No. 13 (March 1986), p. 25. Also see Dennis McWilliams, 'Between the Flax and the Chronicle', HWSJ, No. 13, pp. 10–24, which examines the 'Star-born' theme, pp. 16f.

21. This is the typescript page number. In *The Gold Falcon* Barbara Sincere's letter appears at the end of Chapter 49, and Henry Williamson's reply opens Chapter 50. (Chapter is hardly the right word; they are so short that they are more like scenes in a play, the acts being the section titles: 'Migration'; 'Greenwich Village Eyrie'; 'The Vision in Eldorado'; 'Home-coming'.

22. Edith Walton enumerates many of the fictional characters' real names in this review. First, she points out that the hero, Manfred, is the author of an autobiographical book called *Farewell to Poetry*, which she equates with Robert Graves, *Goodbye to All That*, and that the present publishers had previously published Graves's recent books, and that Graves is an intimate friend of Sherston Savage (Siegried Sassoon) and Colonel G.B. Everest (Lawrence of Arabia). Then a list: Adolf Stucley (Aldous Huxley); Wallington Christie (Middleton Murry); P.B. Bradford (J.B. Priestley); Mark Cradocks Speuffer

(Ford Madox Hueffer); Harold Vigor Tinby (Henry Seidel Canby); Alick Peace (Alec Waugh); David Torrence (D.H. Lawrence); etc. In a revised edition of *The Gold Falcon* (Faber, 1947) Henry used several, but not all of the real names of his characters. But in 1969, in a proposed new edition that I, acting as his secretary, was handling for him, he was again going to revert to the original 'noms-de-plume'. Unfortunately, the publisher pulled out at the last moment and no new edition ensued.

23. In 1956 Henry Williamson wrote a note on this letter to make it quite clear what its contents referred to; his intention was that it should be used by his biographer in due course. In a letter from Ann Thomas to myself in recent years, Ann related that Biddy and her parents were very kind to her, and she did not think they knew her history (i.e. that Henry was the father of her child), which says a great deal about the genuine manners and kindness of Gertrude and Biddy.

24. Ann Thomas recently very kindly returned this letter to me for insertion into HWLEA.

25. *The Diaries of Evelyn Waugh*, ed. Michael Davie (Weidenfeld & Nicolson, 1976). Evelyn Waugh (1902–66), writer of satirical novels, had married Evelyn Gardner (the Hon. Evelyn, youngest daughter of the 1st Baron Burghclere) in 1928.

26. Auberon Waugh, son of Evelyn, in an obituary of his Uncle Alec, as related in Humphrey Carpenter, *The Brideshead Generation* (Weidenfeld & Nicolson, 1989), p. 51.

27. See 'Tribute to V.M. Yeates' dated January 1935, printed as an introduction to the second impression of Victor Yeates, *Winged Victory* (Cape, 1934; 2nd impression 1935). This tribute first appeared as 'V.M. Yeates: A Personal Tribute' by Henry Williamson in *John O'London's Weekly* (26 January 1935), where it had additional passages of quotation which were unnecessary in the introduction to the book itself. This was recently reprinted in *Threnos for T.E. Lawrence and Other Writings*, op. cit., p. 93.

28. *Romeo and Juliet*, Act II, Scene 2. Juliet speaking after the balcony scene:
    'O for a falc'ner's voice, To lure this tassel-gentle back again.'

29. In real life the Renshaw family is related to Ida Loetitia Hibbert, through her cousin Mary (Lady Mary Bagot née Hibbert), who was Loetitia's bridesmaid (see Ch. 4).

30. CHWE is Ann Edmonds' father, Major C. Harold W. Edmonds, OBE, MIEE, M. Inst. T., Director of 'Ormiston's Alumina Ltd.', known to Henry as 'Monk' Edmonds.

31. Henry Williamson arranged for John Heygate to send a telegram as if from Hollywood offering HW a job – to impress the Edmonds and to give HW an excuse to make a dramatic exit. (Information contained within HWLEA.)

32. A large part of this letter is reproduced in Henry Williamson's introduction to *Winged Victory*, op. cit. (note 23). Note that whereas in the letter itself it is 'O fortunate tu', Williamson printed it as 'O fortunatus tu'.

33. Full accounts of this meeting on board the *Berengaria* between Henry Williamson, T.E. Lawrence and John Heygate can be found in *Devon Holiday*, Chapter 7.

34. I. Waveney Girvan, the man who wrote the *Bibliography* of Henry Williamson's early work.

35. Miss Emma Mills was the same who presided over the Authors' (? Writers') Society lecture that HW gave in New York in 1930. She in her turn had reminded him of Mrs Dawson Scott who had instigated the Tomorrow Club (later PEN) which HW joined in 1919.

36. See the *North Devon Journal*, 15 March 1934. I am grateful to the librarian at Barnstaple Library, North Devon, Ms Jamie Campbell, for providing photocopies of the newspaper accounts of this fire (the clipping referred to is not in the archive), and attendant material. There was a further disaster at Castle Hill. The pictures saved from the original fire were brought back to be reinstated in the house after the restorations were completed. As they arrived late in the day they were left for the night in the van in which they had travelled, which was parked in the garage. Van and garage were engulfed by fire during the night, this time destroying the paintings, many of which were priceless; see the *North Devon Journal*, 15 March 1934, and Christopher Hussey, 'The Rebuilding of Castle Hill, Devon, The Seat of the Earl Fortescue', *Country Homes and Gardens Old & New* (date not given on the photocopy provided).

37. These sections were changed before eventual publication and 'Alethea' was never printed – but later transposed for the early 'Lucy' descriptions in the *Chronicle* (in an early TS the name was 'Alethea').

38. This handwritten note was reproduced in the introduction to the second impression of *Winged Victory*, op. cit., and thus reprinted in *Threnos* (HWS), op. cit.

39. Originally there were two gates, 'Top' and 'Lower', which was almost on the crossroads. After HW's death Devon County Council decided the lower entrance/exit was too dangerous and ordered it to be closed.

40. See Ann Welch, *Happy to Fly – An Autobiography* (John Murray, 1983). In this book Ann gives the most casual reference to Henry Williamson; his son 'John Willy', as John Williamson is known in gliding circles, gets slightly more attention. In the Second World War Ann was one of those women who as a member of the Air Transport Auxiliary delivered aeroplanes new from the factories to the operational units, a job calling for great skill and bravery. After the war she became involved in gliding, running the National Gliding Championships where she became a friend of Henry's second son, John Williamson, famous in the gliding world.

41. The second impression of the book is dated November 1934 but it cannot possibly have been published before at the earliest January 1935.

42. Despite continuous rumours to the contrary ever since Lawrence's death, there is nothing whatsoever in this letter to connect T.E. Lawrence with a peace movement to do with Hitler or Fascism, as was to be suggested by Henry Williamson himself, and thus taken up by others in the future. To try and dispel the controversy that there has been over its content, the full text of the letter was printed in my article 'The Genius of Friendship' HWSJ, No. 27, op. cit.

However, due to an error of my own an important phrase was omitted from a sentence on p. 32, twelve lines from the bottom, which should have read: 'I am reading / through Yeates' 60,000 fragment *FAMILY LIFE I wish I knew /* what I thought of it.' This article clarifies all the details of their friendship and the later controversy.

43. Henry Williamson, *Genius of Friendship: T.E. Lawrence* (Faber 1941; reprinted to celebrate the centenary of the birth of T.E. Lawrence, HWS, August 1988). The story of the friendship and correspondence between HW and TEL. Despite careful search of the large file of newspaper reports of this event in HWLEA, I have been unable to find any mention of who was in attendance at TEL's bedside before he died, apart from the various physicians, and TEL's brother, Professor A.W. Lawrence.

44. Ibid., closing sentence.

45. This article does not seem to have been published at this time. Lawrence's executor, Professor A.W. Lawrence, put an embargo on any use of material from Lawrence's letters at this time, thus it would have had to be withdrawn. This article is almost certainly that which was later to be published as *Genius of Friendship*, op. cit.

46. For further background see Richard Williamson, introduction to *The Illustrated Salar the Salmon* (Webb & Bower, 1987).

47. Ibid.

48. A staggart is a young deer that attaches itself to a master buck to learn 'the trade', much as a young man acted as squire to a knight in medieval days, or an apprentice to a master craftsman.

49. Guy Priest, 'Remembering Henry Williamson', HWSJ, No. 4 (November 1981), p. 17; 'Further Memories', HWSJ, No. 6 (November 1982), p. 12; 'More Memories', HWSJ, No. 8 (November 1983), p. 30; 'More Memories', HWSJ, No. 25, (March 1992), p. 35.

CHAPTER 6

1. Books by John Heygate include: *Decent Fellows* (Cape, 1930); *Talking Picture* (Cape, 1934); *White Angel* (Cape, 1934); *Motor Tramp* (Cape, 1935); *These Germans* (Hutchinson, 1940); *Kurumba* (Eyre & Spottiswoode, 1949); *A House for Joanna* (Cape, 1937).

2. Information contained in a letter from John Heygate to HW in HWLEA, dated 1 August 1935.

3. Henry Williamson's son Richard, who knew Heygate well, has many stories of his wild behaviour.

4. In my article 'The Genius of Friendship', HWSJ, No. 27, op. cit., I stated very definitely that there was no actual evidence to connect John Heygate with Nazism. This statement has to be reviewed in the light of this new information. It was very naive not to realize the import of the fact that the Ufa film company was under the control of Goebbels as Minister of Propaganda. Neither did I know at the time of writing that article that Henry Williamson was staying with John Heygate on the day of Lawrence's death. Coupled with the above, this must reinforce my supposition, stated in that article, that the connection that HW was to make between Lawrence and Hitler must have originated in a large part with John Heygate.

5. *Motor Tramp*, op. cit.

6. John Heygate, 'Missing: The Real Englishman', *Daily Express*, 8 October 1931, p. 10.

7. In his letter Heygate mentions funds: 'I have money available at the moment.' He may have been referring to money he was about to inherit from his dying father or, possibly, he may have been claiming this on expenses, either from Ufa or even the Nazi Party direct. As far as I can discern from the papers in the archive, HW thought the money was Heygate's own and that Heygate was making a kind gesture to a good friend.

8. John Heygate, *These Germans* (Hutchinson, 1940). Heygate had attended Heidelburg University in 1924 and had seen how Hitler had freed southern Germany from communism, 'The Red Terror', thus making Hitler a hero to his countrymen. In providing this historical background Heygate makes it very understandable how Hitler rose to power. Doubtless Heygate

had discussed all these points many times with Williamson.

9. Henry Williamson, 'The Tragic Spirit', *Adelphi*, Vol. 20, No. 1 (October–December, 1943).

10. Dr J.W. Blench, 'Henry Williamson and the Romantic Appeal of Fascism', Part I, *Durham University Journal*, Vol. L, No. 1 (December 1988), pp. 123–39. Part II, *Durham University Journal*, Vol. L, No. 2 (June 1989), pp. 289–305. Readers of this excellent analysis must take into account that at the time he wrote it Dr Blench was totally unaware of the true content of Henry Williamson's last letter to T.E. Lawrence, assuming that HW had told the truth that it contained arrangements for a proposed meeting at the Albert Hall which Lawrence would lead.

11. The germ of this concept first grew in my mind in 1986 when formulating a letter in answer to Padraig Cullen, 'Henry Williamson: The New European', *Scorpion*, No. 8 (spring 1985), p. 15: see Anne Williamson, 'Letter to the Editor', *Scorpion*, No. 10 (autumn 1986), p. 44., where I state that a better title for the article would have been 'Twentieth-century Romantic'; see also Anne Williamson, 'Editorial', HWSJ, No. 16 (*Tarka* Diamond Jubilee issue, September 1987) where I stated that *Tarka the Otter* was a perfect example of a novel in the Romantic tradition: its subject matter is nature, it is a prime example of imaginative freedom, has a poetic form, and uses language with vividness, informality, and originality: all parameters of Romanticism.

12. *The Romantic Spirit in German Art 1790–1990*, ed. Keith Hyartley (Scottish National Gallery and Hayward Gallery, 1994).

13. Little, Brown recently took over Macdonald in England. They are reprinting Henry Williamson's *Collected Nature Stories*, a multivolume book containing a selection of HW's best early stories as their contribution to celebrate the centenary of HW's birth in December 1995.

14. The Sitwells – Dame Edith, Sir Osbert, and Sacheverell – were highly critical of forms of writing that did not coincide with their own views. They were particularly critical of the Georgian poets and were modernist in their own styles; thus they would have been critical of HW's style and form of writing. Richard Williamson thinks Henry bought the stuffed bream in an antique shop.

15. *Hamlet*, Act I, Scene 4.

16. Geoffrey West, 'Review', *Time and Tide*, 16 May 1936.

17. *Methodist Times & Leader*, 14 May 1936.

18. The *Bristol Evening Post*, 12 May 1936 and *News Review*, 14 May 1936.

19. See John Gregory, 'Henry Williamson and the BBC', HWSJ, No. 29 (March 1994), pp. 5–22, for comprehensive coverage of this subject. The texts of the broadcasts have been published by the HWS, ed. John Gregory: Vol. 1, *Spring Days in Devon and Other Broadcasts*; Vol. 2, *Pen and Plough, Further Broadcasts*. This also contains a check list of the radio broadcasts.

20. *Goodbye West Country* is dedicated to 'The Migrants' – 'Loetitia, Ann, Robin, Windles, John, Margaret, Robert, Rosemary, and Richard'.

CHAPTER 7

1. Henry Williamson, *The Story of a Norfolk Farm* (Faber, 1941).

2. Giles de la Mare, son of Richard, confirmed in a telephone conversation that the 'cottage on the Norfolk coast' was at East Runton near Cromer.

3. There is no date on the letter but Henry Williamson himself wrote on it '6 weeks before my mother died'. Richard Williamson confirms that there was a tremendous flood in north Norfolk in August 1912, which is commemorated in Stiffkey village on a 'flood pole'.

4. Ann Thomas stated in a letter to me in recent years that she and Loetitia discussed their doubts about this venture.

5. Henry Williamson must have written to his Aunt Mary Leopoldina about the farm project asking her to loan him money or to take a share in the farm, for a letter from her shows that she reacted very unfavourably and did not think the project a good idea at all. She wrote quite sharply

about it, and never made any money available.

6. Guy Priest, 'Further Memories of Henry Williamson', HWSJ, No. 6 (October 1982), pp. 12–19. The novel was never published.

7. The Edward Thomas Memorial Stone on the 'Shoulder of Mutton' hillside at Steep, near Petersfield in Hampshire, is the focus of the Edward Thomas Society Birthday Walk undertaken every spring by its members. For further details see the Edward Thomas Fellowship, Bridgwater, Somerset.

8. See Alan Dilnot, 'Henry Williamson's Contributions to Mosley's *Action*', HWSJ, No. 22 (September 1990), pp. 18–21. It is an interesting point that in his autobiography Sir Oswald Mosley, *My Life* (Thomas Nelson, 1968), Mosley only refers to Henry Williamson in passing, which shows that HW really held little importance to him other than as loyal friend, a point borne out by Diana Mosley, in 'A Tribute to Henry Williamson' in *Henry Williamson, The Man, The Writings: A Symposium*, ed. Father Brocard Sewell (Tabb House, 1980).

9. See Jean Goodman, 'Artistic Friendships', HWSJ, No. 30 (September 1994), pp. 48–53, where it is pointed out that Munnings also had a deep down-side opposite of the up-swing.

10. This incident is related in ibid. See also Henry Williamson, 'A Riotous Artist' (a review of Sir Alfred Munnings, *The Second Burst* (Museum Press, 1951), first published in *John O' London's Weekly*, Vol. LX, No. 1429, 1951, and reprinted in HWSJ, No. 30 (September 1994), pp. 54–6).

11. Letters in HWLEA between Henry and his wife refer to this.

12. Henry unfailingly referred to her as Mrs North in his diary. She was in fact the Hon. Mrs Meriel North, and is portrayed as Lady Penelope Carnoy in the *Chronicle* novels, although the references in the diaries give no indication of the depth of friendship the novel would suggest. Her daughter attended the famous 'free-spirit' Summerhill School at Leiston.

13. Apart from incorporating this episode into the *Chronicle*, Henry Williamson also elected to publish it as a small limited edition *In The Woods* (St Albert's Press,

1960) to help raise money for the *Aylesford Review*.

14. See Edward Seago, *Peace in War*, op. cit (Introduction). After Henry's death his beneficiaries gave the portrait to the National Portrait Gallery, London.

15. In the *Chronicle* Henry describes Phillip striking Lucy during a similar quarrel. Richard Williamson remembers that Henry did strike Loetitia at some point for he remembers John protectively leading their mother out into the garden while her nose bled, so possibly it was at this time.

16. Reginald Pound (1894–1991), journalist and biographer, mentioned Henry Williamson in several of his books. Although they were fairly friendly and there are a few letters from Reginald Pound this is the only reference to him within the archive papers.

17. See Daniel Farson, *Henry: An Appreciation of Henry Williamson*, (Michael Joseph, 1982).

18. This incident can be found in Chapter 18, 'Relief' of *Lucifer Before Sunrise*.

19. One internee, Olive Hawke (Mrs Burdett) wrote to Henry Williamson from Holloway Prison where she had been interned for two and a half years, asking for his help to publish the book she had written, *What Hope for Green Street*. Letters from Jarrolds Publishers and Ethel Mannin show that he did his best for her.

20. Henry himself knew the diaries for 1943, 1944 and 1945 were missing for he made a note (undated) to that effect in the 1946 diary.

21. For confirmation of this fact see 'Records of the National Farm Surveys of England and Wales, 1940–1943', Public Record Office where Henry Williamson's Farm Record is reproduced. Interestingly this official record mentions HW's books about the farm.

22. Lilias Rider Haggard and Henry Williamson, *Norfolk Life* (Faber, 1943).

23. Sir Henry Rider Haggard (1856–1925) was the author of many books of which *King Solomon's Mines* (1885), *She* (1887), and *Allan Quartermaine* (1887) are the best known. Less well known was his work on farming *A Farmer's Year* (1889) of which there is a copy in HWLEA, but it is not possible to ascertain whether Henry

obtained this before or after his meeting with Lilias Rider Haggard.

24. Henry Williamson, *Green Fields and Pavements: A Norfolk Farmer in Wartime*, ed. John Gregory, with an introduction by William (Bill/Windles) Williamson, (HWS, February, 1995). This collection of Henry Williamson's articles from the *Eastern Daily Press* distils the essence of his life and thoughts of the farm era.

25. Reprinted in Henry Williamson, *Breath of Country Air*, Pt 1, pp. 55–6.

26. Macdonald Hastings, 'A Norfolk Farmer's Shoot', *Picture Post*, Vol. 21, No. 6 (6 November 1943), pp. 17–20. Henry himself mentioned the incident (25 October 1943) in 'Pheasants and Partridges' in *The Green Fields and Pavements* series in the *Eastern Daily Press* reprinted by HWS 1995 (op. cit.).

27. *Breath of Country Air*, Pt 4, p. 86.

28. There has always been the suggestion that Henry Williamson offered the farm to Windles to farm on behalf of the family and that Windles refused it. Windles states that this was not exactly so. It was mentioned very casually through a third party. He stipulated that he would need a large tractor to do the job, not the tiny Ferguson; the idea was never mentioned again.

29. See *The National Farm Survey, 1941–1943*, Public Record Office, where the Old Hall Farm and Henry Williamson are given considerable prominence, including mention of *The Story of a Norfolk Farm* and *Lucifer Before Sunrise*. Ref. MAF 32/739/351.

CHAPTER 8

1. These articles are included in Henry Williamson, *A Breath of Country Air*, Pt II, ed. John Gregory (HWS, 1991).

2. St John Horsfall was killed a year or two after winning the Belgian Grand Prix when the ERA he was driving crashed at Silverstone.

3. Underborough was owned by a rich American family who let the Elwins live there.

4. Henry Williamson, 'A Reverie of Exmoor', *West Country Magazine*, No. 1, (summer 1946), pp. 6–9.

5. John Braine was born and educated in Bradford and became a librarian there after the war. At this time he may have been secretary to the Literary Society. His first novel, *Room at the Top*, in the 'angry young man' genre, was not published until 1957.

6. Cyrus Brooks was with A.M. Heath Literary Agents, who had handled Henry's books since A.D. Peters gave up the Andrew Dakers agency, and who continued to handle them right through Henry's life, and afterwards on behalf of the Henry Williamson Literary Estate.

7. Kenneth Allsop, *Adventure Lit Their Star* (Latimer House, 1949). This book won the John Llewellyn Rhys Memorial Prize the following year.

8. Henry Williamson, 'Birth of the Phasian Bird', *Adelphi*, ed. J.M. Murry, Vol. 24, No. 4 (July–September 1948), pp. 199–205.

9. Henry Williamson, 'The Doom of the Peregrine Falcon', *Adelphi*, ed. J.M. Murry, Vol. II, No. 4 (September 1924), pp. 345–7.

10. James Farrar, *The Unreturning Spring* (Williams & Norgate, 1950), ed. and with an introduction by Henry Williamson. New edn (Chatto & Windus, 1968). Henry Williamson's introduction is reprinted in *Threnos for T.E. Lawrence & Other Writings*, ed. John Gregory (HWS, 1994). James Farrar had been a navigator in the war and was killed in July 1944 while engaging a doodle-bug (V1 rocket) in his Mosquito fighter-bomber – his plane just disappeared, presumably blown up with the doodle-bug. He was just twenty years old. There are several references to James Farrar in various issues of HWSJ.

11. See Anne Williamson, 'The Genius of Friendship: Part II: Richard Aldington', HWSJ, No. 28 (September 1993), pp. 7 ff; also, Alister Kershaw, 'Henry Williamson', in ibid., pp. 24–33.

12. Henry Williamson, 'Words on the West Wind', *Adelphi*, Vol. 25, No. 1 (October–December 1948); Vol. 25, No. 2 (January–March 1949); Vol. 25, No. 3 (misnamed 2) (April–June 1949); and also continued in issues edited by George Godwin: Vol. 25, No. 4 (July–September 1949); Vol. 26, No. 1 (autumn, 1949); Vol. 26, No. 2 (January–March 1950).

CHAPTER 9

1. The fact that the caravan survived so well was mainly due to a great deal of work on the part of Robert and Richard who between them maintained it by painting and repairing it every summer.

2. Henry described this visit to France in 'Words on the West Wind', *Adelphi*, Vol. 26, No. 1 (autumn 1949); see also Anne Williamson 'The Genius of Friendship, Pt. 2, Richard Aldington', HWSJ, No. 28 (September 1993), pp. 7–21; and in ibid., 'Henry Williamson, "Dear Friend of Lavandou"', pp. 22–4, reprinted from *Richard Aldington: An Intimate Portrait*, ed. Alister Kershaw and F.J. Temple (Illinois University Press, 1965); and also Alister Kershaw, 'Henry Williamson', HWSJ, No. 28 (September 1993), pp. 24–33. Henry continued with a description of the journey to Milan in 'Words on the West Wind', *Adelphi*, Vol. 26, No. 2 (January–March 1950).

3. In the years immediately following Henry Williamson's death in which I have been administrating his literary estate, the Bompiani Italian editions of *Tarka la Lontra* and *Salar il Salmone* sold very well indeed.

4. Giles de la Mare (Director, Faber), Richard's son, in a recent telephone conversation with the author, said that he knew his father had objected strongly to HW's political views.

5. Review cutting in HWLEA, *Horse and Hound*, 24 December 1949; anonymous short review.

6. Review cutting in HWLEA, *The Scotsman*, 15 December 1949.

7. Janet Wilson, 'Reviews', *Socialist Leader*, 26 November 1949.

8. William Thomson, Canadian by birth, was an artist of some repute, who had trained at the school of Kokoshka in Switzerland. Henry and Bill got on very well together – they appreciated each other's wild streak – and remained friends throughout, although Bill and Margaret were divorced in due course. In about 1964 Bill painted a portrait of Henry, and Henry commissioned portraits of all his family.

9. The Elwins now lived in one of the small group of houses facing the beach next to the 'Black Rock' at the foot of Pickwell Down, Underborough being too big for them now their children were independent. The Williamson family called this group of very modern houses the 'Cheese Rind', which they rather resembled.

10. An entry in Henry's diary for 16 May 1951 refers to his fury at the discovery that Christine had registered the names as Michael Henry, and not Michael Harry as he had presumed: and that Mrs Duffield always called the child 'Christopher', which annoyed him intensely.

11. Henry did later complain that the house had been sold for too little (although he had made about £1,000 profit on his original purchase, a considerable amount in those days). In actual fact it was only £150 less than the price he had suggested. He also grew very irritable over the sale of the unwanted furniture at an auction in Bury St Edmunds at the beginning of November, when he decided most items had been sold for far less than they should have fetched, in his absence, especially his grandfather clocks. Henry added a waspish entry in his diary about this in later years, but it was put wrongly into an entry for 24 March 1946, under an original entry of 'Sale of furniture at Botesdale' which must have been an auction he attended at that time. He frequently told other people that the little three-legged walnut table on which he wrote *Tarka* was rescued by Margaret, who paid 6 shillings for it (inferring that it should not have been in the sale). Henry himself made the original list of all the furniture and effects at Bank House, marking what belonged to 'HW' and what to 'ILW', and what was to be sold and what kept. This particular table was not marked as belonging to anyone (and certainly not as 'the table that *Tarka* was written on'), and Henry himself marked its suggested sale price as 10 shillings. Loetitia marked up her copy of the sale catalogue with the prices achieved at the sale, and against this item she put 'bought by MM [Margaret] for 10/-', which was the actual price suggested by Henry himself. Henry's original manuscript list, the printed auction catalogue marked

up by Loetitia, and a letter from her to Henry dated 4 November 1950 mentioning that 'Margie bought the round 3-legged table, she loved it & wanted it for her studio' are all in HWLEA.

12. George Painter (see Preface, note 5).

13. Ibid.

14. Alan Clark, review of Martin Gilbert, *First World War* (Weidenfeld & Nicolson, 1994), in *The Guardian*, 13 September 1994, and also in the *Evening Standard*.

15. S.P.B. Mais, review of *The Dark Lantern*, *Oxford Mail*, 29 November 1951.

16. At this time Richard was sixteen and a half years old and still at Blundell's Public School at Tiverton. He recollects feeling totally overwhelmed by such an idea at that time, and not knowing how to deal with it. Richard went on to become a naturalist and author in his own right, with a career as the warden of Kingley Vale National Nature Reserve near Chichester. His first book was *The Dawn is My Brother* (Faber, 1958) (runner up for the Llewellyn Rhys Prize, 1960); followed by *Capreol, the Story of a Roe Buck* (Macdonald, 1972); and *The Great Yew Forest* (Macmillan, 1978). He has written introductions to several recent editions of his father's books, and chapters in a variety of natural history compilations; also a weekly 'Nature Trails' article for over thirty years, and many television scripts and appeared in several of his own television programmes.

17. The actual quotation is:
> Not I, not I, but the wind that blows through me.
> A fine wind is blowing the new direction of Time
> (D.H. Lawrence 'Song of a Man Who has Come Through', 1917)

Henry used neither this title nor 'The Wind's Will', which he referred to for a while.

18. E.W. Martin was to prove a staunch friend and helped Henry with such jobs as proof-reading over many years. He contributed an essay, 'Henry Williamson: the Power of the Dead', in *Henry Williamson, the Man the Writings. A symposium*, ed. Father Brocard Sewell (Tabb House, 1980).

19. Sir John Heygate (he inherited the baronetcy and Irish estate at Bellarena on the death of his uncle in 1940) had divorced his second wife (by whom he had two sons) in 1947, after the disastrous denouement of coming home from the war to find she was having an affair with a home-based officer. John went berserk and did some very wild things at that time, spending money prodigiously, which resulted in him having to take out a second mortgage on the Bellarena estate, and then spending the rest of his life working desperately hard to try and keep things together. In December 1951 he married Dora Luz, third daughter of John Harvey and the former wife of Lt. Col. Rollo Gillespie, by whom she had four daughters, who all lived either at Bellarena or nearby. John and Dora were devoted to each other and he was devastated by her eventual illness and death.

20. A transcript of the programme is in HWLEA.

21. For a fuller exploration of the background of this episode, see Anne Williamson, 'The Genius of Friendship, Pt 2: Richard Aldington', HWSJ, No. 28 (September, 1993), pp. 7–21, and F.D. Crawford 'The Weather-Vane Soul of Henry Williamson', HWSJ, No. 30 (September 1994), pp. 5–21.

22. Richard Aldington, *Lawrence of Arabia, A Biographical Enquiry* (Collins, 1955).

23. Henry Williamson, 'Threnos for T.E. Lawrence: Pt I', *European*, No. 15 (May 1954), pp. 44–61; 'Pt II' *European*, No. 16 (June 1954), pp. 43–60. Reprinted in Henry Williamson, *Threnos for T.E. Lawrence and Other Writings* (HWS, 1994), pp. 1–36.

24. Henry Williamson, 'Review of *The Home Letters of T.E. Lawrence and His Brothers*, ed. A.R. Lawrence (Blackwell, 1954)' published in *John O'London's Weekly*, 2 July 1954, and a further review in the *European* (November 1954). Radio broadcast in *Book Review*, West of England Home Service, 24 August 1954, transcript printed in Henry Williamson, *Pen and Plough*, ed. John Gregory (HWS, 1993). Henry Williamson also recorded another talk about Lawrence in a programme fronted by Charles Causley, *Signature*, on 2 March 1955; and a television programme which went out on 28 November 1968.

25. Ruth Tomalin has written many books. She contributed an essay on Henry, 'Patriot's Progress' in the *Symposium* ed. F. Brocard Sewell (op. cit.; see note 18 above).

26. The essay was eventually published posthumously in a collection of essays compiled by Murry's widow, J. Middleton Murry, *Katherine Mansfield and other Literary Studies*, foreword by T.S. Eliot (Constable, 1959). In her compiler's note Mary Middleton Murry stated: 'The series of novels by Henry Williamson, which are the subject of the last essay, were very highly thought of by John Middleton Murry. He considered it of real importance that Henry Williamson should be fully recognized as one of the great novelists of the generation and therefore was most anxious that this essay should be published. After writing the essay, he read *A Fox Under my Cloak*, the fifth of the present series of novels, and noted: "It is altogether worthy of its predecessors".' Two further volumes of the *Chronicle* had been published in between. At the end of the essay Henry Williamson has written in his copy 'Bless you, dearest Jack Murry! . . . Now I must on with Chapter 3 of *A Test to Destruction*.' Henry wrote to T.S. Eliot apropos his Foreword to Murry's book for a short note from Eliot on Faber headed paper is pasted into the front of the volume; 'What you say about my Preface gives me great pleasure and what you imply about your friendship for John Murry warms my feelings.'

27. Henry had two typists working for him at this time. It would seem that Elizabeth Tippett did the first typing from the manuscript and perhaps major revisions, and the other girl, a Miss Walker, did final drafts.

28. Christine currently taught at a little school in Croyde.

29. Colin Wilson 'Henry Williamson and his Writings – A Personal View', HWSJ, No. 2 (October 1980), pp. 9–20.

30. For background see Father Brocard Sewell, 'The Aylesford Review', HWSJ, No. 5 (May 1982), pp. 23–6. This issue also contains 'A Checklist of Articles on or by Henry Williamson in the *Aylesford Review*, 1957–1967', pp. 27–9.

31. 'Henry Williamson: A Symposium and Tribute', *Aylesford Review*, Vol. II, No. 2 (winter 1957/8), ed. Father Brocard Sewell, included: 'Henry Williamson', editorial by Father Brocard Sewell, pp. 33–7; 'Williamson, the London Novels', W. Gore-Allen, pp. 37–41; 'Henry Williamson, an English Proust', Malcolm Elwin, pp. 42–8; 'The Novels of Henry Williamson', John Middleton Murry, pp. 49–55; 'Some Notes on *The Flax of Dream* and *A Chronicle of Ancient Sunlight*', Henry Williamson, pp. 56–61.

32. *Henry Williamson The Man, the Writings: A Symposium*, ed. F. Brocard Sewell (Tabb House, 1980) with contributions from Ruth Tomalin, Kerstin Hegarty, Alexander Burgess, Diana Mosley, Brocard Sewell, Sylvia Bruce, Hugh Cecil, E.W. Martin, David Hoyle, Roger Mortimer, Oswald Jones, reprints of Williamson's own essays originally published in the *Aylesford Review* (see Note 31 above), and the memorial address given by Ted Hughes at a service in St Martin-in-the-Fields, London, on 1 December 1977.

33. These articles have been reprinted in Henry Williamson, *From a Country Hilltop*, ed. John Gregory (HWS, 1988).

34. See 'Out of the Prisoning Tower', *The Spectator*, 22 August 1958, pp. 243–4.

35. The Wedmore had been inaugurated by Miss Millicent Wedmore in memory of her father, Sir Frederick Wedmore, author and critic, and it was an honour to be asked to be the speaker. There are several charming letters from Miss Wedmore in the HWLEA, and to mark the occasion she presented HW with a little volume of her own poems, *From a Cornish Moor* (J. Stevens Cox, 1956).

36. Henry Williamson, 'Some Nature Writers and Civilisation', Wedmore Memorial Lecture 1958, published in *Essays For Divers Hands, being the Transactions of the Royal Society of Literature*, New Series, Vol. XXX, ed. N. Hardy Wallis (Oxford University Press, 1960), and reprinted in *Threnos for T.E. Lawrence and Other Writings*, op. cit.

37. Goronwy Rees, 'New Novels', review of *Love and the Loveless* (and other books) in *The Listener*, 18 December 1958, p. 1046.

38. Henry Williamson, *The Children of Shallowford*, rev. edn (Faber, 1959).

39. Richard Williamson recalls the thrill of hearing and seeing newly imported wolves prowling in the severe frost and cold. Henry was too miserable to take anything in. On leaving the party they could not find the way out and ended up climbing over the fence. Henry worried about missing the last train back, and hailed a passing motorist and demanded that he take them to Liverpool Street Station; despite the driver's protests, Henry won, and the poor man went out of his way to do this!

40. Ted Hughes (1930–), poet and author, Poet Laureate 1984, read the address at Henry's memorial service, published in *Symposium*, op. cit. (see above, note 32).

41. At this time Richard was training in forestry and farm management to prepare for a career in the Nature Conservancy (now English Nature). He was also writing a daily nature column for the *Daily Mail*. Sarah was at a private day school nearby, for which Richard contributed a large part of his small earnings for her fees, as Henry felt unable to afford them.

42. In his introduction to the *Symposium* (op. cit.) Ronald Duncan infers that Henry gatecrashed their holiday party willy-nilly. Henry's diary shows that this was discussed and *then* he went out to order his ticket. He understood that he had been invited. But that may have been due to a misunderstanding. Duncan's style in this contribution is somewhat flippant which in retrospect gives a generally false impression.

43. A short account of their friendship can be found in Kerstin Hegarty, 'Henry', in *Symposium*, op. cit.

44. In Greek legend, Galatea was one of the Nereids, the fifty daughters of Nereus, 'The Old Man of the Sea', who were all fair virgins with golden hair. Galatea was courted by the Cyclops but she preferred a young herdsman, Acis, and when the Cyclops crushed Acis under a boulder, Galatea used her power to change her beloved into a river, to flow eternally.

45. The Savage Club had had to amalgamate with the National Liberal Club due to difficult financial circumstances.

46. Ann Quin, *Berg* (Calder, 1964). This book gained enormous attention when it was first published; quite extraordinarily so since it was brutal and fairly obscene. No critic, including those who helped her to gain two worthwhile travelling scholarships, seemed to have noticed that the book bore a distinct resemblance to S.M. Synge, *Playboy of the Western World*, one of the great plays of Irish drama and first performed at the Abbey Theatre, Dublin, in 1907. In this play a character called 'Widow Quinn' gives the hero Christy Mahon his first experience of love. Ann eventually committed suicide

47. A summary of a talk given by Patrick Garland (who has had a distinguished career, including Director of the prestigious Chichester Festival Theatre) about his friendship with Henry Williamson at the HWS AGM in 1987 can be found in HWSJ, No. 17 (March, 1988), p. 48.

48. Sue Caron, *A Screw Loose* (B & T Publishers, 1977), Ch. 2 'A Glimpse of Ancient Sunlight', pp. 41–59: reprinted in a limited edn, *A Glimpse of Ancient Sunlight* (Aylesford Press, 1986) with a foreword by Father Brocard Sewell.

49. Henry Williamson, 'A First Adventure with Francis Thompson', in Francis Thompson, *The Mistress of Vision* (Saint Albert's Press, 1966). This essay is slightly more erudite and revealing than the following one.

50. Henry Williamson, 'In Darkest England', in Francis Thompson, *The Hound of Heaven – A Commemorative Volume*, ed. G. Krishnamurti (Francis Thompson Society, 1967). This was the text of his presidential speech to the society in January 1967. This volume contains a selection of essays which, although directly concerned with the work of Francis Thompson, can equally be applied to that of Henry Williamson. Henry's essay is reprinted in *Threnos for T.E. Lawrence*, op. cit.

51. All these articles have been collected and reprinted in Henry Williamson, *Days of Wonder*, ed. John Gregory (HWS, 1987).

52. Towards the end of the Second World War Richard Richardson served as a young soldier in India. He regularly sent to Richard Williamson aerogrammes about bird life which he illustrated with the detailed and

intricate paintings and drawings for which he was to become famous.

53. Earl Haig very kindly made copies of Henry Williamson's letters to him available to HWLEA through one of the HWS members, Ian Abernethy, for which I am very grateful. It is from his accompanying letter to Ian Abernethy that the quotation and paraphrase have been drawn.

54. A transcript of this half-hour programme was printed in HWSJ, No. 9, (March 1984) pp. 27–36.

55. Colin Wilson, op. cit. (see this ch. Note 29). The term 'outsider' is a reference to Wilson's second book, which made his name, *The Outsider* (1956).

56. Rolf Gardiner (1902–71) was a long-standing friend, although there is no mention of him anywhere in Henry's papers and only four letters from him exist in HWLEA. His granddaughter has recently found letters from Henry to Rolf Gardiner in their archive and has made copies available to HWLEA, for which I am very grateful. Rolf Gardiner was very involved with the Morris dance movement and the 'Musikheim' in Germany, and also in the land and communal living. He established the 'Springhead Ring' from his home at Fontmell Magna near Shaftesbury in Dorset. Henry and Rolf may have been introduced by Maurice Renshaw who was involved with Springhead as early as 1939 as he is reported in their newsletter as making a report on casual labour-gangs in Scotland, and he ran a Land Service Camp at his North Devon farm with boys from the Plymouth High School in 1940. Like Williamson, Rolf Gardiner came under an undeserved cloud because of his leanings towards Germany.

57. *The Twelfth Man: A Book of Original Contributions brought together by the Lords' Taverners in Honour of their Patron HRH Prince Philip Duke of Edinburgh*, ed. Martin Boddey (Cassell 1971). Henry's contribution was 'Genesis of Tarka', very similar to his 1930s radio broadcast 'The Otter' (see *Spring Days in Devon*, op. cit.).

58. These articles are reprinted in Henry Williamson, *Days of Wonder*, ed. John Gregory (HWS, 1987).

59. Henry Williamson, 'Reflections on the Death of a Field Marshal', *Contemporary Review*, Vol. 218, No. 1265 (June 1971), pp. 303–13. The editor of *Contemporary Review* was Rosalind Wade, wife of William Kean Seymour, a longstanding friend of Henry Williamson. Rosalind Wade gave a talk to the HWS AGM in October 1986, in which she recalled the friendship of these two men. A short resumé of her talk can be found in HWSJ, No. 15 (March 1987) in 'Secretary's Notes', pp. 48–9.

CHAPTER 10

1. Margaret was now separated (and later divorced) from Julian Bream.

2. Nowadays there are notices telling people not to go down the path as it is dangerous. To the Williamson family it was part of their childhood.

3. Joseph McKiernan, 'Flights of Fact and Fancy', review of *The Scandaroon*, in *Evening Chronicle*, 14 October 1972.

4. Penelope Martin, review, *Western Mail*, 28 October 1972.

5. Maurice Wiggin, 'On the Wing', review, *Sunday Times*, 22 October 1972.

6. William Foster, 'Return to Nature', *The Scotsman*, 4 November 1972.

7. Alec Hamilton, 'Henry Williamson', *Guardian* 14 October 1972, p. 10.

8. This early experience may be the clue to Henry's fixation with young girls. (Note that there is no suggestion in this that he ever approached girls under the legal age.) Moreover, it was soon after this that his mother 'deserted' him by not going with him to the war, at the time when he desperately needed her presence for comfort, thus fixing him into a psychological time-warp.

9. *The Wipers Times*, foreword by Henry Williamson; introduction, notes and glossary by Patrick Beaver (Peter Davies, 1973).

10. Edward James, on whose estate Richard and I rent a cottage, was a patron of the arts, especially surrealist paintings. He created the Edward James Foundation for Arts and Crafts at his former family home

in West Dean, Sussex, and handed over everything to his trustees. He did not take quite so placidly to his new role as I made out to Henry, but I hoped that such a ploy would be a good example for Henry to follow. Edward once asked Richard to be one of his trustees, but like Henry he changed his mind frequently (or had it changed for him). He was a lovely man, although in some ways as difficult and temperamental as Henry, and had written a novel and several volumes of poetry. He once came round when Henry was staying with us. I saw him coming up the path and told Henry who was coming; as I went to open the door Henry hid behind it and shook his head at me to gain my allegiance. Edward was used to walking in and staying for an hour or two. He must have been very surprised to find no welcome on this occasion. I don't think these two men would have got on very well together. Both liked to hold centre stage – though Edward was far better at listening to other people's share of the conversation than ever Henry was.

11. See Peter K. Robins 'Adventure Lit His Star', HWSJ, No. 28 (September 1993), pp. 34–9, and also letter from Rodney Legg, Warden of Steep Holm, in 'Letters', HWSJ, No. 29 (March 1994), p. 63.

12. Bernard Price (1933–93) writer and broadcaster, was born in Chichester, where he was known locally as 'Mr Chichester'. He was an expert on antiques, local history and countryside matters. He frequently broadcast from Bristol, hence his appearance as guest of honour on this occasion. Bernard was one of our greatest friends and godfather to our daughter Bryony. He had met Henry on various occasions at our home. He wrote about Henry in his book *Creative Landscapes of the British Isles: Writers, Painters, and Composers and their Inspiration* (Ebury Press, 1983). Henry Williamson features twice: under 'East Anglia', p. 109, and also 'South West', pp. 132–5. Incidentally, the photograph (ibid., p. 125) of Richard Jefferies' home at Coate Farm is one in which Richard Williamson bears an astonishing resemblance to Jefferies.

13. Due to family circumstances, the house was sold some time after Henry's death. Since then there have been several modifications to the original design, including the fact that the first floor has been completely filled in so that the huge cathedral-like room no longer exists. Half of the Field was sold with the house, but the family retain the other half which contains Henry's Studio and Writing Hut.

14. 'The Crake' originally appeared in an American magazine, *Esquire* (date unknown), but Henry stated that it was extensively cut at that time from his original story; see Preface, *Tales of Moorland and Estuary* (Macdonald Futura, 1981). It was first published in book form in *Tales of Moorland and Estuary* (Macdonald, 1953). 'The Crake' tells the story of fishermen in the Devon village of Appledore who are being terrorized by a dreadful portent of death, the Crake, so called because of the terrible noise heard one night, and the deaths that come to be associated with it. In the end, the Crake is revealed to be 'Orca gladiator', a grampus, the killer whale. Henry may have been making one of his well-known puns on the sound of 'whale' and 'wail'.

15. The quotation is from the last line of *Tarka the Otter*.

16. Ted Hughes's memorial address was published in *Henry Williamson: the Man, The Writings: A Symposium*, op. cit., Appendix 3, pp. 159–65.

A BIBLIOGRAPHY OF HENRY WILLIAMSON'S WRITING

This list is offered as a guide to the extent of Henry Williamson's writing. It is not exhaustive, and only first and major editions are given. Students will find further information available from the Henry Williamson Society (see p. 358), from which a fully annotated bibliography will be available in due course.

In order to make this list more readily comprehensible, the two main series *The Flax of Dream* and *A Chronicle of Ancient Sunlight* have been grouped together, although this slightly distorts the chronological order. To avoid unnecessary repetition Henry Williamson is abbreviated to HW, the Henry Williamson Society to HWS, and the society *Journal* to HWSJ.

The Flax of Dream – a tetralogy
  Vol. 1 *The Beautiful Years*, Collins, 1921; rev. edn Faber, 1929: Dutton, 1929.
  Vol. 2 *Dandelion Days*, Collins 1922; rev. edn Faber, 1930; Dutton, 1930.
  Vol. 3 *The Dream of Fair Women*, Collins, 1924; Dutton, 1924; rev. edn Faber, 1931; Dutton, 1931.
  Vol. 4 *The Pathway*, Cape, 1928; Dutton, 1929.
The Flax of Dream, a further revised edition in one volume, Faber, 1936. (This is considered to be the definitive edition, but many readers prefer the original versions.)

The Lone Swallows, Collins, 1922; rev. edn illus. by Charles F. Tunnicliffe, Putnam, 1933. (This was HW's second book.)
The Peregrine's Saga, And Other Stories of the Country Green, Collins, 1923; pub. as *The Sun Brothers*, Dutton, 1925; ed. and illus. C.F. Tunnicliffe, Putnam, 1935.
The Old Stag, Putnam, 1926, ed. and illus. C.F. Tunnicliffe, Putnam, 1933.
Tarka the Otter, Putnam, 1927; Dutton (USA), 1928; ed. and illus. C.F. Tunnicliffe, Putnam, 1932; Penguin, 1937; Puffin p/b 1949 onwards; ed. and illus. film stills, intro. Richard Williamson, Bodley Head, 1978; ed. and illus. photographs by Simon McBride, intro. Richard Williamson, Webb & Bower, 1985; Folio Society, 1995.
The Linhay on the Downs, Woburn Books, 1929.
The Ackymals, Windsor Press (USA), 1929.
The Wet Flanders Plain, Beaumont Press, 1929; Faber, 1929.
The Patriot's Progress – Being the Vicissitudes of Pte. John Bullock, illus. William Kermode, Geoffrey Bles, 1930.
The Village Book, Cape, 1930.
The Wild Red Deer of Exmoor, 1931; Faber, 1931.
The Labouring Life, Cape, 1932; pub. as *As the Sun Shines*, Dutton.
The Star-born, ed. and illus. C.F. Tunnicliffe, Faber, 1933; rev. edn illus. Mildred Eldridge, Faber, 1948.
The Gold Falcon or the Haggard of Love, Faber, 1933; rev. edn Faber, 1947.
On Foot in Devon, Maclehose, 1933.
The Linhay on the Downs and Other Adventures in the Old and the New Worlds, Cape, 1934.
Devon Holiday, Cape, 1935.

Salar the Salmon, Faber, 1935; ed. and illus. C.F. Tunnicliffe, Faber, 1936; Penguin, 1949; ed. and illus. Michael Loates, with introduction by Richard Williamson, Webb & Bower, 1987.

Goodbye West Country, Putnam, 1937; Little, Brown, 1938.

The Children of Shallowford, illus. with family photographs, Faber, 1939; rev. edn Faber, 1959; new illus. edn Macdonald, 1978.

The Story of a Norfolk Farm, Faber, 1941.

Genius of Friendship: T.E. Lawrence, Faber, 1941; HWS, 1988.

As the Sun Shines, Faber, 1941.

The Incoming of Summer, Collins, undated.

Life in a Devon Village, Faber, 1945.

Tales of a Devon Village, Faber, 1945.

The Sun in the Sands, Faber, 1945.

The Phasian Bird, Faber, 1948.

The Scribbling Lark, Faber, 1949.

Tales of Moorland and Estuary, Macdonald, 1953.

A Clearwater Stream, Faber, 1958.

Some Nature Writers and Civilisation, the Wedmore Memorial Lecture 1959 for the Royal Society of Literature. Pub. in *Essays by Divers Hands*, Vol. XXX, the Proceedings of the RSL; Rep. as a separate pamphlet; printed in *Threnos* HWS, 1994, q.v.

In the Woods, Saint Albert's Press for the *Aylesford Review*, 1960.

A Chronicle of Ancient Sunlight
- Vol. 1   *The Dark Lantern*, Macdonald, 1951; p/b edn Alan Sutton Publishing 1994.
- Vol. 2   *Donkey Boy*, Macdonald, 1952; p/b edn Alan Sutton Publishing, 1994.
- Vol. 3   *Young Phillip Maddison*, Macdonald, 1953; p/b edn Alan Sutton Publishing, 1995.
- Vol. 4   *How Dear Is Life*, Macdonald, 1954; p/b edn Alan Sutton Publishing, 1995.
- Vol. 5   *A Fox Under My Cloak*, Macdonald, 1955.
- Vol. 6   *The Golden Virgin*, Macdonald, 1957.
- Vol. 7   *Love and the Loveless*, Macdonald, 1958.
- Vol. 8   *A Test to Destruction*, Macdonald, 1960.
- Vol. 9   *The Innocent Moon*, Macdonald, 1961.
- Vol. 10 *It Was the Nightingale*, Macdonald, 1962.
- Vol. 11 *The Power of the Dead*, Macdonald, 1963.
- Vol. 12 *The Phoenix Generation*, Macdonald, 1965.
- Vol. 13 *A Solitary War*, Macdonald, 1967.
- Vol. 14 *Lucifer Before Sunrise*, Macdonald, 1967.
- Vol. 15 *The Gale of the World*, Macdonald, 1969.

The Henry Williamson Animal Saga, Macdonald, 1960; (*Tarka the Otter, Salar the Salmon, The Epic of Brock the Badger, Chakchek the Peregrine*).

Collected Nature Stories, Macdonald, 1970; Little, Brown, 1995.

The Scandaroon, Macdonald, 1972.

Books edited by HW include:

An Anthology of Modern Nature Writing, Nelson, 1936.

Richard Jefferies: Selections of his Work, Faber, 1937.

Hodge and his Masters, Richard Jefferies, Methuen, 1937.

Norfolk Life, by Lilias Rider Haggard, Faber, 1943.

My Favourite Country Stories, Lutterworth Press, 1946.

Unreturning Spring: Being the Poems, Sketches, Stories & Letters of James Farrar, Williams and Norgate, 1950.

'Introductions' by HW in other books: see individual references within the main text.

Collections of HW's ephemeral writings published posthumously by the Henry Williamson Society:
Contributions to the Weekly Dispatch, ed. John Gregory, 1983.
Days of Wonder, intro. Richard Williamson, ed. John Gregory, 1987.
From a Country Hilltop, ed. John Gregory, 1988.
A Breath of Country Air, Pt 1, intro. Richard Williamson, ed. John Gregory, 1990.
A Breath of Country Air, Pt 2, intro. Robert Williamson, ed. John Gregory, 1991.
Spring Days in Devon, and Other Broadcasts, foreword Valerie Belsey, ed. John Gregory, 1992.
Pen and Plough: Further Broadcasts, intro. John Gregory, ed. John Gregory, 1993.
Threnos for T.E. Lawrence and Other Writings [together with] 'A Criticism of Henry Williamson's
    Tarka the Otter' by T.E. Lawrence, intro Dr J.W. Blench, ed. John Gregory, 1994.
Green Fields and Pavements: A Norfolk Farmer in Wartime, illust. Michael Loates, intro. Bill
    (Windles) Williamson, ed. John Gregory, 1995.

Cassettes:
The Peregrine's Saga, read by Sir Michael Hordern, for the Royal Society for Nature Conservation.
The Perfect Stranger, produced by David Clayton and Neil Walker for BBC Radio Norfolk, 1989.
The Broadcasts of Henry Williamson, Vol. 1, 'I Remember'; Vol. 2, 'The Hopeful Traveller.' Taken
    from BBC archives.
Henry Williamson: Old Soldier, a paper read by Fr. Brocard Sewell with readings by Frances Horowitz.

(All collections published by the HWS are available from John Gregory, Publications Manager, HWS,
14 Nether Grove, Longstanton, Cambridge, CB4 5EL)

FURTHER READING

Farson, Daniel, *Henry: A Portrait*, Michael Joseph, 1982.

Lamplugh, Lois, *A Shadowed Man*, Wellspring, 1990; rev. edn. Exmoor Press, 1991.

Murry, J. Middleton, 'The Novels of Henry Williamson' in *Katherine Mansfield and other Literary Studies*, Constable, 1959.

Price, Bernard, *Creative Landscapes of the British Isles*, Ebury Press, 1983: pp. 109, 132–5.

Sewell, Father Brocard (ed.), *Henry Williamson: The Man, The Writings – A Symposium*, Tabb House, 1980.

The Tarka Trail: A Walkers' Guide, Commentary by Richard Williamson, 2nd rev. edn The Tarka Project (available from the Henry Williamson Society or The Tarka Project).

The Henry Williamson Society *Journal*, Ed. Anne Williamson, published twice a year since 1980, contains reviews, correspondence, reminiscences, work, criticism of, and articles based on research into Henry Williamson's life and writings. Its wide and varied content has greatly added to the knowledge and understanding of this foremost writer.

THE HENRY WILLIAMSON SOCIETY

At a meeting in Barnstaple in May 1980 of a nucleus of keen and interested people, it was decided to set up a society in honour of the memory of Henry Williamson, and so the Henry Williamson Society was inaugurated. Membership grew quickly and now members are from all over the world and from all walks of life; their common bond being an interest in the work of Henry Williamson. The society is a non-political and is dedicated solely to its stated aim:

> to encourage interest in and a deeper understanding
> of the life and work of Henry Williamson.

The President is Richard Williamson, who is one of Henry's sons. Other members of the Williamson family are equally supportive. Mrs Loetitia Williamson, Henry's first wife, has particularly taken a keen and active interest in the society's affairs.

The society organizes two meetings annually. The autumn meeting, the AGM, is held in October in North Devon, with Henry Williamson's Field and Writing Hut at Ox's Cross a major focus. The spring meeting is based in other areas with a particular Williamson connection, for example, the Lewisham area of south-east London, north Norfolk, or Bedfordshire. The programme typically includes a major presentation and society dinner on the Saturday evening, with talks, discussions, slides, displays, walks and visits to places of special Williamson significance occurring during the rest of the weekend. Smaller local meetings are encouraged and draw considerable support. Apart from the organized aspect of these meetings they provide an opportunity to meet and talk with people of similar interest. Several visits to the battlefields of the First World War have also been arranged.

The society publishes a *Journal* twice a year, which contains a wide variety of articles about the writer and his work, which is adding considerably to the knowledge and understanding of this important twentieth-century author. A major project for the society is to collect and publish the ephemeral writings and articles previously only to be found in newspapers and magazines, and several titles have already appeared (see Bibliography). There is also a considerable society archive, housed at Exeter University which, together with the original gift by Henry Williamson to the university in the mid-1960s of a selection of his manuscripts, and the deposit after his death by his literary estate of the entire remainder of the MSS and TSS accepted by the nation under the National Heritage Scheme, provides primary source material for members and research students. A main concern of the society, together with the Williamson family, is the preservation of the author's Writing Hut at Ox's Cross, Georgeham, North Devon, which was extensively renovated in 1985, but is kept exactly as it was when Henry was alive, and serves as a memorial. In 1984, with Lewisham Borough Council, the society placed a commemorative plaque on the house where Henry Williamson spent his childhood and youth, 21 Eastern Road, Brockley, which is the setting for the early volumes of *A Chronicle of Ancient Sunlight*.

Readers wishing further information about the Society should contact in the first instance, the Membership Secretary: Mrs Margaret Murphy, 16 Doran Drive, Redhill, Surrey, RH1 6AX.

All enquiries about copyright matters to do with Henry Williamson's published and unpublished work should be addressed to: Anne Williamson, Manager HWLE, Keepers, West Dean Woods, Chichester, West Sussex, PO18 0RU.

INDEX

Works by HW are listed under Williamson, Henry William, works by. Fictional characters from HW's writings are listed under fictional characters.